Praise for *Jilya*

'These pages helped me heal and get my strength back that grief had stolen from me after losing Mum and Dad. I know these pages will also have the ability to help others understand our culture and the intergenerational trauma we have carried through our lives. This book will definitely open hearts and minds, and it put me on the right track to heal and feel like me again.' **– Troy Cassar-Daley**

'I've long admired Dr Tracy Westerman's work and her unrelenting pursuit of the delivery of appropriate care for the most vulnerable among us. Self-determination and a re-examination of commonly held practices and beliefs when it comes to the delivery of critical mental health services to Aboriginal people lie at the centre of Dr Westerman's work. This book is more important now than ever before as we seek to build an understanding between Aboriginal people and the rest of Australia and of why so many policies have failed to deliver positive outcomes. This book explains why and roadmaps those solutions.' **– Brooke Boney**

'A story of grit, insight and, especially, hope. Tracy Westerman, a luminous pioneer in the field of culture-informed psychology, writes with a powerful urgency and clarity that is sorely needed.' **– Julia Baird**

'Affliction strips us of our humanity – we become nothing – then a miracle happens and we realise the sufferer is us, all of us. Tracy Westerman makes us human and whole – read this and be better.' **– Stan Grant**

'Validation and affirmation on every page. Tracy Westerman's lived experience is our learning moment.' **– Narelda Jacobs**

'Tracy Westerman is wise, strong, empathetic and resilient. She tells the extraordinary story of her life as a young kid growing up in the remote Pilbara town of Tom Price and becoming the first person to undertake her entire schooling there and be accepted into university. She takes us on a fascinating journey that explains how to adapt traditional monocultural and individualistically focused "one-size-fits-all" clinical psychology specifically for Aboriginal people. Intergenerational trauma and racism have scarred not just individuals but also families and even whole communities. This is one of the root causes of entrenched and persistent disadvantage. If we don't understand and model assessments and treatments as Tracy compels us to do, we will continue to fail to close the gap of disadvantage. Tracy shows us a pathway to treatment and healing, not just for individuals, but also their families and whole communities. Everyone who reads Tracy's book will have a much deeper insight into the individual and collective trauma of Aboriginal people. But also an understanding of how those problems and traumas can be treated and addressed.' – **Lucy Hughes Turnbull AO**

Tracy Westerman is a proud Nyamal woman from the Pilbara region of Western Australia. She has a PhD in Psychology, is the owner and founder of Indigenous Psychological Services, and is the founder of the charity the Westerman Jilya Institute for Indigenous Mental Health. She is a recognised world leader in Aboriginal mental health, cultural competency and suicide prevention, achieving national and international recognition for her work. She has received many awards including an Order of Australia, Telstra Women's Business Award Winner (WA) and Australian of the Year (WA).

Jilya

How one Indigenous woman from the
remote Pilbara transformed psychology

TRACY
WESTERMAN

First published 2024 by University of Queensland Press
PO Box 6042, St Lucia, Queensland 4067 Australia
Reprinted 2024

The University of Queensland Press (UQP) acknowledges the Traditional Owners
and their custodianship of the lands on which UQP operates. We pay our respects
to their Ancestors and their descendants, who continue cultural and spiritual
connections to Country. We recognise their valuable contributions to Australian
and global society.

uqp.com.au
reception@uqp.com.au

Cover design by Josh Durham, Design by Committee
Cover photograph courtesy of the author
Typeset in 11.5/15 pt Bembo Std by Post Pre-press Group, Brisbane
Printed in Australia by McPherson's Printing Group

University of Queensland Press is assisted by the Australian Government through
Creative Australia, its principal arts investment and advisory body.

A catalogue record for this book is available from the National Library of Australia.

ISBN 978 0 7022 6869 4 (pbk)
ISBN 978 0 7022 7004 8 (epdf)
ISBN 978 0 7022 7005 5 (epub)

University of Queensland Press uses papers that are natural, renewable and
recyclable products made from wood grown in well-managed forests and other
controlled sources. The logging and manufacturing processes conform to the
environmental regulations of the country of origin.

Aboriginal and Torres Strait Islander readers are respectfully cautioned that this
publication contains images/mentions of people who have passed away.

'Jilya' means 'my child' — for this is about our children.
To ensure that they all have an equal opportunity to thrive.
I dedicate this book to them all.

Contents

Introduction

This book is both a personal and a professional account. It's the story of how I came to be the first Aboriginal person in Australia to complete a combined Masters and PhD in Clinical Psychology, and why that matters. It's also a reflection on the failings of the mental health system and how psychology is practised in this country, and the damage that is done when you operate from a one-size-fits-all, monocultural evidence base.

I am a proud psychologist, but the profession needs to own that our entire evidence base is predicated on cultural exclusion and that this continues as denial, causing incalculable harm. We are a world that does not like difference, and it is literally killing my people.

There remains no Indigenous-specific, data-driven content in any psychology degree in Australia. Nor is there a required minimum standard of measurable cultural competencies in the profession. Instead, we have a 'side order' of cultural awareness – or 'we had an Aboriginal person do a lecture' paternalism.

A fundamental truth was drilled into me during my training as a psychologist: *If you get assessment wrong, you get treatment wrong and you make things worse.* As Aboriginal people, we suffer – more than any other culture in Australia – from what I refer to as 'the big three' when it comes to mental health assessment: misdiagnosis, overdiagnosis and underdiagnosis. So, in 2003 I developed the only culturally and clinically validated screening tools for at-risk Aboriginal youth and adults. Yet universities and governments have ignored them and refused to fund their rollout into high-risk communities. These same universities will claim they have Indigenous content that's clinically informed and data-driven. It's not, and they need to stop lying about it. When at least 50 per cent of clients in mental health, justice and child protection systems are Aboriginal, how much longer can psychology continue to neglect the needs of Aboriginal people?

My own journey with psychology began in the remote town of Tom Price, in the Pilbara region of Western Australia, when I picked up a book that described the profession. I decided it would be my life's calling, despite never having met a psychologist before. I had to educate myself through distance education, and with no-one on either side of my family having seen the inside of a university, it's fair to say the odds were firmly stacked against me.

Yet I have learnt that representation matters. When I completed my Masters/PhD in Clinical Psychology, it became possible for every Aboriginal person to also achieve this. And while it is nearly impossible to be what you cannot see, my journey is a lesson in how it is possible. When I became the first Indigenous person to set up a private psychology practice without government funding, it established a model for other Aboriginal people to do the same.

Later, frustrated at the lack of government response to the unacceptable rates of Indigenous child suicide in our remote communities, I naturally looked to those who, like me, had too many barriers to success. In 2019, I funded the Dr Tracy Westerman Indigenous Psychology Scholarship Program to train up the next generation of Indigenous psychologists. By 2020, I launched my name charity, the Westerman Jilya Institute for Indigenous Mental Health, and to date we have funded – and I am personally mentoring – fifty-five future Indigenous psychologists from across Australia in our highest-risk communities, without federal government support. With just 218 Indigenous psychologists in Australia that contribution is significant and permanent, because locals never leave. In a very short time, my intention to #BuildAnArmy of Indigenous psychologists has captured the hearts and minds of the country. I have now raised over $2 million in scholarship commitments and over $9 million for the operations of the program, all while racking up in excess of 4000 volunteer hours. I will not rest until we have a Jilya base in every Australian state and territory to address the unacceptable inequities that successive governments have failed to.

Having built two successful enterprises from the ground up through sheer will and determination, I hope this is a story of inspiration.

Too many scholarships favour the privileged. Ours don't. Each year we select students from the highest-risk regions and with a mindset of how many gaps they have had to close. Disadvantage is always relative and true leadership should champion those who have had to prove *many* people wrong to get to where they are, who have had to surmount the most barriers to succeed. It is poor leadership that promotes the idea that those who have overcome the least should drive solutions for those who have to overcome the most. We have not had a single student drop out in three years. How? Because representation matters – they can now be what they can see.

This is the story of how I came from the remote Pilbara to become one of Australia's leading psychologists. It's a story of significant pain, but also of healing. Of client trauma, and of never giving up. Of always believing that change is possible.

It is a story of what is possible with drive and determination, and of how hope can be the difference this country so badly needs – especially when many more share it with you.

Ultimately, though, it is a story of love for my people.

And why I built an army of psychologists for them all.

1

Mum and Dad:
When black and white made sense

Mum and Dad – Mavis and Mick Westerman – were two people from completely different worlds who found each other. Dad a whitefella, Mum an Aboriginal woman who at the time of their meeting wasn't even a citizen of her own country. They should never have made sense, but the best relationships rarely do. They complemented each other in ways that were often hard for others to see from the outside. Mum and Dad were simple people with simple values: to work hard, raise a loving family and do everything in their power to make sure their children had greater opportunities than either of them had. Neither of them came from a conventional family – Dad due to dysfunction, Mum due to the consequences of the government policies of assimilation and cultural destruction, which ultimately claimed both of her parents by her teens. So, they were determined to find in each other the salvation they'd sought their whole lives. Every value we were raised with was about the love of family. That's a force that can overcome being born with very little else.

I remember Dad regularly coming home with a bunch of flowers for Mum – no easy feat in the remote Pilbara, but he would somehow manage it. He truly adored her. She, for the most part, would feign embarrassment about it. Showing affection didn't come easy for Mum, but it did for Dad. This gave us the luck of having two parents who understood their roles in raising Aboriginal children in a world that would always need them to be tough yet compassionate and kind.

Dad looked like he shouldn't have been as kind and sweet as he was. Decades of sunburn had weathered his arms so much they resembled rawhide, even eroding the tattoos he got as a young kid in the army, which he'd joined to escape a dysfunctional background. Hard manual labour had made his hands resemble bear claws. They were so large he had to use a pen to dial the phone. Years of bush mechanics and work as a stockman, otherwise known as a 'ringer', had developed in him the kind of intelligence that is the most valuable commodity in the remote Pilbara. Dad had to learn how to fix most things because his survival depended on it, living in such extreme conditions and remoteness where tradesmen and resources were very limited. He was a jack-of-all-trades, able to problem-solve his way out of any situation.

Mum was his opposite half. She was taller by around half an inch, although to try to win her love Dad told her that he was 6 feet tall, could play the guitar and was part Aboriginal – none of which was true. Strikingly beautiful, she stood out as an Aboriginal woman who walked with pride. As a tall kid I always admired her posture and how she carried herself. I found my height to be embarrassing, particularly when I was taller than every boy in my class by a significant margin. But Mum never stooped. I adored this but struggled to emulate it.

For Mum and Dad, black and white together seemed to be easy, at least from the outside. But it certainly didn't start that way.

Black identity and a father's love

Mavis Ball was a born-and-bred Nyamal woman from Marble Bar. She was the eldest of four children, the only girl. Her younger brothers Harold, Eric and Les were all over 6 feet 4, and with Mum at 5 feet 11 (the same height as me) they were certainly a formidable family. She was born in Port Hedland in 1942 to Kitty and Murphy Ball. My maternal grandparents were highly respected in their home town of Marble Bar, more than 150 kilometres southeast of Port Hedland. Murphy and Kitty had been traditionally married by permission of the chief protector. In this generation of the government policy of 'protectionism', written approval from the chief protector was required for almost everything: from buying a pair of socks to getting married. It was an era of complete and utter control over the lives of Aboriginal people – the basis of which continues in much government policy today in its race-based restriction of human rights.

Murphy was a taxi and truck driver, an extremely well-to-do occupation for a 'full-blood', according to the potted history that we, as a family, have only recently managed to glean from Native Welfare files. Murphy and Kitty were hard-working, and they modelled this for Mum and her three younger siblings. They worked hard because they wanted a better life for their kids, and they would die trying. Their efforts were, unknown to Mum, fuelled by a fear that the welfare would come calling for their children. Having greater opportunities, though, was also the false promise of the policy of protectionism – that if you 'behaved', if you 'conducted' yourself like a 'white person', you would be afforded more rights. These rights not only never came, but required denying who you were, your culture and all who continued to practise it – that being, your own family.

When Mum was nine years old, the welfare came calling. She remembers little of what happened other than being on a small plane with two people she didn't know. They had told her parents that she was unwell and had to be taken to Port Hedland. But she was not unwell, and she didn't understand why her parents had been told this. She remembers sitting on this plane and seeing her mum outside, crying and being held up by her aunties. As the plane took off, her mum fell to the ground. Aunties grabbed rocks from the ground to hit themselves with. This is sorry cutting. It happens in times

3

of death. Mum had seen this happen during Sorry Time. But why were they doing this now? She began to cry. As the image of her mum became smaller and smaller in the plane's little window, she did not know where she was going. She didn't know if she would ever see her family again.

Her next memory is of being in a dorm and seeing two 'white people' pacing nervously. As she watched them, her eyelids became heavy. Her face was numb from tears. She slowly drifted off to sleep.

'Mavis, wake up,' whispered a voice she recognised, as strong arms wrapped around her in the dark to pick her up. 'Sssh …' The light from the hallway illuminated her dad's face. Was this a dream? She felt a familiar kiss on her forehead and a hug she had known so many times – when she had fallen asleep around the campfire and her dad's strong, loving arms had carried her to bed – and she knew it was not a dream.

Murphy Ball had found his way from Marble Bar to Port Hedland – all 187 kilometres, through mud and mangrove trees – to bring his daughter back. He then put her on his back and carried her all the way home, back through the mud, the mangroves and the oppressive heat. It sickens me how close my mum came to forced removal. Murphy Ball single-handedly changed the course of all our lives.

Love comes in many forms – it comes in hugs, it comes in 'I love you's – but it mostly comes in actions.

The actions of a father's love had, generationally, saved us all.

It has taken a lifetime for Mum to share the pain and trauma of her early life, and even now it is only in small pieces. She would rarely hug us kids or say that she loved us. That sounds tough, but every single action she took told us consistently and reliably that we were loved. There are layers to my mum that she has never shared. I don't blame her. Looking back now as an adult, I am in awe of her strength and resilience.

I understand now as a psychologist that Mum struggled with racial trauma and possibly complex post-traumatic stress disorder

(C-PTSD), in which memories can become distorted and consequently irreconcilable because of the age at which the trauma occurred. Mum's understanding as a child of what had happened became normalised, which occurs when traumatic things become part of a 'daily' or 'normal' existence – as is common with other victims – but complicating and compounding this was the fact that this was racial trauma that was perpetrated on Aboriginal people by government legislation, and the abuse was then enabled and perpetuated by systems and individuals.

In these circumstances, when those who are supposed to protect are also the abusers, Indigenous people have no power or control over preventing the trauma. Children look to their parents to provide a safe haven. But when the parents are also powerless to stop these traumatic events from occurring, as Mum's were, who can these kids go to for protection? As children we develop a sense of self based on our world being safe and predictable and on being told we are loved and loveable. Homes in which complex racial trauma is evident means that environments are modelled as unsafe by those around us. Love can feel overwhelming because there is fear and anxiety attached to it. Sigmund Freud referred to this as a reaction formation – a defence mechanism against fear or stress; that being, if I truly attach to a child who could realistically be ripped away from me, that would be intolerable.[1] It is therefore better not to show love or affection because this will protect me from the pain of loss. In these complex circumstances, our biology is altered as our nervous system becomes armed to remain activated in anticipation of threats.

For individuals who have experienced abuse, reconciling this takes energy and insight. It also cannot occur when trauma is continuing in their environment. The trauma of child removals is that they were as unpredictable as they were unstoppable.

Dad – Rhodes Arthur 'Mick' Westerman – was born in Collie, in the state's southwest, but his early years were with his mum, Violet, and stepfather, Ray Cross, living mostly around the Goldfields region. He spent most of his teenage years and adult life drifting from town to town, picking up odd jobs. As a result, he was always drawn to remote areas. He arrived in Port Hedland in 1961 alone, with everything he owned in his broken-down old ute. With no family he could rely on, his home was often on the side of the road in his swag. Port Hedland in the 1960s was a harsh environment. It was hot beyond what he had ever experienced before as a kid from Collie raised around the Goldfields, where there was at least some winter relief from the heat. Hedland was stifling – it was not unusual for the mercury to hit close to 50 degrees Celsius during summer. The red dirt and arid climate made Port Hedland hard to like, but – being predominantly a mining town – it was booming with the work opportunities Dad needed.

The local mob saw that Dad was always alone, without a woman or family, and they felt so sorry for him that they decided he needed a dog. The local policeman just happened to have a litter of pups that were crossbred cocker spaniel, so one of them became Dad's. Now, for a tough station man to have a cocker spaniel rather than a cattle dog was quite the comedy act. He called the tiny little black dog 'BoBo' and the locals would say, 'If you ever want to find Mick Westerman, you just have to find BoBo.' The little cocker was his shadow. The story goes that the other ringers would arrive at the station with their 'tough-guy appropriate' dogs, while Dad would turn up in his ute with the pretty spaniel ('non-tough-guy appropriate') at his side. Even though BoBo wasn't his choice of dog, she aptly represented who he was – tough on the outside but soft as they come. Dad had four daughters, so he always had a strong feminine side to him despite his tough-as-nails upbringing and exterior. (To this day, we have always had cocker spaniels. I currently have two, both as loyal, no doubt, as BoBo.)

I am not surprised Dad found a safe haven with Aboriginal people because that is the essence of the culture. I have lost count of the number of whitefellas whose families were dysfunctional or had rejected them who ultimately found solace with Aboriginal people. They looked after Dad and took him in because there is often less judgement from people who've spent most of their lives being judged by others. Importantly, the nature of 'collective cultures' is this attitude of 'what is yours is mine' – no-one 'owns' anything. Everything is shared. That sat well with Dad, who owned nothing but a truck and his swag of clothes and basics. There is this naturalness of looking more to the group than the self, so there is very little thought about what serves you personally. Dad was this way despite having never known this in his family background. He came from two alcoholic parents who were concerned only for themselves, as addicts sadly tend to be. His father, Charlie Westerman, was originally from Glasgow and was a violent drunk by all accounts. His mother – who raised Dad and his brother Tom upon separating from Charlie when Dad was only three years old – was also a heavy drinker, who Dad spent most of his life embarrassed by. Mum would relay to us kids when we became adults that Violet was 'as rough as they come'. No doubt being married to a violent man would have contributed to that tough exterior, for her own survival.

Mum remembers the first time Dad introduced her to Violet. Dad said to Mum, 'You won't like her.' By this stage, Violet had married Ray Cross – a hairdresser, of all things. Violet passed away before I was born, so I never met her. I only heard Dad speak about Ray Cross, who he greatly admired and who he considered to be his 'father'. My dad could fix anything, and he would often tell me that his stepfather taught him everything he knew. I think he also admired Ray for his influence on his mother. I understood that Ray would simply be my grandma's 'wingman' – picking her up when she got herself in a drunken state and making sure she was okay and looked after. But they would regularly go on drinking binges and not come back home, often leaving Dad and Uncle Tom as very young kids to fend for themselves for days, asking neighbours to look in on them. That was how it was in those days in small outback towns.

Dad was one of four kids. Aunty Joy and Aunty Betty (who I never met) went to live with Charlie Westerman when his marriage to Violet broke down. It was a pretty random division of the kids, by the sound of it. Years later, we would finally meet Aunty Joy, who filled in some of the blanks of Dad's background. I don't remember ever having real conversations with Dad about his family and upbringing, just snippets – like about running away at fourteen to join the army, and about being so tiny at 4 feet 11 that he worked as an apprentice jockey. (The Westerman men all go through very late growth spurts.)

We found out in recent years through the wonders of the world wide web and family tracing that Charlie Westerman basically died a vagrant, found dead in someone's backyard. A sad end to a tortured and unhappy life. Aunty Joy would later tell us of her brutal upbringing at the hands of Charlie Westerman. The only time she would see him, she said, was on pay day, when he would show up and 'flog' her for cash. So cruel. Aunty Joy was like the female version of my dad – kind, gentle, loving. I always wonder at that, given what they came from. It was incredible as a kid to see them together.

When my parents met in Port Hedland in the early 1960s, Mum had yet to obtain a certificate of citizenship. It was Western Australian government policy that Aboriginal people had to show 'evidence' as to why they should be accepted as citizens of their own country. Mum had so far resisted doing so – at her core, she was always an activist and understood that the concept was deeply wrong and offensive. To obtain citizenship there was a range of conditions to be met. The first was that she required two non-Aboriginal people to act as 'sponsors' to attest to her having lived as a 'white person' for a minimum of two years. Often this occurred when you were employed by someone regularly, as both the 'reference' and the process were extensive. The station managers eventually convinced Mum to apply for citizenship, and it was something she always felt ashamed of – to the point that although she kept it in a drawer at home, she never showed it to us until we all became interested in our history in our twenties. For me, I was always involved in Aboriginal activism at some level, so it was always going to come up as a topic. Her certificate looks like a passport and was made possible under the *Natives (Citizenship Rights) Act 1944*. Once citizenship was granted, the person was no longer considered a 'native or aborigine'. As the Collaborating for Indigenous Rights website states: 'it was impossible to be both an Australian citizen and an Aboriginal person'.

Every Aboriginal person who obtained the 'dog tag', as some called it, had to deny or 'sell out' their culture. But the promise of being treated as 'an equal' to whites was understandably compelling for those who wanted a better life and particularly so for their children. The 'criteria' included convincing a magistrate that you were 'civilised' and living according to 'white standards' (whatever that means). Additionally, you had to prove you were free of disease, could speak English, and had 'severed ties with other natives' and renounced your Aboriginality – although you were allowed to maintain connections with your 'lineal descendants'.

Mum ripped a part of her photo off during a fit of anger at herself that she had 'allowed' herself to be exploited like this. These policies knew exactly how to dismantle a culture. They knew that the promise of a better future and to be treated as an equal would always be a greater motivator than remaining the same, living a life in which you were 'less than' and opportunities were limited. There is nothing more indelibly traumatic than for that promise to come with the denial of your core self. These internal identity conflicts are rarely resolved because, ultimately, there will always be this idea that you 'did it to yourself'. Mum's guilt around her certificate of citizenship has waned over time, thankfully, but those parts that remain unhealable in her are what continue to drive so much pain in generations of Aboriginal people – knowing that no matter what you do, how well you behave and speak or how educated you are, the world will always look at you and your children as less than.

Of course, these citizenship certificates created a divide between Aboriginal people who obtained them and those who did not. Those who were guaranteed more human rights could only do so by 'assimilating' and 'acting white', denying their culture, leaving behind their families and cultural practices for the promise of a life of equality that never came. Skin colour has always mattered, and a certificate wasn't going to change that reality. The colour of your skin was always what was judged and deemed 'less worthy' depending on your 'colour gradient'. Mum, as a 'full-blood' Aboriginal woman, was on the lowest rung of the ladder. No certificate of citizenship was strong enough to repel racism, a hate that knows no bounds in Australia towards Aboriginal people, as shown by epidemiological studies on its physical and mental health impacts.[2]

So, how do you explain to your children, who you are raising to be proud of their blackness and to stand up against racism – always, even to their own detriment – that you went to court to obtain citizenship of your own country? And that required that you renounced your culture? Well, you explain it as a mother's love. Mum was always determined to make a better life for her kids than she'd had, and in Mick Westerman she found a soulmate.

The love between them was fairly instant, depending upon which side of the love story you believe. Mum was working in the Port Hedland pub, washing dishes – a good job for an Aboriginal girl of seventeen years. When she'd finish work, she would begin the long walk home in darkness. Dad would be parked outside, waiting for the end of her shift. He had completely and utterly fallen in love with her, but was too shy to approach her. Mum would giggle to herself when his car headlights came on and he'd follow her all the way home, to make sure she was safe. This went on for a few weeks until he finally got the courage to talk to her. Stunningly beautiful, my mum – according to our aunties – was always considered to be someone who would do well in life. She had a strength and determination that matched her height, and she held herself with a confidence that drew people to her. Dad was simply transfixed by her. Her poise, strength and dignity were in spite of the trauma of her background, one that was typical for Aboriginal women of her generation. I have often been humbled by the fact that despite the hate, despite the racism and trauma that could never be rationalised, she always taught us to 'rise above it' – that what we could control was how we reacted to hate.

Her parents had passed away when she was in her teens and she was forced to get into the workforce as much as possible, with so many people taking advantage of the non-citizen status of Aboriginal people by not paying wages. She was mostly raised by her two grandfathers and, as the eldest of four children, had a responsibility to work rather than get an education.

Wedding bells happened very quickly for them at the Port Hedland registry office. Sitting at the front of the pub afterwards, Dad and his mates drank 'longneck beers' while Mum had lemonade because Aboriginal people were still prohibited from drinking alcohol by order of the government. So, there they were on their wedding day, not able to toast their marriage with a glass of wine or champagne like any other newlyweds. By this stage Dad was a firm 'white blackfella' – the term we often use for our white brothers and sisters who are so ingrained in Aboriginal culture, so in love with Aboriginal people, that we 'claim' them. Blackfellas had long claimed my dad, way before he met my mum.

Many years later I benefited significantly from Dad's reputation when I walked into my first job in Kalgoorlie and went to my first big meeting with local Wongi mob. I was a twenty-two-year-old kid and terrified. After the meeting, one of the elders came up to me, looked at my name tag and said in a gruff voice, 'Tracy Westerman ... You Micky Westerman's daughter?'

I thought, *Oh shit, what has he done?*

'Umm, yes,' I replied.

After a short pause, while he looked over his shoulder to motion the rest of the mob over, he extended his hand to me and said, 'Put it there, girl.'

That made me smile. I then heard stories of Dad, as a whitefella, working side by side with 'us blackfellas' when no-one else would. It does your head in that this would be considered anything significant, but it was, and it made me feel sad and proud at the same time.

During that first job in Kalgoorlie, I also learnt from Wongi mob that Dad not only worked side by side with blackfellas, but he refused to take wages, as back then blackfellas mostly got room and board for their hard work. Dad took this stand despite having to support us all. Mum later told him, 'That's all very well and good, father' – they affectionately called each other mother and father – 'but we have kids to feed.'

Dad taught me many leadership lessons purely through what he did, through his actions. Dad didn't need a parade for doing the right thing. He just did it. He taught me this value of altruism from a young age. It is what you do when no-one is paying attention, when no-one is watching. When you do the right thing despite there being nothing in it for you. He modelled integrity and it taught me to be more tuned into actions than words.

My work in Kalgoorlie, as hard as it was, was made so much easier by the elders there who vouched for me. I am forever grateful to them and humbled by their love and support. It was my first training ground as a young welfare worker who really had no idea what I was doing. I just knew I wanted to be there and make a difference. Their cultural vouching for me helped to light a fire in my belly, but more than that it instilled in me how important it is for Aboriginal people to support each other. It has stood as the major difference in my life to have so much support from an entire community of Aboriginal people, and particularly given the predominantly white town I had grown up in. Like for my dad, blackfellas became my safe haven and I have never forgotten it.

Tamala Station

Dad was a station man through and through, but as he became a family man he began to understand that station life would limit his opportunities and those of his kids. Having an Aboriginal wife in the era of assimilation made things even more difficult. Tamala Station was one of the first places they were to work together as husband and wife for many years. Dad was a ringer, Mum a shearers' cook who was only paid in room and board as an Aboriginal woman. She recalls that she worked hard with no let up. The ringers and station workers ate and ate and ate. The nature of their physical labour meant that food had to be constantly prepared – and then there was the cleaning. The Pilbara heat and dust were unrelenting. And then there were my three sisters and brother, all under eight years old, to care for. It is a significant testament to the degrees they were prepared to go to for a better life.

At this stage, Mum was so painfully thin that the doctor advised her against any more pregnancies. When she told him she was pregnant again, he apparently 'threw the bill' at her! Living on a remote station meant there were no services around, so when Mum was about to give birth Dad would have to find his way to the nearest town. In my case, it was Carnarvon, in the Gascoyne/ Murchison area of Western Australia. On the night in question, my family were at the outdoor cinema about to watch *To Sir, with Love*, with the great Sidney Poitier, when Mum went into labour. My entire childhood I never heard the end of it – that Mum didn't get to watch the movie as a result. How relieved I was when it finally came on the TV!

Both Mum and Dad had been desperate to have another boy and had already selected a name, Robert. So they were more than a little miffed when out I came – another girl!

Upon that announcement, Mum apparently said, 'Oh no.'

The doctor replied, 'Well, I can't put her back. I can't throw her out the window.'

'Okay,' said Dad, 'we'll take her, then.'

A very inauspicious arrival into the world.

For two weeks, I had no name. Eventually, so that story goes, Mum was reading her favourite magazine, *The Australian Women's Weekly*, and there was a story about someone called Tracy Gillian. (I have never found out who this was, but the running joke is that, knowing my luck, I was named after a serial killer somewhere.) So, that was to be my name – Tracy Gillian Westerman. The final piece of the Westerman family.

Useless Loop

Yes, there is a place called Useless Loop. Go on, have a laugh, get it out of the way! I'm used to it. But it is pretty cool telling people you are from Useless Loop. It gets lots of laughs at international keynotes in particular. This is where I spent my formative years, up to around five years of age.

It is in the Murchison area right next to Monkey Mia, a World Heritage Site. Dolphins in their plenty come to the shore to be fed, which is not great for the natural order of the ecosystem, but it's how tourists have discovered this beautiful natural habitat.

Useless Loop – or 'the Loop', as we called it – became Mum and Dad's salvation. Dad had heard of the salt mine there and the money that could be made. Station life was hard, with little reward. At this stage, it was all about ensuring a better life for their children, so off we went with all five kids in the back of the panel van. Prior to that, Mum and Dad had lived most of their married lives on stations, so it was a new opportunity for them both.

Useless Loop was a closed town that predominantly employed Aboriginal people. Its tiny population of about thirty or so families were all in some way related to us and each other. I have faint memories of our time there, but Mum would often tell me stories about it, saying, 'You used to get me into a lot of trouble.' She would regularly find me wandering off to the 'blackfellas camp' (as Mum used to call it), sitting around the elders, listening to yarns. Anytime I would go missing, she would know exactly where I was. I have always been drawn to mob, to yarns, to our greatest teachers and storytellers. This is something that was clearly always instinctual. Then there was that time she found me sitting on the counter at the store, very confidently telling the lady behind it that I wanted 'that and that and that' while I pointed at my 'order', a whole 2 cents in my hand that I'd managed to find somewhere. Mum was mortified, of course, and grabbed me off the counter before marching me home.

I was what the school headmaster used to refer to as a 'chatterbox'. At around eighteen months old I was already able to form complete sentences. Having four siblings meant that I was like a little toy that everyone wanted to play with, so the environment was incredibly stimulating. My eldest sister, Lorna, who is ten years older than me, took it upon herself to teach me the ABCs and counting.

The school at the Loop was one room, from Year One through to Year Seven. Everyone was barefoot. From the get-go Mum was fiercely protective of her kids. Mike, being the only boy, was spoilt rotten by her and a little pile of trouble. On the first day of school, he had a fight with another boy and ended up getting the cane. Now, in such a small town, half the school was the Westerman family. When Lorna and Sharon came home from school crying, Mum of course asked them what had happened so they relayed the story, while heaving and sniffling through their tears. Mike thought it was a great joke and didn't really share their emotion. What this all meant was that Mum had plenty of time to get pretty angry, and when black women get angry, they start cleaning. When the principal came knocking at the door to explain to Mum why he had given Mike the cane, her hands were submerged in soapy water, scrubbing her frying pans. Ever practical, Mum grabbed one of the heavier pans and quite literally chased him down the street with it. I believe the words, 'No-one hits any of my children!' were yelled, while half the town watched the principal squealing to try to get her to stop.

We laughed about that image and yarn (which got increasingly embellished) for many years to come. In fairness, though, it would have been a pretty terrifying sight: Mum all athletic and tall with her black beauty; a town full of blackfellas egging her on; and a rather large frying pan as a potentially lethal weapon.

But that was Mum. Harm any of her kids and feel the heat. Big-time.

Mum and Dad were hard-working, almost to the point of being workaholics. It's a trait we have all inherited in our family and it often overwhelms the people around us. We find it hard to switch off – not always from work; it can be exercise or socialising or just cleaning the house. We all have this need to always be moving in some capacity. Our home had a very gender-stereotypical division of labour, with Mum inside doing 'women's stuff' and Dad outside doing 'men's stuff'. However, Mum ruled the roost, everywhere. Dad married a strong woman, and he raised strong women. It is often tempting to label people, even though we are all much more than our labels ('labels belong on jars', I always say), but in my view Dad was a feminist. He pushed us girls towards becoming educated rather than having families, as did Mum. He would always tell me, 'Go out and get an education. Don't settle. Don't rely on a man.' It was an interesting juxtaposition, given he was strong as an ox and looked like the toughest human being you could imagine. Stereotypically he should have been saying the opposite, but he encouraged us as equally as he did his son. For a man of his generation, it was extraordinary in hindsight.

He raised us to believe that we deserved the best in any future life partners. 'Never chase after a man, Tracy. If you have to chase them, they don't deserve you.' And as a result, I never have. I would often feel sorry for my male mates when they would come to the Westerman household for the first time to pick me up to go out. They would typically beep the horn and then wait in their car for me to come out. Dad refused to let me go out to the car. A man, he said, has to come to the door.

Every single one of my mates learnt that 'baptism of fire' and from then on would always come to the door. I am so grateful that my dad modelled these clear boundaries for me and my siblings. Because of this, I have mostly been surrounded by kind, honourable men my entire life thanks to my dad and, later on, my brother Mike.

I guess I was first consciously aware of how incredibly lucky I was to have the father I did once I'd left home to go to university. So many of the young women I encountered at uni were limited by their fathers. They were told, 'Don't worry about an education – you are just going to get married and have kids.' Dad wanted me to be strong and independent, to make choices based on wisdom rather than what was socially expected. I had no idea of the importance of this gift until I saw those who did not have it.

Every time I got a good grade at school, my instinct was to run home and show my dad. He could hug you so tight that you would sometimes feel like you couldn't breathe. He adored his family. He understood implicitly what was right and wrong and I have inherited those core values. There was never ambiguity about it for him. As I have grown, that strong foundation has been such a critical part of my success, although it took me a while to understand this – that being guided by strong values will always see you right.

But the greatest gift he gave all of us kids was his optimism. He could be out bush in 50-degree heat, flies everywhere and sweating bullets, but with a cup of tea in his hand and his family around him, he would say to me, 'Life can't get much better, Tracy.'

I'd reply, 'I guess so, Dad.'

But I have been so fortunate to have inherited that optimism. I continue to find the most joy in the smallest things because I know their importance. What a gift to give your children – the gift of hope, resilience and optimism.

Dad was and remains my strongest leadership influence.

Tom Price

Eventually Dad explored better opportunities for his growing family and was offered six months' work in a remote Pilbara town called Tom Price, run by Hamersley Iron (now Rio Tinto), to mine iron ore. The red dirt was even redder and the environment significantly harsher than in Useless Loop: spinifex, gum trees and very little shade anywhere. The mercury would regularly hit 40 degrees before six in the morning, but it was a dry heat. The mining company had built beautiful new brick homes, which came complete with ducted air-conditioning. But as a family we hated being indoors, so we'd put a sprinkler on the shade cloth on the patio roof to provide some coolness when, despite it being stifling, we'd all sit outdoors. It's a funny thing with born-and-bred Pilbara people – our love of the heat always trumps any desire for the coldness of air-conditioning. Even to this day, people are often more than a little stunned when we all retreat outdoors on 40-plus-degree days. It's just our norm.

So, we arrived in Tom Price like the Addams family: five kids, a dog, a cat, and a mum and dad, all squashed into a beaten-up old Land Rover that was a bit like the TARDIS – how can it fit all those humans and animals?

To our knowledge, we were the only Aboriginal family in town. This was overwhelming for Mum, who was still affected by the horrific race-based trauma she'd experienced as a child. She has often relayed how people in Tom Price would avoid her. She said it was like she was 'from another planet'. Her biggest fear was that the welfare could come calling at any time – this was, of course, lost on us as kids, but was ever-present for her as a black woman in a town in which our every move was under observation from a culture she had only ever known as destructive but had had to learn to appease. She desperately tried to reconcile her race-based trauma with raising kids who had to 'get on in this world', as she would say, and the job she did of protecting us kids from it, frankly, was extraordinary. As a result, our upbringing was brutal in the sense that there were no excuses. We had to be better and smarter than every other kid in school. We were the only kids who wore the school uniform, starched to within an inch of its life. Every morning she would tie our hair so tight there was no possibility of a strand getting out of place. Our school shirts were buttoned right up to our necks, to 'preserve our dignity'. Most importantly, god help us if we ever tried to take a day off school – because, you know, we were sick or something. We would be met with the same response each time: 'Well, then you may as well go and get a job at the grocery store marking tins.' Fortunately, we were healthy kids for the most part. Not even the weekend provided any reprieve. If you dared to wake up after six o'clock, too bad – no breakfast. If you decided you were going to lie on the couch and do nothing all day, think again – get outside and do something.

But most weekends were all about exploring local waterholes and having family picnics and barbies. Holidays were family trips in the Landy, visiting all the towns in the state. It was always about family for Mum and Dad.

A few years into living in Tom Price, Mum found out there were two other Aboriginal families in town – the Koster and Zweckel families – and she was finally able to feel 'normal'. She could drop her guard with them as they were also raising Aboriginal kids in a mining town. We all became lifelong friends.

For Mum and Dad, Tom Price showed that their hard work was finally paying off. The town itself was pretty new – all the houses were just a few kilometres from the open-cut mine and were purpose-built for the tough environment. Having a home that was fully functional, though, seemed strange for Mum. When we arrived at the beautiful brand-new four-bedroom home we'd been assigned in Tom Price, she refused to get out of the panel van. I remember her saying to Dad, 'This is like Buckingham Palace. It can't possibly be our home.' Indeed, she would often speak of having lived in houses that had no floor, as if to constantly remind us how lucky we now were.

On our first Christmas, Dad, flush with cash, bought us all new bikes. The photo of all us kids lined up with these shiny bikes is one for the times. The gleam of the silver spokes is almost blinding even in the old polaroid snap.

But coming from Useless Loop meant we felt out of place. When we moved to Tom Price, Mum would say to us, 'Don't tell anyone you came from Useless Loop. That's shame!' So when people would ask us where we were from, we would simply go mute because none of us were brave enough to defy Mum's direct instructions. It's quite funny in hindsight. We might as well have said, 'We just appeared here from Mars.' To be honest, it kind of felt like we had!

It certainly didn't help that there were just a couple Aboriginal families in town. We were very aware that we were representing 'all Aboriginal people' and that we were being judged on that basis. The many times I experienced racism as a kid, I understood that my reaction to it was always about representation. We know that an 'othering' occurs in the minds of non-Aboriginal people, particularly for those who have never met an Aboriginal person – as was the case with most of the town. So my response would immediately be filed as being representative of all Aboriginal people.

Us and them.

As a result, I learnt to educate. I knew that in the minds of those who believed their views to be absolute, my reaction would solidify their perception of Aboriginal people. I had to learn from a young age how to deal with racism as if it wasn't personal.

Racism and identity

As the youngest, I was lucky as I got to stay home for a few years with just my mum until I went to school. She was typical of that generation and didn't go back to work until all her kids were at school. She spent more than forty-five years scrubbing floors as a cleaner, first at the single-men's quarters and then at the school with the education department for thirty years, all to give us kids better opportunities than she'd had. Not once did she ever whinge or make us feel any form of guilt for it. Love won, every time.

Despite Mum's lack of formal education, her passion for politics was impressive. To this day she can name any federal or state politician and tell you their portfolio and relevant background. She watched Question Time for fun. She read the paper (when it used to be real journalism) page by page, every day. We were raised to be politically informed and there was no worse crime in the world than voting for the Liberal Party. 'That's not what black people do,' she would drum into us.

The Pilbara was a union stronghold and always overwhelmingly voted Labor, so by the time the federal election came around the result was already decided in our area. We were the 'dead rubber', for the most part. Dad had just started his own small gardening business when Paul Keating was up for prime minister, and he thought that the Libs understood small business better. So, he decided to exercise his democratic right to vote and voted for the Liberal Party.

When I came home that night after helping on election day (yes, I was also *that* politically active), Dad had been banished to outside the house. The door was closed and Mum was in quite the rage, ranting, 'You won't believe what your father has done!'

Well, I imagined all kinds of crimes against humanity. 'Did he have an affair? Did he break the law?'

Mum looked at me with fury. 'HE VOTED FOR THE LIBERAL PARTY!'

Yes, nothing like exercising your democratic right to vote.

Sadly, the education system didn't match what I was being taught at home. One of my first memories of school was being taught about

Aboriginal people as 'others' who were not like 'us', who were something to be studied. It's also my first vivid memory of a sense of shame. The Social Studies workbook had pictures of two skulls – one was a Neanderthal man's and the other was Truganini's, the last 'full-blood' Aboriginal from Tasmania, whose skeletal remains were on display at the Tasmanian Museum. Rather than the 'lesson' being about Truganini's strength or the disgusting way in which her remains were treated, it was that Aboriginal people had evolved no further up the evolutionary scale than Neanderthals. I remember the assignments referred to Aboriginal people as 'savages', as not having any civilised way of life. The lack of any celebration of Aboriginal people as heroes in leadership or for their contribution to this country remains. The weaponising of teaching black history in school has become about 'critical race theory' or teaching 'white guilt', when it is simply about owning or acknowledging the truth of our history. A history denied is compelled to repeat itself.

I was mortified and immediately felt a sense of shame. I have since understood that racism manifests in the same way as trauma by activating the same responses of fight, flight, fawn or freeze. (I will discuss this in more detail in later chapters.) As a fair-skinned Aboriginal kid, I can completely relate to this. I experienced this fight-or-flight activation whenever racism occurred, and it would occur because my Aboriginality was 'invisible' in being so fair-skinned. The anticipation of racism then became greater for me. My heart rate would speed up and I'd feel like I was going outside of my body. Ultimately, though, it instilled a sense of internalised shame, despite coming from a background in which I was always taught to be proud of my culture. I understand it now as being part of 'black identity formation', which I discuss in detail in Chapter 4. This sense of shame, of not 'fitting in' and of feeling different, commonly leads to an internalised rejection of culture, which is mostly developmentally based and age specific. I certainly went through this, feeling 'embarrassed' about my dark-skinned relatives or simply when I saw Aboriginal people on TV being represented as drunks or criminals or all the other negative stereotypes that dominate the media representation of Aboriginal people. Fortunately, like most Aboriginal people, I also figured it out. Identity is a complicated construct to understand and it's difficult to reconcile that you are different. Most of us want to fit in when we are little kids. The idea that you 'stand out' for any perceived negative reason causes internal stress and identity struggles. As a psychologist, most of my suicidal clients have identity struggles because of racism, either from within their own mob or from non-Aboriginal people. Why? Because our identity can protect us from harm. People who have the genetic, biological luck of resilience (as I had) tend to cope better with external stressors like racism because they have a strong sense of who they are – or more accurately, they have better coping mechanisms. If you add being Indigenous as an extra layer, your identity becomes more about how the general public feels about Aboriginal people. The difficulty with this is that your identity is affected by labels, stereotypes and simple 'group membership', which can drive a lot of your self-worth. Sadly, studies are increasingly showing the adverse impacts of racism, with up to 30 per cent of depression and 70 per cent of trauma symptoms in black people accounted for by racism.[3] The cumulative effects of this are significant. Yet as a country we continue to give racism a 'free pass' as an explanation for suicides, mental health issues, incarceration rates and child removals.

As a psychologist, I know that the first step to healing is to validate the client's pain. At a level of basic human compassion, however, if someone tells me that they are in pain, my first instinct is to acknowledge that pain and not to dismiss them as 'playing the victim' or by saying that they need to harden up or that 'all lives matter'. Yes, all lives do matter, but statistics tell us that all lives clearly do not matter equally. I want to live in a world in which we *don't* have to say 'Black lives matter' anymore. But until we move from denying our racism to acknowledging it, progress will always be slow.

I borrow the ideas of Jane Elliott, an American teacher who developed the famous blue-eyes, brown-eyes social experiment in 1968. For those who don't believe that racism drives poor outcomes for Aboriginal people – that is, doesn't drive our higher incarceration rates, our higher suicide rates, our higher child removal rates – I ask you a simple question: would you trade places with a black person? I wonder what that answer would be.

The good news is that a strong sense of cultural identity can alone buffer the impacts of racism. As a therapist, I have long focused on understanding the tools that Aboriginal people need to manage racist events, rather than ignoring their reality.

Black parents have always understood that they need to raise their kids to be aware they are going to be treated differently because of the colour of their skin. Many black kids I have worked with have told me stories of how their parents will tell them to 'look small' and to not make themselves obvious, to keep their heads down when they walk the streets. It's a horrific burden for a child to carry, and one that non-Aboriginal parents do not have to concern themselves with.

However, there is a fine line between protecting kids from danger by preparing them for racism and feeding an idea that the threat of racism is everywhere or that every 'white' person you encounter is automatically racist. Black parenting ain't easy.

So how can Aboriginal parents raise robust kids who are proud of their culture and have a strong identity in the face of so much objective racism? Well, environment is critical and, importantly, the only thing parents are capable of exercising some level of 'control' over. They can, at a minimum, create an environment that teaches their children not to generalise their experiences of racism in a way that makes the outside world inherently and overwhelmingly threatening. Internalising racism leads to poorer outcomes in our kids. So, when a child experiences racism, it's an opportunity for parents to teach, to ensure that the child develops cognitions that ensure positive psychological adjustment in the future. To show what I mean, let's look at two different parenting (environmental) responses. In the first one, the parent reacts to their child's experience of racism by saying, 'Don't worry, son, that's just the way white people are.' In the other, the parent says, 'Don't worry, son, sometimes *people* are just mean.'

I had the latter environment. As a result, I didn't generalise my experiences of racism in a way that I perceived every interaction with a white person as racism, activating my fight-or-flight response and ensuring that it remained activated and led to poor outcomes. In the former example, the child's cognitions get altered in a way that feeds this view, which activates their fight-or-flight response because racism is perceived as threatening. The body naturally arms itself when it feels in danger, as part of its survival mechanism. So, if racism is perceived as being everywhere, the fight-or-flight response is constant, which means a higher risk for a raft of psychological issues, such as anxiety, trauma responses and depression. Sadly, many of the suicides I have responded to have had racism implicated as causative. Much of the research is now showing that racial trauma is very real and remains unaddressed in therapy by therapists.

But what about environments in which racism is so entrenched that it is literally almost everywhere? Well, stick with me on this one. I was a child welfare worker in Kalgoorlie for a time, and that had to be the most overtly racist place I have ever lived in. In fact, it got so bad that my brother and I started wearing Aboriginal flag pins on our clothes when we went out, hoping it would help us avoid the constant racist comments people would just drop in general conversations. The twenty-four or so Aboriginal kids on my caseload had never known a white person to be kind to them. So, I would construct social environments in which some of my white friends and colleagues would hang out with them – otherwise known as 'Rent a Whitey'. Yes, I am being humorous here.

Now, this may sound odd, but there was method behind my 'madness' (and by the way, it's not racist when I do it ...). I would be very deliberate in my language: 'See that whitefella over there? He's really a nice fella, hey?' This would create a 'white person, very kind, does not compute' scenario, in which ingrained cognitions – such as 'All white people are racist' – could be internally challenged by exposing them to the very thing they did not agree with. Their cognitions would then become altered through evidence to the contrary of what they believe to be true.

My white friends now ask me, 'So, Trace, are we coming around your place to "act white" this weekend?'

'Yep,' is my answer. 'Be as white as you can possibly be.'

To be able to laugh at racism is probably one of the better gifts of resilience. And although finding humour in racism might sound strange, the logic of racism is so illogical it's often easy to laugh at it.

Frankly, racist diatribes haven't changed much since I was a kid. It's the same four or five common themes, so it's pretty easy to develop a prepared, rehearsed script for them all and rattle them off without having to react as much to it emotionally. But it takes time to develop these tools.

The reality for me is also that, as an Aboriginal person with lived experience of racism, and as a psychologist who has always had a 100 per cent Aboriginal caseload, I don't have the luxury of not addressing what is predominantly causative of poor mental health outcomes.

I understand that thoughts feed the fight-or-flight survival activation, so it's about providing the tools that enable my clients to challenge those thoughts. These protective strategies provide a greater buffer to racism than the racism itself. That's not easy – and, importantly, it should never be solely the responsibility of victims to develop the tools to manage racism in isolation from strategies to reduce racism. So, in the past ten years I have started applying the psychology of behavioural change in combination with the neuroscience of racism in my workshops. It's powerful and not something anyone else does, because it is a combination of complex behavioural change as well as understanding not only that racism is not just individually felt, but politically and collectively felt as racial trauma. Racism involves many complex behavioural traits, some of which appear kind and even sound anti-racist but that have as their goal the denial of racism and the pain inflicted on Aboriginal people.

The notion that racism is unconscious is controversial as it is often read as 'letting people off the hook' for their racism. However, I am coming at this from a position of science and of behavioural change as a process. We understand that insight is the starting point to any change. We also understand that people react to difference as infants and that these reactions remain as stress reactions in the brain.

The concept of the racial empathy gap (REG) has established that the capacity to feel empathy and pain is affected by colour and cultural identity – that being, the pain of black people is appraised differently and even felt less than the pain of white people. This can be seen in the significantly lower physiological arousal in white participants for black people experiencing pain than their white counterparts.[4] So, altering that means putting people who perpetrate racism into experiential activities to make what is 'unconscious' conscious, but do so in a way that leads to behavioural change. I have done these workshops with many thousands of people to date – with police, with child protection workers, with teachers. The aim, of course, is to reduce the REG.

This sounds straightforward, but it is extremely 'high risk' as a program and requires a psychologist at the helm, because we are primarily focused on why people change. Indeed, a phenomenon known as the other-race effect (ORE) tells us that blackness is perceived as significantly more personally threatening, which feeds a disproportionate stress-based reaction to cultural and colour differences in racial interactions. In the United States, the George Floyd murder was one such event of ORE disproportionate reactivity. In Australia, there are numerous cases of deaths in police custody, such as Cameron Doomadgee, Ms Dhu, Mr Ward and Joyce Clarke. All these cases showed not only ORE reactivity but REG responses from the broader public and systems, which focused more on the 'less worthiness' of the victims than on the unacceptable actions of police and systems. As a result, there has never been a conviction for an Aboriginal death in custody in Australia because the systems and individuals feel justified in their disproportionate reactivity.

The workshops I run are critical and, to my knowledge, they are the only psychoeducation-based workshops applying racism neuroscience and behavioural change occurring in Australia. The Kumanjayi Walker case, like the George Floyd case and many others, was a 'perfect storm' of ORE. Yet, in the aftermath, no-one was talking about it as a causal factor. Fear of blackness is what resulted in these deaths. Access to higher-level thinking becomes more diminished and impulse control is compromised. Yet people were saying that the police need better conflict-resolution skills or better communication skills. No, they don't. They need to develop insight into their physiological reactivity to blackness (ORE) and to cultivate the tools to reduce it. Conflict-resolution skills are useless when stress reactions dismantle your ability to apply them. This is just basic human-condition stuff, but no-one is brave enough to admit to it in these systems and address it.

I used to hate these workshops because I had to hear a lot of racist stuff throughout them. You have to become okay with hearing it, though, to allow people to gain the insights they need to learn strategies to shift their racist thoughts and behaviours. Yes, it is like therapy, and I do a lot of 'live' challenging with volunteers telling me their most racist thought-drivers. It is absolutely powerful stuff and there have been many moments where you could hear a pin drop. Those are so important because they change people for the better, and I see it in the room. And people keep registering for the workshops because they are so powerful.

I have learnt to do things I don't always love for the greater good, and I know that these workshops will take Australia to a better, more honest place.

True change doesn't happen with denial. But getting at truth requires personal insight. It's relative to your ability to react emotionally to the pain of others. We have a racial empathy gap in Australia, where the pain of Aboriginal people is not being felt. It's not being validated. It's being celebrated.

The psychologist in me is not at all interested in just talking for talking's sake. Putting people in scenarios that make their racism conscious to them, and doing so in a way that ensures behavioural change, is hard. That's a challenge I have taken head-on because while I can work with Aboriginal clients about how they manage racism – in themselves and in their children – it is never the case that victims of racism are 'more responsible' than the perpetrators of it.

Racism and Mum: Taking it on

My mum never took a backwards step when it came to defending her kids and taking on racism, which modelled the behaviour for us kids. In fact, today they would call her fierce. I recall the time when my brother Mike and our cousin Darren volunteered to be waiters at the Year Ten dinner dance. They were both dressed in suits. Photos were taken. They looked so proud. But when they came home, Darren was upset. When Mum asked him what happened, he replied, 'One of the girls said we looked like the black and white minstrels.'

Well, that was that.

'Into the car,' said Mum. Off they went to the girl's house. Darren and Mike were mortified and tried to hide under the back seat.

When they arrived, Mum ordered them out of the car. 'Come with me.' Striding to the front door, she knocked loudly. The door opened and the girl's father was greeted with a demand for an apology. Out came the girl to apologise to Mike and Darren, who by this stage were hoping that the earth would open and swallow them both up.

That was my mum. No-one was going to mess with her. She set the standard for me and all my siblings. She always had our backs. I've lost count of the number of times she called out racism from people.

I remember her saying to me when I was a teenager, 'You kids are not whingers. You always get along. So if you say something is not right, then it has to be because you were raised to tell the truth.'

And she was right. We were never a problem for her. But being one of the only black women in an overwhelmingly white town and taking racism on anyway? Man, that was brave.

A lot of people throw that word at me in relation to the advocacy work I do. I don't know – you just learn to stand up for what is right when it is modelled for you. I don't think that's brave, but

I understand why people may feel that way if they have never seen it before. I have always stood up, even to my own detriment, because I believe it's your responsibility when you have a voice to stand up for those who don't have one. What is the point of having an education if you don't use it to educate others? It's a responsibility more so as a psychologist to educate on issues that people will often find painful, but through that pain can come a greater understanding.

I have now learnt probably the greatest lesson of all: that my disadvantage is my greatest advantage.

I don't need to have racism explained to me because I have experienced it.

I don't need to have disadvantage explained to me because I have lived it.

And that's why solutions should always belong in the hands of those who have also 'closed many gaps'.

2

Education:
The most powerful weapon

'Education is the most powerful weapon you can use to challenge the world.' These words from the great man Nelson Mandela have always been so poignant to me. My parents mirrored that in our home every day. They understood that the *only* way we would have a better life than they had had was through an education.

Education has taken me beyond any expectation I ever had for myself. Everyone probably assumed I would stay in the Pilbara and not do much with my life. But I have learnt that coming from disadvantage should never limit you nor define you. My education has seen me travel the world and the width, depth and breadth of this country several times over. You can lose your physical health, you can lose your mental health, but an education is something that no-one can take away from you.

I hope that I stand as an example to Aboriginal people – to those from remote backgrounds, to those who do not come from familial, educational or generational advantage, or anyone who is struggling with the voices around them of lowered expectations – that anything is possible.

But I am also conscious of the fact that there has been a lot of luck in my disadvantage – luck that many Aboriginal people do not have.

My story

So, there I was, living in a remote mining town where resources were limited and pretty much everyone worked at the mine. By the time I was fifteen Dad had progressed to being a 'white hat' – a supervisor, who would wear a white safety hat to denote their status, while the workers would wear orange ones. (It was a 'don't drink the Kool Aid' type cult – those mining towns!) Mum and Dad were finally earning good money and had enough savings that we weren't struggling as much anymore.

My brother Mike had managed to get himself into Mining Engineering at the Western Australian School of Mines in Kalgoorlie; Lynny had accepted a traineeship with Hamersley Iron and decided to remain in Tom Price; and Lorn and Sharon had both long left home, as the two eldest in the family, and were starting families of their own in Tom Price.

I was about to begin Year Ten, but the local high school didn't do many tertiary entrance subjects for Year Eleven or Twelve. Almost all my same-aged peers were sent to private schools just before they turned thirteen, with their parents having no choice but to spend all their wages on high school fees to give their kids the same opportunities that most 'city folk' took for granted. So off I went to Perth College in Mount Lawley at the ripe 'old' age of fifteen to embrace the opportunities (and astronomical cost) of a private school.

It was probably my own fault that they sent me, because I had recently stated very proudly that I wanted to become a psychologist, after reading about the profession in an occupation finder at school. It sounded like a great thing to do, but at that age I didn't have any complex understanding of it, just an instinct that helping people was something I would be good at.

I'd always found it easy to relate to people and to get them to talk and feel comfortable. I was a student councillor for multiple years running, a top athlete and a scholastic over-achiever in the small pond I found myself in, which gave me the confidence to be a people person.

However, the odds of becoming a psychologist were pretty stacked against me on multiple levels. First, there wasn't anyone in Tom Price who had done all their schooling (including from kindergarten) and managed to get themselves into university. Second, I had never met a psychologist in my life. Third, no-one on either side of my family had been to university or had a tertiary education (except my brother, who had just started his mining engineering degree), so I didn't have the generational advantage of having formally educated parents as models for this, unlike many others. This also meant not having the 'privilege' that my peers took for granted – having parents who could help with your homework. Mum's education was limited to primary school and Dad's was not much better. Lastly, Tom Price was not set up for scholars or academics – the vast majority of my mates had either gone off and found work at the mine or had ambitions to do so after they finished the equivalent of Year Twelve, and taking trades and 'secretarial-focused' subjects. It was certainly tempting to do the same after seeing your mates driving around in brand-new cars and having disposable income, not doing the hard yards of years of study, that's for sure.

So, I caught my first-ever airplane to seek the opportunities in Perth that my small town could not provide. I was one of two Aboriginal kids at Perth College and while I loved the girls I met, I absolutely hated the boarding school and the restrictions I suddenly had on my movements and choices. In fact, I hated it so much that I lasted a solid six weeks! I refused to get back on the plane after the Easter holidays, much to my parents' anger and disappointment. Interestingly, it was my brother Mike who was the most disappointed, which speaks to the way we were being raised to reach for the stars. He was no doubt rightly concerned that I was giving up my dreams out of fear and that I would spend my life in the same small town as a result. But boarding school was simply the wrong environment for me. As someone who had so much freedom at home, I found it overwhelming and frustrating to do everything by a routine and a bell, asking permission anytime you wanted to move beyond the dorm. I admit I didn't cope at all well with it.

The school was also very strongly Catholic. Being forced to go to Scripture on Sundays was something that I had put up with as a kid, but I felt increasingly repelled by the Catholic Church. To me it represented nothing but hypocrisy and pain. Culture and religion have very rarely ended well for Aboriginal people. Mum had us all baptised as Roman Catholics, mostly out of fear. Certainly, the only stories I heard about the Catholic Church and nuns from my mum were brutal. She told us about the constant floggings she copped in the missions. One of the worst stories was from when she was a kid. She had beautiful black hair, which her mum would groom every day. It gave her a sense of pride. When she got head lice, the nuns decided they would chop off all her hair and pour kerosene over her scalp for good measure to make sure the lice were gone. My grandmother's heart broke when she saw Mum: completely bald, with visible cut marks all over her head. But what could she do about it as an Aboriginal woman? Absolutely nothing. She wiped Mum's tears away, dressed her in her uniform and sent her back to school as though nothing had happened.

I remember the nuns would regularly knock at our door to ask for donations, and Mum would scrape together a few cents to give to them. So many times, though, Mum would hear them knocking and panic that the house wasn't clean enough, even though it was always spotless. As the youngest and the last kid at home with Mum, I recall one day Mum sent me to answer the door – with all my blonde hair and whiteness – with clear instructions to tell the nuns she wasn't home. Unfortunately, at four years old, I took that a bit literally and Mum was mortified when she heard me proudly tell the nuns, 'Mum told me to tell you that she's not home.' Mum frantically came out from her hiding place and tried to do a bit of damage control.

On another visit, when I was no more than five years old, I was standing in the lounge room and heard the nun say, 'You have a very clean house for an Aboriginal.' Mum reacted like it was a compliment. That was her generation – such a comment from a nun to an Aboriginal woman was high praise indeed. Even at that young age I felt this was not right, and it has always stayed with me.

As I got older, the Scripture classes that used to be 'fun' – with singing and being praised for reciting passages from the Bible that you didn't really understand – increasingly started to make less and less sense. (Even now I can recite many of the passages of the Old and New Testament by heart.) Two things stood out for me. The first was when one of my sisters had a baby 'out of wedlock' and the church refused to baptise my nephew. Then, when another of my sisters remarried, she wasn't allowed to have the ceremony in the church because the Catholic Church did not believe in divorce. It was this type of thing that made me question the 'God loves all of his children equally' rhetoric that was preached at us so often in the Scripture classes. When I was forced to hear many of these teachings again at private school, it put me off staying there even more.

Back at home, I had no real idea what I was doing other than getting away from what I saw as the 'prison' of private school. I slipped back into Year Ten and frankly felt so relieved at being back with my mates and family that I found myself being called to the deputy principal's office for a good hard lecture! Mrs Massey, the first female deputy principal of our school, was probably the coolest woman I had ever seen in all my fifteen years of 'worldly' experience. She stood out in my mind for being a high-achieving woman, but she was also just cool. She was always smartly dressed and had a bob haircut. I was in awe of her. She seemed so sophisticated, but more importantly she had bucked the trend of all leaders being men. I loved that about her. The fact that she gave me the 'come to Jesus' talk I needed stands out to this day. Her words to me were, 'Tracy, you are a smart young lady. Your academic record is impeccable, but the way you are going, you are heading for a string of Cs. You can't continue to rely on your natural smarts anymore. If you are aiming for university, you have to put effort in and you have to put it in now.'

I am so grateful for that conversation and I still remember every moment of it – its impact was that great. By the end of the year, I managed to get straight As across all of my subjects. This gave me choices for Years Eleven and Twelve, but of course I had no intention of going back to a private school in Perth. So, the only option was to do my tertiary entrance subjects through distance education.

Distance education was completely under-resourced at the time – and still is – and it was extremely challenging not having constant physical access to a teacher. However, it was critical for giving kids like me an opportunity to reach for the stars while remaining in our communities until we felt robust enough to break through the safety net and go down to the city. I would most likely not have become a psychologist without it. I recently advocated for the restoring of funding for school of the air and distance education when Western Australia's state government tried to defund many of these services in remote communities. Education should be available to everyone – not just those who are already privileged through greater access or economic or familial advantage. I stand as a success story of the distance education model, and I am sure that there are many others.

Distance education was difficult though, as you really had to work ten times harder than most students; it's different to school of the air, which has an actual classroom set-up. However, it taught me to be independent and self-sufficient in my learning. I would get my monthly assignments, post them back to a tutor in Perth, who would then mark them and post them back. The high school just allotted me 'free class periods' to sit in a room with my assigned work. There was no other support. I was just very lucky that Mr Young, our geography teacher, was a former distance education teacher and had also taught history. He simply took it upon himself to help in any way that he could.

I was also very fortunate to have the best group of friends possible. There was a handful of us who were probably seriously doing distance education for university entrance, including my best friend Karen Button, Steven Lloyd (who is still one of the smartest and nicest people I have ever met – a deadly combination),

Andrew Reyne and my other bestie Rachel Wright. We supported each other as much as we could but, ultimately, we were pretty alone. I met my distance education teacher once in those entire two years, which is pretty incredible to write down now.

We were all good kids and a dream for our parents because we just didn't get up to anything bad; if we ever tried (like once attempting to smoke a cigar on New Year's Eve – yes, truly 'naughty' stuff), we were all so loud and innocent that we would ultimately give the game away. I was a complete sports nut and that was pretty much a full-time job – playing basketball, softball, water polo and even soccer at one stage, but I truly loved running. I was a sprinter, excelling in 100-metre and 200-metre sprints. Long jump, high jump – I would have a go at pretty much anything and everything, athletics-wise. My dream was to become a full-time professional athlete and although studying was important to me, sport was more so. Even to this day, running remains my first love. I truly couldn't exist without it. Basketball was almost an obsession. I would regularly be down at the outdoor tar courts in 48-plus-degree heat, shooting hoops to the point of rarely missing a shot. I always had a Spalding basketball somewhere not far away from me. I have always been driven, no matter what the task, and study was no different. I have never really known how not to do 'full force' with anything I set my mind to.

Year Twelve is always an incredibly stressful year, but it was even harder doing it all alone. By this stage, I was one of just a handful of people trying seriously to go university – with Karen, Andrew and Rachel – as most other students had already decided on apprenticeships at the mine with Hamersley Iron. The problem with this was that our tertiary entrance scores were subject to a process of statistical moderation, which meant that because only four students in our school were sitting the exams, how well each of us did would dramatically affect the moderated scores. After the 'mock' tertiary entrance exams, I remember (but didn't fully appreciate at the time) our deputy principal imploring all twenty Year Twelve students *not* to sit the tertiary entrance exams if their goal *wasn't* to go to university, as it would have such a huge impact upon the scores of those of us who did want to go.

Some took the advice, but many didn't. As a result, despite getting 93 per cent in my history exam, my statistically moderated score was 73 per cent, which could have been devastating to my entrance into university. I was pretty angry about it, to be honest. Clearly the difficulties studying in a remote region were not fully understood by those decision-makers in the city, and in their wisdom they made it even harder. If anyone thinks that education is *not* for the privileged, then I am happy to be an example of that through this book.

At the time though, my obsession with getting into university was so great that I did nothing but sleep and study. Mum coped with it beautifully. She would put a plate of food in front of me, say nothing, then walk away. She had dealt with four other kids by that stage, so she understood the value of silence for stressed-out teenagers.

When I heard the familiar sound of the postie dropping off the day's mail, I knew my tertiary entrance score had finally arrived. It was a hot day as usual and I was restless. Holidays in Tom Price were always like that. There were only so many times you could go down to the milk bar or cut laps with your mates, which, when you were on your P-plates, was tops in entertainment!

It felt like my entire future was in that envelope. As I slowly ripped it open, I suddenly couldn't breathe. I had so many feelings. My legs felt weak and I had to sit down. I knew I needed a score of at least 370 to get an offer from the University of Western Australia (UWA). I was absolutely desperate to go there. It was one of the top 100 universities in the world and to me represented a reality I could only dream of being a part of – old-school academia and world-recognised to boot.

My eyes desperately scanned down to the bottom of the page.

My score: 384.

I was buzzing! I had officially become the first person to complete their entire schooling, from kindergarten to high school, in Tom Price and get into university. The hard work was behind me now; it was time to head back to Perth. This time was different, though. I was now ready to leave the comfort and security of my Pilbara upbringing.

The big smoke

So there I was, a kid from the Pilbara, desperate to learn everything I could to equip me to deal with the most complex mental health issues facing my people. In the 'big smoke' of Perth, man, did my fellow students think I was daily entertainment. I had never caught a bus or been on an escalator. One day I ended up on a bus all the way from Nedlands to Fremantle – travelling more than 13 kilometres past my stop – simply because I felt it was too 'shame job' to press the button to let the driver know I wanted to get off, with all those eyes on me. I remember thinking how brave people were to do that! I was so anxious about crossing highways I would literally wait for a group of people to follow them across, such was my fear of being hit by a car. It's funny that when I travel to Melbourne and Sydney even now, I still do the same thing. I guess you can take the girl out of the bush ...

Everything was so fast-paced I couldn't keep up. Perth to me was overwhelming and scary. I was living at St Catherine's College, and thank god because I felt safe and grounded there. I could at least find my way to the food hall, no problem. College also gave me a backup sisterhood. Mostly they just laughed at me, but they were great girls. We had a group of ten or so of us who became firm mates. There was the Esperance crew: Sandra, the future accountant; Christine, the graphic designer; Clare, the marine biologist, who would gleefully tell us at dinner how many epidermises she had ripped off in her biology class (we soon banned her from updating us on her day). There was also Karen, who had been my best friend since primary school. We were two Tom Price kids in the big smoke with no idea what we were doing, but we had each other. We were in the same dorm but at different universities, as Karen was training to be a dental therapist at Curtin University. I loved every minute of my time there. Probably a bit too much! It was like a smorgasbord of fun for an eighteen-year-old who had only met a few hundred people in their entire life before. And I genuinely like people, which is probably an essential part of the psychologist job description.

Although I adored college life, I didn't enjoy university itself, which I truly didn't expect given I had worked so hard to get there, but ambition just didn't come to me until much later. University is so much about discovering yourself. Every ounce of my energy was still reserved for sport at this life stage – basketball, running and sprint training. Making study even less interesting was that I only had twelve contact hours a week. Of course, I was ill-equipped for this and assumed that going to the lecture was all I needed to do. I didn't realise that there was this thing called pre-reading, which added an extra three or four hours of reading for every contact hour.

The culture shock was the most impactful. I didn't name it at the time; that has only come with hindsight. I didn't have the luxury of 'just learning' like my peers. Most days, it felt as though someone had parachuted me in from a different planet. I must say, though, that the exchange rate was pretty good – for every $1 in Pilbara money, I got $1.01 in Perth money (yes, that's a joke). I remember sitting in my first lecture theatre and staring back at me were around 800 pairs of eyes. This was almost bigger than my home town. I was only one of four Aboriginal people studying first-year psychology at UWA and the other three 'had to do it' as an elective, so they would not go on to become psychologists. I felt so honoured to be there, to be walking in the footsteps of so many people before me, but I was also overwhelmed at being only one of a small number of Aboriginal people who ever did. And definitely the only kid from the Pilbara who did. And what made it worse was, frankly, how white the system was and how it spoke only to those from privilege. Words that I had never heard before dominated conversations and I didn't have the 'script'. I would regularly be in tutorials with people who I just felt silly or 'less than' around. They all seemed so mature and sophisticated. I didn't know anything about the complexities of city life or the nuances of the written phrase. I didn't even know what a bibliography was and bombed out in many assignments because of it.

The campus was beautiful but large, so I missed many classes purely because I couldn't find my way to the lecture theatre. Its population was over 10,000 at that stage – to me it was frightening that so many people could be in one place at the same time. Libraries were a nightmare. I would go there, not be able to find anything and then walk back to the safety and sanctity of my room at college. I felt overwhelmed and not 'good enough' to be there. I knew absolutely nothing about the world, really, even though I excelled at history. I had only ever been on a couple of planes before and had never travelled outside of the state. Everything I knew was based on what I learnt in my small home town.

Feeling completely out of my depth for the first time in my life, I found the fun of the city way too tempting and a convenient distraction. I have always been an extrovert, and it was easy to just focus on fun when I was around a lot of people my own age at college. There was always someone who was prepared to take a 'study break' and come out with me. I became a victim of a self-fulfilling prophecy in which I found the system so overwhelming that I stopped being serious about doing well. I also needed to discover an entire world I had never known – being around so many educated and smart people studying so many different disciplines. I drank in conversations with so many students, went to pubs and nightclubs, and, of course, did so much sport. It was just fantastic.

University was also just too theoretical. Psychology was all about science, much of which I found was impossible to relate to human beings, let alone black ones. It didn't help that the word Aboriginal was not mentioned once throughout the entirety of my undergraduate degree. Psychology is based on a scientist–practitioner model – the science informs practice. The problem is the science has been informed without Aboriginal people, so I couldn't relate to any of it. There are many things in psychology 'proven' by science that defy logic. Practitioners are then trained based on faulty science. However, when I was being trained in the 'science' as an undergrad,

I internalised this as being my own deficits – my inability to learn, my failure to understand it and, ultimately, to become a psychologist. I now understand how education systems favour the privileged while crushing so many Aboriginal people because of it.

By 1991, I had nonetheless managed to complete a Bachelor of Arts (or a BA, which we used to say stood for 'Bugger All' because that's what it qualified you for) with a major in psychology. For the first and last time, I had a terrible academic transcript – a string of Cs. Having had to do most of my tertiary entrance subjects through distance education had made me completely ill-equipped for the system I was entering.

I have since learnt that academic transcripts often don't reflect how smart you are, just how many barriers you have to overcome.

So, I left university having basically given up on my dream of becoming a psychologist. It was just too hard to reconcile it with the reality of what Aboriginal people were experiencing every day. I had also suffered so much damage to my self-esteem because of my transcripts that I was like a wounded dog who just wanted to get away from it. It was much later that I realised how the university system had failed me and my people.

How was it possible to have a suicide rate that was double that for non-Aboriginal Australians, an incarceration rate that was nineteen times the rate for non-Aboriginal people, a child removal rate ten times the rate for non-Aboriginal people and not have *any* training as a psychologist on how to work with Aboriginal people? This profession is supposed to respond to all pain, not hierarchically organise the relevance of that pain.

Giving up my dream sounds like it should have been tough, but it really wasn't, and I didn't feel that way at all. Even now, I am so thankful for every single struggle I have had because they've all led me to where I am today. Fortunately, what I didn't lose was my desire to work with my people. So, I boldly applied for a job with the Department for Community Development in child protection – mostly because my brother, Mike, was in Kalgoorlie by then and that was where the job was based.

My catchment area was the Western Desert communities. As the only Aboriginal graduate welfare officer in the entire district, I had no real choice but to take on Kalgoorlie as well as occasionally get out to the surrounding communities, where many of my clients and wards of the state were based.

I would never have gone to the Western Desert if university had made sense to me. I would never have been faced with every complex human behavioural issue it is possible to be challenged by. I would never have become the psychologist I am now. Remote communities are the hardest work you will ever do. There is no backup, no-one you can refer complex clients to. You have to deal with what is in front of you. But, if you can withstand the challenge, they will also make you a significantly better clinician. They force you to consider your privilege and feel the love of those who do not have it, every single day. So many clients would come to see me because they understood that I could help them; I could advocate for what they needed because I had the words; and I had natural empathy for their pain as an Aboriginal person. I suddenly became aware that I had this privilege of being heard and listened to, and it was the first time I respected the value of my education and understood the responsibility it came with. It lit a fire in me. It was these communities that restored my faith in myself – that made me believe that I could actually do psychology.

3

Changing Psychology in Australia: Developing evidence for culture-bound syndromes

In more than two decades as a psychologist, I have never had a learning curve as significant as those years I visited the Western Desert and those remote communities. I am so grateful it was my first experience as a future psychologist, and more grateful that I have never gone into these communities as a 'visitor'. I was there to do complex trauma, suicide prevention and traumatic grief interventions, and it was always at the request of the community themselves based on my growing reputation and 'vouching' from one community to the next.

Too many people never have the privilege of working at the cutting edge of cultural complexity like this. It's easy to take a 'safe' path in psychology, to work with what is predictable – and nothing about Aboriginal communities is either of those things. Over the years, I have had so many clients come to me who, on the face of it, looked floridly psychotic or who were having complex attachment and trauma-based issues that would level any clinician. In the Western Desert, I'd only had three years of psychology training. On top of this, the community would consistently attribute symptoms to cultural phenomena, whereas I thought they were due to clinical disorders. I was a 'baby' culturally – not only because of my age, but also because Aboriginal culture is so complex and hierarchically status organised. In addition to having no training to guide me, there were no practising Aboriginal psychologists who could guide me through it. When clients were experiencing spiritual visits, for example, the community would say, 'He's right' – meaning that he was just going through a cultural grieving process or that he had been 'sung' or 'cursed' because of cultural wrongdoing. However, my clinical training told me that he was experiencing command hallucinations – the definition of which is someone believing their thoughts are being controlled by an outside source. How on earth do you unpack the difference between someone experiencing psychosis and someone seeing spirits of deceased loved ones as part of cultural grief?

I had to think on my feet because nothing had been published that accepted a spiritual dimension could be anything other than a diagnosable mental illness. The professions of psychology and psychiatry had no evidence to support a different set of beliefs attached to mental health, which meant that the so-called science just didn't allow for it – but those who were determining the 'science' were definitely not Aboriginal people.

So I picked up a notepad and drew two columns on a page. On one side I wrote 'Similar' and on the other side 'Different', and then listed the ways in which spiritual visits were similar to psychosis and how they were different. This was the simple way I started developing an 'evidence base' around distinguishing between psychosis/ schizophrenia and culturally appropriate spiritual visits – and this was only *one* culture-bound syndrome of many that I had to make sense of.

It was instinctual for me as an Aboriginal psychologist to unpack and validate these realities rather than pathologise them. Although it was truly frightening to take on my profession and tell them they had it wrong, it defies logic that Aboriginal people have up to three to four times the rate of psychoses and schizophrenia as non-Aboriginal people, given the prevalence of schizophrenia is pretty stable across cultures.[1] However, there remains little published literature that guides clinicians appropriately to determine cultural differences from schizophrenia outside of a handful of articles.[2] It's not uncommon to go to Aboriginal communities with a population of a few hundred and they often have up to a dozen or more Aboriginal people who are diagnosed schizophrenics. It's impossible for these rates to be correct.

I remembered a fundamental truth drilled into me during my training as a psychologist: *If you get assessment wrong, you get treatment wrong and you make things worse.* Here is an example of what happens when you get assessment wrong. An Aboriginal man reports he has been 'sung' ('cursed') by lore men for a cultural wrongdoing. He's placed in psychiatric care and diagnosed with command hallucinations. He's put on medication. His visions of lore men persecuting him become worse due to his failure to resolve the cultural wrongdoing. He's then confined in a psychiatric ward for his own safety. He starts having spiritual visits calling him back home to Country. He's diagnosed with clinical depression, but he's suffering from a spiritual disconnection from being away from Country. His medication is increased. His spiritual visits become severe and he self-harms. His medication is increased again.

This is too often an Aboriginal person's reality when they have contact with the mental health system. Cases like this have become my bread and butter as a psychologist, either through my own clients or consultations with clinicians across Australia, with this type of cultural phenomenon being misdiagnosed, treated clinically and not being resolved. For psychosis and schizophrenia, this usually means prescribing anti-psychotics.

When I first started going into remote communities, I noticed – and the community themselves would regularly flag – the number of medications that were being prescribed, too often as the sole treatment of choice. In a very remote community, I had an elder whose son was diagnosed with schizophrenia. The elder said that one day he decided to time how long the mental health nurse spent 'treating' his son, which was essentially administering medication. He said that the nurse getting out of the car, administering the injection and getting back into the car took a total of eight minutes!

My early observations of the transactional nature of mental-health service delivery have become more normalised over time. Nurses drive from community to community solely administering anti-psychotics, or mental health workers have a basic interaction rather than deliver complex therapeutic interventions.

In fairness, governments are not funding prevention or therapeutic services in remote regions, and the ones that are there are burnt out and overwhelmed. Universities have also dropped the ball when it comes to culturally informed treatments. There are also the difficulties of isolation and attracting staff willing to cover vast catchment areas, often without backup. The Kimberley, for example, which has the highest suicide rates in Australia,[3] has a catchment area of some 48,000 kilometres. It's impossible for mental health clinicians to do anything impactful in these circumstances. I consider myself to be a pretty good psychologist, and there is no way I would go into a high-risk remote community with no backup or support. But we expect that of our workforce every day, and then we wonder why they burn out and why remote areas continue to consistently have our highest-risk communities.

In the Kimberley region, for example, less than 1 per cent of the population access a clinical psychologist. It is unknown what percentage of that is Aboriginal clients. However, the waitlist for psychologists in the wealthy eastern suburbs of Sydney is two months.[4] Therapeutic services are predominantly based, accessed and funded in urban environments rather than in our highest-risk communities, which are consistently the most remote. The fact that we do not geomap data to show these hotspots means we don't fund commensurate with need. To say our government has let these communities down is an understatement, and it is as true to say that they stopped caring about them – or pretending that they do – decades ago. As I mentioned earlier, this is called the racial empathy gap (REG) – the pain of these deaths is just not felt as equally as the pain of other deaths by suicide that are more 'relatable' to politicians. The in group/out group dynamic explains a bit of it, of course, but the REG explains the balance.

Rather than explore cultural causes and interventions, the medication dosage is increased or changed to another brand because, remember, this is the 'treatment of choice'. But when these clients are experiencing a culturally related spiritual visit or have been 'cursed' or 'sung', medications don't work. They don't result in any symptom relief. Dosing up patients with anti-psychotics beyond the point of it being therapeutic is dangerous, but it's considered 'best practice'.

The other problem is that the duty of care of mental health professionals does not include being culturally informed. Just as our training was so singular in its cultural exclusion, too many practitioners don't appreciate their responsibility to understand a client's worldview and to have the tools to engage with them at this level. If this was a clear ethical requirement, the treatment of choice would look very different – not just in terms of access to traditional healers or Nungkari (we Nyamal people call them Maban) and culturally specific treatments, but also in the profession insisting that practitioners understand that context is vital when it comes to assessing what is 'normal'. 'Normal' is culturally relative, which from a psychological standpoint means that clinicians' basic duty to establish what is impactful or what 'impairs functioning' is relative to cultural context.

For me, my go-to ethical principle has always been the 'principle of least harm' – what is the least harmful approach for my client? You could choose to medicate an Aboriginal person who is experiencing culturally related distress or you could explore and facilitate cultural resolution and have a far greater chance of symptoms being reduced or, often, completely resolving.

What is best practice culturally is too often at odds with the principle of least harm when it's predicated on clinical best practice. This should be fundamental in the training for all in the mental health profession, but it isn't. No wonder Aboriginal clients fear contact with the system. They are so resigned to the idea that medications will be the sole treatment that they resist getting professional help. As one elder recently said to me, 'That fulla has got so many pills in him you can hear him rattling.' I've heard someone else say, 'That one has so many pills in him he glows in the dark.' When the treatment of choice is psychotropic medications, it leads to fear because people are being nullified out of their symptoms. And all the community see is that the person they knew is no longer there.

The efficacy of psychotropic medications has been debated in relation to treatment generally,[5] so it is of great concern that there remain no clinical controlled trials with Aboriginal people, as we are extremely vulnerable given our isolation, remoteness and medical literacy. Self-medicating is often a core component of depression, for example, and the range between a toxic and therapeutic dose becomes incredibly problematic in this combination of factors. With up to 85 per cent of GPs prescribing them, it indicates that a medical, disease model is consistently the sole focus.[6] It seems like a 'quick fix' but it's lazy. It doesn't give the client and their community the tools to respond to the disorder – nor does it ensure that mental health workers are required to provide these tools.

Why cultural treatments are so important

If cultural issues aren't explored, cultural treatment becomes an associated impossible reality for clinicians.

Get assessment wrong, get treatment wrong, make things worse.

Cultural issues need cultural treatments for things to resolve. Cultural treatments involve cultural interventions from an appropriate hierarchy, from elders to Nungkari or Maban, or through specific rituals (going through Sorry Time). But the fear of exploring cultural causes – and, therefore, cultural treatments – overwhelms the average psychologist because this is not within the scientific evidence base they are trained in. Then there is the reality that these treatments are highly complex, particularly with a culture so secretive and taboo that you could unwittingly cause damage for your client. It takes an extraordinary amount of dedication to be culturally effective and to be respected culturally.

But clinicians face a global industry of the monocultural nature of psychopathology, of disorders informed by a singular cultural view – tested only with non-Aboriginal people. What this translates to is significant ongoing barriers and feelings of stigma for Aboriginal people in need of critical mental health treatment when accessing services.[7] For example, in Queensland, the Northern Territory and Western Australia, up to 77 per cent of 'intensive family therapy support programs' are engaged with by non-Aboriginal families.[8]

The sad reality is that Aboriginal people only access the treatment they need when it is mandated, either through prison programs or via statutory child welfare requirements. I have heard too many stories of families so desperate to help a loved one that they call the police to get them locked up, so they can then access treatment programs. It's not a decision that any family, let alone our most at risk and vulnerable, should have to endure.

What does cultural treatment look like?
The man who was sorry cutting

A remote area nurse who I worked with years ago would regularly have 'mob' bring people in to see her because they were sorry cutting, which is a common cultural grief ritual. It involves hitting or cutting parts of the body as a way of releasing pain for the person who has passed away and is specific to Sorry Time (sometimes called Funeral Time). These rituals are displays of respect for the deceased. However, in my research, communities consistently reported that Sorry Time was more ritualistic in areas that were more remote. It also involves specific people who had specific relationships with the deceased and is often separated by gender, such as 'women's wailing circles' (this is not the traditional term) in which predominantly women wail in distress for the deceased.

The nurse would regularly see people who had sorry cut to the point that they were at risk to themselves – for example, hitting their head so much they caused significant gashes. The nurse was told to 'patch them up' so that they could go back and continue their Sorry Time. This obviously presents significant conflicts with the nurse's duty of care to 'do no harm'. Another ethical dilemma lies in her responsibility as a health professional to assess and manage the risk of her clients.

So, how should she have proceeded? These cultural practices present significant challenges in separating self-harm that is individually generated from those that are culturally sanctioned, collectively initiated behaviours. The physical signs or cuts are likely to be confused clinically for a deliberate, personal act of self-harm. Non-Indigenous practitioners have to consider the cultural appropriateness of these behaviours, which differ not only from their own worldview and beliefs, but also from the clinical (mono-cultural) diagnostic information available to them.

But there are also several distinguishing characteristics. First, we know that sorry cutting never leads to death.[9] So, the principle of least harm means allowing an Aboriginal client to go through their specific, collective grief process to ensure their grief will then be resolved, rather than remain unresolved.

Second, the ritual of sorry cutting is meant to *release* rather than *create* pain. The cutting of skin is to resolve the pain of loss, and to also demonstrate respect for the deceased. It's vital to be able to determine the difference between behaviours which represent deliberate self-harm from those which represent a culturally appropriate expression of grief.

Third, individuals appear disconnected from pain during sorry cutting. In my paper on culture-bound syndromes I discuss the idea of differential pain tolerance, which has been noted in several cultures worldwide whereby rites of passage that outwardly appear painful are clearly not experienced as such. One example of this occurs during the Tamil Hindu festival of Thaipusam, in which participants engage in various acts of devotion and control over their senses, including piercing their skin, tongue or cheeks. It is therefore worth considering whether dissociation is at play in sorry cutting, and whether dissociation is indeed a practised cultural phenomenon. To engage in these rituals in a way that ensures that pain is *released* rather than *felt*, there must arguably be a dissociative element involved. However, this creates problems from an assessment perspective because self-harm also has a dissociative element that enables the person to not experience it as painful. This commonality is significant, as it makes it difficult for the clinician to separate cultural sorry cutting from self-harm without exploring the 'triggers' and relevant cultural context to these behaviours.

Despite the similarities, it is clear that sorry cutting is vastly different to self-harm. Simply being able to explore what has triggered the behaviour – external, collective cultural grief resolution as opposed to internal resolution of psychological pain – and then assessing if the individual's report matches the community context: that being, using similar idioms, language and terms of distress to describe the behaviour; it fitting with cultural grief protocols within the context of Sorry Time; and it's sanctioned by the community.

A standard Mental Status Exam (MSE) requires that there is an assessment of 'self-harm'. My lived experience is of hearing too many stories of Aboriginal people being sectioned in psychiatric wards because practitioners have confused sorry cutting for self-harm and felt terrified, rightly, of failing in their duty of care if someone is at risk to themselves.

Importantly, sorry cutting has a clear end point to it, tied in with the conclusion of other cultural behaviours and rituals that mark the end of Sorry Time. However, what does differ is the specific grief *rituals* from one community to the next. Context is therefore important. So, the 'intervention' is to ensure that all of the behaviours and processes specific to the cultural context of Sorry Time are enacted. The therapist then monitors their client's outcome. The sorry cutting should conclude as the cultural grief is resolved.

You can appreciate this is terrifying for the average clinician, because 'duty of care' always has a cultural context of 'what will cause the least harm' to their client.

The girl who had spiritual visits
My desire to work on cultural treatments gathered momentum when I left the beautiful Western Desert communities and Kalgoorlie and

moved to the city to be a 'baby psychologist'. My first client was a twelve-year-old Aboriginal girl who was having spiritual visits from her cousin-sister, who had died two years previously and was telling the girl to 'join her', as in 'end her life' like she had. I'd erroneously thought that culture-bound syndromes only existed in remote areas, because that's where 'real' Aboriginals live, right? Well, now all bets were off …

Again, I turned to my trusty 'similar/different' idea that I'd used in the remote communities. It had become a little more sophisticated over time, through clinical experience with many Aboriginal clients and, of course, yarning with elders. I knew I had to differentiate spiritual visits from psychosis and schizophrenia across the core symptoms upon which clinicians rely. But I also knew that I had to determine and manage her risk to self.

No pressure!

Suicide risk assessment is different with Aboriginal people. The risk indicators are not the same and neither is how you extract information from Aboriginal clients, in terms of communication styles but also in gender differences and areas of taboo information. I will discuss this more fully in Chapter 8, but for now, I will say this: everything we do is narrative, built around a story and always visually based.

To discover if something is culturally related, we ask questions like, 'What is the main yarn you are telling yourself when you feel worst in yourself?' Or 'What is the main image you see?' Aboriginal people will always tell a cultural story, and getting at this content is important when it comes to assessing for cultural versus clinical context and triggers.

There is also a normalcy of the spiritual dimension within Aboriginal culture, such as seeing, hearing or feeling spirits of the deceased. This means that, straight off the bat, two of the diagnostic criteria out of five for the diagnosis of schizophrenia are met. This includes hallucinations and delusions, which are both evident in cultural spiritual visits in grief reactions and within the culture-bound phenomena of being 'sung' or 'cursed'.

Generally, psychosis looks at two core areas: whether people have delusions, and whether they have hallucinations. To convince the industry that these were, in fact, culturally appropriate spiritual visits, I understood I had to provide evidence of difference across these two areas.

First, delusions are what is referred to as 'false beliefs' – beliefs not based in fact. The person believes something despite overwhelming evidence that disproves it. They continue to believe it anyway. It used to be difficult to explain the concept of delusions, but then Donald Trump happened ... 'I won the election.' 'No, you didn't.' Despite overwhelming evidence, he believed it anyway.

However, cultural relativism then comes in and – as we know – when determining what is 'normal', context is important. So, does Aboriginal culture say that spirits can visit us? Twenty years of clinical experience and my entire life as an Aboriginal person definitively says, 'Yes.' So, the belief that spirits are visiting you from an Aboriginal context is not delusional, because it is culturally relative and appropriate. The culture believes this is possible. That's the first differentiating characteristic. The individual then needs to describe the experience using the same words and language that their specific community uses (we call this 'idioms of distress'). This is the second stage of the assessment process, in which the individual view needs to be consistent with the community context. For example, some communities have spiritual visits, but some don't. When they do, they will use specific words and dialect to describe them. They will understand how they look and manifest. Individual and community contexts must match each other. To assess this, the clinician is responsible for having this information via cultural mapping of community context and community norms. It is important that we are objective when it comes to assessment.

The second distinguishing characteristic of delusions is that those who are psychotic/schizophrenic tend to have a particular *type* of delusion, of which there are many – delusions of grandiosity, of paranoia, of reference, and so on. With schizophrenics, delusions always generalise out to every interaction and experience, but for

Aboriginal people, our beliefs (that are often viewed as delusional from a 'white, clinical' context) are always specific to the experience (such as a death or being cursed) and do not generalise out to all experiences. For example, if a patient is reporting visits from a deceased relative, they will not report 'visits' or 'perceptual disturbance' occurring without this relevant content and context attached to it.

For our young client, she'd had a death, that of her cousin-sister. Her community confirmed this and also normalised the spiritual visits by echoing the words she used to describe how they manifested.

All of this was consistent with a culture-bound spiritual visit rather than psychosis.

Let's now unpack the other component of psychosis: hallucinations. These are when patients experience things that no-one else can hear, see or touch. There are several differentiating characteristics from cultural grieving, which is what I hypothesised our twelve-year-old client was experiencing based on the content of the visits (her deceased cousin) and that death was a trigger. The first is that if cultural grieving is 'resolved', then spiritual visits are always comforting to the individual. This is very dissimilar to psychosis, whereby agitation and distress are concomitant with the hallucinations. Hearing voices can then feel overwhelming, and the agitation feeds the compulsion to comply with the voices. The obvious compulsion is, 'Maybe if I just do what the voices are telling me to do, they will stop.' Auditory command hallucinations are extremely difficult to live with as complying with the voices doesn't make them stop. It's why those who experience them have very high rates of suicide.

With Aboriginal people, cultural spiritual visits are not distressing or disturbing. However, they will manifest this way if something has been 'missed' in the grieving process. Visits can then take on a tormenting form.

So, the first question I ask my Aboriginal clients when they report spiritual visits related to grief is: 'When that fulla visits you, is it a good feeling or not a good feeling?' If Sorry Time has concluded, the response is usually something like, 'He right,' which means everything that needs to be done culturally has been done. If they say, 'Not a good feeling,' I then explore what has been missed in the grief process. This begins by asking, 'What happened when the person passed away?'

As there are numerous grief rituals that differ from tribe to tribe and which represent Sorry Time, practitioners' cultural competence is critical. They need to understand the cultural norms of their client's community and be aware of local customs, such as the cutting of the deceased's hair by a close relative, smoking ceremonies and sorry cutting, as already described. If specific tribal rituals are not fully concluded, spiritual visits will often become troubling – as they had with my client, with her cousin telling her to 'end her life' like she had.

When you have an Aboriginal client, you also need to explore and enact cultural solutions in addition to managing clinical risk. One example is if they were away from Country during Sorry Time when a close relative passed away, you might ensure they had some strands of the deceased person's hair or 'dirt' from their spiritual Country. At all times, any cultural intervention should occur in consultation with close family relatives. The treatment 'outcome' is then of monitoring the visits to see if they are no longer troubling or impairing the individual's function.

Another aspect that distinguishes spiritual visits from psychosis is that there is a consistent separation of 'self' from the 'entity' – for example, 'I am being "sung" by' or 'I am being visited by'. In many cases of psychosis, the individual *becomes* entwined or indistinguishable from the entity – for example, 'I am god', 'I am the devil' and so forth. This is never or rarely the case with culturally appropriate spiritual visits.

Finally, the content of hallucinations is consistently of a cultural nature. Visually, it may be spirits appearing; aurally, voices take on a consistently cultural form. It follows that if the disorder is culture-bound it will consistently manifest itself culturally.

So, for our twelve-year-old client, the images she was reporting told a story of missed Sorry Time, of not returning home to grieve and make a spiritual reconnection with land and Country. Therefore, the intervention was to get her back home to Country, so she could do her Sorry Time. We would then monitor the visits to see if they were still distressing while assessing her risk of suicide.

Once home, the visits became comforting to the girl. They no longer presented in a way that had a narrative of risk to self.

The outcome for her would have been very different with a singular clinical focus.

What is cultural and what is clinical?

After seven years, I got pretty efficient at figuring out the differences between culture-bound and clinical disorders. The term they use for this in psychology is diagnostic formulation. It involves weighing up the evidence to determine what is the most likely explanation (from an assessment perspective) of a client's distress. This is important, as up to 70 per cent of mental illnesses have symptoms in common. If you add culture-bound syndromes into the equation, it becomes even more difficult to get assessment right.

My 'similar' and 'different' columns were a great starting point, but the process eventually became significantly more technical. I established four stages that clinicians could work through to assess culture-bound syndromes.[10]

Loosely, these were:

1. practitioner cultural competence and cultural competency work. It is about getting practitioners to become aware of their attitudes and beliefs about Aboriginal people in order to shift their behaviour towards their black clients, but also not relying on clinicians to understand when their biases were impacting their work. This is the problem; the profession makes a lot of assumptions about cultural competency without any guidance to ensure that competency.
2. the client's individual beliefs and cultural connection

3. context, which involves ascertaining whether the culture-bound syndrome exists in the client's community and whether the client's description – the words they use and how it manifests – matches the community view. Assessment is objective – you are looking for inconsistencies.

4. community capacity – the existence of elders, Nungkari, lore people who not only hold knowledge but are also vital to 'treatment' and assessment accuracy. If someone says they have been 'sung' ('cursed') by lore men, for example, they need to have lore men in their community who agree that they have done something wrong to justify why they believe what they believe.

Effectively, I had to create an evidence base where there had never been one before. It was hard work and at times seemed insurmountable. I had become adept at challenging individuals, but systems – that is another whole level of impossible. Systemic racism is the cause of pretty much all the escalation in mental ill-health, and individual practitioners are regularly destroyed by it.

As an example, in 1998, during one of my first consultancies in the Northern Territory to look at the efficacy of mental-health outcome measures with Aboriginal people, I was challenged by the expert committee when I said that information about culture-bound phenomena was not included in mainstream tools. They said, 'There is no evidence that culture-bound syndromes exist, Tracy.'

I responded, 'You are completely correct. There is zero evidence ... [pause for dramatic effect] ... in the world in which you live. Because no-one has written this stuff up in an academic journal doesn't mean they don't exist. You go into any Aboriginal community for the last 40,000 years and they will know of these things. The evidence is there, just not in a form you can relate to.'

A compelling 'argument', no doubt, but one that was too readily dismissed as opinion, rather than considered science. Remember: systems will not change unless you give them irrefutable evidence of cultural difference. The only way that could be achieved was by putting complex culture into science through publishing it in an academic journal. The problem is that, as I recently ascertained, just 0.043 per cent of the 920 papers published across the three Australian Psychological Society journals since the society's 2016 apology to Aboriginal and Torres Strait Islander people are by practising Indigenous psychologists – and most of those papers are mine.

Publishing academically is a minefield because you are still being 'critiqued' by academic 'peers' who do not understand Aboriginal culture at all. Indeed, it took my paper on culture-bound syndromes close to two years just to go through peer review.

In training they teach you how to hone your clinical instincts. They teach you nothing about differentiating clinical from cultural. How can one person possibly change that? I had no idea; I just knew I had to. The damage being done was too great to ignore.

Changing psychology

Regular headlines would beam across our TVs and newspapers about the scourge of suicides devastating our nation. At the time, Australia was in the top third of all industrialised nations for suicide rates. The news reports would contain a litany of all the things the government was doing to address the issue. The final sentence would always be, 'And Aboriginal people have double the rate of suicide as non-Aboriginal people.'

Full stop. Nothing else.

I thought, *Where are all of the interventions the government is funding for Aboriginal people?*

I had begun to work at the Midland Child and Adolescent Mental Health service as a provisionally registered psychologist. As a clinician with a 100 per cent Aboriginal caseload, I would be referred client after client who had made a suicide attempt. I had to meet many in hospital. Of those who survived their attempt, about 50 per cent were relieved that they did, 30 per cent were angry that they did ('I can't even get *that* right') and the balance were in shock – numb while processing the pain of survival, stunned at being in such despair that death seemed like the best option. This was often the case when alcohol or other drugs were involved.

We know that the first twenty-four hours after a suicide attempt is when people are most at risk for further attempts. That's why we have – or *should* always have – suicide watches. However, many are sent home, either alone or to unprepared family who have no idea what to do, and sometimes with a referral that is often not followed up.

How could they be sent home? Because risk, of its nature, changes. Once someone is 'no longer' at risk, they are discharged. But risk assessments' effectiveness depends on cultural competency and whether clients feel safe to express that to their clinicians. And, of course, just as risk can be reduced, it can also escalate again.

It's no wonder so many families – black and white – feel completely let down by a system unprepared and often unskilled in the complexity of suicide risk assessment.

Indeed, continuity of care is such an issue that a recent study received media attention because it found that more than 81 per cent of presentations to hospital for self-harm or to frontline services (usually police) were by Aboriginal people.[11] However, the report had no detail of what happened to those individuals in distress after frontline services had presumably responded to them. There was no indication of any follow-ups.

When someone presents to services in distress, it is the most challenging thing they can admit to – that they are struggling and need help. The system should not be making it harder for them, and it should certainly be tracking where these at-risk individuals go afterwards to link them with critical prevention opportunities.

We know that Aboriginal people are more than twice as likely to die by suicide than non-Aboriginal people, but we also know that an Aboriginal child is *at least four times* more likely to die by suicide than a non-Aboriginal child.[12]

I have always said that the words *child* and *suicide* do not belong in the same sentence.

So, how on earth do you start to address this?

My work at the 'cultural coalface' in Kalgoorlie and the Western Desert communities had given me a bit of street cred, but most importantly it undid the damage of my first experience of university. I felt, like most Aboriginal people who cannot understand white systems, that not being able to do this thing called psychology was about my deficits, but it was actually about the system. I needed to understand complex behaviour in Aboriginal people *first*, so I could then go back to uni with relatable experiences to link with the scientific theory, because the way they were teaching it did not include any Indigenous context. I now had that, and I was craving the theory I needed to understand it at a deeper level to try to help these communities.

Fundamentally, we shouldn't be trying to understand risk factors *after* a child has died by suicide. We should be able to clearly identify the indicators beforehand and do all we can to prevent it.

I had no idea how I would do it, but I knew I had to figure it out. At that stage I had completed my bachelor degree, and so I applied for a Masters in Clinical Psychology. I got offers from all four Western Australian universities, and I chose to go to Curtin because it had a reputation as the best clinical psychology school in the country and I wanted to be trained by the best in the business.

A year into my masters, I was approached by the lecturers to consider doing a combined masters and PhD. It had only just become available as an option. The idea was pretty overwhelming for someone who, frankly, thought completing high school was beyond them. Then there was the pressure of being the first Aboriginal person to ever do it and wanting to do something that would make a difference to my community. It was a lot to consider.

When I'm overwhelmed by something, going for a run is my go-to. So, I threw my joggers on and off I went. I knew I would find the answers in my zen. The familiar thud on the pavement mattered little. I had a focus – not to find a solution, but to let go and be in a mindful zone. An elder once said to me, 'When you are struggling with an answer to a question, stop struggling and the answer will come.' That to me is mindful running. It's how I run marathons –

I don't think about it. My physical training is like that; my writing is like that. I am like that. I hate anything that is forced. I have made my biggest life decisions and had my greatest breakthroughs on a run, when my mind is free from pressure and I am in the moment.

The Swan River was as beautiful as always. It was easy to tune out. It was easy to be aware of my feet and how hard they were hitting the ground. It was easy to have a sense of my body and how heavy I was feeling and what was weighing on me. The best sensation as a runner is feeling light. Your feet make very little contact with the ground. Your breathing is rhythmic and not laboured. Your body isn't slouched. As the glistening of the Swan River became more hypnotic, the eureka moment came.

All roads lead to assessment.

Every single person in the mental health profession does assessment. It is the starting point to literally everything.

I started becoming aware of my thoughts and tuned in to them.

If you get the assessment wrong, you get treatment wrong and you make things worse.

What if the reasons Aboriginal people were dying by suicide were *different* to those for non-Aboriginal people? What if the entire mental health industry misunderstood the risk factors? Every community I had been into at that point kept telling me that there were 'no warning signs' when someone died by suicide or made a suicide attempt. Or was it that we were looking for the *wrong* warning signs?

Researchers have long explored the idea of suicide causal pathways – the 'why' of suicide – but solely with non-Indigenous people. We know, for example, that 98 per cent of those who died by suicide had a diagnosable mental disorder.[13] It is also firmly established that depression increases suicide thoughts and attempts, and when severe depression is comorbid with substance abuse it accounts for between 50 and 60 per cent of suicide deaths in non-Aboriginal people. This is no surprise, as alcohol is a depressant and feeds the cycle of depression.

Understanding causal pathways has been critical to suicide prevention efforts in non-Aboriginal populations. First, it informs public awareness campaigns about early warning signs. Second, once you can explain why people are dying by suicide, you can logically determine the 'what' (to do) – as in, best practice treatments for the 'why' (such as for depression and for alcohol and drug use). Research further indicated that if we could determine best practice treatments for depression, there would be a 50 per cent reduction in suicide deaths. See how important causal pathways are!

However, causal pathways are very different to risk factors. The idea is that if you eliminate a cause, you eliminate the result (the suicide). Risk factors might increase the 'odds' but by themselves do not explain or eliminate the end result (suicide). Alcohol is a strong risk factor for suicide, for example, but it's not a cause. Governments consistently get this distinction between risk and cause wrong, so they'll restrict alcohol and call it suicide prevention. It's not. It's alcohol restrictions.

Unfortunately, there had been *zero* focus on determining Indigenous-specific suicide risk factors and therefore there was no evidence with which to determine unique causal pathways. Therefore, best practice treatments could not be established for Aboriginal people. See how these things have a knock-on effect?

But without culturally valid assessments, none of this would be possible. I realised that culturally informed assessments could be the answer to every 'closing the gap' issue. (I discuss this further in Chapter 11.) If you get assessment wrong, you fail to accurately measure the impacts of treatment and to gather robust data on what is working. There was no data in Australia on treatment outcomes for Aboriginal people. I knew that no-one had grabbed a bunch of depressed Aboriginal people and tested treatments of best practice to reduce their depression. So, we were not measuring anything in terms of treatment impacts to skill up a workforce around what is effective.

Further, no funded programs had shown they were reducing suicide or mental health risk. That is something that needs to be front and centre of every single conversation on Indigenous suicide prevention. Millions and millions were funnelled into interventions and programs that had failed to demonstrate any measured outcomes. Even more millions were directed towards restricting the human rights of our most disadvantaged, then people wondered why improvement had not occurred.

I realised that my PhD topic had to be about developing unique assessment tools for Aboriginal people. If the spiritual dimension was being diagnosed as hallucinations, clinical treatments would not work. Aboriginal people were being sectioned under the *Mental Health Act* due to 'deliberate acts of self-harm', but they were sorry cutting. I had seen Aboriginal people put into violence prevention programs when they were administering traditional payback or lore. People were suicidal because they were removed from traditional Country and put in prison or in psychiatric units. Old people were choosing to die rather than go to regional areas for treatment.

I had seen many of my clients improve without standard clinical interventions and with the help of healers (Nungkari) or lore people. But how do you prove that to people, particularly when the culture-bound syndromes that I spoke of were mostly ignored or dismissed?

My PhD resulted in four unique assessment tools, one of which was a psychometric tool known as the Acculturation Scale for Aboriginal Australians, which enables cultural mapping of a client's connection to culture and kin. This allows practitioners to explore cultural engagement and connection with Aboriginal clients and was co-designed with Aboriginal communities. To be clear, it does not measure culture; it places an onus on practitioners to explore individual cultural connection and cultural identity rather than make assumptions about connection – usually based on skin colour or whether people are based in the city or in remote communities.

The lore man

The case study of the lore man shows how this tool has significant value in distinguishing cultural norms from clinical 'risk' – otherwise known as the cultural defence or cultural formulation in assessment.

A forensic psychiatrist had undertaken a risk assessment on an Aboriginal man charged with 'grievous bodily harm'. She questioned him about the circumstances of his offence to explore two areas that indicated the likelihood of future criminality. First, do they deny that they did it or do they accept responsibility for their actions? Second, if they accept responsibility, do they minimise or mitigate culpability? For example, someone may say, 'Yeah, I did it, but they provoked me', or 'I didn't hit them that hard'. This is loosely what forensic risk assessment looks at: exploring factors that increase the likelihood of future criminality.

So, the forensic psychiatrist started to tell me the story of this Aboriginal client she was assessing, and as she was talking I joined some dots in my head, based on knowing the community reasonably well. She mentioned he was a 'lore man', although she had no idea what this meant.

Essentially, the role of a lore man is to administer payback or punishment on behalf of his community for wrongdoing or transgressions related to men's business. The most complex aspect of lore is that its rituals and practices are known only to those who have been initiated as lore men. So, this means that disclosing 'lore information' is a transgression at the highest level and is punishable under traditional lore.

A lore man will *never* disclose any details about lore. This secret aspect of Aboriginal culture is what separates it from all others. In fact, Aboriginal culture is the most secretive culture in the world.

I have had to do assessments on lore men, and it is incredibly challenging because lore men don't speak to women. But when you are the only Aboriginal psychologist in Australia who has a PhD focused on culturally informed psychological assessment, it means you have to find a way.

I have learnt how to extract information to the benefit of my client. To make meaning of their behaviour but doing so in a way that doesn't transgress traditional lore and put me in danger culturally.

I have done assessments on lore men who have been 'sung' culturally and look psychotic.

It is difficult not only to extract information safely, but also to convince mainstream systems that these men really have been sung rather than experiencing psychosis or, worse still, 'hiding behind their culture' to excuse violence.

So, when the psychiatrist questioned the lore man about the circumstances of his 'offending', his inability to disclose lore was being assessed by her as a 'denial of a crime and minimising his role and responsibility in that crime'. Fortunately, though, she rang me because her instincts were telling her that she was missing something.

'Have you done a cultural map on this guy?' I asked her.

'What's that?' she replied.

'I am going to email it to you and walk you through it,' I said.

I sent her the Acculturation Scale for Aboriginal Australians, which could then be used as a 'cultural defence' as it assesses engagement in traditional cultural beliefs and engagement with traditional cultural lore.

This man had not woken up and decided to cause harm to another. He had an obligation to administer punishment on behalf of his community. This is what is referred to as a very different criminogenic profile. And in all instances of law and lore, context matters. But if you are not assessing cultural context, then you are not providing accurate assessments.

Strangely enough, the psychiatrist had actually done the right thing clinically, in terms of the assessments she had available to her. But she had done the wrong thing culturally, and she would never have been able to determine the difference without guidance and a culturally informed assessment.

Cultural relativism is a really challenging thing when you are working across cultures. But assessment is objective, not subjective, and context is important. Not every Aboriginal person who harms another will have this type of lore context upon which to make meaning of behaviours. Nor will the community validate this reality in every circumstance, either. But assessment should ultimately tell a client's story. And the story to explain here is this: Why did this man wake up and decide to harm someone else? The cultural map told all of the story. The clinical assessment told none of it.

In 2003, I became the first Aboriginal person to graduate with a combined Masters and PhD in Clinical Psychology. This was such a proud moment, and I managed to get an A average for the PhD, with two international markers and one Australian marker. I was so honoured to have Israel Cuellar give me an A+ as his *Handbook of Multicultural Mental Health* (with Freddy A Paniagua) had been my bible throughout my entire PhD. (Okay, it was so expensive that I actually 'borrowed' it permanently from my supervisor, David Hay – we used to joke about that quite a lot.)

Graduating was not just a personal achievement, though. I understood that, when I became the first Aboriginal person with a Masters and PhD in Clinical Psychology, it had become possible for every other Aboriginal person to also do this, because representation matters.

Most importantly, the findings were extraordinary. I established, for the first time, that there were different risk factors for Indigenous suicide, with impulsivity and anxiety (which I believe is actually trauma – more on this in Chapter 8) accounting for 64 per cent of the variance of suicide risk. I am not surprised that we found this in a good population size because in years of clinical practice and talking with bereaved families and communities, there was a consistent theme – that the suicides were 'really quick' with no 'warning signs'.

As suicides were continuing to escalate, I understood that we had to establish this through research to save lives. If the risk factors were different, that was so critical. People were being trained to look for the wrong indicators. Communities knew it, but it was vital to have this validated. Based on my research, I created the Westerman Aboriginal Symptom Checklist – Youth (WASC-Y), for patients between thirteen and seventeen years old, as well as a version for adults (WASC-A).

Over 50,000 practitioners across Australia have now been accredited in the WASC-Y/A tools. However, there has been zero government support or funding to enable its rollout or ongoing validation. The lack of acceptance of my findings and screening tools by governments and academic institutions has shown how entrenched systemic racism remains, and this is something I have only just started to talk about publicly.

I have had bosses of big health services come up to me at the end of one of my three-day workshops in which they have been accredited in the five unique psychometric tools I developed, and say, 'This training was so great, Tracy, but you know what we desperately need? Culturally informed assessments in our service. Do you know of any?' In these moments, I have to count backwards from ten in my head before responding.

Distressingly, though, in 2016 I provided expert evidence to the WA parliamentary inquiry into Indigenous suicides. I extensively discussed the WASC-Y/A and how assessment is critical to suicide prevention. They asked for copies of the manuals and tools. By this stage, around 20,000 practitioners had been accredited in the tools, which I cannot imagine being matched by many psychologists in this country, so practitioners had long embraced its importance. I was being contacted regularly by practitioners across the country to tell me that my training and tools were helping them to save lives. However, the parliamentary inquiry made no recommendations for a rollout or implementation of the WASC-Y/A.

Eighteen months later, thirteen Aboriginal young people had died by suicide in the Kimberley, which triggered an inquiry. The inquiry concluded that none of these thirteen children had had a mental health assessment. Despite my optimistic nature, this broke me. The coroner made no recommendations about improving assessment, but around 21 per cent of her recommendations were about alcohol restrictions and assessing for fetal alcohol spectrum disorder. In other words, there was nothing about suicide prevention.

The ABC called me after I posted on social media my disgust at the lack of recommendations about Indigenous-specific risk assessments and the existince of my tools since 2003. The wonderful late journalist Russell Woolf asked me: 'Dr Westerman, had your assessments been rolled out in the Kimberley, could lives have been saved?'

Live radio is tough; you have to think on your feet. I'm not going to be the person who says on radio when bereaved parents could be listening that this could've been the case. Instead, I said, 'Sadly, in life, we don't get a do-over. But what I can say is this: every single parent should expect that our governments fund equal and basic access to mental health services, to basic assessments. The government has fundamentally failed our most vulnerable communities, and generationally so.'

I admit, I got off the phone and cried that day. For all those lives lost. For the many more that would be lost due to ignorance and racism. This is not about ego. It's not about money (that accusation has been thrown at me more times than I can count) – and I have had to do most things for free as a result.

It's about children killing themselves.

I will forever be disgusted by the lack of inroads and, frankly, the complete lack of desire from our governments to properly address this critical issue.

The last piece of the cultural assessment puzzle

Another outcome of my PhD was that I validated the existence of culture-bound syndromes for the first time in Aboriginal people. However, it took until 2021 to publish it.[14] It won the Australian Psychological Society's Altmetrics Award for the biggest reach of any published paper that year. This is because clinicians are struggling literally every day with these issues but they are being told that there is 'no evidence' these cultural-bound syndromes exist, let alone being trained in how to deal with them.

The paper details four stages of assessment that ensure clinicians can effectively assess and treat *any* culture-bound syndrome. I am so proud of it, but it was also the most terrifying thing I have ever published. I was terrified of getting something wrong, of putting something in the general public that had the potential to harm a culture that is so steeped in its secretness. By that stage I had, of course, trained people in culture-bound syndromes for a long time. But training is different because you can contextualise this information over a few days.

The nature of a publication is that it is static. Every word is open to individual interpretation. So, I sat on it for nearly twenty years. I had to develop the confidence that came from seeing these issues everywhere I went across Australia. More accurately, I had to develop 'street cred' culturally as well as clinically. But what really pushed me to publish it was that I was constantly told within the hierarchy of the profession that there was no evidence that these 'things' exist.

I wrote the paper, hoping that it would be the start of a flood of similar papers that would validate what I had found and improve on what was known. That's what science demands and I am pretty hard-nosed in science, because I *have* to be. Because big systems do not move unless they are provided with irrefutable evidence of cultural difference. But science also requires that we have no ego when it comes to the challenging of our work as it means the evidence base will become larger and improved, and that's vital. I also wrote the paper because for too long, the science has failed Aboriginal people and practitioners in determining what works. This was unacceptable neglect.

When my paper was published, it represented that critical validation from the scientific community. This was a 'big deal' and confirmed it was a seminal paper. However, it was only published in 2021. How many Aboriginal people had suffered – and continue to suffer – from a lack of culturally informed assessments and treatments? It is incalculable.

In the following chapters, I'll explain why it was so important to develop assessment tools from the 'ground up' – by Aboriginal people, for Aboriginal people. These tools have helped so many of my Aboriginal clients with various culture-bound syndromes that they had either denied, were ashamed of or were fearful that authorities would view these issues as representing a pathology and so they buried them. This includes people from 'wrong way' relationships and those experiencing racial trauma or traumatic grief, and it often required understanding complex cultural rituals, such as Sorry Time and returning to Country, that needed to be incorporated within standard psychological treatments. It's certainly not what they teach you in any psychology degree at any university, but that is the excitement of working with Aboriginal people. There is no script. You have nothing to guide you. But if you are a true clinician, you will find a way. Because treatments should always fit clients, not the other way around.

And too many clinicians forget that.

4

Black Identity:
Stories of internalised racism

Identity is a complex and powerful construct. It can protect and insulate us from harm, but it is also dependent upon the public regard in which we are held by others. With just 30 per cent of Australians regularly socialising with Aboriginal people,[1] which ensures negative stereotypes and prejudice continue unchallenged, and accounting for around 66 per cent of the association between interpersonal racism and depressive symptoms, identity struggles have been predominant in my work as a psychologist. Most of the suicidal Aboriginal clients I have worked with had identity struggles at the core of their impulses.

The average therapist is completely untrained in how to work with identity issues, which means that resilience is rarely a therapeutic focus.

So, how *do* you treat cultural identity?

If someone says to me, 'I am Greek' or 'I am Italian', I reply, 'Cool.' When I say I am Aboriginal, the consistent response is, 'Yes, but how Aboriginal are you?'

I used to say, 'Just my foot is Aboriginal,' but my better answer now is, 'Every. Single. Bit.'

I have never asked anyone how Chinese or Greek or Italian they are. The questioning of Aboriginality has become so normalised in Australian culture and is even weaponised: 'Why are you *claiming* Aboriginality?' The origins of this, of course, are the assimilation policies in which governments would literally 'colour-code' Aboriginal people and treat people better or worse in accordance with their 'Aboriginality', based on skin colour alone. The objective was to 'breed out' the Aboriginality of people by separating us – the 'full-bloods' were kept separate from the 'half-castes', and again from the 'quarter-castes' who could 'almost pass as white' and were therefore afforded more rights, privileges and often 'better treatment'. This, of course, led to Aboriginal people turning on each other. Divide and conquer: this will get the job done every time.

I was recently asked for proof of my Aboriginality by an organisation who wanted to send their staff to my training workshops. I refused to provide it. I was disgusted that, even for a contract for service, if you are Aboriginal then payment is seen as some kind of 'handout' rather than a fee for your hard work. I wondered if any of the non-Indigenous services they contracted required a 'proof of whiteness' beforehand? Or how many non-Indigenous services delivering programs into Aboriginal communities required a statutory declaration from those communities and a three-part test that demonstrated their track record of being culturally informed and effective in those communities? This would at least ensure that the process of funding was on equal ground and based on *outcomes*.

This red tape is tying up Aboriginal people in business, while non-Indigenous businesses don't face the same barriers and, as a result, compete for Indigenous funding often unchallenged. The falsehood that claiming Aboriginality comes with significant monetary benefits and a whole raft of privileges fuels such questioning. Those who 'fake' their Aboriginality are rare exceptions, not the norm. It is not a free-for-all for anyone to easily and readily 'tick a box' of Aboriginality.

The reality is that we are the only culture in Australia that has to go to extreme lengths to prove our cultural identity.

There are many cultural groups that have identified roles, whereby someone from a particular culture or with a distinctive cultural skill base is employed for a specific position. Migrant communities, quite appropriately, have people from the same cultural background to provide services, because sharing cultural identity, language, values and beliefs not only improves outcomes but in many instances saves lives. Some studies have shown that if a practitioner is from the same culture as their patient, this can reduce infant mortality up to threefold.[2] With up to 68 per cent of Aboriginal people dying from preventable conditions, you understand that this is not a privilege or a 'handout' but an absolute necessity.[3] The reality is also that Aboriginal people want to remain in remote communities, where the highest-risk individuals are dying from preventable diseases. It saves lives, results in better outcomes and therefore saves a hell of a lot of money.[4] The problem is that the racial empathy gap means when you say 'preventable death', it is too often processed as blame. Can you imagine blaming non-Indigenous people for getting cancer or heart disease? This drives the significant shortfall in health-based funding, an estimated $268 million. The Northern Territory has long been calling for such needs-based funding.

Yet for Aboriginal people there is a yardstick that no other culture has to endure to prove our identity, so that we can access health services commensurate with our need. Proof of Aboriginality requires a three-part test: having a statutory declaration from an Aboriginal Community-Controlled Organisation confirming your Aboriginality; showing that you're an active member of that community and mob; and finally, being accepted by that community as an Aboriginal person and having established links there that have been confirmed by elders.

When the late Jack Charles – arguably one of the most famous Aboriginal people in Australia – was asked to provide proof of his Aboriginality, it was clear that no-one seems capable of exercising common sense on this issue.

We are the only culture in Australia that was required to sever ties with our family and kin and to denounce our culture in order to gain basic human rights in the form of citizenship of our own country – like my mum had to do. We are also the only culture for which it was government policy to 'breed out' our Aboriginality and systematically destroy our culture. And now we are the only culture in Australia that must *prove* our cultural identity to access basic services.

We have also never received restitution for any of this destruction of our culture, with the national apology occurring hundreds of years after forced removals began. I discuss the intergenerational trauma impacts of the Stolen Generations and the denial of it as a post-trauma variable later in this chapter.

How is black identity formed?

While there is limited research that has conceptualised the formation of black identity, it is nonetheless consistent across 'black' cultures, representing a common 'minority group' struggle. The concept of 'black identity formation' was first described by William Cross in 1971, who proposed that it involves five 'phases'.[5] His model offers insights into how black populations develop psychological robustness.[6] The psychological and developmental construction of black identity is arguably the most critical factor in addressing risk. Why? Because racism is an established, enduring and inescapable risk factor for suicides and mental ill-health. It is also impossible to eradicate. Therefore, it is extremely difficult at the treatment level to address what is a core driver of suicide risk.

So, understanding what buffers or moderates racism remains crucial for prevention. My PhD explored why some Aboriginal people seem to 'cope' better with racism than others. This was challenging because there was no data-driven clinical research with Aboriginal people on resilience, let alone what specific factors moderate risk. However, we did know of many protective factors that had been delineated with non-Aboriginal clients, and it was logical that some of these would apply – for example, cognitive style, problem-solving capacity, effective communication skills. I have also focused heavily on these factors in my clinical practice.

My WASC-Y tools have a cultural resilience subscale in them and this has provided evidence on the extent to which cultural resilience buffers mental health and suicide risk in Aboriginal people. It's critical research that will provide a good basis for ongoing expansion into clinical interventions by providing clinicians with a specific focus. In defining these variables for the first time, it makes them capable of being altered through therapy and as part of treatment plans and measured outcomes. Current assessments do not incorporate anything Indigenous specific, which means practitioners are unaware of how to address unique risk factors (especially racism), and protective factors that buffer risk as part of standard therapy.

Providing a black identity 'treatment' framework

I start the session on black racial identity in my workshops by showing people a video that's called 'The Doll Test'. It's quite an old social psychology experiment in which the instructor asks young 'kids of colour' (probably four or five years of age) questions about two dolls in front of them – one is black, one is white. First, they are asked to establish which doll is white and which doll is black by pointing at them when instructed. The interviewer then asks them about how they perceive the doll, such as, 'Which doll is the nice doll?' and 'Which doll is the ugly doll?' The children consistently point to the black doll each time a negative description is given. The follow-up question then is, 'Why is that doll ugly?'

The children respond with things like, 'Because he looks like me.' This and similar answers show that children internalise the concept of black being bad and white being good from a very young age.

When the video is finished, I immediately facilitate an understanding of what is occurring from the perspective of black identity development by asking these questions:

- What age were you when you became aware of cultural difference for the first time?

- What had happened to make you aware?
- Was it a negative or a positive experience?

The answers to each question are always pretty consistent, and I always do a 'show of hands' to make this point to the group. First I ask, 'How many of you were between four and eight years of age?' The vast majority will raise their hand, whether they're Aboriginal or non-Aboriginal – although when I have a group of just Aboriginal people, everyone *always* says yes.

Then I ask, 'How many of you had a negative experience?' Again, most of the group will raise their hand.

I have come to understand that these common experiences are due to the intersection, at key moments in our lives, of child cognitive development and black identity formation. Most people have their first recalled experience of cultural difference as an experience of racism. I say 'recalled' because it is about the stage of cognitive development – the fact that this is a negative experience is relevant to forming racial identity. The Swiss psychologist Jean Piaget's theory of cognitive development provides us with direction regarding a child's ability to discern difference. Before they turn four, children don't see difference or react to it. They have very little prerequisite to who they like or want to be friends with. They don't react to colour differences. All they really care about is mutual play and mutual interest.

Developmentally, children start to be able to see and then react to difference between four and eight years of age. Indeed, research reveals that both black and white children between the ages of three and six display white-biased choice behaviour, whereas by around age nine black children begin to display black preferences, while their white counterparts remain Eurocentric.[7] Research further shows there is no evidence of reaction to blackness at age five, but it shows up at age seven and becomes prominent by age ten.[8] This is based on brain reactivity – the emotional centre of the brain, the amygdala, is measured for reaction to difference, indicating reaction peaks at this stage of development. For black kids, what this means is they are just internalising external messaging about what it means to be black.

Social scientists believe that identity is connected to an individual's growing self-concept in addition to how they view themselves as part of a collective group. I certainly have experienced this, both personally and through my clients' stories. In other words, the person asks themselves, *How do I feel about my group and how do I think others feel about my group?*

The next part of the explanation comes from the work of psychoanalyst Erik Erikson, who was interested in the role played by social interaction and relationships in development and growth through a person's lifespan. Erikson's theory was based on the epigenetic principle (interaction between our genes and our environment), which suggests people grow in a sequence that occurs over time and in the context of a larger social development based on their community. Most importantly, Erikson believed people experience a conflict that serves as a turning point in development. This is particularly relevant to the different stages of black identity, which I have seen clinically with my Aboriginal clients and will describe later in this chapter.

Kids are naturally drawn to models, usually their parents, who they want to look like, be like and act like. When they perceive, between four and eight years, that cultural identity is permanently fixed, their developmental 'crises', if you will, is to reconcile what this means.

In my clinical work and training of practitioners, I have borrowed William Cross's theoretical framework for the Aboriginal context, but I have also incorporated my clinical observations (and personal experience) with theories of child and cognitive development to make it more clinically useful and applicable as a developmental process. It is powerful for my participants and probably the most useful model when it comes to addressing identity-based conflicts in Aboriginal clients.

As well as understanding 'black identity' within an Aboriginal context, my PhD also resulted in the Acculturation Scale for

Aboriginal Australians. The psychometric tool was applicable to the case of the lore man, discussed in Chapter 3, where it was vital in explaining the relevant cultural context of the criminal act he was charged with, which would otherwise have been absent from his assessment.

The tool can be used across several critical levels, including correcting cultural errors in mainstream tests and utilising it as a 'cultural defence' strategy for Aboriginal people in court systems. It can also be used to determine fitness to plead, a fundamental right in the Australian judicial system – that being, the accused should not stand trial if they do not understand the mainstream judicial process and are therefore unable to instruct legal representation. It is noteworthy that while there are examples of guidelines for the interrogation of Aboriginal suspects, there are no specific guidelines around determining 'fitness to plead'. When this can be quantified – as a psychometric tool – it means that systems cannot refute it.

In therapy, the Acculturation Scale can be used as a method of treatment. It may sound bizarre, but it can be used as a tool to 'treat' cultural identity. Acculturation is essentially the 'nuts and bolts' of identity, and black identity formation is the 'model' of robust black identity development. In combination, this applies a scientific rigour to the development of culturally informed treatment plans by making identity the focus of therapeutic outcomes. At the end of this chapter, there are a few case studies that show the power of taking a comprehensive identity-based focus. At its core, it ensures that practitioners who mostly operate from a completely different set of beliefs are essentially 'forced' into their client's worldview and become more aligned with important cultural treatment goals.

What are the stages of black identity formation? What can they look like?
Stage 1: Pre-encounter – internalised black self-hatred
This first phase is the most difficult as it involves internalised racism as a form of self-hatred. The good news is that it is a developmental phase that seems to peak between five and eight years of age, as already noted. For most Aboriginal people, it is not permanent and

they move beyond this phase, but those who often end up as clients have remained stuck there, unable to reconcile their identity, and this has continued into adulthood. Often neither the patient nor the clinician realises that this is destructive to the self. The concept of 'rejecting culture' has never fully been understood as a possible outcome of racism.

For kids who are at this initial stage, it's primal and it's about self-preservation. Identity is at its essence an individual journey. As a kid you don't want to 'stand out' for any perceived negative reason. When you are black and see the extent of racism in the world – feeding a dominant narrative that everything white is good and everything black is bad – then there is a natural developmental, stage-specific instinct to comply with the norms of the dominant culture to fit in. This manifests itself as either internalising the hatred or becoming racist towards your own people. Either way, it is the most challenging phase and brings the greatest internal conflict related to black identity.

Take an example of an Aboriginal child who has been removed from their family and placed into foster care with a white family (which happens in 65 per cent of cases). They start to internalise racism by repeating the negative messaging about their own people, such as, 'I don't want to go back to my family because they are drunk and violent.' At a young age it is easy to internalise the racist public narrative that you are bombarded with. Children will commonly endorse rather than question such messaging when they are developing their own sense of black identity and at the stage of cognitive development when their ability to think is more concrete than abstract.

Child welfare then often respond by not 'making' them go back home to community. To which I often respond, 'Well done, you have just made something temporary permanent.'

The four-year-old who was terrified of black people: Treating black self-hatred

I recently had a referral for a four-year-old girl who was so terrified of black people that she was a danger to herself. She would literally run away when she saw a black person, and she had such terror that she had recently run into traffic! Now, this is an obviously shocking story, but to make it even more shocking – the girl was also black. The welfare system came to me, not knowing what to do. They had avoided trying to deal with the situation. And with avoidance, things get worse.

Systems struggle to apply science when it comes to racial trauma and associated reactions. So, it is about managing the stage of development. For this girl, it meant first normalising blackfella conversations, then exposing her to Indigenous issues in her environment (such as teaching her foster parents to talk about Indigenous issues and encouraging her to watch Indigenous TV shows), and then providing slow exposure to family members and other Aboriginal people until her distress dissipates. This is all about exposure to diversity – the brain then learns to create positive rather than negative associations to 'blackness'.

However, the average therapist is completely untrained and terrified to deal with cultural identity and normalise these conversations when they have never experienced it themselves. In my training, I talk about 'distress tolerance to blackness' in therapists and frame this up as exposure. The first time you have an identity conversation, you will feel 10/10 stress, the second time 9/10, the third time 8/10 – until these conversations become normalised.

It's pretty basic, but they are primal human reactions. Most psychologists avoid and then forget there is still an individual within the cultural layer who is in psychological pain.

Identity is a long, complex, developmentally specific journey and all of us need time to reconcile and figure it out. It's not something an individual child can manage, particularly one who is being raised outside of their traditional culture.

All people have 'stages' or 'schemas' – essentially, our mental models that are secured in our long-term memories – that develop over time about our culture and, for black people especially, these become crises that need to be resolved. To help with this, black kids should be bombarded with messaging that is positive around who they are, what they look like, think like and act like. Instead, they receive the opposite.

It's a manifestation of racism that kids will internalise it for a period. This often means separating themselves from other Aboriginal people: I am a 'good Aboriginal', I'm not like 'them'. These are all-too-human reactions that are understandable for children (and adults) who are black and in the minority. It's a bit like, 'If you can't beat 'em, join 'em.' I certainly experienced this myself as a kid, as I discussed in Chapter 1. And I have had too many Aboriginal people in therapy who have told stories of trying to 'rub the black off their skin' as a kid, or who have started to develop racism towards their own mob – or a sense of 'shame' at being Aboriginal. This was particularly prominent during the rise of Pauline Hanson in the late 1990s, and again during the 2023 referendum. Fair-skinned Aboriginal kids asking their dark-skinned parents to drop them off at the corner, so they could walk to school and prevent anyone 'discovering' that they were Aboriginal.

This is the collateral damage of racism: our children.

Understanding racism as trauma also explains why there can exist a repetition of race-based traumas.[9] For example, when I was working in welfare, I would often see parents who had been horrifically abused in missions taking their own children back to those same missions. This is a core feature of trauma: repetition compulsion, whereby people subconsciously repeat the patterns of their own trauma to the point that it looks as though they have brought the trauma on themselves.

When traumatic memories and images are attached to anxiety based on self-preservation, they become overvalued and fixed. In this state, repetition compulsion becomes about trying to attain the normalcy or familiarity of the past. It's the seeking of homeostasis.

Repetition compulsion is not a conscious desire. No-one has ever said, 'Being traumatised is so much fun. I can't wait for *that* to happen again.' Its origins are in our biology, as if we are drawn to what is familiar. However, post-trauma there is often an associated control element; for example, 'I expect my children to be removed, so I am going to control the circumstances and conditions under which it occurs.' This is control they have not felt as victims.

A further element of trauma repetition compulsion is that parents who have experienced the destruction of their culture will encourage their own children to 'act white' as a survival mechanism. This is why, when we lived in Tom Price, we were the only kids who wore the school uniform. We did not grow up learning our traditional dialect or culture, which angered me as an adolescent. However, as an adult, I completely get it. My mum – as an Aboriginal woman with a fair-skinned, blonde-haired kid – understood the very real risk that I would be removed from her. If the authorities had seen us practising our culture, the fact that I could 'pass' for white would have put us in danger. So, the smartest thing my mum could do was to ensure we 'fitted in' and didn't stand out. Our survival depended upon it.

Although I felt a lot of anger as a kid for not being taught our language, I now understand as a psychologist that uttering language was traumatic for Mum – and still is. She speaks full Nyamal, but I didn't know this until I went to my uncle's funeral with her when I was thirteen years old. I just assumed that she didn't speak language. Mob were coming up to her and talking in dialect and she understood every word. However, simply saying the words was retriggered trauma for her. Mum was raised in the era when you were literally flogged for speaking language or practising culture.

When black people become racist to black people

At this stage, an Aboriginal person's internalised self-hatred can manifest as seeing other Aboriginal people as less capable or intelligent as white people. I've had the same kind of experience as many Aboriginal people, in which I've turned up to meetings and another Aboriginal participant has brought along a white psychologist as an expert. Often, I've had significantly more educational qualifications – let alone cultural qualifications. It hurts as I was raised to always back other black people – and there is no greater pain as a black woman than to have black people dismantle or white-ant your work.

Racism does not just happen *to* black people; it also happens *through* black people. Lateral violence, racism turned inwards – these are ultimately outcomes of unreconciled black identity formation, whereby those who've experienced extreme racism platform its non-existence. The politics of respectability is a phenomenon whereby privileged members of marginalised groups comply with dominant social norms to advance their group's condition. It is pro-assimilation.

We saw it in dramatic action during the Voice referendum in 2023, in which Senator Jacinta Nampijinpa Price and Warren Mundine represented this view of cultural blindness. And in the United States, Candace Owens and Condoleezza Rice have used their own success to argue that racism doesn't exist or that it creates no real barriers for other black people. This then means that disadvantage isn't real; rather, it's all the fault of black people ourselves for not taking advantage of the opportunities afforded to us 'equally'. It's a dangerous rhetoric. The most dangerous form of racism has always been cultural blindness.

My own success from disadvantage came with a lot of advantage. I had parents who loved me. I always had a meal. I always felt safe. That's luck. I had parents who worked hard and who modelled for me the value of hard work. This meant I was already a generation ahead of many people my age who didn't have that luck. Yes, I have achieved more than anyone (including myself) ever thought possible, but that doesn't mean that racism doesn't exist.

What I have always acknowledged is that the lightness of my skin has also made a significant difference. Being able to 'pass as white' has afforded me better treatment than my darker-skinned cousins and relatives, whose skin colour has always been an additional barrier to their achievements.

Internalised racism often involves a politically conservative position in which black people will promote a white ideal as the true and only mechanism by which equality is possible. It's a failure to understand the clear difference between equality and equity. No-one is saying that no white Australian has experienced struggle, trauma or hard times – just that the colour of their skin or their cultural identity was not the reason for it.

It provides a dangerous cover for racism because if it is coming from black people, it surely cannot be racist. But gay people can be homophobic, women can be sexist and black people can be racist towards their own.

The problem with the argument that 'we are all Australians together' is that it means marginalised communities must adhere to the dominant cultural norms in order to receive respect. This creates toxic situations in which marginalisation is allowed to continue by feeding the idea that there is a significant advantage for black people to just assimilate. It promotes the idea that cultural recognition and respecting diversity is 'virtue signalling' or that wanting to address historical or current racial identity-based trauma comes from a 'victim mentality' or is just pointless symbolism. That validating race-based trauma results in no practical outcomes for victims, as though this kind of trauma matters less or creates less harm.

The denial of racism doesn't mean black people will not be persecuted. Assimilation should never be a goal. It stems from a 'model minority' stereotype. When black people promote this as an aspiration, it simply creates solutions that are based on and bolster assimilation-based solutions to disadvantage, leading to a loss of cultural identity and the denial of race-based trauma. We now know, through irrefutable science, that these solutions fail to address the causes of human behavioural change by reducing racism and addressing its impacts.

The Aboriginal lady with cultural dissociative identity disorder

Dissociative identity disorder (DID), previously known as multiple personality disorder, is controversial. It has been made even more so through its portrayal in movies such as *Split* and *Sybil*, in which people create multiple personalities as a coping mechanism for trauma and particularly complex childhood trauma. However, DID has not really been explored at a clinical level in terms of internalised hatred based on cultural identity, outside of the significant book by Israel Cuellar and Freddy Paniagua.[10] In my clinical experience I have encountered clients whose rejection of their culture followed a similar course to DID, although given the absence of empirical studies on this I can only talk to my clinical observations of it.

There was an Aboriginal woman at an assessment centre I was running for a mining company many years ago. She was there simply to be assessed for a number of roles that had come up for Aboriginal people. It was supposed to be a twenty-minute test of trainability, administered by myself. I also always had a chat as part of the assessment process because you learn much more about people this way than through test results. As we were chatting, she started to say the most racist stuff I had ever heard – and I had heard some pretty racist things in my time. What I can repeat is her saying, 'Aboriginal people are okay, they just need to take a bath occasionally.' I thought, *Did she just say THAT?* But then she said worse and I started to think, *Oh no, she did-n't …*

Oh yes, she did.

So, I put the test aside and asked her about her childhood. (Come on, I'm a psychologist; we are always going to ask you about your childhood, right?) She started to describe a horror story of being adopted out to an incredibly racist white family, who basically fed her a steady daily diet of racism. Well, when you are a black kid in a white family, you can't beat them, so you have to join 'em. You become the very thing you are bred to become. It is also a critical marker for intervention.

So, what was interesting, though, was that she was at an assessment centre for Aboriginal people, so there was something within her that was clearly drawn to her identity in a complex and damaged way. The question was whether she was there to seek out evidence that confirmed her racism or that refuted it. Although I wasn't her therapist, I did have a duty of care – not just as a psychologist but as an Aboriginal person who understood identity struggles. When she spoke, it was in a detached, non-emotive, almost monosyllabic tone and about things that were extremely racially traumatic.

Clinically, I knew what dissociation looked like. The physical self remains but the emotional self 'goes elsewhere' – there is a disconnect between what is being said and what is being felt, and it's a learnt survival response. It is a core coping mechanism for trauma, so I was familiar with it.

How you 'get in' and provide necessary client (victim/survivor) insight is by pointing out the incongruence between what the person is describing, what they are saying ('it had no impact on me') and the traumatic content of what is being said. Such validation is a necessary part of treatment and moving forward. Depending upon the individual's coping mechanisms, there may sometimes be a physical reaction. In this case, the woman's veins were popping up in her neck as she described her childhood and some of its more traumatic events. So this provided the 'in' – telling her that I'd noticed that although she was saying it had no impact, her body's reaction suggested otherwise. What's that about?

The other thing I had going for me was that she was surrounded by Aboriginal people who debunked every myth and stereotype she was told to believe her entire life. Cognitive drivers are critical to challenge because they are central to triggering physical responses and behavioural ones. I call this my 'trauma triad', whereby thoughts activate a physical response, which then activates behaviour (often avoidance). I hit up each of these three components to ensure that trauma reactions are lessened or softened. So, with her (and others like her), I am first very deliberate in my language, saying things like, 'See that Aboriginal man who doesn't drink?' or, 'That Aboriginal man is a fantastic dad.' It sounds bizarre but it's all about challenging cognitive distortions by providing evidence to the contrary of what people have been led (or bred) to believe. This re-scripts these distortions based on evidence because language matters. If we stop these thoughts, the physical activation becomes lessened. It's more complex than this in therapy itself, because I frame it so clients have insight and the tools to manage it over time, but you get the idea.

As I have had to do in desperation with many of my kid clients who have known nothing but racism, I ultimately 'expose' them to the opposite of what they believe, so they can challenge the veracity of those beliefs, which we know cause damage by internalising the racism. And it's another very misunderstood and unaddressed consequence of racism turned inward.

I am finding in my workshops that this issue is an elephant in the room when we talk about outcomes of racism – that you internalise it. And, yes, this can manifest as Aboriginal people being racist towards their own.

Stage 2: Encounter – collective fawn trauma response

This phase is typically precipitated by an event (or a series of events) that forces you to fully understand and acknowledge the impact of racism. It tends to be your first conscious recognition of racism, which is tied in with your developmental phase, as noted in the first stage. This creates what is known as cognitive dissonance, which essentially means that you hold two competing ideas in your head – your cultural identity and the dominant white culture you must survive in. For example, being socially rejected by white friends or colleagues (or reading new, personally relevant information about racism) may lead you to conclude that many white people will not view you as an equal. You react to this racism along the lines of, 'How dare they talk about my mob/family like that?' But this phase is challenging because while you are becoming aware of the extent of racism and of how the characteristically negative public regard in which Aboriginal people are held affects your identity, you also realise that this is a *permanently fixed reality* for you because it coincides with cultural constancy, as already noted. At the same time, there is also awareness of the dominance of white culture.

During this phase of identity development, it can often look like the individual – and then the collective – is 'complying' with the dominant culture as the extent of racism feels overwhelming. It is why, as I argue in Chapter 7, racial trauma needs to considered a distinct trauma category. An aspect of this is understanding that there is a standard developmental process that underpins identity but, for Aboriginal people, there are the additional burdens and unique characteristics that define black identity. I describe it as being similar to the emerging 'fawn' trauma response.[11]

What is fawn? And why is it about trauma survival?

It involves ingrained behaviours that look like compliance, co-dependency and servitude, but they are initiated to avoid additional trauma through appeasing abusers. Fawn responses can be subconscious and hardwired as well as conscious survival reactions. In more than two decades of clinical work with Aboriginal people, I have seen this as the predominant trauma response. Blackness is simply who you are, so when cultural identity is the core reason for abuse, it is both inescapable and enduring, and therefore fawn is the only trauma response that is available to survive.

Fawn is an emerging trauma response that is 'other' rather than the fight, flight and freeze self-directed trauma responses. At its core, it is a survival mechanism and exists as a range of appeasement-type behaviours, which are entirely dependent on the nature of the abuse itself. It can look like subservience and compliance with abuse, and can be critical to survival and particularly when flight (running away) and fight (defending yourself) are not possible due to the nature of the trauma. It's a particularly common survivor response in intimate partner violence when the relationship dynamic is being controlled by the perpetrator due to unequal power.

Obviously, 'blackness' is an inescapable reality. Racial trauma is based on identity and so it is enduring, which means that fawn is arguably a greater trauma default. However, due to its dynamic, it can look to untrained observers as though abuse is not even occurring. It can manifest, for example, as victims deliberately provoking reactions in abusers as a method of controlling the conditions and circumstances under which the inevitable pattern of abuse occurs. 'Hot', explosive anger is harder to predict and more likely to result in harm to self and others (particularly if children are in the relationship dynamic), so pushing emotional buttons controls and manages the anger. With research showing that abusers also consistently use 'rough sex' in intimate relationships, for example, even complying with sexual intimacy often forms part of these fawn behaviours.[12] Appeasement is aimed at controlling the trauma event and associated anger, which then dissipates and is able to be managed by survivors. Environments are then calm in the aftermath. These reactions and patterns are biologically hardwired. As you can appreciate, the power differential between, say, a young black female victim and an older white male represents multiple layers of trauma that are both individual and systemic.

Another common dynamic is survivors defending their perpetrators long after abuse has occurred. This is, again, fear based. Survival is an ingrained mechanism in humans and compliance enables this, depending upon the type of abuse. However, it is problematic that as a victim's response to trauma such compliance has received little attention in the literature. This is a significant gap in our understanding of trauma responses both at the level of individual and collective post-trauma.

Collective fawn response and why our highest-risk communities are those with the highest proportion of black people

It has never made logical sense that those regions with the highest proportion of black people are more, not less, oppressed and often make up the bulk of the statistics around suicide rates, incarceration rates and child removals per capita. For example, South Africa had apartheid yet more than 80 per cent of the population was black. Despite 32 per cent of the Northern Territory's population being Indigenous, the 2007 Intervention happened, 92 per cent of children in care are Indigenous and around 92 per cent of the Territory's prison population are Indigenous.

Looking at the child protection statistics in Western Australia, high removal rates consistently occur in regions with the highest proportion of Aboriginal people. These regions also have the least access to intensive therapy and attachment-based programs. In the Derby–West Kimberley region, where around 60.3 per cent of the population identify as Aboriginal, 100 per cent of children in out-of-home care are Aboriginal; in the Pilbara that's 96 per cent; in the Goldfields, 87 per cent; and in Mid-West Gascoyne, 86 per cent.[13] However, if we remove these four regions, which are also the most densely populated Aboriginal areas,[14] from the seventeen child protection districts in the state, removal rates fall from 57 per cent to just 39 per cent.[15]

It seems counterintuitive that when you are in the majority, you are more oppressed. However, trauma repetition compulsion as a collective fawn trauma response makes sense of this. This stage of black identity formation then speaks to both individual and group-based oppression in which helplessness is a more dominant force, whereby communities feel powerless in the face of statutory organisations who have historically wielded considerable power over Aboriginal families.

The Northern Territory, the Pilbara, Far North Queensland and the Kimberley have the most human rights restrictions in the country. Cashless welfare cards and alcohol regulations also make up the bulk of our over-representation statistics. Human rights restrictions and oppression have been directly linked to poor mental health outcomes, producing a sense of hopelessness and helplessness. For example, since the Intervention suicide rates in the Northern Territory have increased by 160 per cent. Infant mortality was already at levels comparable to those in developing countries, and the average birth weight of Aboriginal children has decreased by 200 grams.

Collective fawn as black identity formation can look like a phenomenon known in psychology as the 'bystander effect', in which individuals seem compliant and as though they are not standing up to injustice or abuse, or are not offering to help. The probability of intervening is inversely related to the number of bystanders, and when you are in the 'minority' (out group) there is an extreme power differential (in group), meaning that fawn (as compliance) is the only option available. Over time, it becomes collectively ingrained as learnt helplessness. The Northern Territory Intervention and a raft of other human rights violations against Aboriginal people have occurred while people 'stood by' or looked as though they supported the racial discrimination behind these policies.

You also see this in communities agreeing with alcohol restrictions. Underlying this social construct is that Aboriginal people have learnt that we must in some way trade our human rights for basic safety. It's not actually about the alcohol – it's about our human rights being currency, but this ultimately feeds our powerlessness. It becomes very difficult as a therapist to challenge this core belief and driver when it is reinforced every single day. And you cannot humiliate someone out of addiction or off welfare.

It was disappointing that the government put alcohol restrictions back into Alice Springs as a 'solution' to youth crime in early 2024. As I noted in an interview with the ABC, once you remove human rights restrictions (for example, alcohol restrictions), there is a human reaction.[16] That often means a period of 'chaos'. But chaos is a necessary part of change. So, if you go back to restrictions in response, you essentially take people back to the starting point of the behavioural change process. What should have happened instead was the introduction of significant supports to allow for the 'chaos' and predictable behavioural responses. This could have included services for the management of complex detox, for example.

Of great concern is that collective fawn occurs because Aboriginal victims view systems as being a greater danger than individual perpetrators. We are seeing this in horrifying cases in which victims have been erroneously labelled as perpetrators by police, and this is happening so often to Aboriginal women that they fear police more than the actual perpetrators.[17] (I have discussed this in an article on coercive control dynamics.)[18]

There has been a 148 per cent increase in the incarceration of Aboriginal women since the 1991 Royal Commission into Aboriginal Deaths in Custody,[19] which is clearly linked to increased child removals. Additionally, a growing category of child removal is 'emotional abuse', whereby children are being removed because they've been exposed to violence – which essentially means the victim of the abuse is being punished for being a victim.[20]

Have your child removed, be incarcerated by police or cop the abuse. When the systems that are meant to protect are also perpetrators, fawn as a survival response to these multiple layers of violence becomes understandable as a dominant appeasement reaction. This is particularly when black identity is not only the reason for the trauma, but also both inescapable and enduring as a factor in your trauma.

It is true that trauma is inherently political. However, Martin Luther King Jr said that riots and protests are the language of the unheard, of the oppressed.[21] There is no greater injustice than that which minimises or hierarchically organises your pain as less than – or remains silent and indifferent to it.

Stage 3: Immersion – all black and all in

In Stage 3 of black identity, you are now 'all black' and everything is now about embracing your cultural identity. There is still difficulty, though, with reconciling identity and an internal conflict between the 'two worlds' you know you must walk in, so this stage can be conflictual and extreme. Typically, white-focused anger tends to dissipate during this phase as more energy is directed towards developing black identity and self-exploration. This exploration results in emerging security in a newly defined and affirmed sense of self.

For some, however, there can be stagnation in white-focused anger. There is a critical discussion around the difference between racism and prejudice – that being, can black people be 'racist' towards white people, given that there is a lower power base at play? Black people can be prejudiced, yes, but not racist.[22]

This speaks to racial trauma. Racism results in cultural destruction; prejudice, on the other hand, can cause damage or hurt feelings, but cultural identity is not the reason for it and it has less of the trauma variables implicated in its impacts than does racial trauma. In Chapter 7, I discuss racial trauma as culture stress, which evidence shows can lead to poor psychological adjustment and is linked with poor physical and mental health.

Stage 4: Internalisation – contentment

This stage, which I call 'contentment', is where we all want to be. You are now comfortable in your identity and have developed the tools to manage racism better. The things that used to be a struggle no longer are.

Identity salience is a core feature of this stage. What this means is that those who are at this stage put their Aboriginality 'front and centre' of how they see themselves. A good question that indicates this is, 'How would you describe yourself?' I would answer, 'I am Tracy and I am Aboriginal.' My black friends and family may describe themselves as parents or as their occupation, and their Aboriginality may not even come into the descriptors. This is a basic starting point for what is a highly complex issue.

The bad news is that those at this stage are more tuned in to racism, so they perceive it more than most. The good news, though, is that they are more robust culturally to be able to cope with it.

One of the stresses in this group of individuals comes from feeling compelled to take on every cause and every single act of racism on behalf of those more vulnerable. The other type of stress comes from lateral violence from your own mob. Research tells us that the stronger and more robust your cultural identity, the better your outcomes – in terms of education, employment, health. So, success often comes hand in hand with this stage. Lateral violence can occur when that success becomes a source of jealous attacks from within your own culture.

In sum, identity discussions are complex. I've had to unpack a lot of racial trauma in my clients as significant damage had been done to their identity and this can occur laterally and hierarchically. This has differed depending on the age of the client. Those who were directly removed as children tend to have more trauma triggers – for example, denial of culture can be a survival default – while the current generation often struggles with history and parents who raised them to deny their culture to protect them. There is also the obvious struggle with skin colour and the public view of what an Aboriginal person 'should' look like that makes identity contentment extremely challenging in different ways for everyone. The pay-off, though, is that the clinical and therapeutic impacts are always significant.

But it is about the individual's responses to cultural change (acculturation) and what 'stage' of black identity is predominant, based on psychological and behavioural indicators and self-reporting. The missing piece of the puzzle, though, is how their environment facilitates or impedes robust identity formation.

A story of identity as stress: The ice-cream cone 'wrong way' kid

G was a kid who was a day-to-day proposition. I took to travelling around with him in my car when I went to lunch or whatever. G liked to roam – you couldn't confine him for very long. He would be placed in a hostel or with a short-term carer, and within hours of dropping him off you'd get a call that he was gone. He was a 'desert' kid who was used to freedom. He'd had very little parenting and was a loner. All of twelve years old and on the brink of becoming a chronic solvent user. I would regularly be called by police to pick G up after they had found him in a ditch or walking the streets by himself at all hours of the night. The smell of kids' breath when they've 'come down' from a solvent had become commonplace for me by then, but it still stopped me in my tracks. G would often have the remnants of glue, paint or some other solvent on his face or skin and, of course, his breath.

You couldn't help but love him, though. He was such a sweet-natured little guy and desperate to be loved, like a little puppy without a home, following you around everywhere you went. Incredibly smart, G was one of those tragic kids who break your heart every day. What a tiny bit of love would have done for him was as sad as it was obvious, but he was reaching that point that all kids reach where he was becoming incapable of routine and fearful of being loved by anyone, which was why he would bolt from every placement. For kids like this, they can't tolerate routine or calmness because they have never known it, so they disrupt it by leaving (like G) or provoking conflict or a crisis. Repetition compulsion is so hardwired. Foster carers are not prepared well enough for it, especially that it will get worse before it gets better. Routine is always how humans thrive, but these kids who have never had routine have never thrived or been their 'best self' as a result. It takes time for new emotions and routines to become tolerable.

With G, although he would bolt from every single placement, he always came back to me. Always.

Whenever I was woken from a deep sleep by a phone call from the police to collect G, I would not hesitate to throw my trackies on and rush out in the middle of the night. The police would often contact me so I could calm him down, particularly when he was so high on solvents that he was becoming aggressive towards himself. It's always interesting why kids externalise or internalise. G was incapable of hurting anyone else, but he would tell me horrific stories of how the police would taunt him, spitting at him in his cell or calling him the sorts of names that you'd think would demean grown human beings. It always angered and disappointed me in equal measure the extent to which so many police chose to reduce themselves to this type of behaviour towards a twelve-year-old. To say I had no respect for them would be an understatement, but we had to deal with them almost daily. Often we had to rely on them, and I hated that. I sucked in more anger talking to police in those years than I had in my entire lifetime. Anger is not a comfort zone for me, but I was able to access it pretty easily every time I walked into a police station and some copper had a lot to say about G. Like my mum, I hated racism in any form and would always stand up to it.

One night when I was getting G, one of the coppers said to me as G and I were leaving, 'That kid will never amount to anything. I don't know why you bother.' I shot back, 'Because he is a frightened child. That you don't understand that tells me all I need to know about you.'

I hated going into the police station. I would freeze cognitively and say very little, just wanting to get things done then get the hell out of there. The historical stuff was clearly part of it, but it was also based on what I saw every day and the stories I would hear from kids. I would be in court with these kids who most of the time had no idea whether they had committed the crime they were pleading guilty to. 'The copper said I did it, so I must have.' This again reflects the other-race effect and drives the significant racial profiling of innocent black people, which shows up in Australia in the over-policing of Aboriginal people. For kids, we also know that a horrific 87 per cent in prison have *not* been convicted of a crime – they have been charged with an offence by police and have been refused bail by a magistrate.[23] The average Aboriginal kid spends *seventy-one* days on remand.

When they ultimately get in front of a magistrate, most of them are found innocent.[24] We now have data coming out of Queensland which shows that Aboriginal kids are admitting to crimes they did not commit just so they are released from prison.[25]

These are children! And let's be clear and stop calling where they are sent 'juvenile detention centres' – they are prisons.

Yet there is this view still that juvenile court is just a 'slap on the wrist', so the legal representation should be about plea deals rather than fighting the charge itself. It is truly horrifying and so many people outside of my profession genuinely struggle to believe this is how the system works. They think I am making it up. So many people live in a bubble in which none of this reality impacts their children, their families.

From a position of evidence, the earlier you put a child in prison, the greater the likelihood they will return to prison. Indeed, 94 per cent of children who go to prison will return before they turn eighteen. The strongest predictor of criminality is its early normalisation via an early prison sentence.

I can put it a better way. In two decades as a psychologist, I have yet to see a child come out of prison better off because of their time there – psychologically, emotionally or in terms of their contribution to society. But Australia is distinct from other countries, in terms of its love affair with prisons. Here, prison is a first resort, whereas in New Zealand and Canada it's a last resort, which means the incarceration and crime rates of their indigenous people are significantly lower than Australia's. I have written extensively on this topic over the years, including on raising the age of criminal responsibility, because of the many Gs who are a constant part of my caseload.

But there was something special about G, and when I was just twenty-three years old I seriously considered adopting him because he just had no-one who seemed to want him. It was striking to me. Aboriginal people always have families and a sense of community. Why didn't G?

The day it all made sense

G had been picked up by the police for stealing an ice-cream cone. He was locked up because no-one was able to bail him. I turned up, as always, but the hostels were full and there were no foster carers available. G had reached the end of the road with a list of minor offences that shouldn't have landed him in kid prison – mostly sleeping rough and having no responsible adult, roaming the streets at night and stealing food. It drew the attention of the relentless 'justice' system, so he ended up in front of a magistrate. Kids would often end up being sent to prison in Perth for what was known as a 'twenty-eight-day hold' for psychological assessment. Because we were remote, access to a psychologist only occurred via this mechanism. It is pretty outrageous that kids were being put in prison for assessment, but there we were (and still are).

In the meantime, despite the children's courts being sealed to the public, the media got wind of G's latest activities and that he was looking at being placed in custody. Cue the talkback radio and newspaper headlines. 'The ice-cream cone kid' was G's new name.

As a welfare officer you would end up in juvenile court at least once a week with one of your 'kids', as I called them, having to provide some formal or informal pre-sentence report or other information that the magistrate would use to determine a sentence. Occasionally an Aboriginal Legal Service lawyer would speak to your client, but that was rare. To the credit of G's magistrate, he stood the matter down while we tried to find further information about G's background. His words were something to the effect of, 'All I hear is that Aboriginal people always take care of each other. There is always family somewhere. Am I seriously looking at placing a child in prison for twenty-eight days because he is hungry?'

I almost said, 'Welcome to every day of the week, your honour,' but I stopped myself.

So, off I went, desperately trying to figure out the mystery of G. He had a really strong cultural background and strong cultural connections that were visibly trackable through family groups and names that I knew around the region. Yet we couldn't find a single placement for him. It didn't add up.

Getting back to the office, I was exhausted. There were days when the pure volume of what a welfare officer must deal with was just too much, and this was one of those days. Phones were ringing off the hook, but I had to push everything aside and figure this out. G's files were six thick volumes. I grabbed all of them and went back to the very start, attempting to piece everything together.

Volume 1: G is born and immediately adopted (not fostered) out. This made no sense across multiple levels. First, adoption is a rare thing in Aboriginal communities and particularly in the late 1980s, when G was born. Second, he was adopted in the Murchison. There is no 'dreaming' or cultural connection between Western Desert mob and Murchison mob. I got a large piece of butcher's paper and started to sketch his cultural map, which is very different to the genograms or family trees which are taught at university. It wasn't just his biological relations; it was also his skin relations. Assigned to Aboriginal children when they are born, skin groups 'determine how relationships are constructed and conducted within the person's community'.[26]

As children grow, they are taught to relate to people based on their skin group. The 'skin' will determine who they can marry, who they are able to speak to, speak about, be near, make fun of and so on. In line with this, Aboriginal people often talk of marrying people who are 'straight (skin)', or 'right way' for them. Alternatively, an individual who is from a skin group in which traditional marriage, communication or close proximity cannot occur is referred to as 'wrong way' or a 'wrong way relationship'.

The mother's skin group determines the child's skin name. In G's region, skin groups were extremely complex and there were multiple numbers. This meant that he had multiple mums, aunties, uncles. But what became very clear as I worked this through – the family tree literally took up an entire wall! – was that G was a 'wrong way' kid, whose biological parents were in a 'wrong way' relationship. Everything made complete sense now. G had been adopted from birth and rejected by his community for being a 'wrong way' kid. The simplest comparison I can provide non-Indigenous readers with is that these kids – depending, of course, upon the community context, values and beliefs – are treated as though they are the products of incest. So, the fact we could not find any placements was unsurprising.

In 'wrong way' cases where G was from, the skin is still determined by the mother's side, so they were who we needed to talk to. While his biological mum was not the most present mother and a chronic alcoholic, our conversations with her at the very least led to G coming back home and spending time with his 'old people'. This started slowly and his stays eventually became longer and longer.

It wasn't a perfect outcome, but it was better than what G had previously. Had we not unpacked his cultural map and his cultural identity, I have no idea where he would be today. G was just one of those kids you always wanted to believe could find a better life for himself. It is rare that those wishes come true.

As a psychologist, I have written a lot about identity because it has been the most significant factor in all of my clients' suicide impulses and mental ill-health. Although identity is an individual journey for all of us, the public commentary around 'how Aboriginal' someone is has led to many Aboriginal people not exploring their history or genealogy and, in many cases, the continuation of generations of denial in families due to racism. Stolen Generations people are the obvious collateral damage of this.

So, I have chosen to take a public stand on the issue because I can afford to do so.[27] I know my cultural connections. I know my 'mob' – and that is luck. Assimilation policies, although devastating for my family, at least did not result in our cultural connections being severed or destroyed. This was not the case for significant numbers of Aboriginal people.

I was a member of the Australian Indigenous Psychologists Association for a short while. As one of the country's first psychologists of Aboriginal descent, and with a track record of more than fifteen years at that time, I was asked to sign a statutory declaration to prove my Aboriginality to simply be a member of the group. I pulled out immediately and have not rejoined since. I remain disgusted that an Indigenous psychologists' society – that is all about being trauma-informed and understanding the harm of assimilation policies on Aboriginal people – perpetuated this trauma on me. They all knew that my cultural connections were irrefutable, but they still insisted on it. It was shameful conduct.

I will never play that game. In leadership, you often have to take a stand for others more than for yourself. I am happy to 'take one for the team' and be accused of being a 'fake' Aboriginal. I say, 'Bring it on.' I often receive direct messages via social media from people thanking me for taking a stand, because they are too afraid to do so themselves. Identity is a personal issue. Why has it become so public? Why are people so consumed by it?

There are now social media sites run by Aboriginal people to 'dob in a fake Aboriginal'. Many of my clients searching online for their identity have been targeted. They weren't trying to benefit from any 'privilege' – they were simply wanting to explore their family background and confirm their genealogy. They then became so afraid of being targeted further by one of these groups that they buried their desire, too fearful to explore it.

The fact that this 'fake Aboriginal' and 'Aboriginal privileges' narrative often comes from our own people is an outcome of colonisation. It is Aboriginal people turning on each other out of fear. The idea that we are weeding out 'frauds' who cannot prove their Aboriginality is resulting in Stolen Generations people whose cultural connections were destroyed as part of government policy becoming collateral damage. So, the very people we are trying to protect are those who are the most harmed.

The Stolen Generations lady who found her culture

It's common that those who were removed and raised to not know their culture speak of a 'knowing' or 'longing' for something, of being drawn to Aboriginal culture despite not knowing they are Aboriginal. I have lost count of the number of Stolen Generations people I have had as clients who have told me that they always knew that they were Aboriginal long before it became a fact. They found out the 'family secret' via direct or indirect means or through searching their family histories once their parents had passed on.

However, finding out about your Aboriginality as an adult is not an easy path. It is significantly complex not only because you go through all the stages of black identity formation you missed as a child, but also because, sadly, you are likely to lose friends and family along the way as a result of racism. There is also the tragic, common experience of feeling rejected by community when you return. To be honest, I am not entirely sure it is always a simple rejection. A big aspect for Stolen Generations people is not being prepared sufficiently for reunification. When we reunify adoptees with their biological parents, comprehensive psychological preparation and risk assessments are undertaken. For people from the Stolen Generations, it is the opposite – they are just thrown back into the environment with the hope they will cope. This is what happened to my client H, who was completely unprepared for the eventual rejection she received.

When I first met H, she presented as a shattered woman – stooped over, not able to make eye contact, speaking in such a soft voice I struggled to hear her. She was so tiny and fragile it looked as though a stiff wind could blow her over. It was painful to watch her try to muster up answers to my questions.

Then we turned to the topic of identity. I often self-disclosed my own identity struggles because it normalised them for Aboriginal people. I wanted to make the point that even though I came from a strong cultural background with an intact, loving family who instilled in me a sense of pride in being Aboriginal, I still found the process challenging.

In Western psychology, self-disclosure is a no-no but with collective cultures like Aboriginal culture, mainstream training is always at odds with what works, and this is one example. Self-disclosure helps by enabling you to be authentic and making your relationship with your client central. You engage in the process of lived experience and this has always worked to shift Aboriginal clients through a lot of pain, so I have always done it. But self-disclosure must solely be to benefit your client. That's the yardstick. Not to use clients to resolve your own issues. That's not valuable or ethical self-disclosure.

We chatted a lot about identity and I said to her, 'In a perfect world you would have gone back to your community, and everything would have made sense. That hasn't happened for now – don't think of this as a permanent state of affairs. It is most likely a temporary one. So, let's see what we can do to feed your sense of culture in here.' I pointed to my heart.

Her eyes lit up for the first time. We then did cultural mapping through the Acculturation Scale for Aboriginal Australians to develop a cultural treatment plan for her. We came up with clear goals and ways she could learn aspects of her culture, to 'treat' her cultural identity, but in an incremental way controlled by her. The first thing she wanted was to learn her language. That was easy – I said I knew language centre mob who could teach her 'proper way' language. There were many other things we did over several months, such as discussing a future reunification, including an assessment of the psychological risks around possible outcomes (good and bad). Within only a few months, the difference in H was like night and day. Over time, she felt ready to go back to her community again, this time prepared psychologically and culturally.

When you feed your internal sense of identity, like H, you will find your external place. H is an elder now. She has found her contentment. H taught me so much. Mostly she taught me that cultural identity is a rollercoaster of pain when it is unreconciled. It can take you down so many painful paths, but if you never lose faith, it's worth every struggle.

5

Grief and Loss:
The psychologist and lived experience

I had done grief counselling with people before, but I didn't get it. You never truly do until you've lived it. For me it was my dad's passing, when I was just twenty-six years old, that remains the single most impactful loss in my life. Grief can make you compassionate because when our emotions are stripped bare, it reveals who we truly are. Dad's death humbled me, but it also made me a much better psychologist. This process is referred to as post-traumatic growth. It is the great paradox of loss, of pain, of trauma – that its aftermath can lead to something positive. But, of course, this is highly dependent on the nature of the trauma, individual coping mechanisms and the support available to make meaning of the loss.

When I started out, I was a twenty-two-year-old kid trying to understand my clients' pain and loss. I had empathy, but I didn't understand because I had never walked that journey. I thought I did understand, but I didn't. I wonder how many of my clients must have looked at me and thought, *What would this kid know about trauma, loss and grief?* If they suspected the answer was *nothing*, they would have been right.

But the challenge for every psychologist is to understand when lived experience is a strength, and when it blocks therapeutic progress. If you're a member of the Stolen Generations and working with Stolen Generations people, or a victim of violence and working with a victim of violence – at what point do your personal experiences hinder client progress? On one hand, if there's been suicide in your family and you're working with a suicidal client, can the therapy become about your own loss? On the other hand, do you need to have the lived experience of your client in order to be effective?

Lived experience is always only as helpful as the extent to which it is benefits your client. If a client's failure to leave their violent partner triggers you so much that it becomes about you – rather than hearing their reasons for staying and gently shifting them towards a safer choice – then it is no longer effective.

After losing my dad, I couldn't see people who had lost parents for a while. That's healthy. I knew that I was still too raw with grief. The smartest thing you can do as a therapist is recognise your limitations. We are human and lived experience can be extraordinarily helpful, but it can also lead to compassion fatigue and burnout.

I have worked with groups of bereaved parents whose children have been murdered or lost through suicide. It sounds like these sessions would be hard and traumatic. But this assumes that therapists are just giving and that helping does not feel good or reward us as well. We know that when we help others, the brain reacts chemically in its reward centre. As humans, our most basic need is to feel a sense of connection to other humans. Nothing achieves this more than helping others.

In grief, there is no such thing as a long time ago. The best description I have heard of grief is that it is unrelenting. It never lets up on you. To this day I miss not having a dad. But when he died, society's response to my grief was that I should bury it, spend all of my time and energy 'getting over' my loss.

The trouble with grief is that it didn't get the memo that allows you to 'get over it'. Buried emotions will always show up physically – through anxiety, weight loss, weight gain ... After the death of a loved one, there is always an associated sadness with every emotion. When you are happy you want to share it with the person you have lost, and then the guilt kicks in that you feel happy without them. When you are sad, you want their reassuring hug that it will be okay. When you struggle with life's challenges, you want to go to them to guide you through it.

My dad missed so much of all our lives, and that will never be okay.

Great loss never leaves us, but neither should it. In therapy, our focus with grief, trauma and loss is to soften our reactions to triggers, but to also make sure that grief is not buried.

It is the overwhelming nature of grief that levels people, because we are simply not prepared when our first major loss happens. The unpredictability of what triggers grief reactions and their loss of that control are central themes in my clients. Not being able to stop the loss when you know it is coming. Not being able to predict what will trigger a memory.

My dad's death was unexpected. He was misdiagnosed as having irritable bowel syndrome by his GP, when he had six tumours the size of golf balls in his liver. The most painful thing was to watch my dad being stripped of his dignity and pride. I saw the pain on his face when he couldn't mow the lawns or fix the car and was forced to look on while others did it for him. Cancer does that. There is no dignity in cancer, either for those who have it or for their loved ones watching them dying from it.

When he was finally sent down to Perth after eighteen months of being 'treated' with dietary changes, the damage was irreparable. I will never forget picking him up from the airport. His physical appearance took my breath away. This robust, healthy, tough station man was reduced to half his physical size. Fear was etched on his face. I had never seen my dad frightened before. Ever. He was just fifty-nine years old. He loved his wife, loved his family, and he was too young to die. That's what his face told me.

I tried not to reveal my shock at how emaciated he was. The challenge of watching someone you love confronting death is that you have to bury every feeling you have because it is not about you. It is about being strong for them. As a psychologist, I had been taught this, to remain neutral. But perhaps that's wrong. Perhaps the fact that we bury our feelings is not helpful. I felt like crying, but I didn't. I smiled. Dad smiled back at me. He always hugged me – *always* – but this time he didn't. I felt relieved because I didn't want to truly acknowledge how much his body had wasted away, or how much what was happening to him wasn't just 'food allergies' but something far more serious.

The things you hold on to in the aftermath of loss is why grief is so individualised. As a psychologist, it always surprises me what my clients ruminate over and can't let go of. It is usually not the most graphic part of the death. For me, I was angry for a long time that we weren't prepared for Dad's death. No-one at the hospital ever told us that he was dying, even at his last breath.

When my emotions overwhelm me I go quiet, as if my energy to speak is best used instead on wishing, hoping, that what is unfolding is not really happening. I have always been this way, emotionally paralysed and avoidant in traumatic situations It's a common feature of what is called anxious-avoidant attachment. Avoidant attachment can often look like emotional strength, but it is actually emotional fear. The emotional comfort range is narrow, resulting in heightened reactivity and extreme reactions to intolerable emotions. Perhaps if I wish it away it won't happen? Words are often lost on people in those circumstances and all you can do to support them is to just be physically present, making sure they do the basics – eat, sleep, drink – and helping with the practical things that need to be done, such as speaking to funeral directors, deciding on a coffin, getting access to the will. Everything will feel overwhelming to them and a potential trigger. With each task they tick off, it's another reality check that the person they love is really gone and that's too much to bear.

The night my dad died is still as vivid to me as if it occurred yesterday. I remember my partner at the time, Chris, pulling into the hospital carpark; I remember sprinting through the endless and familiar corridors of the hospital. How many times had I caught that same lift? How many times had I smelt that hospital smell that masked so much death and so much grief? But I could cope with it because, in my mind, that is what always happened to 'other people'. My dad was just being treated for something he would survive. I never allowed myself to think about the possibility of him dying, as if inviting the thoughts in would allow it to happen.

I finally reached the ICU, where Dad was. He hadn't woken up from his surgery and remained in a medically induced coma. His hands were swollen from the fluid that had accumulated in his body. The nurses muttered something about 'fluid in the lungs' which I couldn't process. All I could think about was Mum not being there.

I spoke to the nurses and then the doctor. Not one of them said, 'Your dad is dying.' I know that sounds silly, but I was only twenty-six. I didn't understand what was going on. We were in a hospital – surely they could fix this?

Finally, after what seemed an eternity, my sister Lynny arrived with Mum. Lynny was six months pregnant with her second child, but all I could think about was Mum. Thank god she was there because if I'd had to tell her that Dad had passed away, it would have been just too much to bear. I was thankful for small mercies.

She looked at me with so much pain when she asked, 'Is Father going to die?' as if I had the answers. I didn't.

Mum held his hand. And, as if he knew that she was there – in death as she had been in life – he took his final breath. The love they had for each other made it okay. It remains both the most traumatic and beautiful moment I have ever witnessed in my life.

I watched him pass away, watched his heart monitor beep, beep, beep, beeeeeeeep. Then nothing. Just silence.

I felt like shaking him. *Dad! Wake up!* But of course I didn't. I couldn't fix this. No-one could. We just had to deal with the pain now.

For months afterwards I couldn't listen to a beeping sound. A lab in one of my lectures had a computer that constantly beeped – it was so triggering.

Trauma is generalised in that there are similar 'clusters' of symptoms. For example, a significant general symptom is that the trauma will be re-experienced. For some it's through a sound; for others it's a smell or a repetitive dream. Triggers are unpredictable because they are specific to an individual's trauma or grief experience. For example, I had one client who after the death of their parent couldn't hear an ambulance siren without freezing. Another client would be triggered by the smell of their parent's perfume. It is this individualised manifestation of trauma and grief that makes it hard to 'get back to normal'.

But you can't go around grief. You have to go through it.

Grief is too often processed as self-blame, shame or guilt. You can always find something to blame yourself for – something you 'failed' to do or that you feel guilty about. When you laugh, you feel guilty. When you feel 'relieved' that the suffering is over, you feel guilty. Not jumping every time the phone rang was a 'relief' after my dad passed away, as was not having my heart in my mouth every single time I rang the hospital for an update on his condition.

I do a lot of 'reframing' with my clients who have experienced significant loss. Our beliefs and faulty thinking can keep us stuck in grief. So, rather than feeling guilty about my sense of relief, I can reframe it as feeling compassion that my dad no longer has to suffer. Changing perspective like this results in softening these triggers. Hopefully you get the idea.

I also had the bittersweet reconciling of being there in my dad's final moments. The 'bitter' is that it initially made the grief so much harder because it was so graphic. Everything became amplified: the sounds, the hospital smells, my reactions to it all. I couldn't process it for many months. These triggers were the harder ones to deal with and required more effort to soften. The brain copes by dissociating from this irreconcilable pain and memories, which means that details can often be 'lost' as a post-grief reaction. I was glad my siblings didn't have that extra burden to their grief, although they didn't see it this way. But the 'sweet' part was that I had that time with him. Nothing was unresolved between us. I didn't have that added layer of pain that others often have with the loss of a parent.

Although grief is individualised, the worst times are always at night, when everything is quiet and you are alone with your thoughts, unable to escape from processing the trauma. And I was experiencing trauma symptoms. *Everything* was about Dad's death. The flashbacks made it impossible to stay asleep, because every time I closed my eyes I was back there, reliving it all again. So sleep had to be avoided. I wasn't into sleeping tablets; it's just not how I roll. Mum and I eventually found solace in sleeping together, holding hands. It was like that for a while.

Back to normal, but what is normal?

For me, it was just a week of 'grieving' before I had to somehow get myself back to university. I was at the start of my fourth year in psychology and had the added pressure of needing to average at least 75 per cent across all of my subjects to get into Clinical Masters, so I couldn't afford to take a moment off. Getting into the program then, of course, as my irrational reaction to his death, became all about making Dad proud, and I became obsessive as a result. I remember sitting on the hospital floor when Dad was at the end stages of his life, drugged up with morphine for the pain and often hallucinating. He would regularly wake up asking for me, so I took to sleeping on the floor next to him with all my books around me.

That first day walking back to the uni campus, it was painful just to breathe. Every step felt like a marathon. That's something that's so misunderstood about grief – the physical impact it has on you. I was terrified someone would mention my dad and I'd fall apart. We didn't have digital news in those days, so everyone read the *West Australian* newspaper, and lots of people would have known about Dad's death. My grief felt like a beacon, being talked about and judged. It didn't take long for a fellow student to matter-of-factly say, 'I read about your dad. I don't know how you are here. If this happened to me, I would be absolutely devastated.'

Hiding behind my very dark sunglasses, I wanted to scream, 'I *am* absolutely devastated! How dare you judge my pain!'

But I couldn't find the words. I was afraid that expressing them would unleash a tidal wave of grief, of anger, of hate, of blame, of every emotion there is that I could not control. And control was so very important to me, as it is with literally everyone who experiences sudden death, trauma or loss. But for me and my siblings, dignity was also how we were raised. To always be appropriate and 'rise above' everything that was thrown at us. It was ingrained in us to always take the 'high road'.

In that moment, though, I hated the values we were raised with. I wanted to be undignified in my grief, but I couldn't. So I just nodded as tears streamed down my face, as my breathing sped up to the point that the pain in my chest became overwhelming and I felt my heart would burst from my chest. I couldn't formulate any thoughts and my body became paralysed. I wanted to get out of there and escape, but I physically couldn't. This is called a freeze state and is part of avoidant attachment. It happens more often than people give it credit for when triggers of critical events occur and emotions come like a flood and overwhelm us.

After a while, as my heart rate came down, the physical control came back. I jumped in my car and drove back home to the solace of grief. I did so much crying in that car. It was where I didn't have to pretend – where I didn't have to arm myself against the unpredictability of when I would be reminded of my loss. At home it didn't matter if I fell apart. No-one judged it, because they were feeling it too.

Hiding our pain is not brave – revealing it is

Dad's sister Aunty Joy, who had experienced so much loss in her life, said to me: 'It takes a while for the fog to lift. One day you will wake up and it will be just a bit less painful.'

For most of my non-traumatic grief clients (I'll explain the difference soon), this 'softening' tends to start after twelve months. This is only because by then you have gone through every major event without your loved one: your birthday, their birthday,

Christmas, Easter, the first anniversary of their passing. However, regardless of how much time has passed, birthdays and anniversaries are always the most triggering times for the bereaved. Because of this, I have got hundreds of pop-up reminders on my calendar to message clients who have lost children or relatives – to let them know they are in my thoughts on these days. I don't always get a reply, but that's okay. It's about being there and understanding that it's always when Sorry Time is over and you are left alone with your grief that is the hardest.

The thing you are not prepared for is the extremes – going from the overwhelming love and support you get during the funeral, the wake and Sorry Time to everyone returning home, back to their normal lives, and you are left alone. It is the most high-risk time for the bereaved.

I channelled my experience of grief into writing a free resource called 'Grieving Aboriginal Way', which helps with the standard phases of grief but also adds cultural aspects to this process. The primary part of this is spiritual visits of deceased loved ones. That is such a common aspect of grief for Aboriginal people and it is consistently 'hidden' for fear of systems pathologising these normal aspects of grief. I discuss this further later in the chapter and how important my culture-bound syndromes paper has been in shifting the monocultural nature of how grief is being appraised as 'normal' or not, based on a Westernised view of it.

My brother Mike was a huge support after our dad's death. He guided me on a few things, like, 'When you see it in the paper, it becomes real, so just prepare yourself for that.' He had unfortunately experienced the death of his childhood sweetheart a few years previously in a car crash. I watched him go through it. I watched him unable to eat or sleep, having to bury his grief just to function. I remember the two of us driving to Broome together in his panel van for twenty-seven hours straight. I understood I had to keep him busy while his brain caught up with what had happened and processed the unimaginable. It was a sort of 'grief watch' and I just knew he needed to have someone with him.

Grief is ultimately an individual journey, though. The brain takes time to process the permanency of loss. It just takes time.

Loss is such a central theme with all my Aboriginal clients, and hearing their traumatic stories is a necessary part of the job. Our training teaches us there is a fine line between caring too much and burning out, and caring too little and becoming ineffective and compassionless as a result. As an Aboriginal person and as a psychologist, I find this line even more challenging because although my personal experiences of racism have been my most valuable therapeutic tool, they have also been the most likely to render me helpless.

Vicarious trauma occurs when listening to clients' traumatic stories and witnessing traumatic incidents hurts those who are there to help. It's recognised and increasingly understood in supervision and workforce support, but not nearly as much as it should be. There is often this view that because you signed up for the job, you should expect what is coming and be able to cope. However, studies show that a significant proportion of mental health professionals have their own experience of mental ill-health and even more of us burn out because of it.[1]

So what happens when those in the helping professions come with pre-existing lived experience of trauma, and are treating clients with significant trauma in systems that perpetuate trauma through systemic racism? While there is considerable literature supporting racism as having a similar impact as trauma, systems have not caught up with that reality and fail to understand it or respond as part of standard supervision, support or evidence-based structural change.

In government-mandated services, the struggles are significantly more personal. My first job out of university was as a child protection worker. I understand how hard it is because I've walked the journey, working in the same system that forcibly removed Aboriginal children from our families and then denied they did it until 2008 when the federal government formally apologised.

What becomes of your Aboriginal clients in a system that fails to see who they are beyond another black kid destined for a cycle of intergenerational failure? What happens to them if you leave? Who cares where they end up? Cop the racism or abandon a vulnerable child – that's the impossible choice.

Imagine having a child caught in the grip of mental illness and there is no-one to help. Imagine if when they do get a psychologist, the cultural barriers between them are so great, any opportunity for healing is effectively lost.

Healed people can heal people. But for the therapist, it's about therapist insight.

Suffering, grief and pain can paradoxically have transformative power. Post-trauma, the brain is capable of making significant changes, reorganising and recovering. Post-traumatic growth is a psychological transformation that follows stressful events, like grief, to enable you to find purpose in your pain.

For me, having to be present for others initially gave me a practical focus, but it was also a great excuse to avoid pain. This had a devastating effect on my processing of grief because I could ignore it – until six months later, after suffering from migraines, hair thinning and adult acne (yes, isn't grief wonderful), I finally had to allow myself to feel it.

Your greatest fear is that your memory of the person you lost will fade over time. It doesn't. That's the thing about the people who shaped who you are – you never lose them. In every tough decision I've had to make, I was guided by the wisdom of my dad.

Because of my dad's death, I am now significantly better at feeling what I need to feel. I am no longer afraid of emotions, but it has taken a lifetime to get here. When my beloved dog died a few years ago, I just allowed myself to feel in the moment. I remember catching a plane shortly afterwards for a work trip and when the air hostess asked me if I wanted a coffee, I burst into tears – as part of my new healthy response to grief. Strangely, I wasn't offered another cup of coffee for the remainder of my trip. Clearly, the woman in seat 6A doesn't like coffee!

Laughter and grief – a powerful combination that represents the emotional rollercoaster of loss.

Is all grief equal? Traumatic and non-traumatic grief

This is a question I get asked a lot, as if you can 'rate' grief. It's obviously asked the most by clients, who have sought out therapy because they are struggling, which they often frame as 'everyone else has moved on' or through some external references of grief reactions and societal timeframes. Any personal loss is awful and life-altering, but there is a distinction between traumatic and non-traumatic grief. This means that there are absolutely certain types of loss that increase the odds of complicated grief (CG) and are more likely to be associated with comorbid post-traumatic stress disorder (PTSD) and other psychiatric disorders. Certain factors can compound the psychological impacts of loss.

For example, the loss of my dad had things in it that made the grief process both more difficult and 'easier' than other types of losses. First, the bad stuff: I had to watch my dad die, and it was graphic and took a long time to heal from; it was unexpected, based on the medical advice and his relatively young age; the nature of our relationship (parent–child); and my relatively young age. While all these things compounded my grief, there were things that moderated it as well – for example, the fact that I had three months with him before he passed. Nothing was left unsaid or unresolved between us. His death was non-violent. He was a loving and supportive father. I was young, but an adult and less financially and emotionally dependent. It was still an irreparable loss, though. One that I continue to feel today, almost three decades later.

While bereavement is stressful whenever it occurs, studies consistently show that the greatest and most enduring grief is faced by parents who experience the death of a child.[2] This grief can persist long after the child's death and more often becomes complicated grief disorder and can also include PTSD. With infant and child deaths up to 3.9 times more likely in Aboriginal communities – and the death of a child by suicide being four times more likely – Aboriginal families have a significantly higher chance of suffering such grief.[3]

A child death causes impenetrable and unhealable trauma and this is where the complex therapy is needed the most. The central theme of this therapy is always a struggle with guilt and associated shame from the idea that the death could have been prevented by their actions or non-actions. It's a necessary part of 'bargaining' with yourself through the grief process, and hindsight is a tragic part of this – we blame ourselves based on knowledge we didn't have at the time.

Family and friends often do not know how to respond and therefore withdraw, inadvertently creating a 'conspiracy of silence' – in terms of not knowing how to help or what to say, but also often going through that same bargaining process, which may manifest as inadvertent blame on the parents. The bereaved will often find solace in other bereaved parents because they understand the journey. They can find the words when no-one else can.

Unexpected death

In 2016 my firstborn nephew, Lee – an award-winning tradesman – went to work on a mine site in the Pilbara and was crushed to death. It remains impossible to find words to reconcile this pain, which has continued to resonate through my family. For his mum to lose her son; for my mother to bury a grandchild.

I was just thirteen years old when Lee was born. He was the 'unofficial nephew' for all my peers. At thirty-two years old, he had just started out in his life before it was violently and unexpectedly cut short. This was a very different devastation to the loss of our dad because when a loss occurs with a relationship of this nature, you always feel as though you have somehow failed in your duty to protect them.

When a death is unexpected, it can lead to depression and anxiety symptoms and substance abuse, as well as other psychiatric disorders and a heightened risk for prolonged grief reactions. Additionally, increased exposure to unexpected death – such as suicides, which are significantly more prevalent in Aboriginal communities – is associated with a monotonic increase in the number of total psychiatric disorder episodes, with some studies indicating it increases the odds by up to four times that of the general population.[4]

Violent death

When the death is violent, this contributes to the increased likelihood of PTSD among the bereaved, and acts as significant, salient and enduring trauma triggers. Numerous studies have reported that a variety of mental disorders – such as depression, PTSD and other anxiety disorders – coexist in bereaved individuals with complicated grief (CG), and one study indicated that 75.2 per cent of patients with CG also had a major depressive disorder and PTSD as comorbid disorders.[5] In those bereaved by violent death with CG, the prevalence of PTSD was reported to be as high as between 43 per cent and 65 per cent.[6] It is common after unexpected and violent deaths for grief to remain unresolved in close family, in addition to trauma that is magnified due to the circumstances surrounding these deaths.

An additional component that is rarely discussed is the shame and stigma that the bereaved often feel after a violent death, because the circumstances of the death are either unknown or attached to the criminal justice system, such as in deaths in custody or murders. There is often a lack of explanation of why their loved ones died and too often with murders and unexpected and violent deaths, there is also public questioning around why their loved one was targeted because there is this natural inclination to want to make meaning of deaths that seem to make little sense. Sadly, violent deaths are significantly more prevalent in Aboriginal communities.[7] Having undertaken numerous reports on heavily publicised violent deaths, I have seen how media attention and ongoing legal processes often results in protracted and compounded grief.

The foregoing means that there will likely exist a greater cluster of co-varying disorders which can be complicated by the interaction with PTSD symptoms.

Cultural factors that exacerbate grief

In addition to the traumatic grief variables noted above is the lack of worth given to bereaved Aboriginal people, which further compounds our grief. This includes the silence from media and political leadership in response to the deaths of children, the less newsworthiness and sympathy attached to Aboriginal victims of crime, and societal racism that places a greater sense of blame on Aboriginal victims of crime and the bereaved, which I discussed on Mamamia's *The Quicky* podcast.[8] Finally, there is a greater likelihood that Aboriginal people will receive less justice from the legal system or often no justice at all.[9] Research has consistently supported a strong interaction between the victim's race and judicial outcomes.[10] Meyers argued that compared with high-status white people, poor and/or racialised crime victims are often depicted as more blameworthy for their victimisation.[11]

There are numerous factors that exist uniquely for Aboriginal people which compound grief. I have discussed the idea of 'racial trauma' for a long time, both in educational workshops as well as in my clinical and assessment work. There are several pre- and post-trauma variables that are racially mediated and specific, and they exist to increase the likelihood of trauma in Aboriginal people. Most of this is in the reaction to trauma. For example, there have been a number of horrific cases of young Aboriginal people dying in traumatic circumstances. The most profiled was Cassius Turvey, a fifteen-year-old Aboriginal boy who was murdered on the streets of Perth in an unprovoked vigilante attack. While there was a clearly established racial motivation for the crime, both the then-premier, Mark McGowan, and the police commissioner, Col Blanch, denied this.[12] This is consistent with the continued denial by leadership of the realities of racism being a factor in crimes perpetrated against black Australians. This refusal to face the truth – confirmed by significant statistics of racial profiling due to the other-race effect – is deeply embedded within the psyche of our country, despite overwhelming evidence of its health and mental health impacts on Indigenous people.[13] The silence of our political leaders at the deaths of our children was highlighted by Jacob Kagi of the ABC, who noted that in the weeks after Coroner Ros Fogliani made an 'urgent' plea for authorities to act after the suicides of thirteen Aboriginal youth in the Kimberley, not a single question was asked in the lower house of the WA parliament about the coroner's report or what the government was going to do about it.[14] The ABC also reported that only nine of the ninety-five members of parliament brought up the inquest in any way, in either chamber, in 2019. This was not new. Suicides in the Kimberley have unfortunately now become generational, silent and unknown to most Australians.

What was of such importance that rendered the deaths of these Aboriginal children irrelevant to the state's political leaders and, frankly, to our country? There is no greater injustice in this world than to be invisible, to feel as though your pain matters less. It is dehumanising and dismisses the trauma that these bereaved families face on a daily basis.

Put simply, it is evident that trauma itself is inherently political. Politicians and government bureaucrats, especially arms of the state, and the media have long been central players in the magnification of trauma, including by denying the cause of the critical incident, minimising its severity and impact, and failing to help. Psychologists know that the first step to healing comes from trauma being validated through acknowledgement. If this doesn't happen, it develops whole new dimensions and intensifies. And trauma becomes systemically generated when governmental bodies and societal structures – including the media – fail to show they care by responding inadequately or unfairly.[15]

Aboriginal people are forced to expend considerable additional energy convincing authorities that race was the sole factor in our victimisation. Holocaust survivors have talked about the impacts of racial trauma in this way – not only its biological and attachment-based impacts, but its role in preventing healing when it is dismissed.[16] You cannot heal when your energy needs to be spent fighting for recognition that you experienced trauma in the first place. If the death occurs in a place where people should feel safe in the arms of the state, the trauma and resulting responses become significantly compounded. When those who are supposed to protect fail to do so, the trauma can generalise to affect all interactions with law enforcement. Up to 40 per cent of Indigenous deaths in custody occurred because medical assistance wasn't provided when requested,[17] and in *all* these cases police and judicial systems have been completely absolved of any wrongdoing, despite some of the most horrific cases of cruelty at the hands of police. In addition, the proportion of Indigenous deaths in custody where not all procedures were followed in the events leading up to the death increased from 38.8 per cent in 2018 to 41.2 per cent in 2019.[18]

The lack of accountability in many Aboriginal deaths – including in custody, in hospital and mental health systems – has combined to significantly maintain trauma responses. As it stands, no police officer has been held criminally responsible for the death of an Aboriginal person in custody.[19] Despite this, police across Australia continue to investigate their own officers for wrongdoing in relation to their duty of care or criminal negligence. The absence of conviction or sanction effectively means that there is no deterrent to individuals in these systems repeating their actions. Specifically, victims' core fear is that trauma will be repeated.

In Australia, Scott Morrison (in)famously said, in response to the murder of George Floyd, 'We have our problems. We have our faults. We have our issues. There's no doubt about that. But when I see things like that, I'm just very thankful for the wonderful country we live in.'[20] Let's look at some of our George Floyd moments:[21]

- Ms Dhu died in custody of septicaemia and pneumonia for having $3600 in unpaid fines. A victim of domestic violence, she had been taken to hospital twice, but sepsis wasn't detected so she was sent back to custody. The inquest found she was subjected to 'inhumane' treatment by police, including being called a 'fucking junkie'. The then-premier Colin Barnett defended the police, stating that they had a 'very difficult' job to do. No charges were laid.

- Mr Ward, a respected elder, blew over the limit. He was put in a police van and transported for four hours without air-conditioning in at least 40-degree heat. He was literally cooked alive. No charges were laid. If you left your dog in the car and it died the same way, you would be charged criminally. The attorney-general also decided that there had been no 'reasonable prospect of conviction' for Mr Ward.
- JFW lost consciousness after being held on his stomach during a citizen's arrest. After his death, no charges were laid.
- Ms Mandijarra lay dead on the floor of a watchhouse for at least six hours before police officers noticed. No charges.
- LV went into respiratory failure while being held down, handcuffed and injected with a sedative by police. No charges.
- VW was locked up for shoplifting and denied bail. She was found dead three days later in lock-up. She had been heard crying for help in the cell, but her cries were ignored. No charges.
- Ms Day was arrested for being drunk in public – not for being a public nuisance or aggressive, just intoxicated in public. She died in custody when police failed to conduct mandated checks and didn't see her sustain the head injury that caused her death, which was captured on CCTV. No charges. On the day Ms Day was arrested, the same police officers took a heavily intoxicated non-Aboriginal woman safely home. Black women are ten times more likely to be locked up for public drunkenness than white women.
- David Dungay Jr died after guards rushed into his cell to stop him eating biscuits, dragged him to another cell then held him facedown and had him injected with a sedative. Before he died, David said twelve times, 'I can't breathe.'
- Veronica Nelson died in custody after suffering malnutrition and gastro. Her cries for help were captured on CCTV and intercom over four hours. They were all ignored by staff. A 'review' by prison services found no problem with her care. The coroner was scathing of this review, which was

government-funded and therefore not independent, and he described Veronica's death as 'cruel' and 'inhumane'.

- John Pat was a sixteen-year-old boy beaten to death by police in front of (Aboriginal) witnesses. His autopsy revealed a fractured skull, haemorrhaging and swelling, as well as bruising and tearing of the brain. Pat sustained massive blows to the head. Officers were acquitted. His death sparked the 1991 Royal Commission into Aboriginal Deaths in Custody.
- Cameron Doomadgee died in a police cell after being locked up for singing too loudly. He died from massive internal injuries, including broken ribs, a ruptured spleen and his liver being cleaved in two. The pathologist compared his injuries to those of a plane crash victim. Queensland police marched in protest at charges laid in the lead-up to the trial of their fellow officer, who was not only acquitted but also compensated.
- Joyce Clarke's family called police to do a welfare check. When they arrived, Joyce was carrying a large bread knife and small pink scissors. It took a police officer sixteen seconds to arrive on the scene and shoot her dead. The officer was charged but found not guilty after the jury deliberated for just two hours.

I was there in 2006 when half-a-dozen tactical response police officers were at a verdict announcement for one of the Bowraville child serial murders. This over-policing indicated a lack of empathy for the victim's family and caused them distress. As I wrote in my expert-witness evidence for the parliamentary inquiry into the family response to the murders, 'Of further distress to the family was that the tactical police occupied most of the first two rows of the courtroom, forcing the family members to hear the verdict in the back rows and some in standing room only.'[22]

Yet there was no anger and no rioting, as was clearly expected by the police. Can you imagine if this over-policing had occurred in any case where three white children were murdered? It wouldn't. That the police put more resources into policing the victims than catching the perpetrator stands as one of the most disgraceful acts of racism I have ever seen. I was so angry for the family. Seeing them all so overwhelmed with pain, I also understood how grief was paralysing all of them.

I have seen Aboriginal people be incredibly dignified after receiving horrific treatment by systems and institutions – from police and the justice system through to the media – in the aftermath of a loved one being murdered. I have often wondered whether this poise is a consequence of the 'othering' we experience as Aboriginal people, as we are judged harshly if we express what is 'normal' pain, including anger.

In loss, you need to express anger to soften it. However, although anger should be visited, you don't want to live there. Most clients come to me because they can't get past anger. There's a lot of crying in my grief and loss groups. I have no problem with that because grief is frequently pushed down and not encouraged. So, for these parents, being provided the space to cry means that they are in touch with their emotions again. We are shaped to deny emotions for many reasons. For parents, it is instinctual to protect those we love; for others, the nature of the death is so graphic, so unexpected, that it's impossible to reconcile.

What has a big impact is the reaction of others to the death. The normal grief responses of reactive depression, shock, anger and bargaining can become stagnated if you don't get the reaction you desperately need and expect. When it doesn't come, you retreat into yourself because it's easier than risking the pain of reaching out, revealing raw emotion and being let down. This means that attachment is affected in a way that is self-protective.

A bereaved mum who was one of my clients said she felt 'proud' that she was looking after her lost son's dog. She went into all the practical reasons she was proud, but they had nothing to do with the real importance of it, which was about attachment. After her loss, she gave everything away – she moved house, adopted out her own pets. So, looking after this dog was actually much deeper; it was about attaching again. There is always a risk of loss with any attachment. But to risk it all and do it anyway – that's so important.

Cultural competency of practitioners

Of course, we also look to individual coping mechanisms or conditionability. I'll discuss this more in the chapter on trauma (Chapter 7), but that is why therapists need to be drilled in not only the theory of grief and cultural manifestations of grief, but also individual responses to loss and associated treatment based on this. However, most critical is the therapist's capacity to personally manage the load of the type of grief that Aboriginal clients present with.

My caseload has always been full of clients who have been exposed to so much trauma and violence that it's been near impossible for them to find a therapist not only skilled enough to work through all the significant layers of it, but robust enough psychologically to handle it. It's pretty common that many Aboriginal clients give up trying to find a therapist as a result.[23] I often think during therapy sessions, *What psychologist could possibly manage this level of trauma?*

I have dealt with my fair share of grief in my clients. We have a mortality rate that is double that of non-Aboriginal Australia, an infant mortality rate that is commensurate with those in developing countries, and a suicide rate that is double that of mainstream Australia. When an Aboriginal child dies in Australia, 27 per cent of them will do so by suicide.[24] That is more than four times the rate of non-Aboriginal children.

But statistics are cold and inhuman. When you look into the eyes of a parent who has lost a child, it is something that never leaves you. For these parents, the grief is intolerable. There is always some way to blame themselves for the loss because of a parent's duty to protect their child. Suicide bereavement just makes that blame greater and the burden more significant.

I have worked with more bereaved parents than I can count, and every one has left a mark on my soul. I am forever humbled by their strength because living with such pain is strength. How do you put one foot in front of the other every day when blame is coming not only from yourself, but also society. I have done surveys in community workshops on myths about suicide, and one of the questions that you have to agree or disagree with is, 'People who die by suicide come from bad families.' A whopping 67 per cent of people endorse this.

But what actually drives this seemingly uncaring view is fear that it could happen to their child. So people have to find a reason as to why it wouldn't define their child. It's a very human reaction, but it is also why significantly more work needs to be done with suicide prevention at a whole-of-community level, because bereaved families are suffering from the death of their loved one and it's being compounded by the community reaction to it.

Parents and loss: The mask of grief

Though a person can be an orphan, or a widow or widower, there is no word for someone who has lost a child – perhaps because it is simply too awful. A group of bereaved parents – thirty of them – were in the room; all had lost children to suicide.

We got through the first ten minutes and then as soon as I said, 'Okay, we are going to talk about grief and loss,' one of the parents (who had a massive box of tissues in front of her) just burst into tears.

It was one of the most emotionally overwhelming moments I have had the privilege to be in – to be invited into this type of pain. As this beautiful lady continued to cry, the other parents surrounded her and hugged her until she stopped heaving with tears.

She finally said the most poignant words: 'I feel like I have been walking around with a mask on for the last seven years since I lost my son.'

As I gave her the space she needed, I gently said, 'It's so powerful to me that you have dropped that mask straight away in front of all of us. Is there anywhere else that you drop this mask?'

She said, 'My son's room. It is exactly as it was when he passed away. Nothing has been moved. I go in there and I cry and cry. It's the only place I can do that.'

'Is anyone else with you?'

'No. I don't allow my kids or my husband to see me like this.'

'Why?'

'Because I have to protect them?'

I have found that the greatest gift you can give as a therapist is to be present, listening to every single word and remembering the themes and words spoken over successive sessions. This is the point at which you have to use your skills and instincts to reframe how people have made meaning of death.

You cannot ever be passive in therapy. Every word is relevant to the client's processing of their grief. There is nothing more insulting to those who are grieving than a psychologist forgetting the names of family members or who is related to who. It's about showing respect for your client's pain and being aware of the themes of their grief, which is ultimately where the work lies to shift their pain. I have close to a photographic memory (if one exists), but I also care very deeply about my clients. It's that simple.

So, although it seemed that the bereaved mother was making a statement – 'I have to protect them' – I framed it as though she'd asked it as a question. I gently said to her:

'Here's something you need to hear. You are all in pain. You are all walking around with masks on, trying to protect each other from pain. As a mother you will feel this even more. You have experienced the most unimaginable of losses – that of a child. *Your instinct is always to protect your children from pain, but in doing so you have buried memories of your son.*

'For your children and your husband, they need to see that it is okay to express pain. Trust yourself again as a parent. Create opportunities to talk about your son. You need to open the door – the one to your son's bedroom, and the emotional one.'

She said, 'Yes, I know I do.'

These are the days I remember why I became a psychologist – to hold someone in pain and feel as though you have had a role in walking them through to the other side. It's impossible to process grief without understanding the pain that got you there.

Sharing pain that has never been shared with anyone else is a privilege. Psychologists have the honour of doing that, every single day.

Loss is a complex journey. You grieve for the person you have lost. You feel angry with them. You think you have failed them. You feel guilty – and then it goes around and around again. Doing it alone is a given. Grief is an individual journey, but suicide bereavement can't be healed alone. There are too many complexities to it, too many questions that will always remain unanswered. You can't answer them alone, but you *can* certainly blame yourself alone without an objective, 'external' reframe.

Grief is often fuelled by misplaced guilt, which is not included in the Elisabeth Kübler-Ross model (discussed shortly). There will always be something you failed to do or say to the person who is now gone. Exploring this as a therapist is difficult because you do not want to add a layer of burden by raising it in therapy, but you also need to ensure any sense of guilt is objectively challenged and reframed. How do you do this? By creating narratives about the death of their loved one and listening deeply to any emotional shifts in that narrative and pointing it out.

It is critical that any 'guilt' felt comes from the client themselves because that is insight. Clients will often not use the word 'guilt' but it's in their actions and behaviours, which are linked to emotions. This is the complex aspect of grief that those who are stuck need help with, through others who don't feel that sense of blame. Hindsight is a wonderful thing, and we blame ourselves harshly because of it. That's not what healing looks like.

There is no normal anymore, just a different normal

When we lose the people we love – our core attachments – we are never the same. Focusing on trying to remain the same is wrong, and any counsellor or therapist who tells you that needs to hand in their therapist card. To suggest you can return to 'normal' not only lacks empathy but sets you up to feel as though you have failed some yardstick of grief resolution. We spend so much time encouraging people to 'get over' loss because most of us, including therapists, are afraid of pain.

That's why I encourage the expression of emotions in my clients. It's vital to try to process emotions rather than direct people to make sense of aspects of loss that are often outside of their control to change, or towards others' actions that make no sense. This is where therapy goes wrong for bereaved parents. Loss is not something to be fixed. It is the emotions attached to it that need to be understood and processed because this is what often blocks healing. What we tell ourselves, our self-talk, the thoughts that drive our emotions are where the true therapeutic work needs to be undertaken.

In my grief workshops, I guide people to first make meaning of what they're feeling, and to try to reconcile it. Most importantly, I also help them develop a deep sense of self-compassion. Some of these powerful parts of therapy are done in a group. Aboriginal people learn primarily through a group but, regardless of the cultural background, groups are helpful for those struggling with personal grief by offering a relatable yardstick and a comparative experience, which well-meaning friends, family and random strangers can't.

Aboriginal clients also find comfort in group therapy, as opposed to individually, so although having thirty bereaved family members in one room sounds completely nuts, the collective nature of Aboriginal culture means that we effectively help each other through pain. Often the most powerful outcome is normalising grief responses with other bereaved parents, rather than being judged by those who have never walked it, never lived it. So we concentrate on allowing people to feel, express and validate emotions that have often been denied and locked down for years.

There are a couple of focused activities we do, and I am a big believer in having themes as key words that I repeat to my clients, so that they can retrieve them as mantras during their toughest times. I am also a big believer in explaining to people why I am asking them to do certain tasks and activities. Knowledge is power, and it's important for clients to feel empowered by understanding the theory behind therapy and why we do what we do.

The workshops begin with an explanation of grief. The most famous model of grief is by Elisabeth Kübler-Ross, which has these stages:

1. denial (shock, numbness)
2. anger
3. bargaining
4. depression
5. acceptance
6. finding meaning

I ask people whether this fits for what they have gone through or where they predominantly are. I explain that people can go backwards at any time and sometimes leap stages. Grief is an individual journey. I also give examples from my own personal loss to help them understand this more practically.

This group therapy is vital because grief in Aboriginal communities is always shared. It's about an entire process known as Sorry Time whereby grief is communal and out in the open, with nothing hidden. That is powerful. As Aboriginal people, we have had to exist in predominantly mainstream worlds in which bereavement leave is only reserved for the loss of close family – and you get just a few days. The problem with this is that Sorry Time takes time. And this long process is critical to ensure that grief does not become unresolved culturally or 'pathological', such as through troubling spiritual visits or sorry cutting that results in unintended harm to self (as discussed in Chapter 3).

There is also the nature of skin groups, which mean Aboriginal people have relationships that come with deeper obligations and meaning. This is particularly the case during the ritualistic process of Sorry Time. The journey is a collective rather than an individual one.

So, given that we are no longer able to grieve in the way that our Sorry Time traditions have always required us to do as Aboriginal people, and that we experience loss at such a significant rate, the obvious question is: where does all the grief go?

Rebuilding self-worth: Individuation from the mob

Ask an Aboriginal person a direct question about themselves and you'll get very little information. We see the group as more important than the self, so it is often forgotten how important it is to teach those from collective cultures how to 'individuate' – to form not only a sense of self but a love for that self. This process is a natural default for most individualistic cultures and happens around the age of seven, as noted in Chapter 4.

For my Aboriginal clients, I start this process with a really easy, short activity:

1. Write down everything you can think of that is great about you.

It is always humorous to see clients, particularly in group situations, write lines and lines. They often look quite proud of themselves for coming up with a litany of things. But, of course, I know what is coming.

I then instruct them:

2. Delete anything that involves someone else.

At this point, the lightbulbs go off in a number of ways. Their faces generally drop as each point is deleted. For collective cultures, everything that is great about them is based on their relationships.[25] This is what is known as a 'high-context culture', in which relationships are critical. It's also no surprise that the vast majority of suicide behaviours (threats/attempts/deaths) in Aboriginal populations are triggered by an intimate relationship breakdown. We are more likely than non-Indigenous people to base our sense of self upon our relationships. Romantic or core attachment conflict also strikes at the centre of how we see ourselves. So, in these instances, emotions can overwhelm. Throw inherited trauma and compromised attachment into the mix, it often looks like an overreaction to interpersonal conflict. Developing a robust sense of self, then, becomes the starting point to addressing this attachment-based trigger as a core driver.

Often the reaction to this exercise can be deeper than it appears. I have had people break down and cry, unable to think of anything that is great about them as an individual.

When people struggle with the task, I phrase my next question like this:

3. If you can't think of anything that is great about you, think of someone who thinks you are 'deadly' or great. What would *they* say about you? e.g. I am a good listener, a kind person etc.

Asking the question indirectly is less threatening and more comfortable, and leads to answers flowing out.

I then instruct them:

4. Write these great things down on stickers somewhere, and tell yourself them *every day*.

These bereaved parents and all the individuals I have worked with who come from abuse and trauma are simply full of self-loathing. Trauma will do that to you. Self-loathing is always the default for parents who have lost a child, and even more so if they have lost their child through suicide. In the group activity on self-worth, there are always protests such as, 'We don't think like this,' or 'We don't talk like this.' But like any ingrained behaviour that is hardwired into us, it can be unwired. It just takes practice. And this is exactly what I tell them.

Exposure therapies and repetition, repetition, repetition

So, to help them start to build their sense of self as an individual separate from 'the mob', I get the group of bereaved parents to do another simple exercise that also works for those who are suffering from depression. It's referred to as 'Pleasure versus Mastery',[26] but I call it 'Skilled versus Fun'. It is common for those who are experiencing reactive depression from trauma or grief to isolate themselves from others – even though the more isolated you are, the more depressed you become – and to stop doing things they find fun or are skilled at. So, I ask them to write a list of what they find fun and another of what they're good at, saying that they have to inject these things back into their lives as repetitive practice until they become ingrained and routine.

Given the collective nature of Aboriginal culture, we also often skill up a 'tag team' of family members and allocate a task to do with the person each day. It's about two things: sharing the emotional load of supporting those who have depression and reactive grief and trauma, while also addressing a few of the core areas of depression, including isolation and movement.

Finally, the great thing about incorporating community is that they are then tuned into knowing what to do and the skills remain in the community. Everything I do, I am skills building. I am trying to work myself out of a job! What is the point of an education if you cannot use it to educate our most disempowered? The less educated people are about their mental health, the less empowered they are to find solutions and to pass those solutions on. So, I teach my clients what to do through 'buzz words', and it is always great when they repeat them back to me in therapy. That's an empowered client. That's a client in control.

They are then also educated around behavioural change. It takes around 1000 repetitions to rewire the brain so that a new behaviour becomes ingrained and automated. This neuroplasticity means that maladaptive behaviours are altered by becoming within a person's control. Control is such an important driver for those in grief, for those in trauma – everything is about routine and repetition and predictability. But what I do is tie it in with individual self-efficacy through increasing their capacity to tolerate what has become intolerable through their loss.

Tolerating the intolerable

So, once we have our lists of things they enjoy and are good at, the plan to implement it is important. This needs to be done in a way that ensures no-one will interrupt them – for parents, their pleasure activities have to be scheduled when kids are at school or otherwise unable to disturb them.

We then develop what I call a 'guilt-o-meter' – this is a visual self-rating of feeling guilty, zero being no guilt and ten being as much guilt as they can imagine. Sitting with the 'discomfort' of self-love is often intolerable for people who have lost children. For other types of loss, it is about sitting still and not allowing distraction and avoidance to become the default response to emotion, which includes positive feelings that have often become less tolerable than guilt.

I had two sisters in my bereaved parents' group who both lost children to suicide. It was horrific and heartbreaking and the pain throughout this family was palpable, complex and entrenched. So, healing starts with rebuilding people from the foundations. This is why these types of emotional tolerance-based activities are so important. However, they need to be undertaken in a safe, gradual and controlled way as they release a tidal wave of emotions that have been controlled and repressed for a long time.

Remember, the repetition of these themes is vital to client self-efficacy. Everything I do with Aboriginal people has to be practical and based in real-life scenarios, and it has to be repeated in therapy so it becomes automated in real life. These key words are repeated and repeated:

- control
- routine
- repetition
- softening reactions
- developing tolerance for emotions

The main thing, though, is respect. Clients need to be treated with the respect to understand the theory of healing. My Aboriginal clients actually respond the most to the respect and empowerment they feel in my therapy.

You need to feed yourself first

With the two sisters, they had to literally practise love and tolerating it. You can't be a great mum, a great sister, a great partner, unless you feed yourself first.

It started with each of them picking their most pleasurable activity. One sister loved to soak in a bath; the other one loved to read books. Neither had done these in the several years since they lost their children. They both made a plan to do their activity on a Friday night when the kids would spend the evening with their grandparents, so there was no excuse. Their instructions were to tolerate the activity until they reduced its rating on the 'Guilt-o-meter'. The idea behind exposure is that the more you face the 'feared' activity, the less you fear it; however, in grief it is actually about the emotion you tolerate the least. Over time, positive rather than negative associations are linked with the activity and emotional tolerance improves.

The first feedback is always funny. The sister who liked to soak in the bath was able to 'tolerate' it for a sum total of one minute. She said that her Guilt-o-meter started at a 12/10 (her words) and she managed to get down to a 10/10 of intolerability. What this meant was that she spent about twenty minutes filling the bath and around one minute sitting in it. That's okay, it was still progress. Progress is any movement, big or small.

She now soaks in the bath for hours. Water bills aside, there's nothing negative in that. She no longer has a visceral reaction to these focused 'tolerating love' activities, which was predominant for her before therapy, and it has extended out to cuddles with her other children, her partner and, ultimately, attachment. Love felt like an intolerable emotion because it was tied in with deep self-loathing.

It's gradual, small and large at the same time.

Permission to feel, rather than avoid

Another exercise I get the group to do is to give themselves permission to feel other emotions that I have observed they find intolerable and so avoid. Families who have suffered public losses – especially those involving coroners' inquiries, court cases and a litany of things that distract from grief – are the ones that often manifest avoidance. Each person has different tolerances for different emotions and with these two sisters, self-love was a common theme. They could find more than enough things to 'hate' themselves for – the list of things they didn't do or 'should have done' – all a normal part of grief. But what I am interested in is those normal grief processes that become pathological, in the sense that people remain in those phases, unable to move.

In those circumstances, distraction from pain becomes your best friend. It's a much easier alternative and gives you a rest from vulnerability. I have worked with a significant number of family members involved in very high-profile murders and deaths, and it is a common thread that the grief experience presents as though nothing has been resolved. It's as if the death occurred yesterday. That's what avoidance means.

So, I first establish the emotion/s that are the most intolerable and use practised repetition to increase their tolerance. For example, so many clients who have lost children in brutal circumstances do not cry in therapy. So, they have to practise crying – I give them 'homework' to give themselves time to cry. It must be controlled, confined away from others, to ensure that it becomes a safe place without the possibility of interruption.

It's tied in, though, with being aware of two things. First, what is an evident image or thought when they are crying? This is the crucial stuff – the core beliefs keeping people stuck. We cannot deal with grief, trauma and flashbacks unless we understand them, and that means stimulating practice. We also monitor sleep patterns and rest and do a lot of physical grounding exercises, such as breathing re-training, anxiety reduction and management, as well as cognitive self-talk work. The impact has been more dramatic than I initially thought it would be, and it is consistently a revelation for so many of my clients. Sleep changes are probably the most surprising, although it makes sense that more sleep brings enormous improvements, because it is while you're asleep that your brain processes the most

Grief and Loss

salient aspects of grief. However, clients can start to avoid sleep as a way of avoiding the emotions that arise from processing their grief. What you do not want is for sleep to take on a negative association, and this can happen for people dealing with the particularly graphic death of a loved one.

When something has completely shattered your world, the best way to feel a sense of safety is to establish control through routines. Grief and trauma do not do well with changes in routine. So, setting routines around bedtime achieves this, as well as a 'looking forward' positive association with these night-time routines, in combination with the practised emotional-tolerance routines.

I tend to use repetition of grief theory with my Aboriginal clients, because anything that is highly mobilised in people's brains often means they can access it readily. So, I say the same phrases again and again: 'Routine is your friend', 'Everything is about *control*.' The reframing of words is just as important, to soften their reactions to triggers rather than get back to 'normal' or 'get over' grief.

A client whose child had died in especially awful circumstances, and who faced multiple other critical events around the death, was constantly being woken at night by their dreams. They would struggle to remember a single image from the nightmare, instead referring to it as a 'kaleidoscope'. What they meant was that they couldn't recall what was waking them up as flashbacks. This made it difficult to process them therapeutically. They would come into therapy angry at themselves for 'overthinking', which was badly affecting their sleep. A breakthrough came as the result of the simplest reframing, but it's a therapist's job to point out these things that seem small.

'It's not overthinking,' I said. 'It's processing.' By compartmentalising it, the processing of the graphic parts of the trauma was then controlled and gradually started to soften.

The next session, they were able to recall one of their nightmares in detail.

Now, this type of shift is often lost on clients, so the therapist needs to explain how significant these changes are.

One of my clients recently told me about something that triggered her that she did not expect (this is the nature of triggers – they are unpredictable). Instead of avoiding what she was feeling, she sat in her car and cried and cried and cried. She was someone who didn't even cry at her son's funeral.

There is always something to distract you from your grief. Always. But the impact on my client of feeling what she needed to feel was significant.

Hiding our pain is not brave.

Revealing it is.

What about cultural grieving?

I first encountered the complexity of cultural grief practices in the Western Desert, and this always involved a spiritual visit by the deceased, as explained in Chapter 3.

Grief is very ritualistic in Aboriginal communities and traditional grief practices can appear as hysterical and histrionic. Common expressions of grief are intense and prolonged periods of 'wailing' by (mostly) female elders, the ritual of sorry cutting, and the cutting of hair. Sorry cutting often involves hitting oneself with things like rocks or sticks. It is these open and intense expressions of sorrow that enable grief to be resolved with support from the whole community. The rituals are also displays of respect for the deceased.

For Aboriginal people, bereavement therapy is complicated not only because of the extent to which we are exposed to death, but also because grief practices differ. Resolution of grief is not just about walking people through clinical 'stages' of grief; there is the additional layer of enacting grief practices.

In 2000 I was asked to develop a resource on grieving for Aboriginal people by the Ministerial Council for Suicide Prevention, which had decided to send 'bereavement packs' to people who had experienced sudden death in their families from suicide. Surprise, surprise, the council realised that they were sending these widely to Aboriginal people, but they had no cultural content on grieving. I found the process to be pretty cathartic, if I am being honest, as

I finally had the opportunity to normalise the spiritual components of grief, and in a nationally distributed document no less.

It also became handy for when I ran groups with bereaved families. Probably one of the most powerful of these was with a group of families in a small town whose children had been murdered, and they had never had any therapeutic response to their loss. When I first drove into this community, I immediately picked up on the negative spirit of the place – being a spiritually tuned-in person myself. When we got through the levels of distrust from families – from the systemic failures of police to mental health services to the justice system – we were able to do one-on-one work with them and spiritual visits were raised and normalised, as we commonly do in therapy with Aboriginal people. Every single individual had experienced this but had denied it, afraid that they'd be locked up and considered 'crazy'.

It is why I always say to therapists that *validation* is arguably one of the most crucial aspects of our role – to name and to normalise. That's why my work on culture-bound syndromes (as described in Chapter 3) has been so important. It named what had never been named by the 'system' before, and it normalised so many things for Aboriginal clients who have suffered in silence for too long.

After a while of this individual work, we were able to do group work with the families. At the start of the session, we normalised spiritual visits. Immediately, one of the aunties said, 'That's happening to me.' Another said, 'That's happening to me as well.' And on it went. You could have heard a pin drop in that room. So much fear and so much buried grief. We achieved more healing in that ten minutes of disclosure than we would have in years of individual therapy.

Normalise. Validate. Heal.

Community grief: When triggers are inescapable

In whole communities, as is the case with individuals, grief healing also often involves visually changing environments which are identified as triggering. A good example is a small town that smoked culturally the area where a murder had occurred, to eliminate negative spirits, planted trees and plants, and created memorials for the deceased there, transforming it into a place of love and healing. You cannot heal from trauma when you are being constantly bombarded with visual reminders of the trauma.

I also do this at postventions, where activities are done after a suicide death to address risk in surviving individuals and communities. We have found that after many suicide deaths, the place in which it happened is literally left as it was. This often means the ropes are still hanging on the trees where the person has taken their life. We have even been to communities in which young children were playing with the ropes. Everything is left because people are paralysed by grief.

We know that children mimic and mirror when they are grieving and in trauma, so what the environment models is crucial. In one study, the data showed that 100 per cent of child suicides between the ages of ten and fourteen were by hanging.[27] This is a direct consequence of behavioural contagion, but also of children not being able to articulate how they feel post-trauma, so they are more likely to model their distress by re-enacting the trauma. Research guidelines by Mindframe have shown that when a method of suicide is discussed in the media, that method then increases in the general population.[28] So, it is vital that media reporting on suicides is managed in accordance with journalism ethics as it has the potential to give vulnerable people a 'script' or 'how to' instructions.

In Aboriginal communities, word-of-mouth news means that suicide contagion efforts have to respond at a whole community level. The first thing we do is have elders smoke the area, and importantly we change the look of the environment to create a positive rather than a negative association and ensure that people aren't being re-traumatised through visual triggers. For example, a tree is no longer just a tree; it is a graphic and salient image of the suicide death, so we need to visually 'rebadge' it by changing the look of the environment immediately. Finally, we then do training with the community about how to talk to children about suicide.

It is the hardest conversation they will ever have, but the most important. It is best it happens with parents and those who love them, rather than some other source, such as mainstream media, social media or their peers.

Children and grieving

There is also the reality of how children grieve when they are exposed to so much death and so much attachment loss. I have worked with kids who've become selectively mute due to family violence. I have seen kids develop separation anxiety when a parent goes to prison or a sibling has died by suicide. How do you explain death to children? How do you explain suicide to children?

Well, you need to explain it concretely, not in adult, abstract ways. For example, don't say, 'We lost Granddad,' as children will take that literally and start looking for him. If you say, 'Your sister went to sleep and didn't wake up,' children younger than eight – who are not able to differentiate fact from fantasy or understand that death is final – will be too afraid to go to sleep. Kids between five and eight years old are egocentric, so they will often blame themselves; for example, 'Granddad left because I was naughty.' Everything is their fault or responsibility. Often they may 'forget' the person has died – 'Yes, Granddad is still dead.' There is nothing worse for kids than having an incomplete narrative. It confuses them and they take adult explanations for things literally. So, you need to explain death concretely: 'Grandad's heart stopped beating and he is no longer alive.'

It might sound brutal, but you need to make sure that young children (even those as 'old' as twelve) understand what death actually means – that it is final and that the person will not be coming back. It needs to be explained in a developmentally appropriate way, and not in a way that adults think will 'spare' the child from pain.

Separation anxiety after loss

When children experience loss or trauma, routines are critical to their healing process. You need to be like a drill sergeant. As humans we thrive when our world is predictable. That's why we pretty much do the same routines every single day: get up, make a cup of tea, have some Weet-Bix ... (you get the point). For children, this is even more true.

A client of mine whose husband went to jail had a child who experienced significant separation anxiety. The child refused to be away from his mum out of fear that she would also 'leave'. The mum responded to his tantrums at the school gate by taking him home and not making him go to school. In effect, this broke his routine. The saying 'be cruel to be kind' exists for a reason. This mum needed to get her son back to school. The first day would be really hard, the second day less hard, but the child would eventually gain comfort in his routine by learning he could leave his mum and she would still be there at the end of the day.

Longing for Country as grief

For Aboriginal people, grief is also not just about death; it's about Country, spirit and where we are from. Longing for Country is a thing. And I don't mean Slim Dusty, Keith Urban, Troy Cassar-Daley. The other Country.

Kids who are removed from their traditional land struggle. So much of the necessary research on childhood trauma, abuse and neglect focuses on attachment with people, but for Aboriginal kids, their removal from Country also has a profound impact. As a therapist, I have found this to be an additional factor that must be addressed.

This idea that you can 'treat' longing for Country started fairly organically. An Aboriginal girl in one of the kid prisons was referred to me. She was from the remote Pilbara, where I grew up, so I instinctively brought some spinifex, gum leaves and red dirt. (I had just been home and always take the opportunity to bring a bit of Country back with me. I find it therapeutic.) I'll never forget the image of this poor kid when I walked in. She was slumped over on a chair in the corner of her cell. I called out her name. No movement. But as soon as I sat down next to her and started pulling all my 'artillery' out of my bag, her body language completely changed. She sat upright and a slight smile came over her face. It was instant.

I began to seriously think about how I could use this therapeutically for the many Aboriginal people who were away from Country. There is a high rate of suicide in psychiatric wards and prisons, but there are other issues that involve Aboriginal people being away from Country for extended periods of time: long hospital stays, kids coming down from their communities for school, fly-in-fly-out employment in the mines, and so many sports that require people to leave their community to find opportunities in the city.

I had the idea of applying gradual desensitisation therapies to Country, which are exposure based, and I use them for grief as well as for trauma. They are informed by the simple phobia literature – for example, if you have a fear of cockroaches, we develop what is referred to as a 'fear hierarchy' of exposure. A 1/10 might be a cockroach 50 metres away; a 10/10 is a cockroach on your hand. The client becomes gradually desensitised to the feared object through thoughts, physical control and behaviour (not avoiding the object).

So, I started doing this with kids in prison. The first level was just talking about Country but making all their senses alive by taking them on a 'journey'. 'When you wake up, who is the first person you see? What sounds do you miss? What smells?' etc. If they get upset, you just keep them in the 'story' (that's the exposure bit) until their distress reduces.

Again, it's about creating a positive rather than a negative association. The next level is watching videos of home or video-calling loved ones on Country. Eventually, we bring Country to them. The girl in the prison had her cell look like the Pilbara. Every day, she would wake up and put her feet in red dirt.

We have since had this used in prisons, in psychiatric wards, in schools. The focus is on awareness, insight and self-efficacy, so that clients can make the connection between their low mood and their longing for Country. When people feel down, they can go and sit in Country. We had the prison look like the Pilbara, the Kimberley, the Murchison – every area of the state.

The warden said to me, 'I don't know what you are doing with these kids, but I have never seen them so happy.'

In standard mainstream practice, the healing or therapeutic resolution of grief never includes the critical cultural layers. I hope this chapter changes that.

6

Love, Fear and Attachment:
Why change is so hard

Not all trauma is equal, and not everyone exposed to traumatic events will develop post-traumatic stress disorder (PTSD). While there is individual conditionability, there are certainly types of trauma that increase the odds of PTSD developing, and this chapter is about those critical, entrenched and enduring complex factors. These are referred to as complex PTSD (C-PTSD) and are mostly about bad luck. Some are just born with more robustness than others. Some have traumatic home lives and backgrounds in which abuse is normalised, while others experience traumatic events that are so significant their impacts are immeasurable, so by themselves they can increase the likelihood of PTSD.

But what happens when traumatic events are perpetrated on you simply because of your cultural identity? These types of traumas are inescapable and enduring and need to be considered as a separate category to PTSD and C-PTSD. Once the unique characteristics of this kind of trauma are understood, treatment can be more focused and effective. Racial trauma has had little attention or empirical focus in Australian psychology, resulting in generations of practitioners untrained in the core trauma variables that affect Aboriginal people uniquely. Worse than that, there are entire populations of trauma survivors who continue to suffer from a lack of validation of their trauma and who, based on the data alone, represent the bulk of the suicide, incarceration, child removal statistics. I refer to these families as the 'intergenerational incarcerated, removed and traumatised', and argue in Chapter 11 that this is the basis for solutions to 'closing the gap'. In this chapter, though, we'll look at some of their stories.

What we do know is that trauma tends to feed trauma – in our genes, in our biological vulnerability to it, and in our environment. PTSD involves 're-experiencing' the trauma – the past becomes permanently present. Trauma triggers are as unpredictable as they are individualised, and many battle them without anyone knowing that they are. But are we really doomed to repeat our past?

Our attachment styles – how we relate to others, especially those we love most – are based on what is modelled for us (nurture) and what we have inherited through our genes and in our biology (nature). I learnt as an adult the impact that my mum's trauma and my parents' relationship had on my own attachment style. I find it easy to show love (like my dad) and be caring, but I find it more challenging to accept love (like my mum). At times receiving love can feel overwhelming, as it did for my mum. While I enjoy a hug as much as the next person (thanks, Dad), I struggle in the reliance aspect of relationships. I prefer self-reliance and self-sufficiency, not depending on others. It's probably why I went into a helping profession. Psychologists are trained to cut off their feelings and compartmentalise them, so in many ways it's probably why the profession draws people to it like me, who find service and showing compassion and love for those they're not intimately attached to easier. There is significantly less threat to attachment loss, but the reward centre of the brain is still activated.

My clients with C-PTSD from childhood trauma often present with a lack of 'tolerance for love'. This is particularly common when their protector or carer has also been their abuser; the resulting 'disorganised attachment' affects the development of the victim's neural pathways. When you are a child, you are completely vulnerable and dependent on adult carers for survival. You rely on them for protection and safety, but instead of love and comfort you receive pain and harm. This means that your brain becomes trained to remain on alert. Over time, cumulative abuse can lead to the nervous system being in a constant state of alert because the threat is unpredictable. This threat activation enables survival and is why complex childhood trauma is extremely difficult to heal from. As humans we are hardwired to want to be loved; the biological hardwiring for caregivers is even more so because of this dependency for survival. So, childhood trauma can mean there is a biologically based association between 'love' and harm or threat. For these clients, love can evoke strong, often visceral responses. Love can become what I refer to as an 'evocative cue'. It is often missed by trauma therapists because love is supposed to be a positive emotion.

While the field of trauma is complex and emerging, the attachment field is even more so and the training is just the starting point of understanding how these complex issues manifest in clients, especially Aboriginal clients. It requires extensive experience to understand it well. The application of theory with complex trauma clients is where true clinical and then cultural instincts are developed, and the volume of trauma experienced by Aboriginal clients simply overwhelms the average clinician, as noted in Chapter 5. It is why too many people who seek trauma therapy often feel disappointed in the outcomes.[1]

Attachment disorders are psychiatric conditions related to the maladaptive development of emotional connections to others. John Bowlby, whose seminal research described the relationship between an infant and their parent (typically a maternal figure), considered this early bond to be both developmentally and psychologically crucial because it creates the first internal working model of attachment.[2] His work was then extended by Mary Ainsworth, who devised an attachment classification system called the Stranger Situation

Procedure (SSP).[3] Essentially, Ainsworth observed how infants reacted to their parent leaving and then returning, and identified distinct attachment classification patterns – secure, avoidant and anxious – each with a unique development, psychological style and mental health trajectory. Main and Solomon then expanded the work of Ainsworth with a fourth attachment style known as 'disorganised attachment', in that attachment to intimate others seemed to exist in opposing states of desire and resistance.[4] These opposing states are a byproduct of the relationship between a parent's attachment (caregiver responsiveness) and the infant's resultant sense of security.

Neuroscience demonstrates how infants are hardwired for connection and are highly responsive to caregiver stress. This is all amygdala-based. However, critical and additional factors that are not understood or addressed as a focus of treatment or assessment when it comes to Indigenous families are racial trauma and how it affects caregiver responsiveness and infant attachment classifications. Understanding this is easily the most urgent priority in the prevention of Indigenous child removals.

Let me explain. Though there is undeniable evidence for the existence of racial trauma, it is not incorporated in standard attachment assessments. We know that racial trauma compounds caregiver stress and responsiveness to children. Given that caregiver stress remains the strongest predictor of infant attachment and its resulting classifications, its absence in all of the 'gold standard' attachment assessments currently used in court systems is having a devastating impact on how attachment disorders are being classified.[5] Indeed, the literature finds that there are three 'gold standard' attachment assessment tools used to assess attachment classifications, none of which have been validated with Aboriginal people.[6] This includes the SSP, the Adult Attachment Interview (AAI) and the Attachment Q Sort. Indeed, the SSP has never been undertaken with Aboriginal children. So, there remain no attachment norms against which to determine treatment impacts.

Attachment constructs are also poorly understood in court systems generally – regardless of cultural background – with many tests used in custody evaluations being problematic.[7] Cultural attachment and contexts are so badly understood as to be dangerous. Specifically, racial trauma as a separate trauma category means that there are unique pre-, peri- and post-trauma variables that increase the likelihood of caregiver stress responses. For Aboriginal people, the origin is in forced removal from primary attachments, which has, from a position of science, increased the likelihood of intergenerational trauma.[8] The additional relevant factor is that this removal was race-mediated, which meant a greater absence of control over threat of imminent and unpredictable child removal. It also meant that trauma responses had to be constantly enabled as a survival mechanism to ensure protection from impending threats. How this then impacts on caregiver responsiveness to children is what is unknown, and it remains unexplored in research in Australia.

We also understand that prolonged trauma leads to trauma responses becoming normalised.[9] Forced removal policies continued for decades, ensuring a climate of intense fear and helplessness. Forced and race-based child removals, which increase trauma vulnerability, are highly likely to impact upon caregiver stress and a child's resulting attachment to caregivers under these additional layers of stress. The hypothesis is that, as an Aboriginal parent, racial trauma increases threat responsiveness; there is a fear of truly attaching to a child if they can be ripped away at any time. That would be impossible to cope with, so secure attachment feels biologically unsafe, leading to attachment being 'avoided' or, more likely, that attachment looking 'disorganised'.

This is critical because of two important findings. First, when infants who are classified as having disorganised attachment are paired with adults who also have disorganised attachment, they are uniformly recommended for removal. However, it should be also the case that possibilities outside of maltreatment are also considered as explanatory: for example, that the caregiver is in a state of anxiety, trauma, fear and/or racial trauma. This is particularly important as research has shown that up to 15 per cent of 'low-risk' infants (infants who had no abuse in their backgrounds) were incorrectly classified as having disorganised attachment (a category for maltreated infants).[10] This has been hypothesised to be purely a byproduct of caregiver stress, presenting in infants as disorganised attachment rather than abuse.

Forced removals mean that parents' attachment to their children becomes about fear, anxiety and amygdala (biologically) based threat.[11] It is therefore more likely to be about this approach – flight paradox rather than maltreatment. We also understand based on Chapter 3 that racial and collective trauma is ill understood or addressed, and that fear of systems (having children removed when reaching out for basic assistance and help) feeds much of this race-based anxiety.

Further compounding this trauma and increasing the likelihood of trauma transmission has been the associated government denial of the impacts, extent and evidence of forced removal policies until the 2008 National Apology to the Stolen Generations.[12] In the lead-up to the National Apology, former prime minister John Howard said: 'In some cases, children were wrongly removed; in other cases, they were removed for good reason; in other cases, they were given up; and in other cases, the judgment on the removal is obscure or difficult to make.'[13] Senator Jacinta Nampijinpa Price's comment ahead of the 2020 referendum that colonisation had had a 'positive impact' for Aboriginal people was simply a continuation of this denial.[14]

The damage that the denial of race-mediated trauma creates is incalculable. Victims come to therapy to name trauma as trauma. They present with behaviours that are problematic to themselves and their loved ones, but they often lack insight into the fact that their behaviours are trauma-based reactions. Validation of trauma is a critical therapeutic first step to healing, as it provides the necessary insight for victims to understand that they are victims and that their symptoms are an outcome of trauma.[15] So, the successive and decades-long denial of forced removal has virtually guaranteed the intergenerational transmission of trauma by existing as a critical post-trauma variable.

Secure attachment is the goal. We understand, based on the existing research, that children who fall into the disorganised category can become securely attached.[16] However, this is predicated mostly on a treatment focus on the variables that impede caregiver responsiveness to children. Not understanding racial trauma compromises any ability we have to halt that future trajectory of ongoing child removal and escalation. For example, a study was able to show that addressing caregiver stress (depression, trauma) resulted in the 'disorganised' proportion reducing from 60 per cent to 25 per cent.[17]

It is vital therefore that we develop not only unique assessment tools that validate racial trauma variables but also associated treatment interventions capable of reducing it. This needs to be front and centre of every discussion we have around Indigenous child removals and 'closing the gap'.

Pat Crittenden's work argues that attachment that looks 'disorganised' is actually organised or adaptive.[18] I tend to agree. I see it as 'approach avoidance', as it means people are unable to approach their carers for love and comfort, counter to our hardwired instincts. The predictability of primary carers' love calms neural pathways and aids emotional regulation by enabling children to develop the capacity to self-soothe during stress. The paradox of abuse and pain is that pain repels you and places you in a state of reactivity, but relationships are also crucial to heal your pain and compromised attachment.

What this means is that love – through triggering these sensations – can become 'intolerable' and lead to clients avoiding showing it and/or not being able to comfortably receive it. This primal post-trauma reaction is visceral – I have had many clients say that it is a sick feeling in their stomach. In some, it is based on deep self-loathing; however, it is consistently driven by either a conscious or subconscious intense fear of loss and rejection.

I have watched it play itself out across so many dimensions and particularly in the child protection field – parents not 'showing up' and being absent from their child's life. This is often about being afraid of attaching to children who are very likely to be taken from you. It isn't about not loving your child. It's about the fear of losing them. If you don't attach emotionally to your children, it will be easier to cope when they are taken from or reject you. This has been hardwired into many Aboriginal people through generations of forced removals. But on the surface, it is perceived as confirming the view of welfare services that black parents do not care about their children.

So, what we should be doing is allowing ourselves to feel until our reaction to intolerable emotions begins to soften and becomes within our control. Just as with grief therapy, an essential part of the attachment healing process is giving ourselves permission to cry and to feel anger and sadness. Those of us who have what is known as secure attachment are able to deal with the whole range of positive and negative emotions. This then increases the odds that they will pass this on to their own children. Securely attached parents tend to have securely attached kids, and those kids consistently have the best mental health outcomes.

One of the most tragic things about forced removals is that collective cultures by our nature are more likely to raise securely attached kids. Indigenous cultures that promote kinship parenting in effect not only share the care of children, but have a greater emotional capacity for and responsiveness to children than nuclear, Western styles of parenting. They are also better able to adjust their own emotional tolerance to meet the child's attachment needs.

Parenting in collective cultures means a greater focus on the concept that it 'takes a village to raise a child'. Community and kin are as responsive and responsible as biological parents to the emotional and attachment needs of kids. The result is that kinship parenting can often be erroneously viewed as being emotionally abusive and neglectful, which continues to be the main reason for Aboriginal child removal in 79 per cent of cases[19] – and these children are arguably the most vulnerable to cultural bias. Importantly, those notifications would, from a position of risk assessment, mostly require a family support response and not the removal of children. Also of note is that these Aboriginal families are being racially profiled, with over 60 per cent of notifications ultimately found to be false.[20]

Kinship parenting also often presents as being chaotic, but the core of chaos theory is that 'chaos' is not chaos if it is predictable. Ask an Aboriginal child to map their carers based on the different emotional needs they provide for them (that is, love, safety, responses to fear, responses to pain, responses to joy) and you will see that predictability being mapped out by them.

Child protection services do not currently require staff to undertake a cultural kinship map. Instead, they use assessment tools based on Western concepts of attachment and parenting. Fortunately, in 2019 Queensland discontinued the use of the Structured Decision-Making Tool due to its cultural bias in confusing cultural difference with risk.[21] We now need the rest of the country to follow. There are too many cases where the risk of child maltreatment is being conflated with parenting differences. The history of forced removals – underpinned by the racial empathy gap, discussed in Chapter 1 – means that there also remains a lack of cultural empathy towards Aboriginal parents in child protection systems, making removal seem easier because it is viewed as being less painful than removing white kids. This was a key finding of my comprehensive cultural audit on child protection services in Western Australia and was discussed by me in a national opinion piece on child protection systems.[22]

Emotions and change

Each of us has our own level and type of emotional tolerance that is tied in with our individual attachment style. I am comfortable with anger because I have seen a lot of it in my clients. As a kid, I had to learn to manage my own anger in a way that served me, rather than dismantled me. It wasn't easy but running was always my self-soothing go-to because it enabled me to think, not avoid. I see many people channel their anger into sports but not develop the associated tolerance for it because they avoid processing the triggers and emotions that accompany it. I have always done my best thinking on runs and I understood that to develop a tolerance for anger I had to also process feelings, so that it could aid me in sport and in life.

Securely attached people can step 'outside' of the emotion and not overreact. This also results in access to the higher-level-thinking part of your brain (the cortex) and enables you to think clearly, articulate feelings in those moments and communicate more effectively.

However, as happened after my dad's death, experiences of loss and trauma mean that emotions can become terrifying and it is easier to *not* feel them. My natural attachment style is anxious avoidant and during the aftermath of Dad's passing, I avoided most of my feelings. It was just too hard to allow myself to feel them. We fear not only feeling them, but also expressing them because doing so to those we love opens up the possibility of being harmed or rejected. Being honest about how we truly feel and who we truly are becomes terrifying.

Repetition compulsion is the repeating of the patterns of your own trauma. When traumatic memories are attached to a self-preservation anxiety, they become over-valued and fixed. In this state, repetition compulsion becomes about the seeking out of the normalcy of the past and a desire for homeostasis. There is comfort in what is hardwired in us and the predictable, because change is hard – even good change.

The abuse cycle

People need to understand that the *first* disclosure of abuse or trauma and the reaction received to it is a vital aspect of the healing process. Denial of trauma exists as a significant post-trauma variable and I have had too many victims tell me that not being believed was actually worse than the abuse itself. That makes sense, because of how difficult it is for victims to come forward and how much energy abusers spend ensuring that this remains the case by creating victim shame and a sense of blame and fear.

When you are not believed or have your memories of abuse questioned by the people you have chosen to disclose to, the trauma is compounded. The worst outcome is when loved ones take the side of the perpetrator, which is way too common – partly because abusers understand that abuse is enabled by creating an environment in which they are seen as 'kind and good' by others. Perpetrators are very good at feigning emotions they do not feel. Those capable of causing pain to others are extraordinarily adept at cognitive empathy: the ability to recognise and intuit emotions, and manipulate them. But they lack emotional empathy – the ability to care about the pain they are causing. This cycle is 'crazy making' for victims, who believe the distress about the abuse that is feigned by perpetrators is genuine because the emotional manipulation – the intense flips from 'love' to 'hate' – is so extreme.

As I wrote in an article on coercive control for *ABC News*, 'love bombing' is often the most important stage of every abuse cycle.[23] The dopamine high of being love-bombed makes victims feel they have met their soul mate or best friend, while simultaneously isolating them from critical supports. Once hooked, this serves as intermittent reinforcement for victims by creating what is known as a trauma bond.[24]

The trauma bond also lures victims back as they desperately seek the loving, adoring partner they fell in love with. But the abuser is the real person – the kind, loving one is a mask, created to trap victims. Perpetrators use the tactic of mirroring to make victims believe they are the perfect partner.[25] They love everything you love, share all your values.

A love bomber's displays of love, whether grand or small, are often public. This not only hooks victims but helps perpetrators develop a persona of being kind, loving and dutiful, while setting up the victim to appear ungrateful, high maintenance and 'emotionally fragile' later on.

Over time a perpetrator will often appear healthier than the victim because *they* are controlling the dynamics of the abusive relationship, and are not struggling with trauma symptoms. Any laws against coercive control need to ensure police are properly trained to understand this, so they don't misconstrue victims' behaviour or get duped by the calmness of an abuser.[26] Victims – particularly Aboriginal women – are too often misidentified as perpetrators, which has devastating outcomes and can deter them from reporting abuse.[27] Opportunistic offenders create opportunities for abuse, constantly, and this includes manipulating others. Indeed, there is no greater opportunity for an abuser or a greater power differential between victim and offender than that of a non-Aboriginal man and an Aboriginal woman in a remote community.

Clinicians must also be alert to these dynamics as too often abuse is being missed, such as when perpetrators attend counselling sessions with their victims. Clinicians are not beyond becoming triangulated into enabling abuse via the perpetrator's aptitude for cognitive empathy and victim gaslighting.

Gaslighting also often results in memories and incidents of abuse being distorted. The behaviours of gaslighting can be so extreme others may think victims are making it up or that they are the 'crazy' and abusive one. It becomes difficult for victims to trust their own memory and judgement.

Too many victims of psychological and emotional abuse have told me they've lost count of how many times people have told them what a 'nice person' their abusive ex-partner is, including their own counsellors. The carefully constructed mask rarely drops.

Why do bad people do good deeds? Because it enables their bad deeds.

In these instances, victims usually take decades to reconcile the fact that they were abused. When abuse is not named as abuse – particularly in the case of complex childhood trauma – victims will often blame themselves. In these circumstances abuse is often never disclosed as victims often fear telling others. And if they're not believed when they do disclose, they may never talk about it again. The impacts of this can be irreparable.

A therapist's job is to believe a victim's truth and to validate it. Therapy is subjective – my role is to validate my client's truth and assist them to make meaning of the impacts of abuse and trauma. However, assessment is objective – I am trying to find inconsistencies or fault in what the client is telling me. People often confuse the two roles. When you are going to court, for example, I have to prove that someone has been a victim. I have to show harm. I have to assess that from an objective standpoint. This is different to those who come to me to heal from abuse. I have to unpack their pain. I have to validate what has occurred for them, and this starts with naming abuse as abuse.

Treating trauma: The man who couldn't love

Recovery from trauma, from abuse, is about relationships.

I was doing a workshop with a women's group in a remote area, just a short one on sexual abuse (indicators, signs, what to do with disclosers etc.). It's often the case that when communities learn there is a psychologist in town, and especially a black one, they will seek you out.

Once the workshop had finished, a beautiful older gentleman came into the room. I was chatting to a lot of the women about their personal issues and concerns. The man's presentation told me straight away that he had a story to tell. He was stooped over, just staring at the ground in front of him. He was a fit, charismatic-looking man with a cowboy hat. His rough hands seemed as if they had seen many years of hard work. His eyes told me so much. They held so much pain.

When I eventually got to him after the women had left (and we are talking about a good hour here), he just burst into tears. It took a long time for him to speak. I just gave him space and reassured him, saying, 'It's alright, I'm with you.'

After a while he said, 'That stuff you were talking about [sexual abuse], that happened to me.' A pause. 'And you're the first person I have told.'

This is what I mean about the need for people to disclose to someone and the fear of doing it. Here was a man who was probably in his seventies, and he has held this his entire life.

'So, can I ask, why today?' I said. 'What's led you to get something out that you have buried for so long?'

'Well, I've just had my first grandchild.'

'And what has that meant for you?'

His face was etched with pain when he looked up at me.

'Well, I can't hug her.'

'Why not?'

'Because I have heard that if you were sexually abused, you will become a sex offender as well. That's what the men who abused me told me. That's what I have heard people say.'

There is significant 'shame' in being a victim, and that's what perpetrators rely on.

I told him gently, 'I need you to listen to this. There is no evidence that the abused becomes an abuser in every instance. If that were the case then logically more women would be sex offenders because significantly more women are victims. Obviously, sex offenders don't come from *Brady Bunch* families, and there is often some type of abuse in their backgrounds, but there's also evidence that nature is just as important. The most consistent variable is the normalisation of criminality in their background, but there are also genetic and biological contributors.'

Because I had spent quite a bit of time during my Masters placement working with sex offenders, I was also fairly efficient at assessing attraction to children. Although I knew that this was unlikely to be the case for this man, based purely on his insight that manifested as severe behavioural control – I did this basic checking anyway. As we chatted, he talked about his five children, who he had raised to be exceptional people. He and his wife had a wonderful marriage and, as he spoke, I was struck by how it is possible for people who come from extraordinary trauma to build a loving family. There can be such resilience in those who are able to believe in and create love, safety and goodness, despite what they have experienced.

However, because trauma like this can manifest so variously, other kids who lived in that mission with this beautiful man have all processed it differently and that's because trauma is as generalised as it is individual. We all have our own unique stress-response mechanisms, which are a by-product of genetics, biology and environment. We know that up to 20 per cent of PTSD is a genetic contribution, and then there is a biological contribution, which has been the focus of research.[28] We do understand that trauma can have a biological impact on a person's genes, which can then be passed into future generations. This can alter genetic expression. In simple terms, epigenetics is the study of the biological control mechanisms of DNA, which turn genes on or off or change how genes are expressed. Epigenetics potentially explains why trauma effects may endure long after the immediate threat is gone, and it is also implicated in the many pathways by which trauma is transmitted to future generations. Studies have shown that children of Holocaust survivors with PTSD tended to have low cortisol levels – which is linked to vulnerability to PTSD – even if they did not have PTSD themselves. Of course, how traumatised parents interact with their children also influences their development.

For this gentleman, receiving love felt intolerable, more so than showing love. He described hugging someone he loved as feeling like he was going to 'vomit', and it would become so intolerable that he'd have to stop hugging them immediately. It is common that intolerance for love shows up as a visceral reaction and pushing people away means that you have tapped out of your tolerance for it. But at its core it is a self-protection mechanism learnt from the pain of attaching: 'I am going to reject you before you reject or hurt me.' Mostly, he managed it by avoidance, and his kids learnt long ago never to reach for a hug from their dad.

So, how do you 'fix it'? Well, you get people to develop tolerance for the emotions they do not tolerate well. Why? Because securely attached people tolerate the entire range of emotions, both positive and negative. It is irrefutable that secure attachment has significant links with good mental health outcomes. The trick is identifying which emotion or emotions the individual does not tolerate – this is the tough part of therapeutic assessment and then intervention. Many therapists do not understand attachment theory at the complex level required – the training provides a basic understanding but not how it applies in complex therapy. The ability to work with complex trauma clients is at the cutting edge of the industry. Knowing how to translate this with Aboriginal clients when there is no guiding foundational research becomes impossible for most therapists, without putting enormous effort into professional development and then becoming comfortable in working with clients who have been exposed to extraordinary trauma. This is another reason intergenerational trauma is so endemic in our people.

Some clinicians also fail to understand that testing attachment cannot be done theoretically or without human interaction that 'tests' attachment tolerance. With Aboriginal people, it is critical that everything is done in real life. Everything must be concrete. The technical term for this is 'in vivo' – you cannot determine if attachment tolerance is improving without testing it through human interaction.

So, once we had gone through all the talking and testing, it was clear that love was this man's most intolerable emotion. It was tied in with self-loathing, shame, guilt and all of the other emotions that victims of abuse experience.

The field of neuroplasticity is an exciting area that helps with so much of this. We know that trauma – which can include grief – has an impact on the amygdala, the area that controls emotions and the ability to regulate and tolerate them – this is at the executive functioning level within the emotional centre of your brain. Neuroplasticity shows that after six weeks of exposure-based therapies, the brain goes back to normal. It heals itself.

So, I asked this man, 'When was the last time you hugged your daughter?' He looked up at me with terror on this face, like I had just asked him to give me his cowboy hat (haha).

'Never,' he said.

'Okay. You said she works at the local store?' He nodded. 'Let's go, we're going to go and hug your daughter.'

At this point he became like a paralysed animal I had to drag to the car. I eventually got him into the car and, as fate would have it, as we arrived at the store, out walked his daughter. I knew this because his face lit up when he saw her.

I said, 'Is that your daughter? Because she looks like you.'

He almost didn't want to admit it, but in a soft voice he said, 'Yes.'

I said, 'Alright, get out, you're going to go and hug her.'

We got out of the car and approached the beautiful young woman. 'Hi, I'm Tracy. I've got your dad here and he is going to hug you.' She looked at me like she was thinking, *Who the hell are you?*

As I gave the instructions to 'the man who couldn't love' (which is what I began to call him), he very awkwardly hugged his daughter. Frankly, it was like watching someone hug a wine barrel. It was pathetic. So, I said to him, 'Mate, that's the *worst* hug I have ever seen. Do it again.'

As the daughter started laughing, I said to her, 'Now, your job, beautiful lady, is to make your dad practise hugging you twice a day. First thing in the morning and last thing at night. But he has to extend the amount of time he hugs you for ten seconds each time. Can you do that?'

She nodded, laughing through tears.

'And your job, Mr Man Who Cannot Love, is to force yourself to hug your daughter until you have extended that time. Even if you have to count in your head until you hit that goal.'

A few months later, I got a phone call. It was 'the man who couldn't love'.

All I could hear in the background was the sound of a gurgling little baby – the lovely giggling sound that only a little child can make, which fills your heart with joy.

He said to me, 'Guess what?'

'What?'

'I have my granddaughter on my lap.'

'Yeah, I can hear giggling in the background.'

'I've had her on my lap for two hours and I can't stop hugging her.'

I said, 'Mate, you have a lifetime of hugs to make up for. You hug the hell out of that kid.'

This is the thing about attachment: you can address it at any time. Once you learn how to show love, you can pass that on to your kids. Then they pass it on to their kids. What a wonderful legacy that is. And when that beautiful man rang me a few days later, he said, 'I didn't think I could fix this about myself, just by practising.'

It's possible for change to occur at any time, and that's the most exciting thing about life's journey.

Systemic racism and why child removals aren't the answer

I am yet to meet a parent who doesn't want to provide a better life for their child than they had. However, the reality is that Aboriginal parents are just not being afforded an equal opportunity to do so, as demonstrated by the irrefutable statistics I have gleaned from the national child protection data, captured by the Australian Institute of Health and Welfare.

In my own research, currently in submission, I found there had been a 119 per cent increase in Aboriginal child removals over the past ten years, and a complete lack of investment in developing culturally informed parenting programs. There is not one culturally informed attachment program shown to be effective in improving attachment in Aboriginal children or caregiver responsiveness to children who have been iudentified as being at risk of removal. What continue to be implemented are parenting programs purpose-built for non-Indigenous families. There is no evidence that these programs have a positive impact for Aboriginal families, but there exists significant research showing how ineffective they are in addressing Indigenous trauma, attachment and parenting needs.[29] There is also the overwhelming economic cost of continuing to fund untested, culturally biased approaches, with racism costing Australia an estimated $45 billion a year.[30]

This is systemic racism: ignore the evidence because you're comfortable using mainstream approaches. The child protection workforce – at 94 per cent non-Indigenous – uses the programs because they understand them, but the bulk of the client base – which is 57 per cent Indigenous – do not engage at a level commensurate with need.[31] Nor are Indigenous child protection workers in high-risk communities or who carry generationally at-risk families on their caseloads trained in intensive attachment treatments. This means intensive therapeutic services are significantly skewed towards non-Indigenous families, which has led to rates of non-Indigenous kids in care declining from 56.8 per cent to 42.8 per cent since 2009.[32]

The fact that governments aren't prioritising our highest-risk communities and are instead focusing on our less at-risk, non-Indigenous cohorts means that services are being designed for the relatively privileged while neglecting the least privileged among us.

When a community has had generational removal of children from primary attachment figures, it loses its most critical models of parenting. Our parents and kin, with collective cultures, are our first and primary relationships – those that give us a sense of self and sense of being loved and loveable, no matter what. But if you have never had parenting modelled for you – if your primary attachments have been destroyed – how do you develop a parenting model yourself? How do you develop a sense of yourself as being loved and loveable when those core attachments have been destroyed? And how do you then pass on those core skills to your own children?

As a child grows, this predictability enables them to develop object constancy: the sense of security to attach, without fear of rejection, loss or abuse. The development of object constancy is crucial, and it develops from understanding that the environment (parent) is providing predictable responses to the range of positive and negative emotions, which feels secure and permanent. When environments are both predictable and comforting, over time the child learns to self-regulate emotions independently, increasing the odds of secure attachment. The development of secure attachment has irrefutable links with better health and mental health outcomes into adulthood.[33]

Attachment matters

If secure attachment does not develop in childhood, this compromised attachment will likely pass to future intimate and caregiver relationships. Removal from primary attachments is a pipeline to the justice system and has been connected to mental ill-health,[34] suicides,[35] trauma[36] and educational failure.[37] We see this in practical action with the same families generationally making up the bulk of child protection statistics.[38] For example, data from the Northern Territory reveals that of the 25,500 notifications of child abuse, 71 per cent involved the same children.[39] This is significant and speaks to the fact that we fail to geomap data on child removals and effectively mobilise early intervention resources into identifiable high-risk families and needs-based funding as the most critical prevention strategy.

At a young age, children develop their sense of self and their ego, as well as their personality structure. And, as I discussed earlier, they thrive when their world is predictable and the love and support of their primary attachments are consistent – object constancy means that relationships matter. If this doesn't develop, then relationships become disposable – they become a 'means to an end' and individuals like this cause significant damage to others as a result. How a child makes meaning of this loss is tied in with their individual personality traits and developmental stage, either blaming others or internalising the blame. In the former, children come to believe they cannot rely on anyone to consistently love or support them. If children don't develop a sense of relationship permanency, and this continues into adulthood, then you potentially have an individual who feels they have 'nothing to lose'. With the latter, they can develop a sense of self-loathing and that they are inherently unloveable, as my client did. The 'man who couldn't love' became the man who finally understood that he deserved love. It's amazing what practice can do. But what about kids whose core attachments are unreliable or even abusive?

Childhood trauma, attachment and individuating from abusive parents: The story of A

There is great paradox in the pain of betrayal and abuse. The body responds to betrayal as trauma, and a fear of future relationship betrayals keeps the threat-response system activated. However, it is relationships that are the very thing that will heal your heart. In my first week as a child welfare worker, I was treading a fine line between doing my job and caring deeply for my caseload of wards of the state and kids under care and protection of the state. The thing that was most striking was that all the kids on my caseload were in care because of 'neglect'. Aboriginal kids were rarely in care because of sexual abuse or physical violence. Their parents seemed to fail to attach to their children and just didn't show up. I became interested in this from the very first week. Why do parents fail to attach to their kids? At least, that is how it looked from the outside. They appeared to assume that the welfare was more responsible for caring for their child than they were. Was this part of generational history? That so many children had been removed it had become the expectation? Certainly, Aboriginal parents were completely powerless in this scenario. Time had not improved that.

One kid who, to this day, tugs at my heartstrings was from a remote community. He was twelve years old and starting to become a solvent user. He was a black kid with blonde hair. He spoke in monosyllables, reflective of his non-existent schooling. He was big for his age but shy. He would follow me around the office like a lost puppy. I was twenty-three and felt like his mum from the very first meeting. He had that impact on you – but, to be fair, pretty much every kid on my caseload did. There was no anger in him, despite being shuffled from placement to placement and with a mum who was a chronic alcoholic. She could go little more than a few weeks caring for him before the wheels would fall off. Despite this, he adored her.

Individuating from an abusive parent is such an important part of therapy and healing. Our parents provide us with our first and most significant template for how we view ourselves and ultimately how we learn to attach in all of our future relationships. So, if a child is not able to see an abusive parent as abusive, victim shame turns to self-blame and the abuse becomes enmeshed in their self-concept and attachment. So, my focus with A was to slowly teach him to individuate. What did this involve? Encouraging him to see his mum as human, capable of both good and bad. Often when children develop into adulthood and start to make meaning of being abused by a parent, they do so through extreme attachment reactions.

This is what disorganised attachment category can look like: the parent is either 'perfect' and they want to be around them all day every day, or they are 'evil' and so cut off all contact. Look into the future and their intimate relationships can be the same – unstable, moving from extremes of love and hate, making intimacy both feared and desired. Object permanency has not been developed and, at its extreme, what is learnt is that relationships are disposable – a means to an end. I discuss this in terms of its links with violence in Chapter 11. It is these extremes in intimate attachment relationships that we focus on in therapy and this means that we work through a process of individuation – the earlier the better.

With Aboriginal clients, therapy is always practical. It's always goal-oriented and based on real-life examples and experiences. Too much of therapy is 'abstract' because of the idea that for clients to develop insights, it should not provide answers or solutions. This frustrates Aboriginal clients, who require context because we have what is known as a present-time focus – the future seems abstract.

A's mum's pattern of abuse was clear and predictable. Leading up to an access visit, he would get himself ready and start packing his bag days beforehand. It was heartbreaking to watch the desperation this kid had to be loved by his mum – that's the extreme part of the victim of abuse attachment cycle. It was made all the more tragic because I knew the pattern. I knew it would end in heartbreak and there was little I could do to stop it.

After the packing came the constant narrative of idealising his mother. It would go something like this: 'You know, Trace, when Mum was younger she didn't drink. She was really beautiful. She used to play sports ...' You get the drift.

So I started to gently develop insight into his mum. I said to him, 'That's great your mum used to be a non-drinker and all these wonderful things. That's great, bub ... What happened the last time you went home?'

'It was deadly. She made a nice feed and we watched TV with all of my cousins who slept over. It was so much fun. Mum had her friends over and she was really happy.'

'That's great, bub. Was it that way the whole time? Lots of fun?'

He then hunched over, looking at the ground, and softly said, 'No. Mum had a few drinks.'

'Was she a bit drunk, mate?'

'Yeah.' His head was still down, looking at the ground.

'What happened then?'

'She got mad because us kids were making too much noise. Then she flogged me.'

The use of the terms *flogged* and *flogging* is commonplace in Aboriginal English. It doesn't necessarily mean being physically abused. It can mean being told off – being 'growled' at.

'That's no good. Did she hurt you?'

'No, but it made me sad.'

'That's understandable. Then what happened?'

'She felt bad and tried to hug me, but I pushed her away. The next morning she made a big feed for us all though, and it was real great. We all sat around laughing and laughing. It's so good having everyone around. All my cousins.'

The story of the dynamic with his mum was the same again and again – happy times followed by drinking and violence. The extremes were damaging. A's nervous system was on high alert, which had an impact on his ability to trust, to develop secure attachment.

In these circumstances, there are a number of possible outcomes that therapists can only determine through observed testing. For A, it resulted in a lack of tolerance for calm. He was a high-energy kid who would constantly pace. He found it difficult to sit with peacefulness in his environment. It didn't only translate into foster care placements constantly breaking down due to A's explosiveness; in therapy, he would start to push buttons out of the blue, finding fault in me and in people around him.

For those who have come from violence, a common hardwired behavioural response is feeling that violence is normal or comfortable. They struggle to tolerate calm simply because it's foreign to them. Those with trauma will often evoke crises in their environment as a method of exerting control, because they expect conflict. As a psychologist, I address this by increasing their tolerance for calm through improving their self-soothing strategies.

A manifestation of this for A was that he would search for any opportunity to 'reject' you before you could reject him. When kids come from a background in which crisis after crisis is normal, they are not entirely familiar with routines.

I have seen many foster care placements break down simply because the foster parents were not prepared adequately for the fact that what they see as 'normal' – having routines, safety, a nice bedroom, a calm environment – initially feels overwhelming for traumatised kids because they have never had them before. This should not be sugar-coated for foster carers. It should be explained to them that routines and calmness will evoke emotional reactions until they become normalised and feel familiar. It is important for them to understand that things will get worse before they get better, but that keeping to routines and trusting in them is vital to long-term change. In isolated cases of trauma, grief and critical incidents, we always recommend to parents they get their kids back into their routines as quickly as possible. When the child has experienced significant childhood trauma, like A had, these patterns just take longer to reverse.

This also means that if you are in the life of a child who has experienced long-term and considerable trauma, you need to be as consistent as a drill sergeant. I have seen situations in which external services and clinicians inject someone into the life of a child with complex trauma and they do not understand how vital it is to be reliable. For example, A would literally wait at the kerb for his cultural mentor to pick him up at 4:00 pm. If they got there at 4:01 pm, A would explode. He had spent way too many hours waiting for his mum to show up, and then she didn't. The pain of that hadn't left him.

But the danger of A's disorganised attachment lay in him seeing his mum as either 'all good' or 'all bad' and this tracking him into his adult relationships. A's reaction to this was he would either 'hate' his mum and cut her off completely or live in her pocket. It was too extreme and intense. Individuation is about teaching kids that there is a middle ground, but also how to protect themselves in the process of developing a sense of self outside of parental attachments. For A, this meant learning his mum's patterns of behaviour and predicting when she was likely to struggle to parent him. Without teaching kids this, they internalise these parenting failures and blame themselves. Our core sense of self is absolutely based on how our parents see us and how they treat us, so this self-loathing is not a trajectory we want kids to end up on.

After working through A's experiences by establishing a narrative of how his mum would try really hard to be a great mum and then fall down in her efforts, it was easy to help A reframe his mother's behaviour. 'You can see that your mum is trying to be the best mum that she can be. That's because she loves you. But your experience is that she can only keep this up for so long, then she falls into her patterns of drinking. This has nothing to do with you. It has to do with what she is capable of. So, given all of that, what can you do to make sure that you are safe and okay when your mum is starting to struggle? Let's work on this together.'

Over time, it's essential that kids with abusive parents begin to see their parents for who they are – not all good or all bad, just grey – so they can develop their own sense of self, rather than relying on their parents who, simply, struggle to parent.

Attachment and client resistance: The 'FU' client

It takes a long time to unwire patterns that have been learnt through a lifetime of dysfunction, even for clients as young as A. As a result, there will be many setbacks and regressions. Change will always be small and incremental, and it is a therapist's role to both understand this and point it out to their clients when it occurs.

Every client is resistant to change to some degree, even the voluntary ones, because shifting your thoughts and behaviour is hard. When clients are completely defiant in therapy, it's usually because we, as therapists, have not fully appreciated how difficult this process is for them.

I have always found the challenge of the toughest clients attractive. My caseload was frequently full of 'out of control' teenagers who were damaged and beyond reach, just 'cutting out time' until they entered that 'magical age' of adulthood when they could be on their own. They are the ones that every therapist should work the hardest to help because we know that trauma feeds trauma, so the odds are that one day one of their kids will become your client. I saw this in my own caseload. Every single one of my wards of the state came from parents who had also been in care themselves or who'd had contact with the justice system.

The problem with many therapists is that they do not understand what resistance looks like, particularly in clients with compromised attachment. You have to work through a lot of anger in people who have had significant loss because they have been let down repeatedly and abandoned when things got tough. People like this will push your buttons to test you. They create havoc because they have learnt not to trust or attach to anyone to avoid the pain of rejection. Some people also respond to loss by believing it's easier to make themselves unlikeable, rather than open up and face possible future hurt.

Core attachment is one of the trickiest things to work with. I have yet to meet a client who follows a perfect script. For Aboriginal people and communities, the extent of their inherited trauma and attachment loss means trust is a massive issue.

One of my 'favourite' clients was a kid called V, a ward of the state with a tough-as-hell veneer. She was hard to like – and she liked the fact that she was hard to like. Developmental psychologists say that the major focus of the teenage years is reputation management, and V loved her reputation for being rough and feared. Every time I would find her at some house in which she'd been couch surfing, I would get the same response: 'Fuck you. Fuck you. Fuck you.'

That's all she would say.

But I kept tracking her down. I wouldn't react other than to say, 'How about we just try one less "fuck you" next time I come?'

'Fuck you. Fuck you. Fuck you.'

One day, probably a good twelve months into my 'work' with V, I got an urgent call. V had been in a fight with some girls and she had been poked in the eye with a stick. I rushed to the Royal Flying Doctor Service base where she was forced to lie still for three hours, waiting for a plane to get her to a major hospital. She couldn't move for risk of losing her eye, which was frightening for V but great for me because she couldn't run away, as she so often had done in the year I had 'worked' with her.

She was scared. It was the first time I had seen her like that. So I chatted to her about the latest crap music I was listening to, what her favourite things were to do – anything and everything. In that entire three hours, I was the *only* person who turned up. Not one parent. Not one friend. Just me. We sat there for all that time, together, but no-one else came. This time, there was no 'Fuck you'. I had finally reached the real V, the one who could be a frightened little kid. This V could show her vulnerability to someone and not have it used against her.

I said to her, 'You know what? You're a great kid.'

This time, she had to sit still with the 'discomfort' of someone being kind to her, of letting someone know that behind her tough veneer was just a vulnerable kid.

I have had so many 'tough' kids from remote communities who used to come into the city ('the big smoke') and grab my hand when we crossed the road. So many moments like this took my breath away. The easy thing to do is judge behaviour. It's much harder to understand it and remember that these are just kids.

For V and me, that was the turning point in our relationship. Never again did I hear that familiar 'Fuck you' (although I did occasionally joke with her about it). When she became a mum herself years later, some of my friends who knew V bumped into her and she excitedly asked them about me and what I was doing.

That's the thing about never giving up – it won't always pay off, but when it does, it is worth every single failure. I never ever gave up on 'my kids' (as I called my child clients). I say this to every parent who has had a kid go 'off the rails': never give up on them.

Trust in the values you have raised them with and just love them. The parents who close the door on their kids and cut them out of their lives will never know if they could have eventually worked through it together.

I had a client whose daughter had such a serious drug problem that my client was having to raise her granddaughter. It was out of character for the daughter, but she had suffered pretty significant trauma and drugs are the perfect way to mask pain. Having gone through trauma myself, I get their attraction to numb you and give you some rest from processing painful events. The daughter needed that time. For my client, the only advice I gave her was to always leave the door open, as hard as it was.

So, she would literally leave the door open for her to come home at whatever time, so that she had a safe place to sleep and get a feed if she needed it. That door was never closed, which was gutsy because damage was done and things were taken. But stuff can always be replaced or fixed. Relationships, once broken, are harder to superglue back together. It got to the stage that my client started locking parts of the house. I think at one point there was just an outdoor fridge with food and a couch. Boundaries are still important, and she would leave notes that were clear about those boundaries.

In time, the love that the daughter was raised with started to overcome some of the self-talk that led to more self-destruction than self-love. But it took time. I've always admired my client for loving the child but being clear that her behaviour was not condoned. She set clear, consistent boundaries that she never compromised on.

Being consistent with boundaries is the hard work of encouraging others to change their behaviour. They used to call this 'tough love'. I just call it being consistent, because change takes time. Her daughter is now working full-time. She still occasionally battles some of her demons and the baggage from the damaged relationships during her drug use, but for the most part she is happy, healthy and functioning.

Significant trauma can lead to destructive patterns. Compromised attachment does the same. Ultimately it is based on emotional fear, whereby the person is so afraid of their emotions that it is easier to turn the pain on themselves than express their feelings to others.

If a child is removed from a family, their family never recovers and nor does the child. The entire system has failed to understand the destruction of forced child removals – specifically, that it is generational and that attachment matters.

You rarely find a parent who does not want to do better and to provide a better life for their child. However, not a single program or assessment has been developed specifically for Aboriginal parents based on empirically determined parenting and attachment contextual differences. The result is that in Queensland, the Northern Territory and Western Australia, as just three examples, up to 77 per cent of 'intensive family therapy support programs' are engaged with by non-Aboriginal families.[40] The fact that we are not providing the basic opportunities for Aboriginal parents to heal their families continues to hardwire extreme race-based responses to at-risk Aboriginal children. A culturally competent system would change this.

7

Trauma, Racism and Violence:
The elder who denied his trauma

It was Carl Jung who said that what you resist persists. When we deny something, we cannot grow. The therapist's job is to help our clients develop insight, because that's when change begins. As humans, there is comfort in what is hardwired and predictable. For survivors, that hardwiring means being in denial because surviving abuse requires it. However, healing from it doesn't.

Why do people do bad things? Why do some people harm their partners but not their children? Why do some people who come from extreme violence and trauma not become violent themselves? Is it nature or nurture? This last question very rarely offers anything useful; as we know, it's a combination of nature and nurture – although, as I jokingly say, you can blame your parents for both.

As a psychologist, I have seen clients from normal, uneventful backgrounds who have committed truly evil acts, as well as those with extreme trauma who have gone on to live loving and fulfilling lives. Then there are those with sociopathic traits, who can hide their real intentions from others for a very long time. This is the nature of the personality variables of the classic sociopath.

Where the science has landed on this is that our personalities are a combination of the genetics of our parents. In fact, scientists estimate that 20–60 per cent of temperament is determined by genes.[1] There are certain genetic pulls that are inevitable. I am always fighting against my 'Mavisness' – when I find myself being like my mum, I say, 'Oh no, genetics got me again!'

But genetics are always an unknown factor simply because there are so many other variables that interact to either increase or decrease this genetic likelihood. For example, what separates those who feel anger but can moderate it from those who feel anger and act upon it with violence and aggression? According to a meta-analysis on data from twenty-four studies, up to 50 per cent of the total variance in aggressive behaviour was explained by genetic influences.[2] However, not everyone who has this 'genetic risk' will become violent or aggressive because we are quite adept at regulating anger as humans. It is one of the more dominant emotions that we feel. Anger can also serve as a powerful motivator in trauma survivors as it feels like a less vulnerable state.

But whether someone becomes capable of harming others is a matter of *how* the genetics combine. Those who have at least one sibling from the same parents know this. You will all have different attachment needs, aptitudes and interests, along with basal personality traits that define a common genetic 'pull'.

When it comes to things like psychopathy, genetics can predispose people, of course, but environment is the key difference, and that's the part that scientists are still figuring out. For example, an environment with an abusive parent and an overcompensating one is a perfect storm for sociopaths, narcissists, psychopaths and those with anti-social personality disorder. This situation creates extreme emotional responses, which means that the environment is unpredictable.

Think of it this way: genetics loads the gun, and environment pulls the trigger. Environment is capable of turning genes on or off, which means that genetic and biological vulnerability is capable of going anywhere.

I'm often asked if I believe there's a 'culture' of violence in Aboriginal communities. My answer is that any offender is enabled by a culture – by those who normalise and minimise violence, and who feed their sense of entitlement and demonise victims. Violence is a human issue, not a black person issue.

It's about empathy.

I've worked with only a handful of Aboriginal people who I would consider to be true psychopaths. One came from extraordinary childhood abuse and trauma; the other had little in their background that seemed to form these traits.

Most personality disorders are uncommon, but through the joys of social media – where pop psychologists use these terms to describe bad behaviour – they're being represented as ubiquitous, even normal. Narcissism, sociopathy, anti-social personality disorder and psychopathy all share traits that make it hard, from a diagnostic perspective, to spot them and attempt treatment – mostly.

There are many high-achieving individuals who channel these traits differently and it is often a core aspect of their success – for example, billionaires and CEOs who possess some of the personality clusters of sociopaths. All these disorders feature a sense of grandiosity – the person's belief that they are untouchable and that rules that apply to others don't apply to them. They all also involve a sense of having unique brilliance – the belief that they are special and have extraordinary gifts that no-one else has. These clients can also be quite charismatic and likeable, intuiting and manipulating the emotions of others as well as feigning emotions themselves.

This is what cognitive empathy is, and it makes psychopaths likeable, which enables their behaviour. You look at truly evil people becoming celebrities – they are chameleons, capable of dualistically being evil as well as outwardly funny and kind. People with anti-social personality disorders access these traits to suit their environment and their audience. Ultimately, they do not have a stable sense of self.

As I mentioned earlier, John Bowlby was one of the first to describe the first internal working model of the self as being based upon the predictability of the parental attachment bond.[3] As a child grows, this predictability enables them to develop object constancy; as discussed in Chapter 6, it's the caregiver/parental bond that develops that secure base. The infant feels secure and associates critical bond relationships with security and predictability, which then increases the odds of future relationship attachment security. If this is not developed, relationships feel disposable; they are there purely to feed a sense of entitlement, to be manipulated to suit a need. Abuse and violence is an obvious possible trajectory. Additionally: when environments are both predictable and comforting, it results in the independent ability of the child to learn to self-regulate emotions, increasing the odds of secure attachment.

When an individual has a background in which primary attachments have been absent or abusive it increases the likelihood of emotional instability or lack of object constancy. A 'perfect storm', if you will, for the development of psychopathic traits would be an abusive parent in combination with an overcompensating one, in which the attachment bonds become extreme – love/hate. The overcompensating parent will then indulge a child in response to the abuse – setting them up to have no boundaries; to be hero worshipped and this may be an aspect of the parent themselves being abused by the abusive parent; meaning the child becomes unwittingly a victim of the victim–offender abuse dynamic. When this happens, the person perceives others as disposable; everyone is simply a means to an end. It often manifests as that person going from relationship to relationship, often returning to relationships to further abuse and manipulate. Love is idealised, so when normal relationship bumps occur they are devalued and disposed of.

A psychopath can also manipulate their psychologist or counsellor, the pay-off being that they escape detection and can continue to abuse. If they enter partner therapy, they will do everything to look kind, concerned and dutiful to the psychologist. The fact that they are extraordinarily adept at faking cognitive empathy means that they will speak to feelings but do not have the ability to truly feel them or care about the pain they are causing their victims. As I've mentioned, victims can be vulnerable to further abuse from child protection and police systems, and even from counsellors who can get triangulated very easily by perpetrators, mistakenly thinking that victims are 'unstable' because they are struggling with trauma symptoms while their abuser is not. Psychopaths often appear calm as they are controlling the dynamics of the relationship.

One of the most difficult parts of being a psychologist is finding yourself liking clients who have done terrible things. But developing rapport and establishing empathy is critical to getting the real story and understanding their criminal impulses. Identifying these impulses is what forensic assessment is all about. To get a sense of what drives these kinds of people, you have to put yourself in the mind of a psychopath and try to think like them. That's challenging – to grasp this darkness and find a way to relate to it. It is easier to have empathy for victims, but this process is an essential component of therapeutic change.

But at what point does a victim became a perpetrator? Many of my clients who have done terrible things had long-term histories of abuse and trauma. Some develop loving families around them, like the 'man who couldn't love' in Chapter 5. Some will become the very thing their environment tells them they are. And some will be 'good people' whose trauma builds to the point that they commit an act of violence.

How does trauma do that? The story of M, the Aboriginal elder who denied his trauma, explains this.

The story of M

In trauma, anger can provide you with a rest from vulnerability. It's a necessary part of healing to visit anger, but you don't want to live there. How do we process it to ensure it doesn't lead to aggression? Living in anger is very different to accessing it when you need to protect yourself from further harm.

An Aboriginal elder, who I will call M, in his mid-to-late sixties was referred for assessment. Like many Stolen Generations people, he had two birth dates – the day he was born on the mission, and the day his birth was confirmed by the missionaries. M had been convicted of grievous bodily harm and was awaiting sentencing. The judge had requested a pre-sentence report due to the unusual nature of the offence. M had no history of violent behaviour. In fact, he hadn't even had a parking ticket before. He also had a Masters degree in education. On the face of it, M was a success story – someone who had achieved and lived a 'good life', although file notes indicated significant trauma and forced removal in his background. He was extraordinarily controlled in every aspect of his life, despite having a complete absence of control over his circumstances for most of his childhood.

But his first offence was a violent one. My client had been having lunch at McDonald's with his de facto partner and her two young children – aged seven and nine – who he had raised for six years and considered to be his own. As he approached the counter to order lunch for the group, M accidentally made contact with a fellow diner, who he recognised from his neighbourhood. This man had threatened my client before. He was larger than M by several inches in height and many kilograms in bulk. M said he apologised to the man and thought that was that.

According to M, the man then loomed over him and glared while racially abusing him, calling him names like 'dumb Abo bastard'. He made indirect slurs that to my client made no sense, referencing the 'boongs and coons that shouldn't be let out in public'. The man also threatened to 'get him' when he left the restaurant, and named the make and type of M's car to show that he would not be able to get away.

M stated that during this time he felt himself getting more and more frightened and threatened, and that he did not know what to do. As his fear increased, circumstances collided in the worst possible way when he found himself searching in his bag for something to defend himself with. He came upon a small pocketknife that he used to cut fruit with. His intention was to protect himself and his family, rather than cause harm to anyone. At some point the man approached M, who has since said he does not recall all of what occurred next. His next memory was of seeing a bloodied knife in his hand and the victim covered in blood on the floor.

It was also relevant to the assessment that M was extremely distressed about what he had done, which is one of the most critical aspects of criminogenic factors in assessment. Does the person feel remorse? Do they have insight? Are they motivated to change?

M was bailed by the judge, which is unusual. It had been some eighteen months between the trial and my assessment. In that time M had developed chronic post-traumatic stress disorder along with agoraphobia. He now had an irrational fear of stabbing someone again. My assessment was that the primary theme was self-loathing – he wasn't able to reconcile what he had done with who he was and his principle of never harming others, regardless of the harm they had done to him.

Police reports appeared to contradict what my client had said, in that all the witnesses said the attack was completely unprovoked. A few comments here. First, external eyewitness testimony is different from an internal state – the witnesses didn't have M's templates that defined racial trauma, which is why it is important that racial trauma is seen as a separate and distinct category to PTSD and C-PTSD. Additionally, eyewitness testimony has been shown to have significant racial bias. According to the Innocence Project, mistakes in eyewitness testimony contribute to over 70 per cent of wrongful convictions overturned by DNA evidence. Of these exonerations, 40 per cent were the result of cross-race identifications.[4]

When I first met M, his tiny stature was striking, although it didn't help that I am almost 6 feet tall. He was all of 5 feet 4 inches with a skinny frame. He said he had lost around 15 kilograms since the time of the offence, which was confirmed by police photos and reports. When he sat down, before I could even engage in any dialogue, he immediately said, 'I know you psychologists. You're going to say I had a terrible life. My life was fine. That's all bullshit to provide an excuse for shit …'

Trauma being 'an excuse for shit' – not the first time I have heard that eloquent phrase uttered by victims and perpetrators, as well as those who have never experienced trauma and don't understand how truly debilitating it is.

So, as I spoke with M, he went through his early history. It was littered with trauma but, as is common with Indigenous people globally,[5] it has become 'normalised' because we are exposed to trauma at a level that is extraordinarily high. In these circumstances, incredibly traumatic events will be described matter-of-factly. Some of this is dissociative, some of it self-protective and some is generated by victim shame and self-blame. It's almost as if victims are searching for validation that they have not experienced trauma – or validation that they have. What is clear is that denial runs deep in victims, as does shame.

Most people have a first childhood memory, even a faint one, from when they were around eighteen months to two years old. M's first memory, however, was from when he was seven, and it was horrific. He told me flatly, 'Back in the day, the welfare and police would come pretty regularly, looking for us "half-caste" kids in particular. My community was close to two others, so if they went to one community, they would quickly go to the next and someone had the job of warning the nearby community. It was often that people would suddenly go into a panic trying to get us kids hidden.'

On the day M was forcibly removed from his family, his dad picked him up and ran with him, putting him behind a tree on top of a hill. This was where M would always hide from the authorities, so this familiar process meant his recall was both vivid and detailed. Just before his dad ran back to their house, his last words to M were: 'No matter what happens, son, don't move.'

Not for the first time, M then had to watch his mum, his grandmother and his entire family being horrifically assaulted by the police, much of which he was still unable to speak about decades later. Tears came while he was talking, and then the inevitable 'corrector' and apology for his pain: 'I'm sorry. I shouldn't still be feeling this way.'

It's much harder to watch people you love suffering pain and trauma than experiencing it yourself. It's why terrorists threaten to harm victims' families, because it pushes people's buttons more. The trauma survival response is compounded by wanting to protect your primary attachments – those who feed your sense of self-worth and who you rely on for love and support. From a trauma response perspective, it also means that dissociation is not as available to you as a coping mechanism.

Not only did M regularly have to witness his entire family being assaulted by the police – his estimate was every few months – but there was a very real threat of personal harm through removal from his primary attachments. With complex childhood trauma, because the victim's personality is yet to be fully formed, it can become so enmeshed within trauma symptoms that unpacking what is trauma and who is the 'real' person forms an additional layer to healing.

During his forced removal, there was no 'goodbye' to his family. He was never to see them again. M was sent to a boy's home with other Aboriginal kids. Another additional cultural layer to M's trauma was the 'divide and conquer' strategy of assimilation, in which kids who were removed were 'colour-coded' and put into cohorts based on their skin colour's degree of whiteness. M was classified as a 'half-caste' and so was placed in the section of the mission that was a better standard than that for 'full-bloods' (deemed less worthy) or 'quarter-castes'. As a 'half-caste', M could almost 'pass' for white, and this was the 'part' of him that could be saved through white indoctrination. Assimilation, said M, meant 'breeding the blackfella out of people', and the missions took that task very seriously, from how the kids were dressed to what they were allowed to say. He was not allowed to speak his traditional language. To this day, when dialect 'slips out' he still recoils.

Being a fairer-skinned Stolen Generations kid fed his trauma denial. His belief that his life was 'fine' reflected the indoctrination by the nuns and priests at the mission that he had 'better' treatment. His default when telling stories of horrific trauma was always to say, 'Yeah, but I didn't have it as bad as the blacker kids.'

To that I had to constantly say, 'Yeah, but, mate, it's still trauma.'

M's denial was as much about the guilt of his 'better' treatment as it was about survival. I have worked with dark-skinned Stolen Generations people who tried to 'rub the black from their skin', but fair-skinned Stolen Generations clients, like M, often feel a form of 'survivor's guilt'.

When you feel as though you 'don't belong anywhere', like M did, your identity can become defined by your trauma. This creates the most pain and sets you on a path of lifelong identity struggles. At its core it's about self-acceptance. The questioning of Aboriginality based on skin colour that has become so normalised in this country – by black and white alike – fuels this struggle and ongoing damage.

In the mission, floggings were regular occurrences and would be with whips, brooms, belts – 'pretty much anything that was close by', according to M. They were so brutal it was hard to walk afterwards. The nuns would dress in full habits and shave their heads as if to represent a level of suffering or sacrifice that was to be admired and emulated. To M, it just represented hate, something he learnt to internalise.

As an adult, memories of nuns haunted M in flashbacks, both in his sleep – regularly waking him up with cold sweats – and while conscious. It's common for victims to re-experience trauma in this way. The brain becomes so used to scanning the environment for potential risks that it becomes normalised after trauma has occurred, even though the threat is no longer present. The brain will perceive threats that are imagined rather than real – for example, everyone will start to look like your assailant, keeping you alert and scanning for imminent danger. For M, he couldn't walk past a church, and he would almost pass out with fear when he saw a nun or a priest. Any reminder of the church triggered his fight-or-flight response and hyperarousal.

A client once asked me how I would describe trauma, and this is the best I could do:

Trauma keeps you trapped in the past, looking backwards rather than forwards. Your future becomes limited by forces beyond your control, and now trapped by those you feel unable to control.

As a therapist, I always find it surprising what my client's most dominant trauma memories are. I refer to this as 'salient' imagery – those events, words or stories that are the hardest to process and so dominate and define the trauma narrative. It's the memory that keeps repeating itself in dreams and in flashbacks in day-to-day interactions with others, as if ruminating over it will eventually enable victims to make sense of it.

But it is not always the most graphic experience that's most salient. For M, his most traumatic memory took a long time to get at. He kept apologising before eventually telling me what it was.

He had only 'patches' of memory from his six years in the mission. He remembers always feeling cold and frightened, until he walked into his classroom one day and a Catholic nun, Sister Mary, who was filling in for a few weeks, changed everything for him.

He was immediately struck by her. She was younger than the other nuns and more modern-looking. She didn't have the shaved head under her habit that was so frightening to him, and she was joyful – an emotion he had not known in a very long time, although he was only around ten years old by this stage. His memories of childhood are all about sadness, nothing else. I was immediately reminded, yet again, of how so much of our life comes down to luck. I always felt safe as a kid, with a roof over my head and a meal on the table. I thought everyone had that until I became a psychologist. That's what my parents had insulated my siblings and me from.

For M, meeting Sister Mary reminded him of long-buried feelings and of what he had lost in the blink of an eye. To cope, as any child of that age would, he had escaped through fantasy, creating an alternate world in which little boys got hugs rather than smacks. In this dream, the darkness didn't terrify him and grown men didn't force little boys to do unthinkable things. It was a world of imaginary friends, of his parents' arms around him, of his mum and dad laughing and his siblings playing with him. I have watched many wards of the state and Stolen Generations people do this, constructing stories for the life they should have lived. The pull to fit in and be what is perceived as 'normal' is so strong.

There is so much shame in being a *victim*. And that's what perpetrators rely on. In M's childlike innocence, he 'fell in love' with Sister Mary. This shows why love, as I have argued in Chapter 6, is often an extremely triggering emotion that survivors struggle to 'tolerate'. This was his first primary attachment since his forced removal. He was desperate for her love and attention, wanting her to see him as a 'good' boy. One day in class he was proudly working on something – he couldn't recall what – and as Sister Mary approached him his heart was beating with excitement and the hope that she would notice his great work. He sat upright, gripping his crayon tightly to make sure he was 'perfect'.

Sister Mary picked up his work. She looked at it, and looked back at him. She then shook her head and to the entire class said, 'This here is the work of a dirty little nigger.'

He turned his head away, embarrassed by the tears that had welled in his eyes. Again, he was apologising for his pain and his trauma.

As he told this story, he went back to being that boy again. Psychodynamic theory says that after trauma, our physical self grows but our emotional state tied in with trauma reactivity can remain stagnated when trauma memories are triggered.[6] It's a common trauma response that people can behaviourally regress back to the age of the trauma and this means sometimes mimicking childlike trauma responses – as a form of trauma re-experienced as repetition compulsion already described and repeat their behavioural response as if the trauma was happening in the moment.[7]

M spoke of extensive physical and sexual abuse from 'literally the first week' in the mission. 'My biggest problem was that I was a cute kid – blonde and sweet-natured,' he said. 'It was like I had a target on my back.'

The abuse was so frequent he lost count of the number of times it happened. It was a daily occurrence for as long as he could remember. 'I would be flogged for being bad and flogged for being good.

At some point, I had to try and rely on who I actually was through the haze of trauma.'

'And who are you?' I asked.

'Someone incapable of being bad.'

At this point, his emotions overwhelmed him and his tears quickly became heaving, uncontrollable sobs. It was clear that the realisation of what he had done was painful to him, but as a therapist I had to maintain my objectivity to assess him for the judge's report. There was a victim in this scenario who had been attacked and violently so.

M then spoke of many attempts to run away from every mission he ended up in, until finally at fourteen he managed to escape for good. He was able to stay out of the reach of 'the welfare' by getting paid work here and there and living on the streets with a group of 'other black kids on the run'.

When he eventually found his family in his thirties, he simply could not fit in. He had no sense of attachment to them. There had been too much damage. He felt he had to pretend that his life had worked out okay. The pressure of pretending eventually became too much, though, and he broke contact almost as soon as he had initiated it.

His mum died several years later. His father said losing him and his siblings 'broke her heart'. M said that he doesn't doubt that was true, but he was too damaged to allow himself to care.

Is racism traumatic?

When do victims become perpetrators? In a dramatic split second, M had crossed that line. And in his mind, he had now become the very thing he was told he would become his entire life. Does racism explain it? Is racism traumatic?

Racism denial makes Aboriginal people feel existentially unsafe. Its lack of validation makes the world feel profoundly and imminently dangerous. Racial trauma, like any trauma, sets our neural pathways to constantly be on alert, to enable survival. Post-trauma, racism denial means victims must expend more energy convincing others of its existence and of its central role in trauma, rather than healing from the trauma itself, therefore compounding its effects.

Unlike therapy, in which treatment takes the time that it should, assessments must be done against the clock. And M's denial of his trauma was significantly compromising the assessment. We were effectively going back to the court with a report that had M stating he had 'no idea' why he did what he did, and that he didn't have insight into this trauma or his behavioural reactions to specific triggers and stressors. In short, he would be seen as a veritable 'loose cannon'.

Most importantly, M had such an irrational fear of stabbing someone again that he had developed agoraphobia, confining himself to his home to cope with his uncontrollable and intrusive thoughts. In the court's mind, it would not be a huge leap to view jail time as a mere geographical extension of his self-imposed home detention.

I now had to work out why he had become violent. This involved thoroughly knowing trauma responses and how they can interact with the additional layer of cultural identity trauma and the neuroscience of racism. This is a complex combination of factors that few health professionals understand well in this country.

First, the 'easy' stuff: what we know about trauma responses. There are four primary trauma response mechanisms,[8] although science is always evolving about trauma. First, dissociation makes survival possible during traumatic events as the brain can reduce the person's heart rate, allowing them to 'step outside' of their emotion and access the higher-level-thinking part of the brain, the cortex. This enables them to formulate a plan to survive or, in extreme situations, escape from danger.

Second, hyperarousal is the body in fight-or-flight mode, which is also essential to survival. The brain says 'threat' and forces the heart rate up quickly. Blood pumps to all the parts of the body that enable the person to either run from danger (flight) or defend themselves physically (fight). The downside of hyperarousal is that it limits access to logic and problem-solving skills. Those who naturally experience hyperarousal as a stress and trauma coping response will be more impulsive and tuned into non-verbal cues as indicators of danger, rather than verbal ones.

The freeze trauma response is hypothesised that it is part of the continuum of hyperarousal, dissociation and fawning, but mostly it occurs within all these responses as well as being a separate response.[9] It makes sense because freeze is the brain in a 'holding' pattern, taking a while to 'catch up' with the traumatic event while it's occurring and trying to process it. For example, survivors of the September 11 attacks described people who literally sat on the steps of the fire escape, waiting for people to rescue them. They froze and sadly didn't survive.

The fawn response focuses on others rather than being self-directed. It is a new discussion point in the trauma field and therefore not as clinically explored, though I do unpack this in Chapter 4. It doesn't mean it doesn't exist; it just means it is an emerging field. As already discussed, fawn involves compliance to avoid and de-escalate trauma. For example, those in violent relationships will appease their perpetrators to protect themselves from abuse or will take abuse to protect others, such as children or siblings. Children who are sexually abused by a parent sometimes comply to save a younger sibling from the same trauma.

The fawn response looks like victims being complicit in their own abuse. Post-trauma, compliance can continue with victims often 'defending' their abuser. This is often based on fear of retribution or simply the hardwired pattern of persecution followed by cycles of 'love bombing' to ensure that victims are trained to feel empathy for their abusers. The violence followed by kindness – particularly when fight or flight is not possible due to age or power dynamics – means that fawn is what remains. It is often weaponised post-trauma by perpetrators to convince others that abuse has not really occurred, which is why it is so highly complex for victims to come forward.

I discussed fawning in Chapter 4 in relation to a collective racial trauma response. I've often seen the fawn response play itself out with Stolen Generations people, both at the level of the individual and at a collective level due to denials by successive governments and mainstream society of the forcible removal of Aboriginal children. Remember, it took until 2008 for the government to acknowledge it had happened. That's a long time for trauma responses to become ingrained due to a lack of validation. Victims often come to therapy to name trauma as trauma. They present with behaviours that are problematic to them and their loved ones – or, like M, I assess them once they're facing the justice system – but, of course, they don't understand that their behaviours are consequences of trauma. So, in essence, denying the removals happened has virtually guaranteed the intergenerational transmission of trauma, which (as discussed earlier) happens through genetics, biological vulnerability and environment, as well as repetition compulsion. Denial of trauma is a trauma variable and compounds the initial trauma event or events.

Although they don't use these terms, many survivors describe enacting all four mechanisms throughout their trauma experience.

However, there is a significant difference between having PTSD and experiencing PTSD symptoms. Let's look at the relatable example of a minor car accident. This had happened to pretty much all of us. I break PTSD down as being a cycle of three affected areas, which are the target of assessment and treatment.

First, come the *thoughts*. Just after you have that accident, you want to avoid driving a car because of fear, fed by the brain misfiring and thinking that every time you get into a car you are going to have someone run up the back of you. These thoughts aren't based in reality; car accidents don't happen every single time you get into a car. But the thoughts then feed the second part, which is the *physical reaction* – hypervigilance, flashbacks, hyperarousal – which then feeds the third and final response, which involves *avoidance* behaviours. And the more you avoid, the more you fear. Your thoughts and physical responses to fear cannot be 'tested' by evidence gained through facing your fear.

Because most of us need to drive at some point, though, we have no choice but to get back into the car. Avoidance is not actually possible. When you do get back in, you experience the first two of this PTSD cluster of symptoms – thoughts and physical reactions – but because you are not avoiding the feared situation, eventually these symptoms will disappear. So, it is perfectly normal to have PTSD symptoms for a few weeks.

This is why exposure-based therapies have always been considered the 'treatment of choice' for trauma. Exposure needs to be specific to the nature of the trauma itself, as well as graduated and controlled. It can start by just talking about the trauma event, which continues until the emotional reaction dissipates. The idea is to create a positive rather than negative association with the previously traumatic memories as a method of 'softening' reactions to trauma triggers, in a way that is controlled by survivors.

The problem with triggers is that they are unpredictable and 'come out of the blue', so clients avoid memories as a default, which makes the triggers unmanageable and reactions to them entrenched become entrenched. Exposure can involve just talking about the traumatic event, using visual imagery and, finally, being in the feared situation (like the car example). The type of exposure is completely dependent on the type of trauma and whether avoidance behaviours are impairing the individual. For example, a client whose family member was murdered – in graphic, violent circumstances in a public place – wanted to 'face their fears' by going back to where the murder happened.

My first question was, 'Why? Are you having to avoid it in a way that is impairing you? Are you driving around the block to avoid it?'

Their answer was 'no'.

'So why put yourself through the torment?' I said. 'There are also many other graphic parts of this trauma to deal with that are impactful. There are also many other exposure techniques we can use.'

The other problem is that setting traumatic goals like this means that if the client does not 'achieve' them then they have 'failed' at trauma. They do not have to face every fear to heal, only those that are debilitating – and it is the therapist's job to set these goals and teach clients to be compassionate to themselves during this process.

193

In simple terms, the difference between PTSD and a 'normal' reaction to a critical event is essentially about the length of time in which post-trauma symptoms are present and the extent to which they have an impact on the person's ability to function and live the quality of life they had beforehand. In M's case, he had complex childhood trauma, which is enduring and impactful across multiple areas of functionality. So, understanding the four trauma responses was helpful in building my assessment hypothesis that his violence was part of a trauma-based reaction.

Indeed, racial trauma explained most of M's behaviour, but it didn't explain all of it. Naming M's trauma as racial trauma meant that we could then refer to the science of PTSD and put it under a racism neuroscience lens to explain how it feeds pre- and post-trauma vulnerability and associated reactions.

Assessing the impacts of racism as trauma: Can it be quantified?

Trauma happens to people. They didn't ask for or invite it. When people are told to 'get over' trauma, it portrays trauma as if it's a personal weakness. In fact, living with trauma *symptoms* takes extraordinary strength.

So, why did a sixty-something-year-old man with zero history of violence suddenly stab someone? Can racial trauma explain it? During my PhD twenty years ago, I first became interested in reactions by Aboriginal people to racism and marginalisation, and whether they 'mimic' trauma responses. I didn't have a name for it back then, but I went on to develop an assessment tool for it called the Acculturative Stress Scale for Aboriginal Australians. At the time, it made so much sense to me. Racism as trauma – I had lived experience of it too, and my clients needed it to be validated but in a way that was quantified as traumatic.

To give a lived-experience reality of what this is like: I hate meeting new people, even though I'm an extrovert. I love people generally – which kind of helps when you're a psychologist, I guess – so why do I always feel a sense of dread and stress when I meet someone for the first time? I should note that this is completely confined to people who don't know I am Aboriginal. I am not 'obviously' Aboriginal (I know, internal eye roll) – I am fair-skinned with blonde hair and green eyes. I guess one of us five kids had to get my dad's genes!

The predominance of racism is such that it has literally altered the way Aboriginal people perceive threat.[10] The possibility of racism is threatening because it is personal, against me and my family. This means that my brain registers it as pain. It also requires me to be prepared for when someone inevitably makes a racist comment, and this constant alertness creates stress. We know that the accumulation of acculturative stress after trauma mimics the fight, flight, freeze or fawn responses already described. The anxiety of anticipating a racist comment is too much to cope with, so I mention as quickly as possible the fact that I am Aboriginal.

Collective trauma is badly understood. It occurs when identity-based persecution exists as unique trauma variables for individuals and, based on the data, whole disproportionally impacted communities. The trauma of stolen children, forced relocation, stolen wages and educational exclusion – all resulting from colonisation – have long-term impacts, making PTSD a more prevalent diagnosis for Aboriginal people because of these additional racial trauma variables that are enduring and inescapable.[11] When racism is a core (and often sole) factor in your trauma, day-to-day existence feels threatening and can activate the same post-trauma fight, flight, freeze or fawn responses of PTSD in which the world just feels existentially unsafe.

While the focus of trauma interventions is to help clients develop the skills and resilience to manage traumatic events, clinicians are left untrained to assist Aboriginal clients cultivate the protective factors necessary to form a healthy and robust cultural identity to moderate the impacts of racial traumas. As argued by Cénat, the DSM-5 – the go-to reference tool for mental health diagnoses – fails to capture factors fundamental to racial trauma, including its enduring, constant and cumulative nature and that the trauma is often perpetuated by systems and institutions.[12]

Cultural identity alone has not only served to magnify trauma likelihood, but also added an additional layer to trauma recovery, which must be better understood by practitioners to ensure more effective engagement in therapeutic interventions.

Why culture stress unpacked M's denial of trauma

M was the walking, breathing definition of culture stress. *All* his many traumatic experiences occurred because he just happened to be born Aboriginal. There was no other reason.

So, that was the first part, defining acculturative stress and incorporating this within the trauma response formulation. The 'value' of culture stress is that it named and validated his trauma. Trauma validation enables insight, and insight is a critical aspect of criminogenic risk assessment as it speaks to the person's capacity and motivation to change.

At a level of risk assessment, though, it armed him around his individualised risk factors by not only providing necessary insight by 'naming' what was triggering his trauma reactions, but also ensuring that risk factors that were alterable or dynamic were identified therapeutically. Prior to assessment he remained in denial of his trauma. Culture stress enabled him to tell his story, a history of trauma he had normalised. It also enabled us to draw an objective comparison as compared to 'most' Aboriginal people; M's degree of culture stress was extraordinarily high. Courts love things that are quantifiable. Racial trauma and its impacts become quantifiable once they are defined, as they are through the Acculturative Stress Scale.

At one point during the assessment, M looked up at me and without a thread of irony said, 'I didn't realise how racist I was. I mean towards white people.'

What this meant was that he had no insight into how much he was reading every situation and interaction as racist. Post-trauma involves a 'misfiring', if you will, whereby threats are imagined rather than real. This activates the body's response to threat.

We now go to the post-trauma response mechanisms I've already described. My hypothesis was that M's natural stress response to critical events was hyperarousal. His history provided the starting point for this hypothesis. Remember the little kid behind the tree, watching everyone he loved being harmed? Dissociation was not as accessible in those circumstances.

I then used more objective indicators. Breathing rate provides a good basal indicator of stress. I asked him to count how many breaths he took over a minute. His answer was thirty-five. The average is ten to twelve.

This extremely fast breathing rate further supported my hyperarousal hypothesis. Those who have high levels of basal anxiety tend to over-breathe, and his body had become accustomed to hyperarousal without him being aware it was due to cumulative trauma.

The final element is something I learnt from the work of American psychiatrist Bruce Perry.[13] Remind the client of a salient memory of their trauma and see how their body responds. I first get them to feel their pulse and alert me when it changes. What natural activation to threat is there? For M it was asking, 'Why did you end up in care?' His pulse went through the roof. This added to the hypothesis that his natural response to stress was hyperarousal. Another piece of the puzzle was added, another hypothesis tested.

The assessment had so far established racism as traumatic and defined how this had manifested specifically in M. However, this was a man who had never reacted violently before, despite extreme stress and trauma. So why now? Why had he not been able to access what is referred to as 'internal restraints', those mechanisms – such as self-talk and slowed breathing – that help us not react to external stressors? What was it about this situation that limited his capacity that day?

We had to home in on the environment to finish the assessment puzzle, to see what range of triggers were evident and the relationship they had with his trauma. The presence of the kids was an obvious one. Protecting himself became about protecting others, which – as we've previously discussed – heightened his sense of threat. It also meant that – just like when he was behind the tree – his access to dissociation was more limited. We also know that those who respond with hyperarousal are more impulsive and reactive, and tend to be less able to engage in higher-level thinking and problem-solving.

The nature of complex childhood trauma is also such that the presence of the kids likely represented a living re-enactment of his own childhood trauma. The fact that the kids were around the same age as M was during his most significant trauma memory is important. Intimate attachments also involve a greater fear of loss, so it made sense that M's inability to restrain himself was in part because of the presence of his children and girlfriend.

The next factor within the environment was the threat based on race. But this was clearly not a new experience for M. He'd faced significant racism before and none of it had led him to harm others.

Assessment is about unveiling a narrative, unpacking all the elements that in combination make meaning of why. No single factor could explain M's behaviour.

The common theme for him, however, was that whenever he had experienced racial abuse, it had not ended well for him. That was his lived experience of the outcome of this type of threat.

The smartest thing you can do in assessment is pre-empt what you are going to be challenged on. Be prepared to defend your conclusions. So, I asked him an obvious question: 'If you felt threatened, if you were so afraid you and your companions would be harmed, why didn't you just leave? It's a long way from feeling threatened to stabbing someone.'

Freeze as a trauma response does explain most of this, of course. As we have learnt, it is often the case that trauma responses lead to people freezing. I have worked with many people with relationship-based attachment issues in which they freeze during conflict, when the sensible thing to do when stress overwhelms your capacity to remain calm is to leave. For many, leaving is not possible; paralysis often takes over when freeze (and hyperarousal) is your trauma default. M described feeling as being as if 'my feet were concreted to the floor. I can't explain it any more than that.'

Of course, he also had an entirely appropriate belief that the man would carry out his threats if he did leave the restaurant.

His trauma history, however, had to be explored further to see if it could provide an additional piece of the puzzle. Remember that M had years he did not remember, and this pre-dated his forcible removal? A significant factor in post-traumatic stress is having an incomplete narrative.

Traumatic memories are so emotionally loaded that even the smallest reminders can be debilitating. Without treatment, trauma can feel like a jumbled mess – a mix of salient and unpredictable images, sounds and emotions.

'You have years of memory that you say you do not remember.'

M nodded.

'Is it that you don't remember or that you don't want to remember? Do you understand the difference?'

'Probably a bit of both.'

'Okay. So, either from what you actually know or what you have heard from others, what do you think is so painful that you don't want to remember it?'

'Well, obviously more trauma. I saw a lot of violence as a very young kid. Before the mission.'

'Who perpetrated the violence?'

'Well, it was my dad,' he said, his head down, tears flowing.

His dad was his hero. He protected and looked after him. Remember the kid being put behind the tree? His dad was his constant salvation, but his dad was also occasionally a violent drunk who would beat his family.

It's difficult and sometimes impossible for people who adore an abusive parent to accept that they are abusive. Sometimes 'good people' do bad things. People are rarely all bad, all the time.

For M, his dad's violence was a secret that was buried deep within him, covered by the fantasy world of a perfect family that he created to survive.

After a pause, I felt comfortable to explore a little more as instinctively I felt there was more meaning to be made here.

'Tell me, how many siblings do you have?'

'Seven.'

'Wow. Big family. And what order are you in the family?'

'I'm the eldest.'

'So when your dad would get drunk and beat your mother and sometimes your younger siblings, what would you do?'

'I would stop him. It was my job to protect them. I was the biggest and the eldest and he would listen to me.'

'Could you leave?'

'No.'

'Why not?'

'Because if I left, bad things happened to the people that I love.'

This was the last piece of the assessment puzzle. Freeze made sense. You can deny and bury your trauma, but there it still is ... and healing never finds itself in denial.

So, the man who had denied his trauma for over fifty years now understood and accepted it for the first time, and it took a violent impulse to get there. M then became highly focused on his healing, which included apologising to his victim.

He approached his therapy in the same way he had approached everything in his life – determined to overachieve. He was highly motivated to change. He needed to finish what he had already commenced.

When I first gave M his culture stress assessment, he couldn't stop looking at it. With tears in his eyes, he said, 'This is real. I mean, this is a real thing?'

I said, 'Well, yeah. Why is this so emotional for you?'

'Because my entire life I've been told I am an angry Aboriginal. This [culture stress] makes sense to me. I now know what I need to do.'

Trauma is often referred to as 'the angry disorder' as the main emotion people emit is anger. Anger is a useful emotion to access during trauma – as I have said previously, it provides a rest from vulnerability because it is a high-energy state. You want to 'visit' anger, but you do not want to 'live there'; that would be the therapist 'narrative'. However, we are really looking at the extent to which access to internal restraints are evident and in a way that ensures anger does not lead to aggression.

The anger-reduction model in trauma occurs when the person's anger overwhelms them so much that they cannot express it or deal with it in a functional or adaptive way. This leads to them either turning the anger outwards (as in M's case) or inwards, through internalising disorders such as self-harm and depression.

The concept of culture stress allows trauma to be better explained and, yes, objectively quantified as racial trauma, which will lead to better strategies and insight around managing it. When I see people like M (and I've seen a lot of them), I often wish I had met them before their violent behaviour led them to me. If only I had seen them years ago, before they exploded in anger and murdered someone or harmed themselves. Like M, they hadn't recognised the build-up to it. The more we recognise this build-up and likely triggers, the greater the opportunity for prevention.

Importantly, culture stress is what is referred to as a 'dynamic risk factor' – those things that can be improved or changed through treatment.[14] We can then assess objectively how much improvement has been achieved.

Placing trauma under a cultural lens like this is critical to assessment because it tells the entire story. Mainstream assessments only tell part of the story, and the vast majority of Aboriginal people who come into contact with the justice system are being given mainstream assessments and tests. The 'reasonable person' test is a legal standard in which, based on the balance of evidence, any 'reasonable person' can understand why someone has done what they have done. This is simplistic, of course, but the test becomes incredibly difficult the greater the cultural barriers between the person and those passing judgement. It requires that people understand a very different worldview, one they have usually never been exposed to or had lived experience of.

There is established racial bias in juries, which results in non-white people being much more likely to receive the death penalty than white offenders. In Australia, Aboriginal people are up to eleven times more likely to be in prison than a non-Indigenous person, and twice as likely to receive a custodial sentence than a non-Aboriginal person.[15] The other-race effect, discussed in Chapter 1, means that it is easier for white jury members and judges to believe that 'black is bad' when they cannot relate to the experience of black people. They feel less empathy as a result, and 'reasonableness' is therefore affected by how similar they are to the perpetrator of the crime.

In Canada, it's very different for Indigenous people. The government there implemented, through legislation, the requirement that every Aboriginal person who comes into contact with the justice system have what is referred to as a Gladue report, an assessment that details specific factors that better explain the characteristics of Aboriginal offenders.

This is essentially what I provided for M. It was also one of the recommendations of the 2016 Royal Commission into the Protection and Detention of Children in the Northern Territory.[16] It has so far failed to be implemented. Incarceration rates continue to escalate.[17]

In M's case, the magistrate rang me to personally thank me for my assessment. I will always remember what he said.

'I have sat on the bench for over thirty years and I have seen a lot of Aboriginal people come through the system and in front of me. I have to say that I "get" racism, but I don't.'

'What do you mean?' I asked.

'As a white magistrate, if I make a call on racism, it will open the floodgates for every Aboriginal person to say it was about racism. How do you make a call on it when you don't really understand it? But your report and this idea of culture stress, I understand.'

M ended up getting an eighteen-month sentence, with twelve months suspended. He still rings me pretty regularly.

A few years after my assessment, he rang me and said, 'You remember that horrible thing I did all those years ago? You are the only person who will understand this, but it was the best thing that could have happened. Obviously not for my victim, but for me personally.'

'Why's that?'

'Because it forced me to look at my shit.'

And that's the best way to end the story of M.

Trauma in kids: The baby who didn't cry

M's childhood trauma began when he was old enough to remember it, even though he later buried that memory. But what about when the victim is an infant? How does this affect them later in life? Complex childhood trauma often leads to identity and personality disturbances, in addition to post-trauma symptoms. In cases where the carer is also the abuser, it shapes the child's vulnerable nervous system because they are solely dependent on carers to help them to feel safe, connected and calm.

A foster family had adopted a six-month-old baby, P, from a remote community. His mother and father, both deceased, were traditionally married. The trauma and abuse his birth parents inflicted on him was so extreme that it is among the worst I have heard of against an infant.

One of the most distressing aspects of abuse of infants and small children is that they are incapable of recalling trauma at a cognitive level. I often say that when it comes to trauma, there is nothing worse than having an 'incomplete narrative' because it becomes impossible to link their trauma-based reactions with their trauma experience. However, what we do know is that trauma stress reactions remain 'filed away' in the brain.

The work of Bruce Perry in childhood trauma has led to a significant evolution of our understanding of its impacts. His book *The Boy Who Was Raised As a Dog* is heartbreaking and compelling, and has rightly become the go-to text on C-PTSD.[18] The vulnerability of children and infants for their basic needs means that trauma impacts are at their greatest. This is because the brain develops at its most rapid rate in utero, and it continues this significant exponential growth from birth to age four. At age four, the brain is in fact 90 per cent adult size with most of the key neural networks occurring during this stage. During this vital time for growth, the child is the most ready and malleable. This means that they learn from those they depend on that the world is safe and predictable. When this love and support from their primary caregivers is consistent and predictable, their neural pathways become 'set' and reliant upon this safety. When abuse or harm occurs at this time, when we are at our most vulnerable, it disrupts this basic neural pathway development and leads to disorganised attachment (discussed in the previous chapter). For baby P, his father murdered his mother and then ended his own life, making P and his two siblings orphans. They were all fostered out separately.

Baby P was malnourished and spent two weeks in hospital prior to being placed with his foster family. When he arrived at their home, he had cigarette burn marks all over his body. He also had some bruises. There was a long-documented history of violence between his mother and father, including while his mother was pregnant, when she was hospitalised several times for a broken arm, broken ribs and other assaults. The police were called many times and the community nurse was all too familiar with the family.

So, when abuse like this occurs in infants, how does it manifest? Well, it doesn't always result in people becoming violent, but, as Bruce Perry says, 'It is the rare and strong person that can carry their trauma without having it spill into the next generation.'[19]

When P was fifteen years old, I became his case manager. He had just commenced his offending behaviour and had been charged with the physical assault of a woman. However, there was a question as to whether the assault was sexually motivated. Clearly, when sex and violence become linked, an extraordinarily dangerous individual is the result.

P's adopted family were elderly but extremely loving and, in many ways, completely unprepared for the challenges that P presented as he developed. Being Aboriginal themselves, they encouraged as much contact as possible with his extended family and community. They had successfully raised loving children who were all adults by the time P came to them. When he began offending, it was the first time the family had ever had contact with the justice system.

They struggled to cope. They had provided a loving and caring environment for P and couldn't make sense of his offending behaviour and certainly were not capable of linking his early trauma with his behaviour. How could they? He had been a baby, so he had no memory of what had occurred. The science on the impacts of trauma on neural pathways had not evolved to the extent that it has today. The reality is that, despite these advances in knowledge, how early trauma manifests is still highly complex and unpredictable.

In fact, when I first met P's foster carers, they commented on what a 'perfect baby' he had been. Despite the horror he had experienced as an infant, P was 'so easy' to look after. When I asked them what they meant by that, they replied with words I have found hard to forget.

'Well, he never, ever cried.'

'What do you mean he never cried?'

'Exactly that,' they both confirmed. 'Never.'

Babies cry because they are helpless. They cannot feed themselves. They cannot change their own nappies. They cannot soothe themselves. They are completely reliant on their carers. Crying is the only way they can draw attention to all their needs. So when they stop crying, they do so because crying has previously ended in torment for them. It's unthinkable and unfathomable what that little baby experienced when someone responded to his cries.

Had P been shaped by this early trauma? Had his trajectory into offending been set in stone when he was a baby? It was as easy to hope for the best but also expect the worst. P always seemed on guard. He was a tall boy for fifteen and was quiet and reserved. There was something about him that looked afraid, almost as if he was scared of what he was capable of. By the time he had served his probation for the physical assault, I had gone back to university.

Years later, picking up a newspaper, I saw P's full name in print. He had been convicted of raping a very elderly woman. I felt sick to my stomach.

I thought of his loving foster family and how they would be reconciling this with how they cared for him. I thought of the victim and how horrific this ordeal would have been, and of her family. I thought of the horror of what had occurred.

Was P destined to commit evil acts because of what had been set when he was an infant? The loving home life he had been given seemed to not be enough to have altered what had been done to him. Certainly, an additional component was that he also came from a background in which violence was normalised. His father had murdered his mother, and one of his brothers had also murdered someone. Did he ever have a chance to be anything but a product of nature and nurture?

The girl who stopped talking

When trauma occurs, you have experienced something beyond the 'normal' human experience. When multiple traumas occur, the capacity to cope becomes increasingly limited. And when these traumas happen to children, they cannot articulate how they feel so they will show you behaviourally, like P never crying as a baby.

The lack of control over traumatic events often causes survivors to need to control their environment post-trauma. There is certainly no greater method of controlling your environment than to stop talking. Here is the story of S.

When kids experience significant trauma, they obviously process it very differently to adults. Their stage of development dictates this, as children are still developing their cognitive capacity and their ability to ascribe meaning. They aren't capable of contextualising events and memories, which means that they make meaning of trauma behaviourally rather than cognitively. Diagnostic differences between child and adult trauma symptoms include children being more likely to model and mirror trauma by acting out the traumatic incident in play, and – in most cases – children suddenly changing their behaviour and/or regressing into previous developmental stages, such as toilet-training.

When I first met S, she was just five years old. Her mum attended my clinic with her. Pretty and wide-eyed, S looked like any typical girl that age, but she was very timid, hiding behind her mum, L, and grabbing onto her leg. L told me that she was struggling to get S to school and that S had stopped talking to everyone but herself and her husband.

S's developmental history was pretty unremarkable – normal birth, every developmental stage progressed as normal. She had some instances of 'regressing' verbally in the past, which is a common childhood trauma response. Selective mutism is a reasonably rare condition, which I have seen a few times in Aboriginal kids who have experienced significant trauma.

S's mum had, in her desire to find a better life for her and her three siblings, ended up taking community housing, but it was in the middle of several warring families and they had been caught in the crossfire. S's family had suffered three home invasions in eight months. L's description of them was horrific: mobs of people rushing through their home, breaking glass and furniture, throwing whatever they could. Some wore balaclavas, some hoodies. The darkness concealed most of their identities, but L knew who they were. Too terrified to report them to the police, she had hoped it would eventually die down.

Because L desperately wanted to get out of the 'ghetto', as she called it, I initially advocated for priority housing. However, the ridiculous bureaucracy insisted that because she had already been allocated a home, she could not be allocated another. Dealing with that was frustrating enough, but in between the stress of it all, S had stopped talking to everyone but her mum. Mothers, as we have learnt based on attachment, are the predominant 'safe haven' for children – this is biologically hardwired, but also socially constructed and even more so in Aboriginal communities.

When a child's world feels existentially unsafe, they will show distress behaviourally and in S's case, this meant non-verbally. Mutism seemed functional in the circumstances of trauma that was inherently loud and verbal, all of which could not be controlled. Retreating to a place of quiet was the functional aspect of dysfunction. Regressing developmentally is often a first indicator of a psychological issue in children, but it is always important to ensure they have been thoroughly checked medically to exclude any physical issues. There are not enough practitioners who spend the time being as thorough with assessment as they can be. It is the rigour of therapeutic training, to be drilled in unpacking explanations for behaviours. There are more than 400 mental illnesses defined by the DSM-5, and there are too many that have overlapping symptoms. For example, it would have been easy to diagnose S with some form of developmental delay or expressive language disorder, put her on the National Disability Insurance Scheme (NDIS) and have her labelled for life.

As I've said before: get assessment wrong, get treatment wrong, make things worse.

I was pretty confident we were dealing with traumatic and selective mutism. This is different to mutism, which tends to be more related to generalised anxiety. S had already gone through language development, so it was unlikely to be a language disorder, and she did not have generalised anxiety but rather trauma-based triggers. L described S waking at night with night terrors and describing images of the faces of the assailants and of the home invasions.

That was the good news. The bad news was that it would require a significant alteration of the current environment and a lot of time and effort to address. L agreed that the home had become a place of heightened fear and of constant checking. Every night, they would go through a routine with S of checking windows and doors and making sure everything was locked, to the point of obsession. All the doors had bolts and the family had purchased shutters so that there was no visible glass that could be broken.

The first step was to make the environment feel less threatening. Easier said than done after three home invasions. The family had decided, however, to move suburbs. Their house had clearly been targeted, for whatever reason, and it now represented fear. It is very hard to heal from trauma when you are still in it; still being triggered by daily reminders.

Until then, there were at least a few things that they could do. We know that there is a strong evidence base for the environmental and parental modelling of trauma, and parents should be conscious of this. Although in L's mind the constant checking was making everyone feel safe, it was actually also feeding S's fears. The need to be sure that everything was locked had become both obsessive and compulsive in her. S had even begun checking under the bed, in the wardrobe and anywhere else in the house that anyone could potentially hide.

The goal was to slowly reduce both the length and frequency of checking and replace it with distraction activities. At that moment, the daytime checking was occurring approximately every ten to fifteen minutes.

Additionally, L was to change the bedtime ritual from obsessional 'rechecking' down to a standard process of locking doors and windows that represented her normal, pre-invasion checks. This was scripted out and had to be followed. The rechecking was then replaced with other activities to distract, including a bedtime story and relaxation techniques for S.

The most important thing was for both parents to initially remove all pressure on S to speak, and to convey to her that they understood that there was a fear that made it hard for her to get words out. If she did not want to speak, then she would not be forced to.

The work eventually paid off, and S started to verbalise to more people.

There are many cases of children developing anxiety-based disorders as a result of their parents' post-trauma responses. The Bowraville serial murders, for which I provided an expert witness statement to the NSW parliamentary inquiry, is such an example. The community would describe Bowraville in two ways – Bowraville before the murders and Bowraville after the murders. When three children are murdered within several months of each other in a very small town, it forever alters the ability of people to feel safe, even decades later.

The outcome is that children learn that the world is unsafe. It is incredibly challenging because while anxiety can protect us from harm, our actions in checking for danger and teaching children to follow our lead can exacerbate a sense of threat, when children look to parents for a safe haven – and to tell them that they are safe.

What happens, though, when parents face the unimaginable – the loss of a child through suicide? How do you ever see the world as 'safe' again? How do you address a whole community's anxiety and trauma when multiple deaths by suicide have occurred? When pain, trauma and anxiety have become normalised as a response?

It's why my community work has been the greatest gift to me. Although healing individuals is why any of us go into the profession, so few of us get opportunities to work with entire collectively traumatised communities. It's not just about changing individuals – it's also about the opportunity of generational change because you are changing environments.

8

The Communities and Suicide Prevention:
Why do people choose to live?

In my suicide-prevention training, I start with a statement that speaks to the heart of a clinician's ability to work in this area: 'If you cannot put suicide on the table as an option for your clients, you cannot work in suicide prevention.'

I then ask them if they understand what I mean. Most nod their heads, but some look confused. So I repeat it: 'If you cannot put suicide on the table as an option for your clients, you cannot work in suicide prevention.'

By validating my clients' right to feel the way they do, I have helped many of them significantly shift in their suicidal impulses. It sounds like a stretch, but it can be that simple. What it does is reduce their resistance to change by saving the energy they'd otherwise have to spend explaining their impulses. Once validated, the client can then focus on the flip side – their reasons to live and exploring their motivations to do so.

But posing this question terrifies most clinicians. As I said earlier, all clients are resistant to change, to differing degrees. Therapists create resistance in clients by not properly acknowledging and validating their feelings. Most suicidal people do not experience validation, and instead have their feelings dismissed by others out of fear. That is ultimately why they seek out therapy.

What we do understand, based on the evidence and my clinical expertise, is that suicidal people have diminished problem-solving capacity and restricted cognitions.[1] Their thought processes and capacity to see beyond their pain have become limited. In these circumstances, suicide seems the only logical solution to escape their intolerable psychological torment.

As clinicians, our focus is to relieve that pain and increase the client's options. That starts with reducing their resistance. My way of reducing resistance is to tell them, 'That's one option. You can end your life.'

Then I pause, to let them sit with the validation.

After that, I say, 'Can you think of anything else that you can do?'

The next part is to search for their motivation to live.

As noted earlier, suicidal people have reduced problem-solving and restricted cognitions, so suicide seems like the only option. The moment you get them to think about alternatives and options, this increases their ability to problem-solve and the focus is always to find ways to reduce psychological the burden. This is a critical starting point.

As you get more experienced in suicide prevention, you develop go-to questions for clients, but frankly, it is just about having the confidence to understand not only the pain that drives people to suicide but also what lifts that pain. It is about clinical and cultural instincts. You can't learn it from a book; you can't speed it up because it takes being comfortable with discussing death. You have to hone your clinical instincts at the same time as your cultural instincts. Until my article on engaging suicidal Aboriginal clients was published in 2010 (which still has a massive readership, and speaks to the absence of other literature in this area), the latter was much harder because there was nothing to guide you – no training, no theory, nothing published. This made opening up suicidal thoughts in an Aboriginal client absolutely terrifying.

It's about energy

Another of my other go-to questions as a clinician is, 'What is good about suicide?' The client's answer is often very telling. By asking this question I am looking for emotions such as anger and defensiveness, and I predominantly get them. Many clients flash a look at me, come out of their slumped posture and say something aggressive like, 'What do you mean what's good about it?' This emotion is good. It tells me they have some motivation to live, motivation to argue against the idea of death.

Then my flip-side question is, 'What's less good?' This gets at their essential restraints. If nothing comes back, which is rare, my next go-to is the simplest question: 'What stops you?' Of course, the fact that the client has come to therapy suggests there is a window of hope that they want to live. It might be a faint one, but it's there.

When suicide impulses begin, they come with an ambivalence, meaning that most people will spend time weighing up whether to choose life or death. My role is to get them to tune into this, because insight and awareness is critical to reducing suicide risk. A sense of hope is what we are tapping into here.

People who are suicidal do not stay that way forever. Suicide impulses, of their nature, change. So, how we develop personal insight is by encouraging them to use their own experience of their suicide impulse changing. For example, I'll say to a suicidal client, 'Tell me about the last time you felt this way.'

'I was fair dinkum about it. I'd had enough. I could not stand the pain anymore. I was so angry.'

'What happened next?'

'Well, my cousin come over and got me out of the house. We went and played basketball.' Their energy shifts and their voice becomes animated.

'Ah, so your experience, then, is that things can change. Things can get better.'

This is what rolling with resistance looks like – using their own narrative and experience to guide them away from their suicidal impulses.

Fear is what prevents most therapists from doing this, and that is why skills development in isolation of a therapist's beliefs about death and suicide does not improve their confidence in working with suicide. Hearing someone's reasons for ending their life is hard and terrifying, which is why it is not for everyone. If that's the case, then suicide prevention is not for you, and that's okay. The best thing you can do as a clinician is recognise your limitations. I say this in another way: 'The smartest thing you can do as a therapist is to realise what you are *not* smart about'.

Refer on. Get your high-risk client to someone who is more comfortable with suicidal behaviours, even if it means getting them on the phone to a clinician. So many services, like the Indigenous-specific suicide crisis line 13YARN, provide this critical support.

Suicide risk assessment is one of the most complex areas to work in. It levels the majority of clinicians, no matter how brilliantly trained they are or how much they intend to help. Governments need to understand this and ensure that those on the front line are trained not only in terms of skills but also in terms of attitudinal drivers. It is so important because the data tells us that up to 30 per cent of clinicians will experience the suicide death of a client. It is complex, it is scary and very few of us understand what it is like to feel as though you are holding someone's life in your hands. I can tell you, having spent a lifetime in suicide prevention, that it challenges you at every level. It tests your core values about the right of people to choose death over life. It stretches you therapeutically, despite your training in best practice, and you remain terrified that you have missed something, long after you have left your at-risk client.

Throw culture into the mix and Aboriginal suicide prevention becomes the skill set of very few in this country. Indeed, multiple inquiries into suicides in Aboriginal communities have concluded that a lack of access to culturally appropriate services has contributed significantly to escalating suicide rates. Yet the training continues to fail clinicians – and, by extension, our communities – by not focusing on our beliefs and fears. The expectation placed on the average mental health counsellor to deal with the complexity of suicide prevention is unrealistic and the blame for the loss of lives by suicide, often media-generated during coroners' inquiries, is career-ending for too many. Governments have never understood this, and I have lost any hope that they ever will. They don't give community the respect of providing access to complex services despite death after death after death. They keep funding the same ineffective programs over and over again, and then wonder why suicides continue to escalate.

Assessing Aboriginal people for suicide risk

Until my PhD, no-one had ever considered that suicides were so high in Aboriginal communities not only because there were different causal pathways – which I discussed in Chapter 3 – but because the fundamentals of basic counselling skills and therapy had not been tested with at-risk Aboriginal people.

We are a world that does not like difference, and it is literally killing my people. Psychology is built on cultural exclusion, so no-one had ever really bothered to check or scientifically test these differences. In the words of Ted Lasso, if you assume, 'you make an ass out of you and me'.

The first issue is the pure volume of cultural barriers that exist between practitioner and client, many of which have nothing to do with clinical skills. It's overwhelming. To concretise this further, I always start my training sessions for practitioners with two simple dilemmas I have faced many times in my clinical life.

Example one: An Aboriginal elder comes to you distressed about the young kids in the community. She says that every pension day, they know she is getting her money and food so they come and humbug her. When she says no, they threaten to kill themselves. She doesn't know what to do.

Example two: An Aboriginal male has a history of suicidal behaviours. He has a strong cultural connection and only speaks bits and pieces of English. He has made a recent suicide attempt. The community says it is because he married 'wrong way'.

I ask participants in my workshops, who are all heavily trained in suicide risk assessment, how confident they feel about handling each example.

For the first one there is generally more confidence because these types of scenarios are common in many communities, where what is known as 'suicide gestures' will be used to meet a need. They are utilised by people to manipulate others, get a response and ultimately what they want. The end goal is not suicide, generally speaking, although every suicide threat needs to be unpacked therapeutically because there have been many instances in which people have died where the triggers seemed to be quite innocuous. However, for the most part, these types of suicide gestures can be managed behaviourally.

We have done this before in our high-risk families and communities by teaching concrete, rehearsed strategies of conflict resolution and effective communication in groups, based upon changing the predictability of the behavioural pattern. For example, if the vulnerable days are pension day – that's predictable. Make sure the elder is not at home or have someone there with them to reinforce new skills together when one falls down. If it is 'low level' and there is no aggression involved, teach elders conflict-resolution skills. People learn, for example, about vulnerability and there is no-one more vulnerable than elders. So, clinicians feel more comfortable with this one as it is more about teaching group behavioural change and less about complex aspects of culture. You cannot necessarily change people, but you can alter the predictability of patterns that have become normalised for them and communities.

The second example, however, is where clinicians always struggle significantly. The content of the case study has very little to do with skills in suicide prevention. It is completely about the cultural barriers that exist between client and therapist, which we call practitioner barriers. So, first, gender is a sub-culture in Aboriginal communities: men over here, women over there. Lore is a particularly complex barrier as lore men don't speak to women. And remember, Aboriginal culture is the most secretive in the world.

What happens if you are a white woman – as 79 per cent of psychologists are[2] – trying to undertake a suicide risk assessment of a lore man? How do you do that when the cultural barriers are so great that it renders you helpless? Your clinical training has been ineffective in guiding you around cultural complexity, resulting in leaving a client with unassessed and unmanaged risk.

You are taught at university that change involves a therapeutical alliance. It requires empathy and the ability to understand the worldview of your clients, putting yourself in their shoes. How is this possible when their world is so different to your own? When the reasons for wanting to live or die are not relatable to you?

These gaps can sometimes be unconscious or invisible because the training has not equipped practitioners to identify them and do so in a way that is culturally safe. The training, for example, does not teach you that gender (lore men not speaking to women) and hierarchy (elders, lore men and healers having more 'power') are critical barriers that practitioners have to overcome with Aboriginal clients. Let alone that many of the counselling micro skills that are the building blocks of therapy are often ineffective with Aboriginal clients.

These building blocks – such as open and closed questioning, and reflective feedback – are meant to create client empathy and ensure that practitioners can get to 'the story', but they often have the opposite effect with Aboriginal clients. Closed questions, for example, will force Aboriginal people into an answer, which often leads to people agreeing with the question because of what Diana Eades refers to as 'gratuitous concurrence' or the 'yes syndrome'.[3] Also, self-disclosure is a 'no, no' in mainstream training, but it's essential with Aboriginal clients because as part of a high-context culture, relationships and personally liking your therapist is the most important agent for change.

None of this is taught in standard training, so it is no wonder that therapists struggle. The training fails to explain that the process of extracting information is paramount to outcomes for Aboriginal clients. In risk assessment for suicide, a clinician's role is to identify not only risk but also restraints that stop people. How can they do this when they cannot access that story because of cultural barriers?

Yet practitioners continue to be churned out with training that is tested on non-Aboriginal people alone, and then they are expected to deal with one of the most complex cultures in the world. The system is setting people up to unwittingly do harm, and we don't get into this profession to do harm.

The Australian Psychological Society made a formal apology to Aboriginal people in 2016 for ignoring our history and for the damage caused by exclusion. I am currently working on a comparative analysis of the content of Australian Psychological Society journals with similar ones in New Zealand, the United States and Canada. Across the three APS journals, since the 2016 apology, there have been an average of five articles with Indigenous content published per year. This includes, however, a 'special edition' – if you exclude that, there were just three articles per year. What is even more disgraceful is that my analysis shows that 70 per cent of authors of 'Indigenous papers' had non-Indigenous lead authors. There is a lot of currency in being an 'expert' on Indigenous issues as an academic, without actually engaging with said population at a therapeutic level. Moreover, the APS board still has no Aboriginal representation. Oh, but it has 'interest groups' – because nothing says 'standing in equal power' like giving us our own separate group. Invite highly skilled Indigenous clinical psychologists to sit at the *same* table, and then see what outcomes you get.

If you are sharing space but not sharing power, it's tokenism.

So, how do you overcome these cultural barriers? You teach practitioners how to identify and address them. The greater the differences, the more difficult client empathy is, which I call cultural empathy. There is very little focus on this in a practical sense in training, such as teaching concrete strategies to 'get at the story' based on cultural differences. So, we pose culturally complex client scenarios in our training and get practitioners adept at picking apart the barriers. It is interesting that of these activities, it's not uncommon for practitioners to get around 10 per cent of the cultural barriers. The learning is significant, but it wouldn't be *this* significant if they were trained properly.

Here is an example of a scenario we work through. A lore man having thoughts of suicide is referred by Aunty, who says that the community has said he has been 'sung' to harm himself due to cultural wrongdoing. So, cultural mapping and understanding community context is the most important component of determining the lore man's suicide risk. However, psychology teaches you that engagement is with individuals and their internal pain, not with the community and the cultural context of that pain. There is a greater emphasis on the client-centred approach of focusing on their internal struggle and life-and-death weigh-up alone. The research has increasingly labelled this as reasons for living (RFL) and reasons for dying (RFD). As well as representing this internal weigh-up, these terms also tap into the core suicidal behaviour driver, which is hopelessness – not only in terms of a loss of hope for the future, but also an inability to shift intolerable pain.[4] RFD is now showing up as a much more stable predictor of suicide, and this makes sense in my clinical experience because those clients with more RFD also feel a greater degree of psychological burden that is more overwhelming for them to 'lift'. However, what happens if the RFD and RFL are cultural, which are not explored in standard risk assessments and which are ultimately external to the individual? Does this helplessness and hopeless burden increase? And how do clinicians reduce what is culturally driven?

Narrative processes are always the most effective in suicide prevention because they take people into their high-risk situations and allow them to develop strategies that are more concrete and specific to their individual suicide triggers and impulses. As I've already noted, any strategy based on a real-life scenario and then practised in real life – not only to mimic triggers but to practise those concrete strategies – is highly successful with Aboriginal clients. Narrative also enables clinicians to identify cultural triggers that may be maintaining suicide risk.

So, what's different about suicide risk assessment for Aboriginal people?

Well, the risk factors are different for a start, which is critical and had *never* been explored until my PhD. It makes sense that they wouldn't be the same because we are *so* over-represented in the suicide statistics. There has been a failure to determine risk factors that are specific to Aboriginal people and that should be the focus of clinical intervention and prevention efforts. The difference is not something that psychology or mental health has explored to an extent that underpins the therapeutic focus of the work that practitioners do or explains the statistical over-representation of Aboriginal people. Again, the Ted Lasso line about the danger of assuming comes to mind.

Second, the manner in which assessment is undertaken means that practitioners are taught to sit outside of their clients as 'all-knowing' experts. They are instructed to go through the areas of risk that increase the likelihood of someone converting their impulses and thoughts to behaviour. Meanwhile, the clients themselves are not provided with any practical guidance about what to do to prevent a build-up to suicide impulses (what risk 'feels' like), including internal factors – such as thoughts and physical reactions to impulses – and external factors. It was obvious to me from the start that the greater the client's insight, the greater their control over their suicidal impulses. This was particularly important for Aboriginal people, who were dying as a direct result of having no services available. Frankly, as psychologists we are taught to treat our clients like idiots. There's no reason they should not have everything explained to them in a psycho-educational way. Knowledge is power, and most of our mob are dying by suicide due to a lack of culturally and clinical competent services; in this context, knowledge alone can quite literally be lifesaving.

Getting risk factors wrong has resulted in a significant amount of suicide risk being missed. Due to the different nature of Aboriginal suicides, several entrenched, long-term risk indicators are often absent in Aboriginal people, meaning that we will often appear less at risk then we really are. Institutions spend too much time looking backwards after someone has died by suicide and shockingly little energy on trying to prevent it. The profession itself takes no responsibility for it. It's always *our* problem to fix.

It takes a whole community to raise a child. When suicides are so entrenched, it takes a whole community to ensure a child becomes an adult. And it should be seen as every psychologist's responsibility to help. Child and suicide do not belong in the same sentence. The likelihood that an Aboriginal child will die by suicide is more than *five times* that of a non-Aboriginal child.[5] When an Aboriginal child dies in this country, there's a 40 per cent chance that they will do so by suicide.

I first became involved in suicide prevention not by choice, but because I felt a responsibility to do so. During my PhD, I knew that addressing these suicide rates was always going to be highest on my agenda. I was also 'gently shoved' by more than one elder telling me I 'had to' fix what was going on. In the late 1990s, suicide rates in Australia generally were escalating. To address this, prevention programs began to be funded and, as a result, the suicide rate in some age cohorts of non-Aboriginal people plateaued then remained stable until the 2000s. However, the lack of investment in Aboriginal suicide prevention saw these rates continue to escalate.

I couldn't bear going to any more funerals for children who had died by suicide. I could no longer watch their bereaved parents being blamed for the deaths and having to read headlines that screamed about Aboriginal communities being plagued by abuse and alcohol. It's disgusting and *never* happens when a non-Indigenous child dies by suicide. I have shed a lot of tears over the politics involved in Aboriginal suicide prevention – for my community, for the bereaved, for those who put self-interest above what is right, and in frustration at the 'waste' of my expertise and training. Suicide prevention shouldn't only be for those who can afford it.

My work in suicide prevention started and continues because of the power of community and 'grassroots' voices. When someone says to me, 'I'm just one Aboriginal person. What can I do?' I tell them this story of the two girls from Derby.

As my PhD started to evolve and I learnt more and more about how different suicide risks and impulses are for Aboriginal people, I started to put together original content in my training for practitioners. Although it was basic stuff, in 2001 it was like I had split the atom, given how 'white' all the 'Aboriginal-specific' training in suicide prevention was. In fact, I once said during one of my keynote presentations that I love it when people say they have an 'Aboriginal-specific program' and it's just a mainstream program with dot paintings on the cover. The comment got a standing ovation. I guess it was something people needed to hear publicly. I have never been accused of being indirect in my messaging. I am pretty straight-out, but it's not for shock value. My psychology training has been great in helping me make points because I never say anything I can't defend or that the evidence doesn't support.

At this stage of my career, I started to do a lot of work with David Vicary, a non-Indigenous clinical psychologist who worked in child protection and had just such a love of working with Aboriginal people. He was one of the very few non-Indigenous clinicians who actually got it. He loved the Kimberley and so we started to do more and more work together. In 1997, Dave and I were in Broome delivering a two-day workshop for around thirty people from the entire Kimberley, the epicentre of the suicides. I always feel a massive sense of responsibility when I go into these high-risk regions because of the training's importance, but also frankly because no-one else was going up there to train up the workforce. They were just too scared of what they didn't know. So, the fact that there were two clinical psychologists in Broome – and particularly that one was Aboriginal – was significant.

As the training started, two young girls walked into the room. I estimated they were about fifteen years old. As they sat with the adults, who were all trained mental health professionals, they seemed actively engaged – furiously writing notes and asking questions that belied their youth. These kids had obviously 'seen it all', which both inspired and saddened me. How many of our kids don't get to be kids because of what they are exposed to? I had seen too many of them already.

At the end of the first day, we stayed and chatted. I have a firm policy – or, better put, cultural protocol – of *never* leave a training workshop until everyone is gone, even if it means I am speaking to participants until seven o'clock at night. As we finished the 'yarns' and had packed up, these two kids were still there, waiting. They clearly had something on their minds, and they didn't hold back or disappoint.

'Why are you training these service providers?' one of the girls said.

'Well, that's what you do,' I said. 'You train up services with the idea that they become better at responding to suicide risk.'

'Yeah, but when that fulla try and kill himself, he don't kill himself nine to five, Monday to Friday. It's two or three in the morning or on weekends, when things get rough. We're the ones dealing with it all the time. We're the ones getting pulled out of bed and trying to stop people. We're the ones too frightened to wake up in case someone has died overnight. So why aren't you training us up?'

I hate it when kids are smarter than me, I thought to myself.

'Umm, well, no-one does that. No-one trains community and young people in suicide prevention.'

'Well, you need to come to Derby and train us mob.'

As I looked at them, I felt embarrassed by my profession, but I also understood there was an opportunity here to do something truly significant.

'We are happy to do it,' I said, 'but we don't have any funding. We need to get something to feed people and for the venue.'

I looked at Dave and he just nodded. So, we gave them that commitment. We were both certain this was something that needed to be done, regardless of how hard we knew it was going to be.

What we didn't anticipate was the politics. This would be the start of the attempts to white-ant and dismantle my work, and sadly it predominantly came from Indigenous advisers to government on Indigenous suicide prevention.

Months later we realised that these two girls had contacted the Office of Aboriginal Health about the workshop and had asked for funding for some Derby forums. Fortunately, a wonderful lady called Maureen O'Meara, who just happened to be a Derby local and was reasonably high up in the WA Office of Aboriginal Health (OAH), also saw the opportunity and particularly that it was being generated by young people who had 'sampled the merchandise', so to speak, and were providing strong 'cultural vouching' for the forums.

So, through months of meetings and consultations that were all about the politics of 'outsiders' coming into the Kimberley – and not at all about what the communities themselves wanted – we had to convince the key stakeholders in the Kimberley that a whole-of-community suicide intervention program needed to be delivered in Derby.

All that wrangling was so overwhelming that I almost gave up. But I kept thinking about those young girls and what they had to deal with, so I just manned up and kept going.

Eventually, the service refused to free up any of its suicide prevention funding to assist. However, Maureen was able to find surplus in the state budget and begged for it to be allocated to the forums. This was the princely sum of $20,000 for *everything*: airfares, accommodation, printing, time to prepare, after-hours counselling, venue, food … the list went on and on. And don't even start me on the overwhelming number of hours that we put into preparation, counselling and follow-up. At one stage we calculated that the 'cost' of providing interventions was $194 per person, but we still had to find money for insurance, admin and every other expense associated with running a business because we were just being engaged on a fee-for-service basis, without any guarantee that this would continue unless there was an identifiable 'surplus' in the health department budgets at the end of each financial year. We would hold our breath to see if this was the case every year.

The trouble was that this had to go through the local Aboriginal medical services. They would see 'consultancy fees' of \$20,000 for six days' work and not grasp that it had to pay for everything. It destroyed my reputation and created a false narrative that I am 'all about money'. Yet 'non-profit' services were receiving millions in government funding and not having the same slurs thrown at them or achieving actual intervention with high-risk clients like we were. Nor had they achieved in decades what I had in a week, based solely on the numbers and outcomes.

Dave and I were now very conscious that we needed to deliver on this opportunity, not just because of the ethical and moral responsibility we both felt at a very deep level to the community, but because of the additional pressure of being 'on display' due to the politics surrounding this issue. Many people who had quarantined this significant suicide prevention funding for a long time were more than happy to see us fail. That's blunt, but it's also the sad reality of what has limited the reach of my programs.

Compensation for time is pretty straightforward, you would think, but when you are an Aboriginal woman in private business, you are deemed to be making money from people's pain and trauma. Well, I have also taken that out of the equation by doing most of my community and all my direct counselling and assessment work for no cost for twenty-five years. I have also paid personally for high-risk clients to see a psychologist because of the number of highly funded services that would refuse to free up their funding for them. My personal funding of research and development has just been a given, but it's insanity for someone in private business and as a sole practitioner. My business model has always been about creating an irrefutable evidence base that cannot be challenged – that's the psychologist in me. From a business perspective, product development is high-risk, but paying for it myself has also meant no overheads or sharing of profits, so there is potential for an associated reward; however, that always takes time. The negativity has had very little impact on my business success for those who are interested in outcomes.

Unfortunately, our government personalises their decisions. If you are 'not liked' – because you are critical of them – you are cancelled. I am outspoken. I am critical but not for the sake of it. As a subject-matter expert, I am very clear about what needs to be done and why. Politicians used to appreciate the existence of people like me and respected our expertise. Egos in leadership now mean that if someone doesn't like you for whatever reason, community access to your programs will be impossible.

I was called in to present to the Community Safety and Family Support Cabinet Sub-Committee on 29 April 2019 on the spate of Indigenous suicides. In the presentation, I said that I had shown the WASC-Y/A tools to their 2016 parliamentary inquiry, making the really distressing point that eighteen months after I provided them to their own inquiry, thirteen Aboriginal young people had died without a mental health assessment. I said that this stuff keeps me awake at night. Yet this, like every meeting I have ever had with a politician over the last twenty-five years, resulted in no funding or even public philosophical support for my work.

I have spent two decades watching millions being thrown at unskilled non-Aboriginal practitioners for their untested mainstream programs that have zero measurable outcomes. The difference is that these programs are lauded and seen as altruistic. The irony is that I have never been attacked for my *outcomes* – it's always about having to pay me. As if those who attack me aren't getting paid for their programs. As if they all work for free.

I have been asked more times than I can count, 'Why doesn't government fund you?' And I always reply diplomatically, 'That's up to them to answer.'

But the real answer is that they don't want to pay me – for my time, my tests or my programs. It's as simple as that.

My true salvation has always been in community because they can 'see through you', as one Nungkari from the Northern Territory said to me. What he meant was that we can see your spirit – we know you come with good spirit, a good heart. It is always where the support comes from that matters the most.

As Aboriginal people, the failures have been because we have so few people around the table who aren't either government-funded or a version of it. Worse than that, we need to have leaders who have done more than simply sit on government advisory boards their entire lives. How did this become our yardstick of leadership? 'How many advisory boards have you sat on?' Try building something from nothing, without support or without funding – it's bloody hard. But it is where we all need to be as Aboriginal people, going out with zero safety net and achieving success beyond and despite all expectations.

Achieving the impossible!

So in between the politics of trying to appease everyone – except, ironically, bereaved communities – we had to put together unique content on Aboriginal suicide prevention for *three* different contexts: service-provider training, a community workshop and a workshop for at-risk youth. Even twenty-three years later, these programs do not exist outside of mine. And this content remains the literal 'holy grail' of outcomes that had never been achieved.

I managed to throw most of it together in a few months, but sleep was non-existent. I have always been obsessed with getting things done, mostly to my own personal detriment. I would sit at my computer for weeks without a lot of downtime. I just can't let things go until I have an answer. I pulled out whatever content I could find in books, journals and the little that was online. Fortunately, I had a lot of clinical experience with Aboriginal people and communities. I understood what worked and what was needed. But it was still overwhelming, given that no-one had done it before.

I started with some broad, universal information that was contained in all suicide prevention training: suicide myths, what was linked with suicide risk, what suicide risk 'looked like', how to speak to suicidal clients etc. Then we had to figure out how to deliver this content to the three very different groups, which had never been done before, not just in Australia but also internationally. All that existed were mainstream programs, heavily

227

funded to the tune of millions but making zero impact in those high-risk communities.

I also had to factor in the complexity of working with people who were bereaved, including parents who had experienced their worst nightmare. Yet we were being white-anted for wanting to help. For over twenty years it has done my head in that this was the daily reality, and for many years I had to back out of any work in the Kimberley due to the politics around me, sending my well-trained staff instead. I understood that my presence would lead to so much negativity purely because I was in private business that I had to make that really hard decision.

The Kimberley, having the highest suicide rates nationwide by a country mile, was always where I wanted to work. If you fix the Kimberley suicide rate, the difference between the Aboriginal and non-Aboriginal rates falls dramatically. However, the politics that drove who was able to get in there and who wasn't was too distracting and energy-depleting for me. Fortunately, there were plenty of high-risk communities across Australia that didn't come with the same politics and who adored me and my work. Frankly, the work was hard enough. It doesn't sit well with me, still to this day, that I didn't take it on more – particularly given the massive community support for the work. But I was one person in private practice with no resources; there were only so many battles I could fight.

To date, the Kimberley still has the highest suicide rate in the country. Nothing has changed. Except there has been zero engagement with me or my company since these enormously successful forums were delivered there in 2003.

The program of the day was called 'gatekeeper training', whereby community gatekeepers were trained to respond to suicides. It was yet another mainstream program that had good intentions but failed to address the causes of Aboriginal suicide risk. The greater problem, though, was training people to be suicide prevention workers when they had no previous mental health training or qualifications. As someone with more than twenty years' experience in this field,

I still find it extraordinarily challenging. The idea that this could be taught as a 'one-off' was so dangerous.

Community were being 'weaponised' to respond to the most complex issues for a pittance of what the mainstream services were getting for their ineffective, 'evidence-based' programs. It was infuriating.

We reached a low point in 2019 when, in the aftermath of the Fogliani inquiry, Minister for Indigenous Australians Ken Wyatt announced that people in remote communities on CDEP would be trained to become frontline responders to suicides. At that point you didn't have to wonder anymore why suicides were escalating. It seemed that no-one understood how complex this issue was. I wrote a heavily critical opinion piece titled 'Funding football programs is not suicide prevention'.[6] Someone needed to call out the absurdity of it all and what was being put up as 'suicide prevention'.

Finally, after a few months, we had some basic content. We then had to rely on our skills as therapists, and thank god both Dave and I were pretty passionate therapists. We were also really good at role-playing, which would come in handy because the vast majority of our groups spoke English as a second language and needed to visually see it in action.

What many people fail to understand is that effectiveness in this really complex area has two components to it: content and process. Aboriginal people are more concerned with process and protocols than content. So, although we had good content (well, good enough) and massive amounts of lived experience to answer participants' difficult questions, it was more important that the community was okay with us. So the first thing Dave and I had to do was get permission from the community and earn their respect. Then, when we got the green light, we spent time in Derby meeting elders and key stakeholders. They were long, exhausting days. Getting permission was within cultural protocol, but it was also important for elders to 'check us out' to see if our 'lian' and 'ngarlu' (words for 'spirit') was good. In every single community, this has always been the first part of our work – not engaging with service providers but with mob and elders. It is why outreach services have always been the most effective with Aboriginal people.

What no-one talks about is the 'growling' that elders give you as part of this process. If you have never been growled by an elder, you haven't done community work. It's predictable in that you develop instincts for what is a 'growl' and when you have reached the point of no return. I have seen people spend millions and millions on recruitment strategies and elders have it nailed by a 'cultural growl'. It sorts out who will stay the path from those who won't. Fortunately, my experience is that communities are extraordinarily patient if you come from a place of respect and have good intentions. They are always tuned into that and have good 'bullshit detectors'.

The standard script goes something like this: 'Who your mob?' 'What you doing here?' 'Who have you spoken with?' 'Who you going to deliver this to?' 'How are you going to deliver it?'

Everything is about process and protocols. Get that wrong and no matter how skilled you are or how good your program is, you won't get to deliver it if you do not focus on the key relationships in the communities. I have been able to get into dozens of the highest-risk communities in Australia and this always works. We are really drilled in respect largely because we believe in it and in the power of elders and communities to get things done that are valuable to them.

But that is not where our work ends. The problem with government is that they think this is where their work ends – at engagement, at needs analysis and consultation. Community should only be asked what their needs are. They should not be expected to fix things. That's the role of people like me – subject-matter experts.

After our baptism of fire was over, we were ready to deliver something no-one ever had, with what felt like the eyes of the world on us. The Kimberley had long had the highest rates of suicide and we were doing something that was as high risk as it came. But we knew we had to try. There was significant anecdotal evidence from community, including the young Derby girls, that kids were making attempts or in some cases dying by suicide in the middle of the night or on weekends, when the scant number of services were not available. The existing coroners' reports confirmed it – rather than fitting the 'standard' plan ensuring that no-one would stop or rescue them, most Aboriginal people were dying in places where they should have been stopped, such as on front verandahs of homes in the middle of communities.

My clinical expertise at this stage was a significant 'bonus' (if you could call it that) – I'd had the horrific experience of interviewing around 130 at-risk Aboriginal youth in the past year for my PhD. So I had good instincts for suicide impulses and how to address them in both individuals and communities. I understood not only what risk looked like but also what prevented it.

Suicides in Aboriginal communities look different. If we keep checking for mainstream risk factors, we'll miss the right signs. When I first started screening at-risk Aboriginal kids with the WASC-Y, I developed a set of go-to questions. One of these spoke to the lack of planning in suicidal Aboriginal people and the highly reactive, impulsive nature of their risk compared to non-Aboriginal people. I would ask them, 'When you feel worst in yourself, when you can't stop the thoughts, is it that you genuinely want to die or do you just want the "shit" to stop?'

(PAUSE)

'Do you understand the difference?'

'Yes.'

In 100 per cent of cases, the Aboriginal kids replied: 'I just want the shit to stop.'

Now, this is not underselling how at risk these kids are. What it reflects is a consistency in what defines that risk. First, suicidal people lack problem-solving capacity, which means that emotions feel overwhelming and communication becomes compromised. This is for a multitude of reasons, and it's pretty consistent with compromised attachment styles in which avoidance or anxiety overrides the ability to communicate. Second, suicide does not fit the 'belief system'. Aboriginal culture is one in which there is consistently an external attribution made to causality. So, serious sickness, including mental ill-health, is often attributed to *external forces or reasons*. This external attribution belief system means that when ill-health occurs, individuals will most likely attribute it to some external wrongdoing, which is likely to be culturally based[7] – for example, 'doing something wrong culturally' or being 'paid back' for wrongdoing are common attributions made to mental health conditions.[8] This reflects the intertwining of spirituality and relationships with family, land and culture.[9]

For practitioners, the challenge then becomes 'shifting' external attributions in a way that becomes more individually manageable. While there may indeed be complex cultural realities that need to be understood better, this can also manifest as a dominant external locus of control. In practical terms, my experience is that Aboriginal clients will predominantly default to external reasons for their suicidal thoughts – for example, 'that fulla was drinking', 'his woman was nagging him' and 'he was "sung"' or other cultural wrongdoing.

This is tough because suicide is ultimately about an internal weighing up of life and death, so achieving this shift added a layer of complexity to what was already a highly complex issue – and it had to be a critical part of practitioner training. Why? Because the research consistently shows that those who externally attribute causality have the highest rates of suicide.[10] It also means that there is significantly greater default stigma and blame around suicides for Aboriginal people. Specifically, if there are only external reasons for people dying by suicide, then the attribution or 'meaning made' is often that the person or the bereaved should be 'blamed' for it.

There is a significant difference between what I call proximal and distal risk factors. A proximal factor is the immediate trigger, such as alcohol or an argument with an intimate partner, while a distal one is what is actually causative of suicide risk, such as trauma or compromised attachment. Both need to be addressed in treatment, but blame is consistently solely laid on proximal factors – and this is just one of the specific cultural factors I have found in my research that have led to suicides continuing to escalate.

At the same time as these forums, my PhD was uncovering critical information that suicide risk factors were different for Aboriginal people. Emerging data was telling us that most of the suicides were highly impulsive and often triggered by an intimate relationship breakdown. People in the most at-risk cohorts appeared to have 'overreacted' to conflict and lacked the tools to 'self soothe'.

This is very common in those who have compromised attachment and trauma. Essentially, those who have not developed secure attachment from childhood remain highly reactive, highly impulsive. Trauma, as we have learnt, increases the odds of compromised attachment, which often manifests as heightened reactivity to interpersonal conflict or an inability to self-soothe. This finding debunked and challenged every single bit of theory we understood about suicide causal pathways – and this was significant. If suicides were highly impulsive rather than accounted for by depression, as we understood it to be in non-Aboriginal populations, it is quite literally a 'mic drop' moment for every aspect of preventing Indigenous suicides – from risk assessment and treatment to how policy is formed and practitioners are trained.

Eventually I had gathered enough information that I was beginning to understand the nature of Aboriginal suicides, enabling me to develop unique content. But across *three* different groups and with a psycho-educative focus? Teaching whole communities how to address complex suicide behaviours? That had *never* been done before. No-one who knows me could ever accuse me of taking the easy path.

On to Derby

I mostly used the plane trip to Broome to go through the content. I was just starting out in my career while Dave was already a pretty experienced practitioner, so he was nowhere near as stressed as I was. There was also, of course, the additional stress of the entire Aboriginal community who had suffered for so long from decades of suicides, and me wanting to make an impact for them – no pressure! Boy, was I stressed. I went over and over and over the content until it was so rehearsed there wasn't a minute of space in the entire six days of workshop! I laugh now at this, given that I deliver workshops for days and days without referring to a note. But, of course, everyone starts out like this. Public speaking is the most feared thing in the world, even more than death.

Once we landed in Broome, we drove to Derby. The two-hour car trip helped alleviate some of my overwhelming nerves. Dave and I were best mates and we spent a lot of time laughing. I love the extremes of laughter, sadness, tears and all the range of emotions. Community work is always like that. The times I have laughed the hardest, cried the most and felt the most love have been, hands down, during all of the remote community work.

The workshops were to be held in the King Sound Resort. Like any regional town, Derby was massive on service and food, and I do love to eat, being a fitness fanatic who needs fuel. Everything in small towns is always about food and company. We ended up becoming great friends with the King Sound staff; I think they were initially afraid of the idea of two psychologists coming to town to run a full week of workshops with mob from all over the Kimberley, but that dissipated pretty quickly as Dave and I both love a joke and a yarn and are quick-witted like brother and sister.

On the first day, though, my nerves were at their peak. As usual Dave was too busy making jokes to worry about much, and frankly, that's why I loved training with him. When I struggled, he instinctually knew to take over. He also taught me a lot about just trusting myself to know what I know. I was still a bit 'scripted' in my training delivery, but I was able to let go during the acting parts and the role-plays. We learnt very quickly that the community understood complex things when they saw them in action, rather than written down or through complex explanations. Everything had to be simple but without talking to people as if they are idiots. These guys understood complex human behaviour. They understood suicides and mental health because they had lived with it more than anyone else. So, we had to explain things in layperson's terms, but not disrespect them.

We role-played as much as possible and especially anything they needed to remember, such as risk assessment and signs and symptoms of depression. We also used visuals to ensure this information was concretised. Everything had to be capable of being retrieved from people's memories really efficiently, so we used our knowledge of memory retrieval and cognitive learning differences to ensure that information was more likely to be retained. The work of Judith Kearins tells us that visual memory is a significant learning strength in Aboriginal people[11] – in fact, it's how I learn.

So, for basic counselling skills, through a visual role-play medium we reframed this as 'how to "yarn good way"' with someone you might be worried about. The funniest part was when Dave pretended to be a female client called 'Davina'. Dave is a big bloke who is so white he's actually pink. Mob would call him 'the big pinky'. It was hilarious seeing him role-play being a young Aboriginal girl who was my suicidal client, and the mob regularly chuckled about it. You know something is funny when you have what I call 'laughter afterburn' – something you laugh about well after it has actually happened.

We showed how to deal with conflict 'good way' and 'bad way'. Then we asked the community to pick the differences and practise the 'good way' techniques, observed their application and corrected by role-modelling. (We call this *orienting techniques*.) We also demonstrated that negative self-talk feeds depression through a role-play where Dave yelled negative thoughts from a corner while I showed the non-verbal expressions of the sad, depressed person having those negative thoughts. Then, as Dave yelled out more positive 'thoughts', I started to show a different, more positive non-verbal response. The idea was that the community could see that it was the thoughts that led to behaviours and actions.

We got all the way to teaching complex suicide risk assessments and the signs and symptoms of depression, using mnemonics as visual aids with people who had English as a second or third language. Mnemonics are simple strategies to help memorise information. It is always effective with visual-spatial learners. Again, Kearins's work formed the foundation of the 'how' in all my clinical and community work. I've always delivered everything visually – through role-plays, mnemonics and so on. For example, with risk assessment, each of the components had a letter that represented it so that together they spelt a whole word. The signs and symptoms of depression became, laughingly, ASMICEPISS – each letter stood for a different symptom. People would have a giggle, but they *never* ever forgot it. We know this because we tested the skills retention. Plus, I have had the funny experience of having people track me down in different locations to say things like, 'I went to your training ten years ago … ASMICEPISS! Hahaha!' I am not kidding.

However, this is a really important method to use because it is about tapping into the learning preferences to ensure skills retention. Too many words will never work with Aboriginal people due to language barriers and words requiring context for them to be comprehended.

Going through the suicide risk assessments and depression information was powerful stuff, but heavy-going. There were so many bereaved communities in the workshops that the full day of training was only the start of the actual work we had to do. We would regularly have participants triggered by the content and so we'd have to go out to do makeshift counselling and support. As is the nature of grief and trauma, it was unpredictable, but we just had to deal with it.

The story of T

'Tracy, I can finally stop blaming myself.'

These words from a bereaved parent in our group have stayed with me for over twenty years. If you can lift the burden of grief, even just a little bit, for a bereaved parent, you have more than done your job.

During one of our early workshops, we were doing our usual community consultations (that is, asking for permission to work in the community) when I first met T, who asked to meet with Dave and myself. Her son had passed away by suicide just three weeks prior to us coming to the community.

We spent a bit of time with T and her daughter. They were determined to be part of the workshops, but Dave and I were both concerned that it was just too early and that their grief was way too raw. But T was so very determined to try to understand the inexplicable.

It was one of the bravest things I have ever seen – T determined to face her grief with full force. Despite our concerns, Dave and I both understood that you should never argue with a bereaved parent – or anyone who is grieving – about what they instinctually know they need to do. You can point out the landmines, of course, and then prepare to protect them, but everyone is different.

T represented what I find is most common in suicide bereavement: an immediate and, sadly, often lifelong search for answers. But these are answers that, realistically, they will never completely have. The best we can do is inform bereaved parents of what we understand about suicide and what tends to drive it, but we can't completely explain it.

So, T and her daughter, bless them both, sat through two days of service-provider workshops, two days of community workshops and two days of youth workshops. On day two of the service-provider workshop, I explained the complex relationship between depression and suicide via a visual diagram that I had spent days working on.

Trying to explain this to a group of Aboriginal community/ elders/parents who had not had any mental health training was difficult. Then add into the mix that so many were bereaved. The stress and emotion of those workshops is hard to fully explain. I felt such a sense of responsibility to get it right, and there was so much pain to manage and navigate. We often wondered what the hell we were doing – and the fact that no-one had *ever* done this before meant you couldn't rely on your clinical and cultural instincts to get you through it.

And then you had moments – too many that overwhelm you – when you know you have had a hand in someone's healing. So few people get to do that for someone. And suddenly the time, the pain and the exhaustion become completely irrelevant.

We psychologists get to walk away from suicide bereavement. We don't have to live with the overwhelming pain of it or the constant sense of blame. Our clients don't. The least we can do is show up for them when they need us.

Depression can be the destination to suicide, but not *necessarily* for everyone.

I still use the diagram I came up with then twenty years later in my training. I have given it to so many practitioners to use with their Aboriginal clients. First, I described depression and its various depths. We teach people the major signs and symptoms of depression based on the ASMICEPISS mnemonic – the more symptoms you have, the more depressed you are. However, there is a big difference between having depression symptoms and being clinically depressed.

You need to have had at least five of these symptoms for at least two weeks, in accordance with the clinical guidelines from the DSM-5. You are also assessed for the extent to which your symptoms impair you. We know that 68 per cent of the general population will show signs and symptoms of depression, but only 16–20 per cent are impaired by those symptoms.[12] This is still massive in terms of population impacts. Indeed, up to 280 million people worldwide are likely to be affected by depression at any given time.[13]

Getting it early is critical to prevention. Like any mental illness, although depression is the destination, it takes a while to get there, so the better tuned in both individuals and communities are to the journey, the greater the opportunities for prevention.

There's an apt saying about depression: you are often the last person to realise you are depressed. One day you wake up feeling a bit sad, and then the next day you're a little sadder still. It's often the people around you who are tuned into the difference. So the first thing we do is teach people the signs and symptoms of depression through role-play and a mnemonic. Then we explain the relationship between depression and suicide using colours. You may have a day or so in which you have what's referred to as 'the blues'. This is common – a lot of people have times when life feels overwhelming.

Harmful thoughts are fleeting but easily pushed away. If things get worse, you go into what I call a 'grey' depression, in which everything looks and feels grey. This is when suicidal thoughts start to become more prevalent and harder to push away. You are likely to begin losing interest in things and feel like nothing is enjoyable anymore. People around you are probably starting to notice that you seem different.

As you become more depressed, you lose concentration and your sleep and mood are affected. These things combine to reduce your problem-solving ability. However, they also limit your capacity to formulate and carry out an act of suicide, which requires significant planning and energy. So, although all you think about is suicide, the nature of depression means that you lose the energy and concentration to carry it out.

Black depression is the next stage, in which you can no longer push the thoughts away. They are now starting to really impair your ability to function. You can no longer attend to conversations with friends or family, such is the overwhelming nature of the thoughts of no longer wanting to live. The hopelessness and helplessness you feel to make things better override any ability you might have to shift things. However, again, the depression is debilitating and prevents you from acting on suicidal thoughts. The worst point of depression is what I refer to as 'white depression' – this is also known as clinical depression. This is when you literally cannot get out of bed. From the moment you wake up until the moment you finally get a small amount of restful sleep, all you can think about is the overwhelming pain and wanting to end it all.

This is exactly what T's son looked like. He was in bed for weeks, not interacting and barely eating. Her concern as a mum was completely understandable. Being in a small remote town meant there were scant services, and those that were available had very limited skills. Add being a young Aboriginal male into the mix, and good luck finding someone to help.

The nature of depression is that in around 80 per cent of cases, it is 'self-limiting'. As the patient begins to recover, their energy and motivation return.[14] It doesn't mean you are 'cured'; it just means that there is some relief from some of the negative symptoms, such as lack of sleep, withdrawal from activities and isolation from others. From the outside, it looks as though you are 'better', in T's words. There is some movement. So, when T saw her son get out of bed and make a sandwich, she felt relieved. When he said he was going to visit his cousin, she felt she could stop worrying. His cousin was his best friend. He was in safe hands. He was reaching out and connecting again.

Thank god, thought T.

At this point, T would never see her son again. He left the house, went to his favourite spot and ended his life. She found a note in his room that said simply, 'I love you, Mum.'

When I explained to T this complex relationship between depression and suicide, I told her, 'For what you saw, he looked as though he was getting better. You saw it completely accurately based on his behaviour. He looked better. He got out of bed. This stuff is really easy to miss and even pretty educated people miss it.'

And she said the words that will forever remain with me, 'Tracy, after having this explained to me as you have, I can finally stop blaming myself.'

We can never take away the pain of this type of loss, but if we can lift its burden just a little bit for a bereaved parent, we are doing our job. We can lift misplaced guilt and misplaced anger.

Love is blameless. Suicide bereavement, sadly, never is.

The whole-of-community forums were the start of what would become international interest in my work, because no-one had ever thought or been silly enough to upskill whole communities as I was doing. I didn't realise it at the time, but my publications and media were being noticed in Canada and New Zealand.

Isn't the internet a great thing? We had 117 people come through across the first three forums, and the volume of people who come to our workshops has been consistently as large as that for the time we were able to deliver them. Maureen was stoked, being a Derby local.

The workshops had been scheduled during the Derby Boab Festival (and blackfellas *love* a festival!) and yet people were choosing to come to our forums instead.

As psychologists, we were 'clever' enough to do outcome evaluations. We developed a great questionnaire for community and services that allowed us to track improvements in skills and coping techniques from the start of the workshops to the end. I screened the youth participants with my WASC-Y checklist as this was a targeted intervention, so we wanted to map symptom change. We also did one-on-one counselling and any necessary follow-up, and there was *a lot* of it, often involving complex psychological assessments and referrals into whatever services we could find weeks after the forums ended.

And, yes, this was all for $20,000. If I had been 'motivated by money', as some claimed, I would have gone out of business after the work involved in those forums. But the community work that I have often done for no cost – or that has been the most effort for the least financial return – is still what I jump out of bed to do. The corporate work that pays well for my expertise is far down the rung. I still love it, but not compared to being in remote communities.

After the first phase of the forums, we evaluated all the data and wrote a pretty comprehensive report for the health department.[15] The results were just phenomenal, with increased confidence in understanding signs and symptoms of depression, better understanding of suicide risk, improved intentions to help and, most importantly, confidence in referring a family member into a local service increased significantly as a result of the 'whole-of-community' approach.

I have always been big on outcomes. That's the psychologist in me. I am not fussed about output (bums on seats) – I want to know that we have had a measurable impact, in this case a reduction in risk factors. If people are entrusting me with their time, I'd better be able to show that I can improve things for them.

I am also pleased we outcome evaluated these forums because a lot of people were really angry about us coming into Derby.

Politics and suicide should never mix, but sadly it is one of the most political arenas you can imagine, involving turf wars, empire building – whatever you want to call it.

Long ago I learnt two things that have served me well:

1. Don't get involved in politics. I have never sat on an advisory committee or been part of the 'inner sanctum'. I'm not a joiner of interest groups. It's mostly because I have never had the time. Choosing between working in a community and sitting in a bureaucratic meeting about what should be done – rather than actually getting shit done – is pretty easy. I am a doer, not a talker, and in small business you just don't have that luxury anyway.

2. Never listen to the 'noise'. I accepted long ago that people are going to dislike me. It's never bothered me because I am comfortable with who I am and what my values are. I adore my community because they have good 'bullshit' detectors. The hate I get is always from those who have vested interests, so it makes sense. That's for them to reconcile. I have never bought into it. I believe Denzel Washington said it best – 'You will always be criticised in life by people doing significantly less than you.' Amen to that!

After the success of the first forums, Maureen spent a lot of time finding some cash down the back of a couch for follow-up forums. We then had a final phase of skills consolidation phase. Because we used the same outcome measure, we could track at what point the communities 'got it'. This was when the outcome was the greatest and they didn't need us anymore because they were able to mobilise what we had taught them when someone was at risk.

Our data said that this happened by the third phase of intervention, the first phase being introductory, the second a follow-up and the third skills consolidation. There was this massive impact in terms of skills, but we sort of knew that anyway. We had set up a 1300 free-call number so people could ring us to get some guidance in terms of skills application. We knew the tools and coping strategies were being used not only because they were giving us many examples of risk responses, but because they were using the language we had taught them.

I use key words to represent what needs to be done or understood by the group. For example, we used the term 'tracking' to describe making sure that suicidal people were occupied and busy during high-risk times and that someone was always with them if they were having a crisis when services were not available.

We wanted to be very clear, though, that communities were not solely responsible. A big part of the forum was facilitating community, youth and services meeting up and knowing each other, which is often not the case. Virtually every remote or regional town heavily relies on a fly-in-fly-out workforce and literally no-one knows who the services are. We then developed a clear service-delivery model that was really practical – when services were in town, who they were, where they would locate themselves and how to meet them – and then displayed this information in a central part of town, attached to a picture of the service provider – visual again! We started doing this when more than fifty services began turning up for the training workshops.

We *always* run our workshops on Country so that mob can see the clinicians, and so clinicians are forced to meet the community. Outside of the skills development, it was the most powerful outcome of the forums.

After Derby, we went into Roebourne, Wyndham, Kalgoorlie, Laverton and Mowanjum, but only if there was annual underspend in the budget. The contract for service wasn't operational funding, which didn't enable us to do much else beyond delivery and meant that I had to pay for everything else out of my own pocket. The time it took to write the content was overwhelming by then, as it was to train people to deliver the programs. After a few years we had an amazing team. Two Aboriginal male mental health workers did the men's groups, two females did the women's groups, I did the service-provider groups and we all chipped in to do the youth forums.

After a while, we managed to get such a massive reputation that other states became interested, but it was tough because of the complete absence of operational funding. While we were given contracts for delivering the forums only – that is, nothing for admin, insurance, printing costs etc. – mainstream programs that were just basic training without interventions with community and youth were getting millions and millions. Yet the 'chatter' persisted that I was all about money and not love for community. It regularly frustrated and distressed me, but not for myself. I could easily just march off, hang a shingle on my door and be a very successful psychologist, but I saw the significant impacts of our programs and knew that very few practitioners in Australia, if anyone, had the ability to deliver them.

I spent the better part of fifteen years lobbying federal and state governments for funding to no avail, yet we have achieved more outcomes than any of the heavily funded programs combined. That's an objective fact because we tracked and measured outcomes. No-one else does that, not even the ones funded in the millions.[16]

The years I spent delivering those forums in remote communities, working at the coalface, gave me so much joy among the extremely hard work. Unfortunately, when Maureen moved on from OAH, that was that. No more whole-of-community forums.

Fortunately, other states came calling and we were able to go into Alice Springs, Maningrida and Katherine (Wirli) in the Northern Territory; Tabulam and Bowraville in New South Wales; Echuca in Victoria; and on it went.

We had an incredible group of facilitators, but due to politics we have not been able to deliver these whole-of-community programs since 2009. And that's despite every politician around this issue requesting personal meetings with me. I have stopped meeting with politicians as a result. It just destroys me.

During the Indigenous suicide crisis in 2019, my friends said that they had never heard me being so negative. I was so distressed because I had met with about fifteen state and federal politicians who all promised me that they would fund my work because

'I was the name on everyone's lips' to solve the Indigenous suicide crisis. This was especially true after I wrote some pretty scathing opinion pieces about the disastrous government attempts at suicide prevention. But all of that time was wasted, yet again. When I met with those politicians, they would inevitably come with a few staffers who would furiously write down everything I said. Clearly, it was so they could then use my words to convince people they understood the issues. And, of course, so they could say that they had 'met with Dr Tracy Westerman' when asked what they were doing about Indigenous suicide prevention. So I have stopped meeting with politicians unless there are no photos or staffers and they show me a clear plan for funding a high-risk community or group. These conditions are why I have not met with a Western Australian politician since 2019.

Sadly, it has continued. In 2022, we applied for federal government funding under my charity, which included $1 million in my free work (no wages) and donated intellectual property. We were to skill-up three high-risk regions in the ongoing delivery of these programs and had support letters from every single peak body, state and federal. It would have been the *first* funded whole-of-community Indigenous suicide prevention program tracking suicide risk (measured by the WASC-Y tools) against the suicide death rate. It was a global first, and it was significant work, yet we missed out on the funding.

In the years I have spent delivering these workshops, I have run community interventions that would terrify even the most gifted clinician. As one of my elders said to me, 'Bub, if it was easy, everyone would do it.'

In those workshops we had to deliver complex psycho-educational mental health and suicide interventions in which there were often two or three different language interpreters in the room. For some groups, the majority of people were not literate in standard Australian English, so any written information was rendered useless. We did workshops where mob would come from remote areas and not open the workbook, while sitting next to a psychiatrist or lawyer. My job was to deliver to these vastly different groups in a way that they both learnt what they came to learn. I have turned up to remote communities expecting to deliver prepared content for service providers, only to be told it was actually for parents and elders. In real time I had to adjust the entire training workshop in my head. It's not for the faint-hearted.

One of my 'favourite' workshops was in the remote Northern Territory where the training room was a concrete pad with no walls and a tin roof. It was 45 degrees and there was building going on nearby, so the sounds of angle grinders, drills and jackhammers were constantly in the background. There were kids playing in front of me and through all that I had to deliver complex psycho-educational interventions on suicide, trauma and grief. Down the back of the room were a few rows of cranky-looking blokes with their arms folded. I asked the facilitator who they were. She said, 'They're on a community service order. They've been told to be here.'

To which I replied, 'Let the healing begin.'

There was also a trainee psychologist, who was a white bloke desperate to work with Aboriginal people. He had brought along his beautifully prepared PowerPoint presentation, but by this stage he had become a puddle on the floor. For a year and a half he had asked to 'meet Aboriginal people today' … Yes, that's me being comedic, but you get the drift. I sometimes have to save people from themselves, which is about instinctively knowing when someone is both capable and ready to do remote community work. It takes a long time and has to be handled gently.

I turned to him and said, 'Well, you are going to have to throw that garbage out,' referring to his meticulous PowerPoint. He became even paler than his usual colour and looked ready to vomit.

'Don't worry,' I said. 'We just have to act this whole thing out. Follow my lead.'

I got out a sheet of paper and made a dot-point list of topics we could cover that day. Again, I came up with 'words of the day' and common themes that I could then repeat throughout the workshop so people could understand and remember fundamental ideas and how to use them in real life.

So, the whiteboard looked like this for our two-day workshop:

CONFLICT – GOOD AND BAD
MANAGING ANGER
DEPRESSION – WHAT IT LOOKS LIKE
GOOD YARNING / BAD YARNING SKILLS
SUICIDE – HOW TO TELL IF SOMEONE IS FAIR DINKUM OR GAMMIN

I turned to my trainee and said, 'Okay, we are going to show them some conflict techniques, so you just need to pretend you are angry with me and have a full-on go at me.'

'But I like you.'

'Yeah, just pretend. Say you don't like my shoes or something.'

He dutifully went at me. Now, I pride myself on being a Logie-winning actress, so I went full tilt back at him. You could have heard a pin drop. I then told him to go at me again, but this time I modelled good conflict-resolution skills using a calm voice and a mnemonic I'd prepared. We repeated those words until he matched my modelled calm response.

Again, the participants were completely silent.

When I asked them what was different about the first one compared to the last one, they started talking non-stop. Visually showing people is a great way to teach skills, especially when you are dealing with so many different language groups and often literacy issues. Then you list the techniques. It's practical. It's real life. These are the most effective methods with Aboriginal people. I've taught complex things to thirteen-year-olds and people with English as a second language purely by adjusting my delivery to suit the group vibe. I have always been good at reading non-verbal cues because it has been my complete focus as a psychologist. I am a big believer in energy. I can feel it when I'm losing people, based on the group energy in the room. I can see the disconnect on their faces. I can tell if my language is too 'high talk' and then I adjust, but I can also sense when I am coming across as trying to talk 'too black'. I don't think I have ever embarrassed myself doing this, but who knows. I have to regularly 'un-white' myself when I am in 'my bliss' – in remote communities with blackfellas.

You also have to keep participants interacting and moving. As Aboriginal people, we don't do well sitting still. I need to move to learn. Most of our workshops involve movement as well as role-plays, videos and visuals. If you're teaching real-life skills in real time while in the moment, you can then be confident you have created all the necessary conditions for Aboriginal people to access the skills they need.

It's why I became a psychologist in the first place. I live for this work with my mob.

Ground zero: My lightbulb moment of optimism

When you are on the treatment side, optimism is your most valuable asset because it means you always believe that change is possible.

The work of Martin Seligman tells us that optimism saves lives. Without optimism for the future, we run the risk of suicide and mental ill-health becoming normalised. A self-fulfilling prophecy for those who need to believe in the possibility of change.

One of my most powerful, ground-zero experiences of the power of community was in the Western Desert. It was the late 1990s and the area was notorious, with a global exposé on the extent of petrol- and glue-sniffing in Warburton community. I spent a bit of time there, mostly flying in and out to chase up wards of the state, to support foster carers or to bring clinical psychologists from Perth for complex assessments.

The first time I landed in Warburton I was greeted by the community health nurse, a beautiful lady who came in and out of Kalgoorlie on regular weekly stints for around three years. She gazed at me and said, 'Yep, you look like you can run.' I think she probably said that to everyone just to poke fun, as most people who landed in

Warburton looked terrified. No-one coming off the tiny site airplane fitted in, including me. I felt as if I was back in Hedland as a kid, feeling like the whitest person in the world. I probably struggled with my identity the most when I was in remote areas, to be honest, where most people would have assumed I was white.

Other than that internal struggle, though, I adored it. The more remote the better. There is this thing about seeing 'Country' – for me, it was red dirt, heat and spinifex, and if there was a bit of rain mixed in there as well, forget about it. I was in heaven! I had a constant, overwhelming urge to throw my shoes on and start running through the familiar wide-open bush tracks.

Landing there for the first time, though, was overwhelming. Imagine an area the size of your local footy oval littered with shopping bags, discarded after a substance had been inhaled. It was like Armageddon.

There are literally thousands of basic household substances you can use to get a high from as a 'sniffer', as we used to call solvent users.[17] That makes it really hard to reduce access to 'means'. This was also prior to vehicles being converted to low aromatic fuel and cars would be constantly drained of petrol, which was always the 'high of choice'.

At the time we knew very little about the impacts of solvent abuse on the brain and executive functioning. We now understand this, as well as that solvent abuse is correlated with psychosis. People sniffing glue, petrol or paint get high really quickly, but they come down from that high just as quickly. Different solvents are stronger than others, hence why petrol was always the 'substance of choice'.

When you are on the treatment side of the equation, you must be an eternal optimist because you have to believe in the possibility of change. You also have to believe change can be achieved despite significant odds.

Being optimistic has always been my base personality, thankfully. I don't panic. I don't get stressed. I have anxiety around perfectionism, most definitely, but I've never bought into the anxiety of others. As a psychologist, it's unhelpful as you can add to the anxiety of your clients. I'm also lucky that my dad was a ridiculous optimist. His sense of gratitude was infectious, as was his ability to see good in everything and everyone.

However, I did not truly understand what an optimist I am and how it has been the single most critical factor to my success until I had another 'lightbulb moment', this time about solvent users.

I walked into the old shack that was a makeshift office in Warburton. Five kids were there, all siblings, from age four through to fifteen years, all high as kites. I had come to expect this, having spent a considerable amount of time chasing kids who were high in the bush in the early hours of the morning, on callouts trying to get them home. Fun times!

But this day was different. I looked at these kids. I was aware that I didn't feel pessimistic. I didn't feel helpless or overwhelmed. My training kicked in.

I wondered, *How does a kid as young as four learn how to sniff solvents?* This might sound like a strange thing to ponder, but sniffing is actually a really practically complex thing to do, particularly when you are only four years old.

So, I asked the four-year-old, 'Hey bub, how did you learn how to sniff?'

'My [six-year-old] brother taught me.'

Then I asked the six-year-old, 'Hey, how did you learn how to sniff?'

He said, 'My [nine-year-old] sister taught me.'

And up the line it went.

I immediately understood the possibilities. These kids were learning by group, as we do in collective cultures. From a very young age we are taught to think of the group as being more important than the self. Survival depends upon it in a nomadic culture.

In psychology, though, we are taught that individuals have choices, but this is often tied in with group needs and dynamics. All my kid clients hung out in groups and did everything together – siblings, cousins, mates. It was natural for them.

Cognitive development theory, mostly conceived by Swiss psychologist Jean Piaget, certainly confirms that in Western cultures people learn by group until around seven years of age, but beyond that become more individualistic in their learning.

Learning by group has significant benefits. The obvious one is that you can only become so smart by yourself. Those who are struggling to learn will often rise to the occasion if placed with those who aren't. More than that, there is an obligation within collective cultures to teach each other and to help those who are struggling.

For Aboriginal people, we learn by group from the moment we are born and this never stops. But psychology taught me to work solely with the individual, which is what I did in my few years as a welfare worker. So, I would do the individual work with at-risk kids and then chuck them back into the environment that created the problem in the first place.

So from then on I understood that the only way we would see real change in communities is to teach natural cohorts of families. If a child got anger management therapy, the whole mob got it. If there was a high-risk child, I would observe who responded to the emotional needs of that child to determine an attachment map. Any parenting skills needed were taught to the whole group.

This addressed the environmental factor in ongoing mental ill-health. Change an environment, change an outcome. Because Aboriginal people think naturally in terms of others rather than themselves, this proposition was even easier. If you give people the skills, they will run with them. I have seen incredible change based on this.

Group learning has the most impact with collective cultures, but critically it is also about environments being able to switch genetic and biological predispositions on or off, as noted earlier. Change the environment, change the outcome and sustain long-term generational change. It was how I first realised that we needed to get into high-risk communities and skill up everyone if we were ever going to have any hope of addressing our most complex issues.

How a group can change whole communities:
The story of Aunty J

When communities have nothing, knowledge is power. In fact, it can literally save lives. Every community has an aunty or an uncle who are protectors and know everyone's business. They are elders who, over many years, have sought me out for knowledge because they understand the importance of it.

In one of the communities we were working in with very high suicide rates, there was an aunty who I will call Aunty J. She was a typical elder in the sense that she was fierce and protective of her community, and rightly so.

Aunty J was tiny, about 35 kilograms wringing wet but, boy, she had a presence. You could hear her coming way before she arrived, usually with a lot of F-words – and I don't mean 'friends' or 'flowers'.

One time, I had had a *long* day when I could hear Aunty J nearby. As I tried my best to 'escape', there she was right next to me, like a ninja!

So, of course, I said, 'How are you, Aunty J?

'I'm glad you asked,' she said. *Well, I didn't really*, I thought to myself. Then she started to tell a story that was all too familiar in every remote Aboriginal community, every day. 'I am sick of my nephew.'

'Why? What's he doing?'

'Every Friday night, that fella, he try and kill himself.'

'What do you mean, every Friday?'

'Yep, you can set your watch by it. Every Friday night.'

'So, what do you do?'

'Well, I tell that fucking community health nurse to help and she fucking does fucking nothing and I'm fucking sick of that fucking woman doing nothing to fucking help. She just tells me to go away.'

I listened while thinking past all the F-bombs. I then said, 'Okay, you got that out. Now, for once in your life, just listen.'

Aunty J looked like she had just been slapped, but I understood what was going on. There is no greater distress than someone you love threatening to harm themselves and when you go to the person who is supposed to help, they tell you to go away. In those circumstances – and this is the 'science' now that we apply in our approaches – as noted earlier, the higher-level-thinking part of your brain, the cortex, is not available to you. This means that you are less able to think clearly, problem-solve or communicate effectively.

Anyone who has tried to address conflict in their personal relationships knows this is true. You have planned to say all these lovely things, but then you end up saying none of it because in the moment your emotions overwhelm you and your higher-level thinking becomes reduced.

So, I understood that this was occurring with Aunty J. I also knew that language can marginalise Aboriginal people. Because we don't have access to 'flash' whitefella words, our needs are not met. This is really easily addressed, though, by giving people words. So I gave her a script to rehearse, which was effectively: 'According to Section 28(2) of the *Mental Health Act*, you have to keep my nephew safe for twenty-four hours if he is at risk to himself. I am telling you he is at risk to himself.'[18]

The exact wording was a little simpler than that, but the concepts were all in there. I then made her repeat it again and again. I am very good at playing 'stupid' – it's a gift and a tried-and-tested strategy to get clients to just agree with you to get rid of you.

I have learnt to ask, 'What is it you are going to do again?'

It ensures that they have not only retained the information but will be able to retrieve it in the 'heat of the moment', making the thinking part of their brain less necessary. (It also helped my goal of one less F-bomb, of course.)

The next Friday night, true to pattern, the nephew threatened to harm himself. Aunty J went straight to the community health nurse and instead of the usual F-words, she said confidently, 'According to Section 28(2) of the *Mental Health Act* ...'

It led to a completely different outcome.

This is not complex stuff. I didn't have to do three psychology degrees to teach people these basic techniques. But the great thing about community is that it wasn't just Aunty J who learnt this 'magical information', as she called it. Aunty J went straight to her sister, full of beans, and said, 'Guess what I did?' When she told her, the sister then told her daughter. 'Fair dinkum,' said the daughter. And on it went. All the community could talk about was, 'Deadly Aunty J sorted that nurse out. True!'

Thinking about it always makes me smile. Give someone a fish or teach them how to fish.

More than one person is a group

With our community workshops in high-risk areas, we applied this group-based learning in the planning process. We would ask for the community's 'naughtiest' kids because they were often the leaders. They were just channelling the leadership in maladaptive ways.

When we'd put people in groups, it's incredible how quickly hierarchies would form. Aboriginal culture is naturally hierarchical, and respect is central to that. The kinship map I created as the Acculturation Scale, described in Chapter 3, developed in a way that those who had more authority and 'smartness' would naturally be looked up to.

The second strength of groups lies in their ability to alter genetic or biological 'bad luck', whether through additional vulnerabilities to depression, trauma etc., or by the pure bad luck of having processing abilities that are not as great as someone else's. As I've discussed previously, environment can turn genes on or off. So, if you change an environment, you can change an entire outcome for an Aboriginal kid or family.

The people I train are big on running groups, even basing the failure or success of their workshop on how many attend. The thing is, there is significant generational mistrust of participating in 'a group' – which is predominantly mandated for Aboriginal people and not by self-referral. What we want to be seeing is Aboriginal people self-referring and having opportunities to attend therapy in groups *before* they come into contact with systems and mandated programs. This simply isn't happening. So in these circumstances, I tell my participants, 'More than one person is a group.'

Like in Aunty J's case, start with sisters. Curiosity then occurs. Daughters may slowly join in and on it goes. Start in lounge rooms and in backyards. Skills always need to be transferrable into people's natural environment, where they deal with their situational and emotional triggers. This is where most programs fall down – it's because people are forced into them. They are then undertaken in environments in which stressors such as children are not there, so it's impossible to test whether people's skills have improved.

My international reputation was built through my suicide prevention work, in which I was the first to train entire communities. It is at the core of why I became a psychologist – to skill up entire communities to the point that capacity remains in those communities – and also the foundation of my charity. This is not 'co-design'; it is subject-matter experts training communities in complex solutions. It is not consultation after consultation after consultation. We don't expect elders to have the answers and then weaponise them to deal with highly complex issues like youth crime and suicide. Elders know what the needs are, but they shouldn't be expected to provide the solutions.

That's the job of leadership, and leadership has generationally failed to provide what communities have been screaming out for over decades and decades. Instead, they organise 'elders camps' for high-risk youth. Imagine if a young person died on an elder's watch. In a non-Aboriginal community, suicidal youth would never be sent to a retirement village and it be called suicide prevention. Yet it seems quite okay for our highest-risk, most vulnerable communities.

And when you come with solutions to these complex problems, there are so many barriers that have nothing to do with the community itself that you almost want to give up.

Fortunately, giving up is not in my DNA. As I say to my students: 'Anyone can quit. It's those who find a way not to who achieve great things.'

9

Indigenous Psychological Services: Building the brand

If I wasn't a psychologist, I would be an architect or a builder. Or a full-time athlete, of course. Truth be told, I only fell in love with building because I had no money. When I was twenty-eight, I bought the most run-down house in my street. I love the idea that you are building something that could be there long after we are all gone. Perhaps it's also because so much of what we do as psychologists is not always concrete or tangible. Building gave me that – something that represented my hard work. I have owner-built twice and I've spent two years with a builder renovating my current home.

The house itself was a 1927-style weatherboard on 428 square metres in the suburb of Victoria Park, about 5 kilometres from the centre of Perth. It's considered a pretty nice area these days, but when I moved in it was dodgy, full of pawn shops and used-car yards. Being so close to Curtin University, it attracted a lot of students and was a melting pot of cultures, from Indian to Malaysian to African to Japanese to Chinese to Aboriginal.

The house was simple: two small bedrooms with an outdoor toilet and laundry, a front lounge room and a small kitchen with a good-sized backyard, so it made sense to extend the building out the back. The problem was, no-one was interested in renovating a 'character home' – they simply wanted to demolish it and start again. I was aghast at the idea of destroying history, but the quotes for renovating were far too high for my low wage. I initially decided I would leave it for a while, but the trouble with me is once I have something in my mind, I can't let it go. So, I took on a second job working in Child and Adolescent Mental Health Services in Midland, as a psychologist registrar with a brilliant group of clinicians. Fortunately, one of my colleagues – a social worker called Ash – was also a registered builder. In fact, he was one of the very first registered Aboriginal builders. He 'volunteered' to help me, but he had no idea what he was taking on.

I have always set goals. They're not always big ones, but my determination means that I often pull things off that defy any human logic, and as a result there is zero learning curve to not keep doing ridiculous things. So from five o'clock to eight o'clock in the morning, I would sit at my makeshift office in a half-renovated home, trying to develop a business from nothing, with small contracts here and there, while doing my Masters and PhD. From eight o'clock to five o'clock I would go to work, then until after midnight (or as long as my body allowed) I would flush gyprock (alert – technical building term), hand-sand floorboards, paint walls etc. I'd then do it all over again the next day, and every single day for four years. It was the hardest time of my life, but also the happiest.

My family would regularly come down to Perth to do what they could. I think mostly they came down to check that I was still alive or to tell me how insane I was. There was no door on the house, so every night I had to grab a sheet of tin, my drill and some Tek screws and screw the 'door' on! Mum would have to wake me up in the middle of the night to go to the toilet because it was in the 'outhouse' in the backyard. Once the door was screwed on, you couldn't get out other than from the front door.

Hilarious. Well, not for Mum, of course, but the best laughs are always at someone else's expense, right?

Building was something I surprisingly became obsessed with – a character trait, clearly! I would spend every waking hour painting walls, sanding floorboards, anything and everything. It got to the stage that I had to wear long pants to work because my legs were covered in bruises and scratches from carting tin roof sheets around or some other building mishap. I was broken many times – my low point was hiring a hand sander to sand old floorboards because I couldn't afford the big belt sander and running out of sandpaper after two days of not sleeping because I could only afford two days of hire fees. I remember putting my head in my hands and having a pretty major pity party.

But I always got back up from pure stubbornness. I have no idea how, but I did.

Eventually I had a home I adored, with a *Kath & Kim*-style spa smack bang in the middle of the yard. After Mum read about two people in America who died when they were drinking and fell asleep in their spa and drowned, she would regularly ring me while I was having a quiet beer in there and ask, 'You're not drinking in that spa, are you?'

I would answer, 'No, Mum, of course not,' taking a sip of my beer.

Most importantly, though, I finished my PhD at the end of 2002, which I had managed to do – along with my Masters in Clinical Psychology – in four years. I remember handing it in and feeling so satisfied, knowing that I would officially become the first Aboriginal person to have ever completed a combined Masters and PhD in Clinical Psychology. And I had worked my absolute guts out for it.

Coming from a background in which Mum was excluded from education as an Aboriginal woman and Dad was effectively self-taught, I didn't have the privilege of my classmates, who could go home and have their parents help them with their schoolwork. I didn't have a traditional education. I failed assignments because I didn't understand the things that all the other students just took for granted. And yet there I was, about to hand in my PhD in Clinical Psychology.

The two jobs I had to work to pay for the house renovation – that broke me mentally, physically and financially many times over – gave me a small financial buffer if my dreams of running my private business failed. Given that most small businesses fail within the first year, my odds weren't good. At the time, there were also very few Aboriginal people in private business in Australia, let alone a young Aboriginal woman in psychology.

Recently my sister-in-law, Kirstin, confided in me, 'Mike [my brother] was talking about your book the other day and what a great story it is. He said to me that when you quit your job and went full-time into business by yourself, it was the gutsiest thing he had ever seen.'

My brother, like my dad, is a man of few words, but what he says always has meaning. I have learnt that, in life, the reviews that come from those you love the most always mean the most.

Having finished my PhD, I was determined to build a business from scratch that was all about getting into high-risk communities. I probably understood from the start that I had to do it myself. There was no way a government would fund a private company run by an Aboriginal woman. There wasn't, and still isn't, enough imagination in the world for them to accept that an Aboriginal woman from the Pilbara could be a leader in something. Every tender that would come out excluded private companies from applying. It also reflected how Aboriginal people are still viewed: as not being capable of self-determination or of competing equally – or existing – without government funding.

Having Aboriginal people in the private sector needs to be encouraged. The more reliant we are on government funding, the less we are able to speak our truth. We need to come to the table and hold government to account, because most of the people around the table are funded by government. I have sadly been proven right. In the twenty-five years since I started my business, I've self-funded the validation of every psychometric test and unique intervention program that I've created (and that are all Australian firsts), and

I've watched while major research institutions are resourced in the millions for their culturally biased programs and tools – and yet, I've achieved more than they all have.

It used to frustrate me, but now I think the universe had other plans for me. Not having government funding has given me the freedom to speak my truth. It has also enabled me to do the most important thing – to *represent* that anything is possible, for every Aboriginal person from the bush, with no educational or financial advantages; for all those who have been told that they are not smart enough or not black enough or too black; or for those simply struggling with voices around them of low expectations.

I stood in the front lounge of my still half-renovated but liveable house – the house that had taken every ounce of sweat and every dollar I had earnt (and then some) for the past four years – and I knew that this was where my business would start. I wrote my letter of resignation to the department, which had seen me grow from a kid without a clue to a young woman who now had a clue. I understood what my community needed, and I was going to do everything to make sure they received what all Australians have a basic right to: access to the services they need for their kids and their families.

I was scared, though, as there would be no guaranteed wage coming in. I had a mountain of debt and a house that still needed an enormous amount of work, with no rich family or trust fund to save me. But I had to take the risk. And so, in the lounge of that old beaten-up home that had seen so many laughs as well as blood, sweat and tears, Indigenous Psychological Services (IPS) was born.

Indigenous Psychological Services

I told my family about my lofty plans and Mum, gotta love her, couldn't quite wrap her head around it. For years she said, 'Why did you leave that good government job?'

She was right in terms of losing its security, and of course your parents don't want you to struggle. All she saw me do my whole life was struggle, and going into private business with no safety net was unheard of. Mum was generally always right – that's the wisdom that came from raising five kids. I can say that if I had known how hard it would be and how many sacrifices I would have to make, I am not sure I would do it again. Certainly, I wouldn't do it to the same extent. I would have remained in Western Australia with a reasonably small business and not spent half my life sitting on a plane. However, I wouldn't trade my work with so many communities or being invited into worlds that so few get the privilege to experience for anything.

So, Dave and I would try and grab time after hours and on weekends, so that I could start to design a private business. We were keen to explore whether this was possible and if we could make a living out of it. Many hours were spent in the pub and café coming up with a business idea. With all the optimism that most people have when they start their own business, we applied for a tender to do a suicide needs analysis – which involves speaking to the bereaved and those who had made previous suicide attempts, to work out what their needs were – for the grand sum of just $14,000.

At this stage, I had taken long service leave but Dave, being married with kids, could understandably not take the leap of faith (or stupidity!) that I had. So, while we worked hours and hours on this tender and made absolutely no money from it, the universe looked after us. When the tender was done, we flew to Kalgoorlie to present the results and, luckily, a manager of community relations for the now-defunct Western Mining Corporation, Bob Dalton, was sitting in the audience. He was suitably impressed and invited us to put forward a proposal for a worker-ready program he would commence in Laverton and Leonora.

That contract came together after a few meetings and proposals, so I decided to go full-time into IPS. The money was just enough to 'live on', but because Dave and I were splitting everything down the middle as business partners, I had to find other ways to make a living.

So, despite having only delivered a few workshops, I thought I would try to make a living out of training people in suicide prevention. I spent weeks going through the phone book and searching for contact details on the web. At that stage, I could only afford a very cheap dial-up modem that would drop out anytime I moved an inch. My trusty fax machine – a $375 special from the local Officeworks – got an absolute hammering over the next few weeks as I sent out faxes to government and other organisations for my training workshops. They said, *Register now! Aboriginal mental health and suicide prevention workshop – four days, fully catered.* We had no shopping cart because I couldn't afford a website, so fax and email it was.

The registrations came in bit by bit. Most paid by cheque back then so I had to not only build the business every day, but also check the post, do the banking and stay on top of all the accounts. When the GST came in a few years into my business, doing the accounts became a full-time job. I eventually learnt that trying to do everything yourself in business is a false economy, as I would make such a mess of the accounts that I'd have to pay a tax accountant to unravel it all. Not to mention the number of hours I had lost trying to do the accounts myself well into the night. There are definitely things worth paying for in small business. I have now had the same financial adviser, Tony Munday, for twenty-five years and the same accountant, Mark Bell, for more than twenty years. I trust them with every tax and financial decision and they have always seen me right.

What blew me away was that immediately upon advertising my workshops, people were willing to fly interstate to attend. However, my business acumen was still being developed and I made some heartbreakingly monumental mistakes. Hard work doesn't always equal success in small business, unfortunately, and while taking risks goes hand in hand with success, the key is to always anticipate everything that can possibly go wrong. My problem was that I was way too trusting for my own good. I always assumed people would do the 'right thing' and pay if they were registered. I still remember a workshop in which I had paid for catering for all the attendees (between thirty and forty people) and ten didn't show up. I didn't have a bookkeeper because I couldn't afford one, and I didn't understand the concept of terms and conditions and making sure everyone paid up front.

It was devastating. I'd planned that workshop for months and it probably ended up costing me money to run it. I had many repeats of that type of thing.

There were so many lessons I had to learn in business that no-one could prepare me for. I couldn't see the land mines because I hadn't yet experienced any of them, and had to adjust each time something went wrong. The truth is that when you are dealing with people, you are always learning things. It continues to inspire and stretch me that you can't predict what will happen in small business, and you're always learning and evolving. All you can do is control what you can with what you have in front of you.

I always learnt the most from my mistakes, and I made *a lot* of them. They weren't unrecoverable ones, just mistakes that I could correct through self-reflection and changing my policies to ensure I didn't make them again. Most people have a very low tolerance for risk and failure in business, but I've always seen them as opportunities to learn and do better. I have always been able to bounce back from adversity quickly. However, there were many, *many* moments where I almost walked away from it all.

It helped that I thrive on stimulation and unpredictability. I love waking up not knowing what is going to happen. My close friends often say, 'Twenty-four hours in Tracy's world is like five years in anyone else's life!'

Whether it is in academia or business, being in front of an audience, speaking to media about child suicides or locking kids up in prison – and trying to convince Australia to be empathetic on these issues – or heading out to a remote, high-risk community, or renovating a house with no experience in it or running a marathon, I am there! This goal-oriented, high-energy approach is also what I put into my therapy with clients. I hate the idea of 'talk' therapy. In every session, I need to achieve practical progress with and for my clients. That's the responsibility every psychologist should feel – to honour the client's trust, time and desperate desire to feel and see incremental movement away from overwhelming pain.

So, I realised I had to focus on the basics and things I could control. I understood that intellectual property (IP) had to be protected at all costs. The best money I ever spent was spending two hours with an IP lawyer, Lisa Teller, very early in my business. She was one of the few IP lawyers in Perth back then. Before I saw her, big companies would invite me to lavish lunches and I used to think it was so cool, as a kid from the bush who had never been wined and dined before. But I would leave the two-hour lunch and think, *Man, they just got two hours of IP from me for a tax-deductible lunch.*

I am friendly and optimistic by nature, but I admit my country upbringing meant I was too trusting. It led to a lot of losses. I have always liked that I trust people and still believe in the basic kindness of others, but I realised that in business you have to protect yourself from those who will take advantage. Having said that, I've seen too many people become hardened by business betrayals and by having no-one they could trust. It was either through compromising on their values or not compromising at all and being so extreme that they automatically distrusted everyone.

On the other hand, when IPS began to become successful, I also became very conscious of not buying into the 'hype' and the public adulation. I can do a keynote speech in front of a thousand people and come home and forget I did it. My family and close friends had very little idea of what I did. In fact, my immediate family didn't even hear me speak publicly until I was given the Australian of the Year (Western Australia) Award in 2018, more than twenty years into being a national and international speaker.

I rarely tell anyone about my achievements unless they are public and can't be avoided or hidden. It's just the way I have always been. My family often laugh that they only know where I am or what I am doing because they've watched me on TV or heard me on the radio or seen me quoted in the media somewhere. Some people become enamoured with this public recognition. I just don't get it.

I very deliberately avoid it unless it leads to a critical outcome for Aboriginal people.

The WA Australian of the Year Award was the first time I was confronted with the idea that my work was about me. Because I'd have to talk publicly about myself, I almost didn't accept the nomination. I still remember getting the message from my EA when I was in Kalgoorlie that the Australian of the Year CEO had called. The tone of the message made it fairly obvious that I was a finalist. I finished the training workshop and rang my closest mate, Cate, for advice. I said to her, 'When I make this call, things are going to change. It's a different platform to what I have had.' I had to think deeply about it, as I'd be expected to talk about all the things the media throws at public Aboriginal figures – like 'Change the Date' – and, of course, my personal journey. Then of course, when you are talking about Indigenous child suicides, you have to mention racism and I had seen too many Aboriginal people who were public figures destroyed by it – Adam Goodes being the obvious one. So, I had to make a decision, not just for now but also for the future and those times when I would no doubt be attacked publicly for my stance. Once I rang that bell, I couldn't un-ring it, and I then couldn't whinge about it as it was something I had chosen to take on.

It made me uncomfortable for a very long time. When I won the award, the exposure was overwhelming – I did around fifteen individual pieces of media in just a few weeks. I was asked about every Indigenous issue – the spate of suicides plaguing the country, incarceration, raising the age, child removals – as well as my life and upbringing. Everything was on the table.

But when I did a workshop in Albany, the elders got up to do the welcome and said, 'We are proud people, but Dr Westerman's shown us that anything is possible.'

I teared up. It was at that point I realised that it wasn't actually about me. It was about Aboriginal people, who have been told their whole lives that they can't achieve anything. It was about smashing those low expectations. After that, I was 'good' with being a 'public' figure.

As my brand was building, there were a lot of big companies that understood that engaging me got them a relatively cheap 'we are not racists' card. The award also meant that Western Australia and federal politicians finally wanted to meet with me, but I soon learnt it was all about the photo opportunity. As I've mentioned, I rarely meet with politicians anymore as they just waste my time.

It was great in 2009 to win a 40 Under 40 business award and then in 2020 win the Telstra Small Business Award for WA. These awards have different meaning for me, though, because they are about business success and are 'open awards' in which you are up against anyone and everyone. They were also not just about my accomplishments in my subject matter of expertise. But to achieve both layers of success in terms of awards was incredibly satisfying.

The first IPS office

Back in 2001, a few years into the business, the volume of work started to get too much, so I decided to advertise for a part-time psychologist. It was stressful to take on someone and have to work for their wage as well as mine. Christine ended up being with me for a few years and, boy, did we work hard. She was simply incredible, and we are forever bonded. She eventually went and worked full-time after completing her own Masters degree. I will always be grateful for her friendship and the number of times she picked me up off the ground when I was exhausted and got me to some training workshop I had agreed to deliver. I was at that stage where I said 'yes' to absolutely everything because I was so anxious about the business failing, and frankly it's always good to be able to eat and pay mortgages.

I found an old red-brick home in Carlisle, a small dodgy suburb back then, to rent for $1000 a month. That was more than my mortgage at the time, but I had to get my business out of my house, especially now that it was liveable. As well as the rent, I had to find money to hire a research psychologist and an admin person, let alone having a salary myself. It was stressful but I have never had expensive needs. Being raised in the bush does that, especially by pretty simple parents with simple ideas about what is important – values, family and friends. So, I paid myself $40,000 a year for the first eight years of my business and saved or invested everything I made. And everything I saved went into the business, research, test validation and product development, which included printing the manuals for my WASC-Y psychometric tests. I got a $20,000 bank loan for this so that I owned the materials and wouldn't have to give them up to a major publishing company, which would then take all of the profits.

My business strategy has always been to retain all the intellectual property and market everything myself. High risk, high reward was the idea. As word of mouth spread, it meant I didn't have to pay a publicist or a marketing person, entrusting everything that I had worked for to someone who had nothing to do with its development. It was also about data sovereignty and Aboriginal people controlling their own products and information.

Products are high-risk because they take a *long* time to see any return. The risk was a calculated one, however, as all the ideas came from the numerous interactions I had with practitioners on the ground, so I understood what they needed. The next essential bit was having massive contact with high-risk communities and seeing the shortfalls in practitioner skills.

My business and product ideas have always been 'simple', but extremely complex in their execution. This is the part that requires a skill set that few have. For example, as discussed in Chapter 4, it was obvious we needed a unique screening tool to identify Aboriginal people at risk of suicide. That was the 'simple' part. But developing it? Good luck, given that no-one had ever done it before, in Australia or internationally.[1]

Psychology training drills practitioners pretty strongly in psychometrics. Once I had developed the WASC-Y screening tool for youth, creating the adult version (WASC-A) was relatively easy because I could build on a test that was clinically and culturally valid. The hard work had already been done.

But these tests don't really make money. The printing costs plus money put back into research and validation have made them cost-neutral for most of the last twenty-three years. But their value has come through being able to identify Aboriginal people at early stage of risk and that is life-saving. When people attend my workshops, they are provided with training content based upon empirical evidence about suicide and mental ill-health, cultural competency that no-one else in Australia understands or can deliver. Not to mention my clinical and cultural expertise from twenty-three years of using this information with at-risk Aboriginal people and learning what worked. In short, my audiences could walk away with evidence that was impossible to argue with. I loved that. So many Aboriginal workers would arrive at a workshop looking like they were ready to be made to feel 'less than', having been disempowered by structural and systemic racism within their organisations. Over the few days, though, they would become more confident and come alive as the training wore on. It has always made me smile to observe the effects of their lived experience finally being valued. They would constantly tell me that they felt empowered by the evidence I had and that I could 'take on the whitefellas at their own game'.

What's the point of an education if you cannot use it to educate others, particularly our most marginalised communities?

I then developed another product – the first tests of cultural competence in Australia. At the time, there was zero market for it. I put close to $1 million in time (both mine and research psychologists') over about ten years into developing and validating them. They are now online, but this technology wasn't available when I first developed them back in 2003, so when they became automated it was a truly pivotal moment. People can now go online, purchase them and get an automated strength-and-weakness profile. The tests not only measure cultural competence, but provide people with a cultural supervision plan to improve their skills.

When cultural competency is defined, it then becomes improvable and trackable against outcomes. For example, does improved cultural competency of child protection workers lead to reduced child removals? My work in WA started to establish this link. Does improved cultural competency of police lead to lower incarceration rates? The cultural competency test enables us, for the first time in Australia, to determine the causal contribution of a lack of cultural competence and provides one of the most significant opportunities to 'close the gap' (as I discuss in Chapter 11), but in a way that shows economic and service delivery savings on poor data and outcomes that are already being tracked by organisations.

The cultural competency tests brought in no money for the first ten years. But the long game was creating an evidence base that no-one else had. There was no capacity to track cultural competency skills against practitioner outcomes in mental health, so we were stuck with 'feel-good' output-based approaches to this complex issue – in other words, how many 'bums on seats' attend cultural awareness workshops. But no-one was measuring the impacts in terms of improved outcomes due to cultural competency, because racism is the hardest construct to measure. Once you can do that, though, it becomes easier to track racism as a causal contribution.

Slowly, Australia caught up with the idea of the tests. There was a lot of resistance to looking at racism, so we had to shift the fear within individuals and systems to do so. The training workshops certainly helped as the tests were a fairly significant part of the content, which meant people could understand what they were about. I also gave a lot of free product away, so that the market could see it and promote it to others. Over time, all this started to pay off, but it was risky. Now, cultural competency audits of whole organisations are easily the fastest growing area of my business, and I am slowly realising the investment in terms of my time and money.

I have also had to counteract this ingrained narrative that, as an Aboriginal woman in private business, I shouldn't charge for my programs and tests – and when I do, I am 'sinister' in my motivations. Being compensated for your time apparently means you are a money-grabbing 'snake oil' salesman. I have never heard this type of disgraceful accusation levelled at non-Indigenous psychologists who get paid for their psychometric tests, but it is ubiquitous around me. It's quite a bizarre notion that having invested so much of my time and money in these Australia – and, arguably, world-first products, I must then work for free or give these products away.

Federal and state governments have wasted millions of dollars on mainstream tests for Aboriginal people instead of supporting mine. When you are an Aboriginal woman who is an industry leader, you get treated as though you are a sell-out, while those who are making millions from untested, unproven mainstream tests and programs with no outcomes are considered altruistic pillars of the community. The clear belief is that Indigenous issues are always 'best solved' by non-Indigenous people, despite them having a lower benchmark of science for their programs than I have.

But I have done extraordinary amounts of free work as a reaction to this narrative, to my own detriment, and paid for research out of my own pocket for the greater good. I don't know anyone in small business who does this. I have since learnt, though, that this reaction was from trying to appease and convince unknown others of my morality and ethics. As my mentor Janina Gawler once said to me, I needed to 'get over it'. The narrative is what it is and I am never going to be able to stop it, so why bother trying to? Particularly when I am entirely capable of making massive changes in the private sector because of the lack of red tape.

Seven years in the public sector didn't provide the same degree of autonomy. There wasn't an Aboriginal person in the country who had taken the leap of giving up the security of a regular salary to do what had never been done before, so I learnt not to care. I accepted for the first time that I couldn't control what people thought, but I was pretty good with 'me'. I was comfortable with my intent to make a difference, and the community always saw that. It was just the government-funded bureaucrats who were threatened, and that wasn't about me: there is a lot of currency in being a critic and white-anting anyone who has solutions while at the same time distracting from your own lack of outcomes. I will put my track record up against anyone's, any day of the week, and if I haven't achieved the outcomes I've promised, then don't use me. I have said that, from day one.

But Maureen O'Meara from Derby used to put it much better than me: 'Tracy, the money thing is all they can come up with. I have never heard *anyone* criticising your skills or your outcomes, because they can't. What value do they place on a child's life? You are saving lives and the only people who don't see that have never actually been to your workshops.'

This idea that as Indigenous people our voices are only relevant if we are government funded has been holding us back for decades. If everyone around the table is government funded, then who is holding government to account?

Three years into the business, my workshops were getting more and more popular. It was hard work and public speaking is not easy for anyone; however, if you are good at it, it pays well. At this stage I was quoting $600 a day, which was peanuts by standards twenty years ago – particularly given I was developing and delivering unique content. But what you are 'worth' is a market question. You send out into the universe what you think you are worth and the market responds. It's simple supply and demand. I tell every Aboriginal person I am mentoring that there is no such thing as a 'price for your services'. People get paid what they get paid because they earn their 'worth' – they get the outcomes. If you send a quote to a client and they agree straight away, you're too cheap. If you keep missing out on jobs, you are overquoting. If you have more work than you can cope with, you are too cheap.

However, I did not in any way ever think I could sustain my business just from training. I remember saying to Dave, 'You can't make a living out of delivering training.'

He laughed at me, and I now laugh about it regularly. For more than twenty-three years, training has probably been 80 per cent of my income but it had never historically been something people could make an entire living out of, so it was uncharted territory. Training workshops enabled me to do the 'fun stuff' – the free work in communities, which has always been *a lot*: free counselling, free psychological assessments, free training places.

I also funnelled a hell of a lot of money into research and development, including validation of unique psychological tests, development of unique suicide intervention programs, evaluation of all of my programs and training, and constant mentoring. But it has always been this 'free' work for mob and community that has balanced me out and reminded me why I became a psychologist in the first place.

Having now trained more than 50,000 practitioners across Australia – and that's not including the ten or so keynote presentations I do a year, with hundreds of people in the audience – I am one of the most successful trainers in Australia. And I've done it in a 'bespoke' industry with an arguably very specific and limited market. When I say these numbers out loud, it's surreal and when I first started calculating them using our very trendy client-relationship management system, it became pretty clear that this outrageous number of people was likely an underestimate.

But getting from zero to 50,000 has not been easy. When I started, it was just in Perth and I was getting regular private training, client work and small contracts here and there. I then began to be booked out for the year and to spend half my life on a plane delivering workshops across the state. I couldn't enjoy much of my hard-earnt cash because all I ever did was work. I had overheads from my office and salaries to pay for as well as research. It was not a sustainable business model at any level. If I got sick, what then? If the training revenue dried up, what then? But most importantly, it could have burnt me out very quickly.

So, after one particularly long trip across the country, travelling all day and night, and then dragging myself into the office at six the next morning, I had a 'day off' and it hit me like a tonne of bricks: in my chest, in every part of my body. The exhaustion just took over.

Sharon, who was my research psychologist at this stage, and Amanda, my Indigenous trainee, took one look at me and said, 'You can't do this workshop next week. We are going to postpone it and you are going home and resting.' Despite my protests – fifty people would be coming from all over Australia to attend, and I couldn't let them down – those little buggers made all the phone calls and refused to let me back into the office. It was a lockout!

When I snuck back in after a few days, Sharon sat me down and said, 'I've been thinking about things and it seems to me that if you go down, the whole business does too. If you can't work, then the business doesn't exist. You can only do so many workshops in a year to keep the business running. But if you charge more, you can do less. The market is clearly saying you are worth more than what you are charging.'

It all made sense, but being the simple Pilbara person that I am, $800 a day seemed a lot of money. However, each fortnight, the money I was making was barely covering the bills. It also seemed that the idea of public training was more valuable if you could get people to pay per head to hear you speak. At this time the public workshops were only in Perth but were selling out quickly, with people paying $600 per head for four days.

So, Sharon, bless her, said to me, 'I am going to start quoting you at five thousand dollars a day for your private training workshops.'

I nearly had a heart attack. I felt pure shame to be charging that much, and I immediately told her that there was no way I could ask for that much money. She said, 'Well, you don't have to. I will!'

Realistically, you are worth what people are prepared to pay for you, and Sharon was right in testing the market. As she said, 'If people come back and say "no way", then you'll know your value.'

So, she started quoting $5000 a day, and I felt physically sick every time she sent a quote out. But no-one reacted – there was no problem with paying that amount. It took me a while to reconcile that I was being paid for the incalculable hours, days, years of overwhelming work and driving myself to my limits. However, I also saw organisations blow a lot of money on professional development that didn't improve their staff's skills. I knew I was a really good clinician and that this translated very well into my workshops, which would potentially enable them to save someone's life.

After a while, we were capturing good data, so we decided to see whether there was a national 'public' market for my workshops.

This meant people could pay 'per head' to attend. We started advertising through bulk emails and faxes – first up was the Northern Territory, just to test a market beyond Western Australia.

I then went off on a work trip. On the way home, I thought, *I'll just pop into the office.* As I walked in, there was paper all over the floor. The fax machine had run out of paper from the volume of registrations that had come in over the weekend.

We'd received a total of thirty-five registrations in one day. It was now obvious that I had to consider a second workshop. I ended up scheduling two back-to-back workshops in Darwin. The participants included the highest-profile blackfellas in the Northern Territory who were coming along to 'check out' what I was delivering. This was in 2002.

The early years of going interstate and delivering to wider and wider audiences were just pure stress – not sleeping, writing and rewriting content again and again and again. I was obsessed. I remember the first organisational workshop I delivered that was paid. It was in Carnarvon, Western Australia, for the education department on conflict resolution. I had scripted the *entire* two days, word for word. I laugh at this now, but everyone has to start from somewhere. I was never bad; I was just very nervous. I never believed in delivering someone else's content, and I couldn't anyway because my audience demanded 'answers' to every holy-grail issue with Aboriginal people that no-one was providing training on. So I had to develop it from scratch.

My laptop was on constantly. The only peace I got was on planes before onboard wi-fi was invented, when no-one could reach you. I would memorise every paper that had just come out in case there was a professor of psychology or a psychiatrist in the audience who was across the subject matter more than I was. As my reputation grew, there were people there who would try to embellish their own reputations by trapping me in an area where they could look smarter than me. That's okay, but not when people were paying to hear me speak, so I had to learn early on how to deal with certain personalities – the ones who made it all about them and responded with long-winded, rambling answers to questions or case studies, which ran the risk of ruining the workshop. There were also people who made the training all about them. Then, there was the pure idea that there was someone in the audience who knew more about the topics than I did, which was *always* a possibility because my audiences were so diverse in clinical expertise. As my reputation grew, the audience got even more diverse and the pressure became even greater to perform well. This was the most stressful aspect, which few trainers have to contend with – the audience's extreme cultural and clinical diversity. The backgrounds of my participants included lore people, elders, Nungkari, psychologists, psychiatrists, teachers, social workers, Aboriginal health workers, mental health workers, police, lawyers ... The list went on and on. I had people in the room who wouldn't even open their workbooks because English was their second or third (and often irrelevant) language. The pressure to 'deliver' to this group has always been and will always remain my most important priority because they are the first-responders, unheralded and unappreciated. For professionals, education is often about self-interest; for community, it is about literal survival. To be able to say the right word to determine the correct indicators. The things that most of us take for granted and have learnt to see as normal are an absolute privilege to our remote front-line brothers and sisters.

About five years into my business, when I was becoming established as a national speaker, I was asked by a colleague whether I got nervous talking in front of hundreds of people. I didn't skip a beat with my response: 'Never.'

When I'm working with lore men, Maban, elders and people who I respect enormously – and for who training and skills in these issues have the potential to change or even save lives – that to me is pressure. It is true that when you deliver to an audience that means more, the nerves kick in. So, I had to learn to 'double teach' and 'code switch' in real time. This meant that I would explain the technical theory of depression, suicide and trauma so the psychologists and psychiatrists would learn new content, and then I'd break it down in a way that community could understand but that didn't lose those who were after the complex skills. This is where my community interventions and clinical experience came in handy. I knew what worked because I had not only treated the highest-risk, most complex clients around, but I had also gone into the highest-risk communities and was able to translate those skills across whole communities.

For many years the cogs in my brain would grind very slowly. Every single audience was so different and completely unpredictable in their pre-existing knowledge, literacy levels and understanding of mental health. The only way you can possibly hit the right mark and do so for more than two decades is to read the energy of the group – and of course be across every possible question that could come from any group, both clinical *and* cultural.

So, that's why I have spent literally years and years of my life getting the content right – and that doesn't just mean research and research and research. It means lived experience, it means applied clinical experience with Aboriginal clients, it means the ability to read the energy of a group, but most importantly it means considering every way that any group is likely to interpret the content and being prepared for it.

Public speaking has multiple layers to it that feed nerves, and for a few years my self-esteem was so shattered by being on public display that I couldn't look at training evaluations. I am serious. Even though I never had a negative evaluation, I just couldn't look at them. My self-esteem, which has always been a bit fragile, if I'm honest, took a hammering because self-doubt crept in. Being on public display all day, every day, and trying to figure out or control what people are thinking about you – good or bad – is hard. It's known as *positive–negative asymmetry* – the negative stays in your mind much longer than the positive. It makes sense because the brain's job is to protect you from harm and threats, so it has to remember negative experiences more as these are more threatening to life and to self-esteem.

Then there is the reality of how your messaging gets interpreted differently by individual appraisal and internalisation of it, and finally, the worst part: being judged by an audience you do not know. You cannot control any of it and it's why so very few people are successful public speakers. If the public reaction and lack of market doesn't kill you, then the physical and psychological capacity to do it again and again and again will.

So, of course, like with any form of cumulative and anticipatory anxiety, my go-to position has always been to 'over-prepare' – I have always been a hard worker, modelled by my parents, and frankly I border on being a workaholic if I am completely honest, but it's not about the work – it's about the pressure I feel to make a difference to people's lives and the stakes are too high to get it wrong. The stakes are too high to teach ambiguity about what works when children are dying by suicide at the rate they are.

I've had to be across cultural complexity. I have had to be across clinical complexity and merge the two – and be likeable and be present for *every* participant while doing it!

Then going into different states, different regions and doing the same, without offending cultural protocols. I have had lore men come to my workshops. I cannot begin to explain the privilege of that. And, more than that, for them to come up to me during and after a workshop and tell me, 'You know that as a lore man, I am not supposed to talk to you as a woman, don't you?'

It's humbling beyond any experience you can fathom. And then, the clincher: 'I think I want to be a psychologist, like you.'

I have always been a proud psychologist and making the profession a possibility for my people means that we are showing people how to stand in equal power. That's what my training workshops have achieved and that's what keeps me as excited about it today as I was twenty years ago.

Because the very presence of me makes it possible for every Aboriginal person.

I didn't come from privilege, and representation matters. You cannot be what you have never seen.

But developing training content that is unique has added an additional layer of pressure. I had to learn what content was good and what content was bad, purely by delivering it to an audience and seeing the reaction. That's hard and terrifying, particularly when people are paying. It is that heart-in-your-mouth moment when you wait for the reaction of the audience, and you then have to manage it and make meaning of it in a way that understands how an entire audience has processed it.

I watch body language a lot – and that's of course about my training as a psychologist. I have learnt to focus more on how people look and their reactions rather than what they say. I have had audiences that said very little over days and sucked the energy out of me. It's hard not to take it personally, but I have learnt not to as it is my responsibility as the trainer to carry the weight of it and increase the group's energy when I need to. These groups are like families which I am the head of! They can be individually engaged and interested, but when you throw them together you have a dynamic you cannot possibility predict. That's what makes being a trainer so difficult and, of course, perennially challenging. You have to adjust to every single group and consistently so.

Every day I have put myself under stress because stress is good when it is managed and controlled. The Yerkes–Dodson law says that the relationship between performance and stress is an inverted U-shape: too much stress means performance falls, but just enough stress maximises performance.

Taking yourself out of a comfort zone is stressful, but if you can cope with it and channel it, that is where high performance and impact exist. I don't profess to have managed this fine line, and there have been many times when my desire for perfection has destroyed me physically.

Delivering public training for a living means that you can never have an 'off day' or a moment to yourself during a nine-hour workshop in which you can just 'switch off'. The content is also extremely stressful, so you will often have people react to it and then you have to deal with that. Then you have clinicians throwing every complex and chronic mental health scenario at you when you are trying to eat your lunch. It is unrelenting.

While it is taxing cognitively and emotionally, mostly it is taxing physically. Ironically, if I were to put my success down to one thing, it would be my physical fitness. It has been one of the major differences in my success, and it is something that has also kept me 'sane' – it's self-care but also career longevity in combination.

The brand

My first awareness of the brand that was being built around my reputation was during the expansion of my business into the Northern Territory. It was the first time I had ventured outside of Western Australia in my newly minted business. I got a contract with Menzies School of Public Health, which was literally a handful of staff and one building. It is now a national organisation with thousands of staff across Australia. I am always proud of anything that develops so significantly, particularly from the Northern Territory because of how few resources it has and how over-represented it is in so many of the statistics. The bonus was that my brother Mike had set up home in Darwin. He was working out at Borroloola with McArthur River Mine as a mining engineer, so I would get to spend time with my big bro. We are like two peas in a pod, with mutual respect and admiration. Many people have found it odd how well we get along – with my big sis Lynny, we were the three amigos. Apparently, family aren't supposed to get along that well!

It was just a small contract to look at the 'efficacy of mental health outcome measures with Aboriginal people' (try to stay awake during that title). It was part of a national project looking at the bias in mainstream assessments of Aboriginal people. By now I had submitted my PhD on the WASC-Y, which meant I had some expertise. I was asked by the Menzies people if I would do a presentation for their partner organisations on my PhD. It would just be an hour.

This was the first time I truly understood the importance of what I was doing from the perspective of the Aboriginal community. The presentation was in the 'pink building' of the Northern Territory health department. The room was large – I would say a few hundred square metres in size. As I walked in to set up the overhead projector, the space was packed to the point that there were a few people sitting under the table for the overhead projector. I had heard (it may be an urban myth, granted!) that the director of the health department decided to come along at the last minute but couldn't get in the room. The presentation was on why we needed assessment tools of our own – that our children were literally dying because of the lack of screening tools capable of identifying early risk. To me the development of the WASC-Y was a pretty straightforward thing to do.

By that stage the Northern Territory had experienced a significant spate of suicides, predominantly in the Tiwi Islands, and it had the highest suicide rate in Australia among Aboriginal people (or, as Territory mob call each other, 'countrymen' – a term I adore). So, when they heard about an Aboriginal psychologist who was presenting on her research, they literally travelled for miles and miles. It was, frankly, overwhelming. I remember sitting on the plane back to Perth after being 'mobbed' by dozens of countrymen after the presentation and feeling both pride and pressure at the same time.

I knew then that I needed to expand my reach and get more work in the Northern Territory. Back home, I started to think how that could be done. Back to the trusty fax machine!

The Northern Territory

Having been endorsed by mob, I felt that I could dip my toe into the Northern Territory, which was the holy grail of cultural complexity. But it was terrifying to be from Western Australia and running workshops in a place where you were going to be 'growled' by elders for doing so. Many had either been to or heard of my presentation in the 'pink building' and wanted to learn, but others were there to ensure I was observing cultural protocols. This was completely and utterly appropriate. I have always been so respectful of elders, of the holders of cultural lore and cultural knowledge, and their right to growl me.

It was 2002 and I still remember going into that training. It was held over four days at the Holiday Inn and around 70 per cent of the participants were Aboriginal people, with the balance being non-Aboriginal clinicians. In the group, paying to hear me speak, was Henry Sambono – a mental health specialist I had long respected from afar. I had read some of Henry's articles at uni – there were so very few around that were worth reading – and so to actually be in a room with Henry and one of his sons who came from Tiwi, in addition to a whole mob from Batchelor Institute of Indigenous Tertiary Education, was pressure like you cannot fathom.

On the first day at morning tea, Henry – as calmly and sweetly as only Henry can – sidled up to me and said, 'Tracy, the concern we have with this training is that you are going to teach whitefellas that they can do it without us.'

I smiled, and my smile grew wider as he stood there and started to smile as well.

'Why are you smiling?' he asked.

'You'll see.'

As the training continued, the clinical and cultural complexity became so obvious to the group as to immobilise most of them but, as always happens in my workshops, the Aboriginal participants – who were all too used to feeling 'less than' – grew in confidence by the day. It has always been the case with my training, and I never tire of seeing it.

By day two, Henry was literally skipping into the workshop. On day four, he volunteered to pretend to be a client for me in a role-play. It was absolutely epic and I wish I could have captured it on film. See, the problem with workshops that spend too much time on theory is that they run the risk of participants not really understanding how it is done. I needed to show them. So, my only instructions to Henry were, 'Just go completely over the top, blackfella. Don't go easy on me. Do whatever you need to do to make this as hard as you can.'

So, Henry was my suicidal client, a lore man who didn't speak to women.

I call this type of role-play the 'fishbowl'. All the participants put their chairs in a big circle around us and they have to tick off the skills they have been taught as we demonstrate them, to show they've understood what they are seeing in action.

When we finished the risk assessment after about twenty minutes, you could have heard a pin drop. The group's job was now to ask questions of me and of Henry to solidify how to apply skills that are different to those required for generic counselling training. They were also to ask us, of course, about how suicide risk assessment differs because of distinct indicators and about how we change basic counselling skills to 'get at' the story that suicidal Aboriginal people will present with. I tell them that their relationship with the client is critical. Aboriginal clients need to like you. That's not what they teach us in our psychology training, though. They tell us that it doesn't matter if our clients like us. But it is vital to build trust to a point that clients are willing to share what they have learnt to bury, locked away in a place of true darkness. It is the therapist's job to create that place of safety where darkness is not present, which is always what provides the greatest objectivity and insights, the most important being that although pain and darkness can overwhelm you, they can also pass.

This is what is known as empathy – to walk a mile in someone else's shoes, to understand what it means to feel suicidal. Should the therapist have had suicidal impulses themselves? It certainly helps, but my view is that it is not essential. Why? Because therapy is about the client, not the therapist, and people who have had suicidal impulses can have not only different reasons for them, but different strategies that worked for them. Being able to hear people's reasons for wanting to live or die is what empathy and the therapeutic alliance is, whereas having lived experience can be a mixed bag. This is particularly so if resolution has not occurred, which makes transference and using clients as therapy more possible.

I remember seeing a client who had panic attacks. Some three months into treatment, they turned to me and asked, 'Do you have panic attacks?'

'No, never,' I said.

That's empathy, and it is one of the core constructs of the client–therapist relationship. But what about cultural empathy? Can you truly put yourself in the shoes of an Aboriginal person? The idea is that it is a skill to be able to listen to the story and understand what it feels like to walk in the shoes of an Aboriginal person. It's a core construct to effective therapy yet is not even considered part of teaching therapeutic skills.

It is *essential* that therapists are comfortable having conversations with Aboriginal clients about culture, blackness and identity. This should be normalised but it isn't. It needs to be because that's what cultural empathy is.

As word of mouth grew, I started going into other states. Next up was Queensland and I got my first-ever contract over there. It was to deliver a four-day workshop with social and emotional wellbeing workers throughout the state. It was 2002 and the workshop was to be held on the Gold Coast at Sea World, of all places. I was still absolutely flogging myself with putting content together, and don't even get me started on how nervous I was venturing into Queensland to train Murris – Queensland blackfellas – as well as Torres Strait Islander mob. The pressure was immense, and that workshop stands as one of the most stressful I have delivered (and that's saying something).

I had obviously stepped into politics and got a 'blackfella growl': 'Who's this woman coming from WA and telling us Murris how to do this work?' Day one, the energy was terrible. There were a few friendly faces but a large group was pretty pissed off that I had been engaged to do this training instead of a local provider, and they were not shy in showing me their anger – in their body language and in their response to every question I posed to the group. It was brutal. They didn't like me and, frankly, I didn't like them.

By the end of day two, I was ready to give them their money back and tell them to 'stick it' – but about three-quarters of the group were lovely. I had a day's break before day three commenced. I looked at myself in the mirror and said, 'Toughen up, Trace. You didn't get to where you are by being a pushover. You've handled worse than this before.'

So, back I went, determined to win them over. I understood that you can attract more with honey than with vinegar, so my strategy was to agree with everything they said and make them feel like the most important people in the room.

Slowly, one by one, their energy became kinder. Plus, I was told days later that a few of the participants pulled them aside and told them, in no uncertain terms, 'We protect our own, not set upon them!' I thought that was very sweet.

By day four, the energy was just brilliant. The transformation was amazing, but, boy, I was a shattered mess by the end of it. It was a baptism of fire. One of the people who had been particularly harsh to me came up and apologised at the end of the workshop, saying, 'I understand now why they got you to deliver this training. It is really brilliant. I am sorry I behaved the way I did. And I am sorry as I could have allowed myself to learn so much more from you.' I thought it was incredibly magnanimous of them to admit that.

So, Queensland got a reprieve (haha!) because I was ready to wipe the whole state from any further workshops. Dramatic, I know, but we can all become like little children every now and then when our feelings are hurt.

The next states were much easier, as I guess by then I had racked up a pretty significant reputation. This was mostly due to my keynote presentations, plus word of mouth and the fact that I was the first Indigenous person to graduate with a Masters and PhD in Clinical Psychology. Yes, it mattered having the important 'Dr' in front of my name, so after I graduated in 2003 it added to the business's growing 'street cred'.

So South Australia, New South Wales and Victoria came calling pretty quickly. I now felt more confident in being able to deliver my workshops in different states for different mob. No-one had really been doing that as it was an additional layer of cultural stress to venture into Country that wasn't your own. And I didn't want to go through a repeat of that horrific Gold Coast workshop!

As I wrote this part of my memoir, I received an email from a participant at that training workshop. It started with, 'You probably don't remember me, but I attended your training over twenty years ago at Sea World. It was the most impactful training I have ever done.' How incredible it is that so many who attended that workshop remember it so fondly. I know this because I have encountered so many of them over the years who have either come back to the workshop again and again or reached out to say how much they admired the work.

It's also amazing how people can have very different perspectives of the same thing. That's a *very* good thing!

Reflecting on all this more than twenty years later, it is quite bizarre that I am now booking out a year in advance. After all these years, the demand just grows and grows. This would make me the most successful trainer this country has ever seen. I have always expected people would get sick of hearing from me and I have learnt over the years to reinvent myself regularly. It's not easy to make a living from training delivery and particularly with such a small targeted market. You have to inspire audiences, you have to stay relevant and current and, most importantly, you have to entertain. But my all-time favourite quote from mob when they were trying to convince a bunch of community to come and do my workshops is this: 'When you see her, you'll be confused (blonde hair, blue eyes, fair skin). But the minute she opens her mouth, you'll get it.'

That's among the best vouching ever!

The international attention

In January 2003, I received the following email:

Hi from Nunavut, Iqaluit, Canada. I am here in lovely −45C and reading about your great work in Australia. I am organising a circumpolar suicide prevention conference and would love you to come …

Jack Hicks

This Pilbara girl is not built for cold. And by cold, I mean anything under 30 degrees. That's when the heater goes on in our house. So, that email got immediately deleted.

Several days passed and I got a second email:

Hi, Jack Hicks again. You probably thought that email was spam, so I'm sending again. Really keen to get you to Canada for our conference.

After searching the map and finding Nunavut, I replied but struggled to find the words. Enter Professor David Hay, my PhD supervisor, who was determined to get me to Canada.

David had become like a second dad to me, having lost my dad some ten years prior. I was so grateful for his mentoring and friendship. He was probably the only person on earth I could email at two in the morning and he would get back to me.

So, when I told him I didn't think I would go, he shot back, 'Tracy, you need to get an international reputation. People know you enough in Australia by now. You need to do this.'

However, I was determined not to go. I was such a 'bushy' – international travel had never been a big thing on my list of priorities, partly because I had no relatives overseas, but mostly because there was just too much to do in Australia, in communities.

But then there was a knock on the door. It was David Hay with a pair of Canadian snow boots in his hand.

I said to him, 'You really want me to go, don't you?'

'Yes,' he said.

So, I agreed to go to Nunavut. I then rang my bestie, my sister Lynny, and said 'Hey, fancy a trip to Canada?'

No hesitation from her: 'Oh yes!'

After a few months of organising passports and finding the right clothes to take over so that we didn't die of hypothermia, we were ready to go. There we were, two country bumpkins flying across the world, from 45 degrees to −45 degrees.

We were so excited.

The plane trip from Perth to Sydney and then Sydney to Vancouver took twenty-four hours, and then we had around nine hours there before our trip to Ottawa. Fortunately, there was a hotel at the airport so we checked in for a sleep. It still stands as one of the all-time best sleeps of my entire life. When you are beyond exhausted and you find a hotel that has those beautiful crisp, clean white sheets and big fluffy quilts, you just feel as if life can't possibly get any better. We slept for a good six hours.

Then we were off to Ottawa for an overnight stay and our first-ever look at snow. Of course, we annoyed the hell out of everyone who was crankily shovelling the snow from the sidewalk, while we were running around yelling, 'Look, it's *snow!*'

Their looks said, 'Yes ... we know ...'

Finally, we arrived in the capital and were greeted by Jack Hicks. We then went to get our rented snow outfits (who knew *that* was a thing) and then headed to our accommodation, a bed and breakfast 'by the sea'. Unfortunately, the sea was solid ice!

It was a fantastic two days of presentations with the pre-eminent cross-cultural psychiatrist Dr Laurence Kirmayer, who has since become an amazing supporter of my work. He ended up coming to Australia for a keynote for us five years later.

It was such an incredible reception from Inuit people. They were enamoured with my WASC-Y and our programs that we were building from the ground up. (I believe they call this 'co-designed' these days!) They couldn't believe they weren't doing the same for their own people. On the last day there was a coming together of recommendations by the conference delegates and it was all about my work, which was so flattering and overwhelming.

David Hay knew what he was doing when he insisted I went to Canada. It was one of the best decisions I have ever made. I got the validation I needed and that I would never get in Western Australia, where the suicide rate was the highest in Australia. I accepted that, no matter how much validation these tests received, I would have to fund their rollout myself if we were going to gain any traction on Indigenous child suicides.

It didn't need to be financial; just philosophical would have been enough. That makes me feel angry at the wasted opportunity in so many aspects of prevention.

Not long after that conference, the Canadian government sent a delegation to Australia to look at my work. It recommended that the same approaches be adopted with Canadian Inuit people, and that the WASC-Y in particular should be rolled out, but it noted that they didn't have someone with my expertise in Canada. How nice would it be to have that recognition in Australia of how crucial my psychometric tests are to 'closing the gap'. Soon after that an invitation came from Nome in Alaska, so I took my first trip to the US. Not long after came New Zealand, with Auckland twice in a row and then Wellington. The international reaction was overwhelming but so reassuring.

Success is a tricky thing to navigate. Success as an Aboriginal person is even harder, let alone as an Aboriginal woman, as it is with women generally as we have socially constructed gender roles to battle in addition to having an extremely small pool of opportunity. Not to mention being from the remote Pilbara and needing to do distance education to get into university, as well as having a mum who was not even a citizen in her own country. I was a twenty-six-year-old kid when I started my business.

I am one of those extremely rare people who, when asked if they are proud of what they have achieved, answer pretty clearly, 'I have literally exceeded every expectation I have ever had for myself.' How lucky am I to feel that way every day.

10

The Future:
Building an army of Indigenous psychologists

Imagine what the world would look like if more people felt grateful for their privilege rather than entitled to it.

Through building my business over twenty-five years, I have had the privilege to help so many people and communities on their healing journey, and I cannot help but feel grateful. After all, I was an 'accidental psychologist'. The pride I feel is not about the success; it's about the fact that I have never compromised on my values to get me here. The greatest compliment I have ever been paid is from those who have known me the longest: 'Trace, you've never changed.' But being in the healing profession requires you to always present the most honest version of yourself, so the core of what led me to psychology in the first place cannot really change.

When in 2018 I was named the Australian of the Year (WA), suddenly everyone became interested in my opinion, especially in relation to the spate of Indigenous suicides, mostly in the top half of Australia, that were getting worse week by week. Worse still, the headlines of every death by suicide of a young Aboriginal person were, frankly, gutter media. Those claiming that sexual abuse and alcohol were linked to child suicides were the kinder ones. I have worked with more bereaved Aboriginal parents than I care to count and *not one* of them fit that stereotype. It angered me so much on their behalf, to lose a child and then have to see that every day. As I said in Chapter 5, bereaved parents will always wrongly blame themselves for their child's death – they don't need someone else to do it for them. It complicates grief so much more when people have to also defend their culture, their core identity and their parenting.

I hadn't been on social media very long at that point, but I angrily put this tweet out:

> When a non-Indigenous child dies by suicide, we RIGHTLY look for deficits in systems and how we can do better as a society. But when an *Indigenous* child dies by suicide, we look for deficits in our families and in our culture … When are we going to have more empathy for Aboriginal parents bereaved by suicide?

It got over a million hits. I understand why now, but at the time I really didn't grasp how much people needed to hear it. In my simple way, I thought it was bloody obvious.

If you look at what happened after the suicide death of Dolly Everett – a beautiful non-Indigenous teenager who took her own life – it is how we should respond any time a child is harmed or dies by suicide, regardless of their cultural background. We should march in the streets, develop anti-bullying programs and give significant media attention to the pain endured by Dolly's parents, who suffered what no parent should ever suffer.

We should be leaning in equally to the pain of bereaved Aboriginal parents, but we aren't. We respond differently and that's explained by the other-race effect. It's what the racial empathy gap explains – that the pain of white people is appraised as greater than the pain of black people.

True to form, the Western Australian government responded to this new spate of Indigenous suicides by having yet another inquiry – the fourth into the issue in a decade, all while suicides escalated. In 2019 there was what became known as the Fogliani inquiry, after the coroner leading the investigation. I wasn't invited as an expert witness by Fogliani. Obviously, there were *so* many Aboriginal psychologists with PhDs in Clinical Psychology focused on Indigenous suicide prevention in Western Australia. (Yes, I'm being sarcastic.) But I was quoted in her report. I sent a pretty cranky letter, not only because I was not called to the inquiry, but because they had quoted me without subject-matter-relevant context three times and I wasn't afforded any opportunity to address what is a highly complex area in which there are very few skilled individuals in the country.

The problem with inquiries is that they do little to inform us about suicide prevention. Coroners aren't psychologists, nor do they understand Indigenous culture well. The government's blind acceptance of the coroner's recommendations and its love affair with having Indigenous suicide inquiries has simply compounded ongoing negative outcomes, because here we are, now a few years after the Fogliani inquiry, and the latest data shows that suicides in the Kimberley have continued to escalate.

There is significant currency for governments in holding inquiries. We, as Aboriginal people, feel as if we have been 'heard' yet everything stays the same.

Then there was more political spin, as it took the better part of thirteen months for the government to respond to the Fogliani inquiry. Meanwhile, six more Aboriginal young people had died by suicide.

This unfolding national crisis was invisible in our lounge rooms. There was no marching in the streets, no 'call to action' as a nation. It got worse. In the eighteen months after the Fogliani inquiry, there was not a single question in the lower house of the Western Australian Parliament about the coroner's report or what the government was going to do about it. The ABC reported that only nine of the ninety-five MPs brought it up in any way, in either chamber, during 2018, the year of the inquiry.

Our children's lives deserve more than silence, but that's all they received from our political leadership. It bears repeating: there is no greater injustice than to feel invisible, as if your pain matters less.

But what actually broke me was the finding that not *one* of the thirteen young people had been given a mental health assessment. Of course, I had developed the only culturally and clinically validated tools in Australia and taken them to the 2016 WA parliamentary inquiry into Indigenous suicides. After the Fogliani inquiry, I realised I could either sit around and wait for more children to die by suicide, for more families to have to bury their young people, or I could fund the whole bloody thing myself. In those circumstances, it was a no-brainer.

Challenging politicians, big systems and bureaucracies is something I see as a vital aspect of my leadership. Systems need people who will challenge their biases and their comfortable status quo. But this is not activism for activism's sake. It's being educated and self-determined so that those who have controlled the systems that do not serve Aboriginal people well can no longer have a say. It's about holding these systems accountable and setting the benchmarks for them based on subject-matter expertise, but also taking responsibility for achieving critical outcomes yourself, ones that represent measurable change.

And when I get up every day and take on big battles, it's so the next generation doesn't have to.

The Dr Tracy Westerman Indigenous Psychology Scholarship

I couldn't continue to stand by when I had the tools to make that difference. If they saved just *one* life, it would be worth every ounce of my energy.

The litmus test of progress must be each generation doing better than the previous one. My parents more than did their job. Because of their efforts, I struggle significantly less than they did. I understand that it is my responsibility to ensure that the next generation struggles less than mine has. And I accept that this responsibility is broader and far more urgent for Aboriginal people because we are playing generational catch-up – with whole generations, like my mum, being excluded from education and from being paid for work, and with many of us not having equal access to education or employment, nor the advantage of family wealth to fall back on.

Awards like the Australian of the Year (WA) can provide a critical platform for important causes if you stick to your key message. The opportunities it presented took me by surprise. The number of invitations to major events and the interest from the media and the public was significant, although because it was a distraction from my business I had to weigh up whether to invest the energy. I decided to just run with it and say yes to as many opportunities as possible because the cause was just too important.

My background in public speaking was such an advantage with all the media, interviews and, of course, the schmoozing. Among it all, I had two clear strategies. First, I would not allow my key messaging to be diluted. For example, the 'Change the Date' campaign was developing great momentum and although I am a supporter of this, the danger of being drawn into this general social commentary was that my focus as a psychologist would get lost. Issues of child suicide had to be front and centre of everything I said. So, my strategy was to answer the question but always bring it back to the mental health impacts. This was not always easy as the media were not accustomed to speaking at a complex level about trauma, suicides and the causative factors behind these shocking statistics. But as the first Aboriginal person from the Pilbara and the first psychologist to win the Australian of the Year (WA) and, to my knowledge, the first psychologist to be a finalist, I was highly experienced in training people to have complex conversations about Indigenous mental health, trauma and suicides.

My second strategy was having key words I would either repeat or come back to, so that these complex issues would be accessible and understood by laypeople or the 'non-converted'. Having spent decades delivering so much public training and to such disparate audiences was very helpful because I knew how to talk to community mob and non-psychologists.

My goal was to bring these conversations into the lounge rooms of average Australians and for everyone to care about these realities. I wanted to make the 97 per cent feel as affected by these issues as the 3 per cent are.

I have made a career out of my ability to bring black and white equally into the room. It's not easy to put people in situations in which you have to appeal to them to share their knowledge when they have tension, pain and anger that have gone back many lifetimes. Giving up even more 'power' is a hard ask for Aboriginal people, but you appeal to them based on the shared outcome of community and, specifically, of our future generations, our children. Normalising difficult conversations by identifying and recognising process, group dynamic and body language is a necessary part of a psychologist's job.

It's vital to find a common relatability with issues that too often polarise. The problem with trying to bring the entire country into these conversations was the long history of indifference from non-Aboriginal people, but I had already spent a lifetime living and trying to understand what drove that indifference. The first option was that people were afraid of putting their foot in it and not knowing what to say or do. The second was that they simply didn't understand the issues well. The third was that they just did not care.

In my experience it's mostly the first two reasons, but it didn't mean I assumed indifference didn't drive a vast majority – and that's racism as well as human nature. If something doesn't impact me, my family or my ability to live my life, why should I care about it? However, I could see that extremism was also putting off the people we most needed to bring into the conversation, which was white Australia. It was crucial that white Australia feel compelled to do something about these issues as much as Aboriginal people.

I then started to think about what I could do to harness the incredible goodwill that winning awards was bringing. I had quite a number of ideas. The first was, of course, to get into high-risk communities to deliver our suicide intervention programs and to upskill these communities in my programs, as described in Chapter 8. I knew the programs were having huge impacts, because I had seen and measured the outcomes.

Around the same time, the Fogliani inquiry came down with its recommendations. They were filled with the usual stereotyping of bereaved Aboriginal parents – for example, 21 per cent were about alcohol restrictions and it called for more money for the assessment of fetal alcohol spectrum disorder (FASD), despite not one of the thirteen young people having been diagnosed with it. (In fact, FASD has not been shown to be causal of suicides. I have been heavily critical of what I refer to as the 'FASD freight train', with the disorder becoming an explanation for everything to do with Aboriginal people – from crime to suicides.) On the flip side, there were *no* recommendations about improving mental health assessments. How can you prevent suicide if you cannot assess someone properly? It's the most critical part of prevention. If you cannot assess, you cannot treat, you cannot prevent – and this was my area of expertise.

This is what coroners and inquiries give you – the failure not only to match the evidence that bereaved parents had given, but to provide what communities were screaming out for over decades. I am rarely annoyed, but this time I was angry.

When you have looked into the eyes of a parent who has lost a child through suicide, it never leaves you. This kind of grief is almost impossible to recover from, and the pain of not being heard just compounded that. What was also being missed in all these inquiries was that they had all concluded the same thing: that Aboriginal people were continuing to die as a direct result of 'system failure' and a lack of access to culturally competent services.

That children are dying from want in a world of excess is our greatest tragedy

Because I am from a remote community, I have seen how impossible it is to get access to complex services. And because I am a psychologist, I also understand how terrible the training is in terms of ensuring practitioners are culturally informed. We also know that being from the same culture as your client significantly improves treatment outcomes. For example, in the medical profession, having a black doctor can reduce the infant mortality rate of black patients threefold.[1] In other words, cultural competency saves lives.

So, as someone from a remote area, I got it – there was no access to mental health services. Throw culture into the mix and it becomes a very rare skill set, and for decades governments had failed to respond adequately to something so fundamental.

As an ex-Curtin graduate, I picked up the phone and called Vice-Chancellor Deborah Terry. I told her that I wanted to donate $50,000 for an Indigenous psychology scholarship in my name – this would be $10,000 a year. The wheels moved fairly quickly, which they needed to as we were playing generational catch-up here. By then I had established a pretty significant media reach and was about to deliver my speech as WA Australian of the Year, so it was great timing to publicly announce the scholarship as well. The meeting at Curtin went well and we agreed on a media statement to be released on 10 October 2018.

I had also just been informed that I had won the Curtin University Lifetime Achievement Award, and that the provost at Curtin would close my speech at Frasers Restaurant in the next few days. The universe was aligning and working in my favour, which wasn't lost on me. In 2018 I was also inducted into the WA Women's Hall of Fame.

I don't, on principle, believe that anything you donate or do for free should be publicly announced. My dad modelled this well. You do good deeds just because it is right, not for the accolades they bring (this is known as narcissistic supply). There are many malignant narcissists who operate this way, and it's not true altruism. This meant that publicly announcing the scholarship sat really badly with me, but I also understood that it might guilt other people into donating. This was about Aboriginal children dying by suicide, for god's sake, and I knew that the only way to compel the non-engaged to take action was to use every possible emotional button.

The scholarship becomes a program

Initially, we received dribs and drabs of money from the public, but it was slow-going. I was obsessed with making it a success because I don't do failure. I had my massive public reach going for me, so in every workshop, radio interview, keynote speech and private therapy session, and through constant posts on social media, all I talked about was the scholarship. I completely forgot about developing my business because I saw the scholarship as the missing piece of the puzzle.

But we continued to get small amounts of money, and it was not enough to fund another scholarship beyond my contribution. At this stage, Curtin had five Indigenous students enrolled in psychology, so I was determined to get as many of them funded as possible.

Then, we hit pay dirt! I was delivering a workshop in Alice Springs when I got an excited phone message from Curtin's scholarship manager to ring her urgently. Well, you always know it's important when you get a message like that. So, during afternoon tea I called her to get the incredible news that a member of the public had heard about the scholarship and was going to match my donation of $50,000. I was absolutely overwhelmed.

Of course I rang the donor, the amazing Stephen Grant, who has run art galleries in Sydney and New York with his wife, Bridget Pirrie. As it happened, I was about to go to Sydney to feature in a Country Road campaign for Mother's Day on 'nurturing women' (yes, things were getting silly now), so I was able to catch up with Stephen for a quick chat and coffee en route to the airport. The synergy was there straight away, and we had a pretty effortless conversation about his desire to make a difference after spending a lot of time in the Kimberley and seeing the obvious need for better mental health services there.

Well, it got better. When I landed in Perth after that meeting, I got another excited call from Curtin University – after meeting me, Stephen and his wonderful family had decided to make a $50,000 donation every year for five years, a total of $250,000! I posted the news on social media and it went *off*, so it wasn't long before the mainstream media picked it up. It generated the buzz I hoped it would and I did media for most of that week. At this very early stage, it was *all* about developing reach and a brand.

Soon after, people started to email and contact us to help raise funds. Enter the wonderful Gavin Partridge and Roger Benedict, who ran an annual fundraising concert in Sydney every year on World Suicide Prevention Day, which is 10 September. So the request was, 'We run a fundraising concert every year on World Suicide Prevention Day. We raise anywhere from $40,000 to $100,000 and we were wondering if we could raise money for your scholarship?' The concert included the children's choir and the incredible Simon Tedeschi on piano – and, of course, Roger as the head conductor.

Umm, let me think about that for a minute … Yep!

It was revelation after revelation for me during those years, and the big one was that despite Aboriginal people having the highest rates of child suicide, we had been invisible on World Suicide Prevention Day. Roger and Gavin approaching us to raise funds through the concert made me realise that and it stopped me in my tracks.

Unfortunately, it was also incredibly difficult trying to promote a concert held in Sydney that was fundraising for issues which were disproportionally affecting the top half of Australia. The average white Australian was really not aware of the problem, so it was like pulling teeth to fill seats. It was important, however, to try to engage these different hearts and minds, even if 'Aboriginal child suicides' was a really hard sell. Activism is hard, but black activism is much harder.

So, the concert now became my entire focus in everything I said, especially in every piece of media. It wasn't just about *what* I was saying, but *how* I was saying it. I knew that there are three types of empathy and that all three need to be hit up in order to enact behavioural change and action.

The first is when people can identify emotions in others. That's called cognitive empathy. At a purely social brain level, people pick up on emotion, but that's not sufficient for action. The second type is emotional empathy, which means that you genuinely feel what you say you are feeling. That's also not sufficient, because feelings always shift, particularly when, as a white person, blackness and cultural identity does not have a daily impact on you or your family. So, the third type of empathy is actually the most critical: perspective-taking empathy or empathetic concern.

To compel people to act, I had to reduce what I referred to as 'proximity to audience' – the more we lessen the proximity between the issue and the public, the more relatable it would be and the more they'll feel able to act on their compassion. Comparing the responses to the suicide of Dolly Everett with those of the thirteen Aboriginal young people, there was a stark difference in compulsion to act, purely because every single parent in Australia could relate to Dolly being 'their child'. It's not that people didn't care at all about Aboriginal children dying by suicide – they mostly had the first two empathies, but the last one was readily forgotten because the suicides didn't have an impact on them or their families, or make them feel that it could happen to *their* child, so the compulsion was less.

So, when I spoke publicly, I framed my words to tap into that perspective-taking empathy. It wasn't 'Aboriginal children' dying by suicide but 'Australia's children' or 'ten-year-old children – imagine if this was your child'. I had many parents come to me in tears, saying: 'I have a ten-year-old daughter. I couldn't imagine losing her to suicide.' When people react emotionally like this, that's when you know you have got them. It stirs people to protest in the streets and exert consistent public pressure. The lack of this kind of reaction and the absence of connection to the pain of black people is why we are where we are.

And it's why it was so hard to fill the seats at the Sydney Conservatorium of Music. The concert was an amazing opportunity to promote the scholarship, but selling tickets was painstaking. I had only just started to get a social media following, so was flooding my socials with it. I was using as much of my IPS database as I could to get the word out and was up until *all* hours of the night emailing everyone I knew to try to get them along to the concert and encourage others to do the same. It genuinely shocked Roger and Gavin how slowly tickets were moving, given how easy it had been to sell their previous events. It gave them a firsthand look at how hard black activism is. Getting people to attend to raise money for more Indigenous psychologists to address the horrific suicide rates in Aboriginal communities should have been a no-brainer, but I understood – having already developed a successful business from scratch – that this was a marathon, not a sprint. To reach the 'hearts and minds' of Australians, the development of the brand was a necessary part of that, which could only be achieved through public attention and education.

We finally filled around 70 per cent of the hall, and I made my way to Sydney for the event. Media was again my primary focus, in addition to giving a speech at the concert. Roger and Gavin were a little surprised that I came all the way from Perth, but I understood the opportunity and importance of it.

SBS had requested an interview and would and film the concert, which was great in getting the word out, and then the wonderful Jeremy Fernandez from the ABC interviewed me, which really blew up online. I think the ABC website crashed a few times with people trying to view it. It was a great interview by Jeremy and he definitely asked the tough questions. It was filmed in the foyer of the ABC studios with just one camera operator. The interviews I love the most are the ones that are natural and tap into my instincts as a psychologist. Most of Jeremy's questions were about the 'why' of Indigenous suicides and 'how' to address it. By asking specific subject-matter questions, he showed that he understood the issues well.

We needed media to get this right, and many of them wanted to get it right. I regularly volunteer to write passages of articles about me and my work for journalists that deal with complex subjects, as it's easy to get things wrong. Even the best journalists are grateful for this. I see the responsibility of educating the public on these issues as one of my most important roles.

The evening itself was just beautiful, but so many conversations were about people not knowing much, not just about Aboriginal suicide rates, but about Aboriginal issues in general. We managed to raise $35,000, which was absolutely fantastic as this was at least *three* scholarships for a year, and it also gave us the flexibility to award these to students studying at any tertiary institution. The scholarship was still under the auspices of Curtin University, which limited its reach to Indigenous students enrolled in psychology there. This wasn't going to achieve what we needed for our communities.

Most importantly, the concert planted the idea in my head of hosting a fundraising event in Western Australia, historically the epicentre of suicides and where the data showed the highest-risk areas were – the Kimberley and most of the top half of Australia.

When I got back to Perth, I became determined to organise something, but where to start?

Enter Kim Beazley

I had met Kim Beazley several times throughout 2018. He had become the WA governor that year and came along to one of my presentations. It gave me the opportunity to thank him publicly for what I thought was one of the greatest speeches about Indigenous issues by a politician – his reply in parliament to the *Bringing Them Home* report about the Stolen Generations. The then-prime minister, John Howard, refused to let his government participate in the debate.[2]

There was an immediate synergy between us. My mum had long admired 'the Gov', as I began to call him, and he was very generous with his time, asking on more than one occasion how he could help my cause. Truth be told, I wasn't entirely sure at the time. I had only just started to think about how to use the platform I had. Many of my ideas were just too big and would require government funding, so I had to find a different path. I assumed that once I started funding something myself and working for free that they would jump on board. That didn't happen and it still hasn't, sadly.

When I met with the Gov on one of our usual catch-ups, I put it to him that he become the Jilya patron. His response was, 'Of course! What else can I do?' I thought his executive assistant was going to pass out as the Gov had a long list of people asking him to patron their charities, but he didn't have the time to take them all on. I felt very privileged that we managed to hook the Gov. He said to me, 'You know, Tracy, I have heard many ideas over my time. Many are great but they are just too complicated. This is so simple, this idea of yours – of course high-risk communities need more Indigenous psychologists.'

The announcement got a great response, particularly on my growing social media following. The Gov was one of those rare politicians who was respected by both sides of politics and blackfellas loved him. I had a massive following from mob across Australia and their reaction was universally positive. It was a rare feat. Of course, the idea of aligning with someone in a monarchist role and what that might mean to Aboriginal people gave me pause. Every decision in a start-up must have deep thought behind it, to see where obvious criticism could come from. Ultimately, having the Kim Beazley 'brand' – the values he had shown throughout his political life, and, most importantly, his mentorship – outweighed the worst-case scenario of any pushback. Every decision had to be about amplifying the cause, and the Gov achieved that and more. Many people got on board purely because of his reputation and rightly so.

So, with a high-profile patron, a bit of cash in the pocket and my usual 24/7 energy levels, we were able to go full steam ahead on the official launch of the Dr Tracy Westerman Scholarship Program under Curtin University. The Gov's involvement meant we had access to Government House, including catering and the staff, which was such a relief as it would have been more than overwhelming to try to pay for it all and deal with it all myself.

The night was great and my family all came down from the Pilbara. Along with a few other mob from Perth and the Kimberley, they felt a bit overwhelmed by Government House and all of the 'flashness' around it. The media were great too and it was the starting point of the students being thrown into the spotlight, which they all did so well with. It was also amazing for them to meet the Gov, who insisted on having a personal conversation with all five of them. Two of the initial recipients, Taylah Thompson and Nikki McKenzie, remain in our Jilya family today. Taylah recently submitted her Clinical Masters and Nikki began her Masters this year, after being enrolled in psychology since 2008, no less – that was a *big* one!

The ending of my launch speech has become a bit of a mantra for every year of scholarship intake since. It goes like this:

> You have learnt that your greatest advantage is the disadvantage you all come from. You have not allowed it to define you nor to limit you. That makes the very essence of who you are and what you have lived to be the critical difference in how communities will find the strength to heal ourselves.

There was not a dry eye in the house.

Unfortunately, it didn't translate into any money or donations, so that was the learning – always be clear that you want people to open their chequebooks. We had so many wealthy people in that room, but there was a disconnect between the scholarship and it being affiliated with a university that didn't have my passion or the reach that I knew I could achieve. I've learnt in twenty years of business that people are just really uncomfortable talking about money. I made it become part of my comfort zone and vowed to talk about money in every conversation or else they could stop wasting my time.

The scholarship becomes a charity

I have never been someone who plots or plans. The scholarship just naturally evolved, as most organically good ideas should, and the Gov was right about its simplicity. But I understood that its main pull was because it was being led by a psychologist from a remote area who had overcome disadvantage to put her own money into it, and who was personally mentoring the students. It was a combination of factors that was immediately compelling. It was also an easy story to sell because by then I had spent twenty-three years delivering my programs across Australia and developing massive grassroots support and street cred.

So, very quickly, South Australia said, 'Hey, what about us?' We managed to hook Life Without Barriers – its regional manager, Kyp Boucher, was amazing and funded our first SA scholarship. Moving beyond just Western Australia allowed us to develop the idea of a national program. It was at this point that the wonderful crew at the law firm Herbert Smith Freehills approached us to provide pro bono support so that we could become a registered charity with the Australian Charities and Not-for-Profits Commission (ACNC). It was difficult to expand the scholarship because we could only encourage people to donate to Curtin University, which held the money for the scholarship, until our ACNC status was confirmed. This limited so many opportunities, which was unfortunate.

Finally, on 11 November 2020 we became officially registered as the Westerman Jilya Institute for Indigenous Mental Health ('Jilya') Corporation. We also registered with the Office of the Registrar of Aboriginal Corporations. Now we could really go full steam ahead!

Jilya means 'my child' in my Nyamal language, which resonated with people straight away. (It's also the name of my cocker spaniel, who gets very confused by me talking about Jilya constantly!) It was about providing the best opportunity for a future free of the generational child suicides that have plagued our communities for too long, and not being caught in some self-fulfilling prophecy where suicides are normalised in our highest-risk communities.

We developed our inaugural board, which meant we began planning to extend the scholarships to a national program, as well as ensuring that the three other streams of Jilya – determining causal pathways and best practice treatments, and bringing prevention programs to high-risk communities – could be developed and funded. However, the starting point had to be branding Jilya and focusing on what was 'easy' to sell – which, of course, was the scholarships.

#BuildAnArmy

In an interview with Noongar Radio, I was asked, 'Dr Westerman, what is your aim with this scholarship?' Without skipping a beat, I said, 'I want to build an army. I want hundreds and hundreds of Indigenous psychologists in every part of this country, so never again will a child die by suicide on our watch due to a lack of access to services.'

So, the #BuildAnArmy hashtag started on social media and became branded with Jilya. It took off naturally with my followers and it became pretty cool to have so many people approach me in person or on socials to say, 'I want to join your army.' Branding is always about what resonates, which this clearly was, so we just let it naturally keep building.

Now that we were a registered charity, we could take control of all the money I had managed to raise, which was around $300,000. We then advertised for the inaugural Westerman Jilya Institute scholarships under the Dr Tracy Westerman Indigenous Psychology Scholarship Program, but making it clear that they were now national scholarships. We were shocked when more than forty applications came through. Many scholarship programs have to send money back as not enough students apply.

We realistically couldn't fund them all, so we had to cull them. The shortlisting process was incredibly emotional. At this stage, although we had a little bit of money from the donations that could now come in via the website, I was also determined to find a model which ensured that donor commitments were ongoing. The most effective model that I thought to replicate was World Vision's child sponsorship program – in this case, it would be to 'sponsor a Jilya student' and allocate a student to a donor. I had no problem with pulling at heart strings to get these commitments, but we had incredible donors and it wasn't hard to pitch them the idea of long-term support, particularly if they could get their allocated student through to graduation. So, we managed to secure a few major long-term donors, including KWY Aboriginal Corporation and Life Without Barriers in South Australia, businessman

Garry Brown-Neaves and his family, and many other donors who wished to remain anonymous.

In the lead-up to the launch, I received a Facebook message on behalf of Karen Dell, a beautiful lady I had met during my work in the Bowraville community. It said that Karen's daughter had tragically taken her own life a few days previously, and that she had been a passionate advocate for Indigenous mental health. Her family wanted to start a crowdfunding page in support of Jilya. To say I was overwhelmed was an understatement. Such compassion in the face of overwhelming grief is beyond comprehension, but I have seen this more often than not from bereaved families and parents, who are motivated not only by their love for their child but by wanting to do everything in their power to ensure that another family won't feel the same pain. The scholarship was an incredible legacy for Maddy Dell – it also meant that her family could witness an actual legacy unfolding as a student went through years of study to become a psychologist because of the money they raised.

I was in Northam delivering training when the crowdfunding page was to go live, and I was distracted with messaging Maddy's family to make sure that everything was worded and dealt with in a way they were comfortable with. During my hour-long drive home after the training workshop, the donations reached more than $30,000. I cried many tears, to be honest. I didn't feel worthy of it. I felt so many emotions. I couldn't feel happy, as I had with other donations – I simply sent constant messages of gratitude to Maddy's family and thanked them for their trust.

We ended up with a few students from regional New South Wales, where the family was based, so we let Maddy's family choose who would be the recipient. There were more than $50,000 in pledges, which meant that we could begin the Maddy Dell Scholarship under my program and see a student through to graduation. The family chose Kelly Hyde, who I'd met during one of my workshops in Brisbane. Kelly was about two years into her degree and I had humbugged her to apply for my scholarship. Kell was from Lismore, so that fitted beautifully as Maddy had spent time in the region and was passionate about getting services into regional areas. Kell is unlikely to leave the region, so she is a permanent and practical reminder of everything Maddy was about in life.

Leading up to the 2020 launch of Jilya, through a lot of promotion of the scholarship, we got to the point that it was enough to award thirteen scholarships for a year of study. Looking back, it was probably too many, but I was on a roll and convinced myself that I had a year to pay for their annual scholarships and to tug at the heartstrings of our major donors to sponsor them annually – and that I could easily pull that off. I had never overcommitted myself in business, but I had here. I was also confident that the momentum we were building was just going to get bigger and bigger – plus, I had much more money than I ever had when I started my business. I kept telling myself that if I could start a successful business from absolutely nothing, with no street cred or profile, then this would be a piece of cake. Of course, it wasn't, but I was pretty stubborn and pigheaded when it came to Jilya. I was pushing people in a way I hadn't before, thinking, *Come on, seriously, where is your commitment to our communities?*

The 2020 list included three students from Western Australia (as well as Nikki and Taylah, so a total of five), four from South Australia, three from the Northern Territory, two from Queensland, two from New South Wales and one from Tassie.

The mistakes I made were minimal, fortunately. The main one was not factoring in admin costs in the donations, which meant I not only worked for free (which was completely fine) but funded everything personally, including all of the admin. So, on the advice of a few donors, we added 17 per cent to the $10,000 annual sponsorship fee for any admin and student support, although we didn't touch it initially as I decided I would pay for all admin out of my own pocket as well as my airfares and accommodation travelling around Australia, meeting with 'rich people'. As the scholarship has grown, we have used the money from the fee to fund critical needs for the students – for example, we have a hardship fund to assist with study and research – as well as other study-related support. I hate the idea of spending money on anything other than the students, because too many charities spend public donations on everything but their cause. To date, 100 per cent of public donations to Jilya have gone directly to the students – not on admin or travel or big salaries. I am incredibly proud of that.

The first Jilya concert

After the Sydney concert for World Suicide Prevention Day, I wanted to replicate it in Western Australia as I felt that it would be much easier, with relatively more understanding and interest in the issue of Indigenous suicide. Having it in my home state would also ensure we were self-determined.

The first Jilya concert was a huge logistical undertaking and such a lot of work. It became even more difficult when the global Covid-19 pandemic hit and each week there was another restriction on the number of people allowed to be at events; it significantly impeded the ticket sales and interstate travel was, of course, impossible for those major supporters and donors who wanted to attend. The wonderful Gina Williams AM and Guy Ghouse – incredible local artists who had both experienced suicides in their own families and were involved in the Jilya launch at Government House – were keen to be involved.

I had spent the better part of two months furiously writing to every single profiled artist across the country to try to get attention for this cause. Finally, after rejections from around a dozen of them, I was in Alice Springs doing a workshop. In the evening, I opened my inbox to this email from the manager of ARIA Award–winning artist John Butler saying, quite simply, 'John would be honoured to play at your concert.'

I literally screamed with joy and rang the entire Jilya board. This was the 'big fish' we needed and it was absolutely overwhelming to us as a tiny start-up charity. I then knew that Jilya had 'arrived' – having someone with the profile of John Butler was a very big deal. But, of course, this did add massive pressure to then pull the whole thing off and without any resources to do it.

Then, in addition to the musicians, I decided to add to the pressure and have all the students attend the concert, which meant organising for them all to fly to Perth, as well as hosting something so they could all be in a room together and start to bond. I managed to get a $15,000 pledge from an anonymous donor to assist with the accommodation and flights, but it ended up costing less than that due to a lot of cheap organising, my frequent flyer and hotel points, and the students being great at not spending much!

Getting them all together was so important; after all, we were 'building an army' – or, more accurately, building a family. I desperately wanted these students to support each other and have each other's backs, and to have this modelled for them. I didn't want them to experience what I had from my peers. So, the day before the concert, 9 September 2021, was arguably one of the most stressful and proudest days of my life – and that's saying something. I personally sent Ubers for them to come to my house, where I hosted a lunch, which involved organising catering. The students were overwhelmed with being in that room with each other. It was beyond my wildest dreams to see how exceptional they all were as people and for them to witness this in each other.

To add to the fun of the day, I had been asked by ABC's *The Drum* to come onto the show to talk about the concert. Of course I said yes, but it meant I only had five minutes to rush all the students out of my house and back into Ubers, and make sure the technology was working, before going on live TV.

The lead-in for the story took my breath way. The producers had found all our social media with the artists talking about the concert, including John Butler, and they did an amazing mash-up of it all.

Ellen Fanning did an excellent introduction to the reality of what I was doing – that I was having to fundraise to ensure that young people in our highest-risk communities did not continue to die from a lack of access to services. She asked some good questions about why Indigenous practitioners were needed and I was able to explain some complex issues to a pretty big audience. It felt great, but I didn't realise how great it was until afterwards.

I receive an email every time someone makes a donation to Jilya. It's a fantastic thing to see and I often email the donors directly to thank them. But after six minutes on *The Drum*, I got a text message from my website guy, saying, 'What the hell just happened?! Your website has crashed!' I replied, 'Umm, I've just been on TV talking about the concert and the scholarship.'

'Well,' he texted, 'it's crashed the site, but luckily I was in front of the computer and managed to get it working again.'

Over the next day, we were completely *flooded* with public donations. By the time the concert was ready to go, we had received more than $100,000! The response was simply incredible, but it wasn't just about the money – the donors' comments were so supportive. In just six minutes, Australia had reacted to something I had said and that showed we were on the right track. The level of faith that the country was placing in us was overwhelming, and it gave me the win I desperately needed after finding it so bloody hard to generate ticket sales for the Perth event. Eventually, we made $145,000 in ticket sales. Adding this to donations after *The Drum* and during the promotional phase of the event, we ended up with around $250,000!

That year we were able to announce eleven more recipients of the scholarship, taking us to a total of twenty-six students. It was just fantastic how quickly we had grown. At the same time, we also got a small grant from Lotterywest of $403,000, so we could actually employ people.

The two years of working full-time on Jilya – sitting on the board, mentoring all the students, fundraising and then managing a very stressful business – and, of course, daily activism and media was understandably taking its toll. I lost around 5 kilograms in the lead-up to the concert from stress (and I don't really have 5 kilos to lose), with sixteen-hour days on average of trying to get seats sold and build everything from the ground up, including ticket sites and social media promotion. Fortunately, we had the amazing Vu Consulting, who approached me via social media, to do our PR pro bono. They were pretty shocked with the amount of media and social media interest I had managed to generate, given I am only one person. I had managed 15 million hits across social media and 194 syndicated media pieces across print, TV and radio.

We have arrived!

Developing something from nothing means being prepared for the long haul – facing many setbacks and still believing in what you are doing. Despite how hard it has been, I have always believed in Jilya and how crucial it is to Australia. Believing in something so deeply helps me keep getting back up.

As Jilya grew, I took on the role of chairperson. As much work as it seems to be, given I am so heavily involved in the operations and students, it is important that, as the founder, I retain delegation and authority over its governance for many reasons. First, the vision is mine, but also, I ultimately wear all of the consequences if anything is wrong because my name is on the pamphlets!

I also want the scholarship to be unique, not selecting students based on grades but on the barriers they have faced and the disadvantage they have experienced. I regularly reject students who have distinctions. Why? Because they often have relatively fewer gaps to close than other students. We also, of course, want students who come from high-risk, remote communities, so we mostly select those from, for example, the Pilbara or remote Northern Territory over someone from Sydney or Brisbane. It's not always the case, though, because we spend a lot of time understanding our students and asking them about their personal backgrounds. Pretty much all of them have come from significant family trauma – it is almost a given with all the applicants.

This is about making students into future leaders. Each time I see them I want to see growth in their confidence and as people, to be better versions of themselves. The grades naturally improve once we cultivate that environment of not only belief but also of black excellence.

The application also doesn't ask for the repulsive 'proof of Aboriginality' via a statutory declaration – which, as I discussed in Chapter 4, is deeply offensive to me and also problematic.

In my scholarship program, applicants are required to:

1. identify as Aboriginal and note their cultural links, mob and where they are from;
2. have a reference attesting to their work in Aboriginal communities, with evidence of their effectiveness and impacts (in the US, scholarship applications require a minimum of 400 hours community service – we are heading that way as all of our students have this anyway);
3. have clear desire to work clinically in a high-risk Aboriginal community upon graduation, and that any university coursework or thesis will focus on Indigenous-specific psychology gaps.

The interview process is critical and the common-sense part. We spend a good twenty minutes discussing mob and community links and their passion for helping high-risk Aboriginal communities.

Most importantly, I have these criteria because representation matters. One of my favourite recipients is Tex Garstone from Halls Creek. (Okay, he's actually my favourite!) When Tex received a scholarship, it became possible for every kid from Halls Creek to study psychology, because representation matters. It was the same when I became the first Aboriginal person to complete a Masters and PhD in Clinical Psychology. We have many students who 'represent' and that is what is so powerful about them. You cannot be what you have never seen.

My speech at the 2022 Jilya concert was all about representation. I love this passage the most:

Our students represent to every Aboriginal person who has ever been told that they are not smart enough, that they don't belong. Anything is possible because nothing has come easy to any of them.

We have the first future Indigenous male psychologist from Halls Creek; the first future Torres Strait Islander psychologist from Rockhampton; the first Indigenous psychologists from Tasmania, from Mount Isa. Two Indigenous LGBTQI psychology students – the first in Australia.

Not one has come from advantage. All have struggled through isolation, not belonging and many come from significant trauma backgrounds. All of which is going to make them incredible future psychologists because the best method of understanding how to heal pain is to live it.

As Aboriginal people, we are doctors and lawyers. Some of us lead the world in what we do. We do not need to be rescued or have a lesser standard applied to us. Our students represent what others do not see as possible, simply because they have never seen it before.

They battle for relevance in a world that has never championed or understood Indigenous excellence, brilliance and empowerment. But at Jilya we DO!

The scholarship never belonged anywhere but in the hands of those who have also closed many gaps. Those who have also ticked every box that should not have been a success, because we understand grades and academic transcripts often mean nothing more than that you have had fewer barriers to overcome.

We have had not one student – NOT ONE – drop out in four years. In two decades the government has never managed to have an Indigenous psychologist based permanently in the Kimberley. We have five already who are either from there or wish to work there. How? Because representation matters.

The future

At the Jilya concert in 2022 on World Suicide Prevention Day, I announced the first of our 'equity' scholarships, which I again kicked off with a personal donation of $30,000 a year. The announcement of my initial $50,000 commitment a few years earlier for the very first scholarship attracted other donations, so I used this same effective strategy again. It was becoming clearer and clearer that the $10,000 a year was having very little impact for around 70 per cent of our students. Ultimately, we were playing generational catch-up so we needed to get them out to communities as quickly as possible. Many had to work full-time to afford to study and all came from zero financial advantage to fall back on.

We had the wonderful Julia Zemiro donate the same, and then Malcolm and Lucy Turnbull followed very quickly. It was fantastic how it was becoming easier to get these types of commitments, but that's the thing about developing something from scratch – you are always figuring out your buy-in level. The great thing about the scholarship is that we have been able to constantly reinvent it to get closer to what we are trying to achieve – developing skills in our highest-risk communities, because locals *never* leave. To do this, we need to remove the financial barriers that most in these high-risk areas have, which is frequently their sole limitation to starting or completing a psychology degree. Our mentoring and support then provide the students with self-belief. We are developing a 'family' of our students with this idea that we are all in it together, so that they naturally mentor or support each other as I have with them – in a pay-it-forward fashion.

Now it's really become about representation because of the growth of the scholarship, but also about taking on the biggest challenges that life throws at you and the idea that you can overcome them through self-belief. We have shown what is possible without needing to look outside of ourselves to governments to 'save us'. Jilya represents true self-determination. I call it 'Australia's charity' because it is average Australians who have enabled us to get to where we are.

At the end of 2022, the Paul Ramsay Foundation COO reached out for a meeting during their trip to Perth. They were keen on a partnership, based on my work 'that we keep hearing about'. Of course, I moved everything to be available. Over lunch I pitched Jilya to them and that what we were trying to achieve was significantly beyond funding scholarships. We wanted to establish treatments of best practice specifically for Aboriginal people, determine unique causal pathways and develop the first database of Indigenous mental health by digitising my WASC-Y screening tools, which would give us the opportunity to track and respond to suicide and mental health risk in real time for the first time. Most importantly, we also wanted to upskill high-risk communities in my (donated) whole-of-community intervention programs, so that local people could deliver these programs over time. Obviously, all this was complementary to the scholarship and employing our students to have the first national Indigenous psychology service and keep these skills in our highest-risk communities. It was exciting and involved multiple Australian firsts.

The Paul Ramsay Foundation were pretty blown away with the potential of it all. This was globally significant work and they now understood that, although they made no clear commitment at that point. That's the nature of 'business' – it often takes time. There are multiple meetings and many wasted hours trying to convince people to fund you instead of the many other ideas they hear regularly. Often people only see the end result; they rarely understand or appreciate how much work has gone into getting it.

I was not only working in it at the coalface but also developing a capacity that Australia had never seen before with a ready workforce of highly trained psychologists and putting my twenty years of IP into Jilya. Because this is an incredibly complex, bespoke area, I have always been heavily involved in finding the money and running much of the operation. But we need to develop this capacity or our children will continue to die, and that's just not an option.

Why running remains my salvation

I have learnt over time that tiredness is temporary and my ability to bounce back from it is significant. That's why my physical fitness is a key ingredient in my success and longevity. It probably looks relentless from the outside, as I regularly train for between two and four hours every day, but you cannot have the energy to do what I do without being extremely fit.

I have always had my greatest breakthroughs on a run. I came up with the idea for Jilya on a run, as well as my PhD, but it was when I switched to running marathons that I truly learnt about mental toughness and what I was capable of. I turned to them a bit late in life, and I wish I had figured out earlier that I had the mental strength to run them. Statistics say only 1 per cent of the world's population have run a marathon, and I can see why. I've run three – Bunbury, Perth and Melbourne.

I've trained with some really elite, fit people and the marathon destroyed them. Every Sunday is my 'long run' day and it wipes out my entire day. It's between 30 and 35 kilometres, but it doesn't actually become too tough until you get beyond 30 kilometres. A lot of people underestimate the mental toughness going beyond this distance – there's a saying that 'a marathon doesn't start until the 30-kilometres mark'. I have watched people collapse at this point. I have watched people being carted away by ambulances. I have watched people I have spent hours with on the course running stop and walk, and it is so tempting to do the same. But once you stop you are pretty well stuffed. Your entire body seizes up and you cannot prepare yourself for that sensation. The only thing that you can do to get through the unbelievable pain is to mentally convince yourself to keep moving, and the ability to do that is what ultimately separates people who are able to run marathons from people who can't.

But with each marathon, I have actually learnt so much about myself and there have been so many incredible moments of inspiration. I've seen a guy with cerebral palsy running the Melbourne marathon with support sticks, who I only passed at the 41-kilometre mark; I've seen blind people running with support runners, and a guy wearing army boots and a full army backpack. There have also been *so* many people running in honour of someone they have lost – kids to cancer, loved ones who were murdered – using running to find a purpose through overwhelming pain. At the end of the marathon, it's pretty common that finishers will be crying and hugging each other because it truly strips you bare when you have nothing left physically. All that is left is pure emotions and it is something only other finishers understand. Perhaps I respond to marathons because I have seen so many people go through unimaginable grief, loss, trauma and pain, have nothing left, but then find a place of true honesty and grit they didn't think they had.

In the Perth marathon, I got to that pain barrier of around 31 kilometres and I learnt for the first time what 'mindfulness' could do to propel you beyond what your body would probably be capable of if you focused on how bad you were feeling. Instead, I instinctually knew that I had to find some way to tune out or it was going to beat me.

The music on my iPhone was just starting to grate on me, so I had to focus on something else. The guy in front of me was running at the exact same pace as me but he looked like he was running much more easily, so I just focused on his energy. It sounds weird, but it was about getting back into a nice rhythmic flow and 'borrowing' that flow. I started to watch his feet hit the ground, and I tuned out to everything except that: the pain in my legs, the chafing all over my body, the fact I still had 10 kilometres left to run. I tuned out to everything except his feet hitting the ground and became entranced by the rhythm. That's mindfulness. You are not aware of anything – not pain, not how much longer you have to go – except for being in the moment. I did that without realising it for a good 5 kilometres until that awful feeling of wanting to stop had passed.

I have never forgotten that moment – to take your body as far as you think it is capable of and then find a way to still keep going.

My marathon training got me through one of the only truly dark times in my life; it gave me a reason to get out of bed and to literally put one foot in front of the other and this became my daily goal until I was able to process emotions better. Studies are now showing that exercise and movement is as effective in treating depression as psychotherapy, by forcing you to stay with your pain and somehow find a way out of it. Marathons require you to set practical goals on every run and that alone feeds self-efficacy and mastery, which often reduces depression. I think I can run them because I am that way in life. I am someone who can tolerate a lot of pain. I can tolerate a lot of stress. But ultimately I am a person who always needs to find a way, despite the odds. Marathons were initially mostly a psychological battle because they forced me to 'slow down' – my background was in explosive, fast sports, which allowed for very little thinking time and were convenient distractions. Marathons forced me to sit with so many feelings and thoughts on those long runs. I am so glad I discovered them because they have humbled me and helped me to find that 'extra gear' when I have needed one – to believe that nothing is insurmountable.

There have only been a few times in my life when I have felt so exhausted that I thought I couldn't get back up again. The end of the 2021 concert was one of those moments, and I struggled to convince myself that it was all worth it. But as a psychologist, I also understood that, as I say to many of my clients, 'Never make major life decisions when you are in crisis. Because when the dust settles, you will always inevitably regret a decision made on an impulse or one you can't take back.'

Tiredness is temporary.

Around the same time as the meeting with the Ramsay Foundation, I travelled to Sydney to talk to some big players. The trip netted quite a lot – another $30,000 equity scholarship, and MP Ben Franklin, who I had met at his request, pledged a fantastic $168,000 for NSW-specific scholarships.

This was all excellent and it meant that we increasingly had scholarships at the magical $30,000 a year mark, meaning that these students would be able to work less and study more. However, the lack of operational funding was going to start hurting us, despite getting around $100,000 in public donations for the past two years plus a great amount of support from the Myer Foundation, Future Generation and many more pledges that saw a really healthy 'bank balance'. The commitments to what was now forty students meant that we were actually overcommitted in terms of long-term trends in funds per students, and I don't like being panic-driven. I have not been successful in my life by overcommitting myself or living outside of my means, and the situation was making me really uncomfortable.

The text message that changed everything

So, with this weighing heavily on my mind, I flew to Sydney to deliver a four-day workshop. After a long day, I was on the phone to my EA when a call came through that went to text conversion. The message read:

Hi Tracy. It's Dominique from the Paul Ramsay Foundation. I just wanted to call you with some good news that the proposal we received from you we submitted to the board and they have just approved to fund scholarships and research over three years. I think it was $4.3 million.

Not only have I kept that message, but I screenshot it so I never lose it. Suffice to say I read the message and *screamed*, throwing the phone in the air from the excitement. I am surprised the hotel didn't ring security!

I then rang each board member to tell them the wonderful news. They just couldn't believe it. A few happy tears were shed that night. When I finally had enough composure to ring Dominique back, she said the most amazing words:

Tracy, we have travelled into every single part of Australia and literally *everywhere* we have been we have had people *beg* us to fund you so that they can get access to you and your amazing work. I mean *every single* community. It is such an honour to support your work.

Jilya has accomplished so many firsts and we will no doubt achieve a significant amount more. We have shown that we can empower each other to make a critical difference. To achieve what has never been achieved. To do better. To be better. To represent all that is possible.

In 2023 we were able to get a significant number of the students across to Perth for the Jilya fundraising concert. We also held the first formal Jilya Student Conference, with support from the Novotel and

Mercure hotels and, of course, the Paul Ramsay Foundation money. It was two days of student professional development, including training on attachment theory by Dr Lynn Priddis; Dr Sam Cooms (one of our Jilya directors) on publishing as an Indigenous academic; Dr Leanne Holt (the previous Jilya chair) on racism in academia; and I did two presentations, on Jilya research opportunities and managing the media.

Much of my role with the students is simply to reinforce a lot of the value base of what we are about because we are making future leaders. The attacks will come and the only way to withstand them is to be clear about your values and consistent in how you communicate them. I have gone through a lot of media and taken on some complex issues publicly, and this experience is really what I bring for them. However, I also put my research on display to be critiqued and challenged during the conference, and I model that for the students as a leadership growth trait. I want to make it clear that *no-one* is beyond critique, because that is what science demands. I encourage them all to be brave enough to be prepared to be proven wrong because this is what makes for better outcomes – when our scientific hypotheses are either proven or disproven. They are a bit shocked by it, but probably the main trait that has got me the furthest is that, when it comes to leadership, I lack an ego. Ego-driven leaders always need to be right. They will surround themselves with people who will never challenge them to be better or smarter.

My father once said to me, 'Tracy, not standing for anything – that's the least black thing I can think of.' He taught me that leadership is about integrity over self-interest, and the talent you nurture because of it.

In the conference, the students also presented on their postgraduate research. It was simply incredible to see how so many of them have developed, now we have been watching them over four years. These are not just average students; they are getting first-class honours and being granted entry into Clinical Masters and PhDs. (Though we don't select them based on grades, when you create an environment of self-belief, of black excellence, the grades come naturally.)

During the concert, as we do every year, we get all the students up on the stage. In 2023, it was so full that someone remarked that we will have to get a bigger stage. In years to come, I hope we break the stage!

We also began fundraising to develop the first National Indigenous Psychology Treatment and Assessment Centre. Our students are now graduating – six in 2023 and another six at the end of 2024 – and we have recently employed two of our students in the 'Jilya family' as research psychologists. This is where the real work begins – as they graduate and work with me to take on the big challenges this country has failed to address for too long. We also started looking into establishing our own dedicated Indigenous psychology journal. This is what has always been needed – we must control and cultivate our own research. Looking to white systems to peer review our work when they do not understand it has stymied progress on so many critical issues.

We also awarded eleven more scholarships, taking us to fifty-five in total. This year, we specifically targeted Alice Springs, now that we have five students from the Kimberley. However, Alice was different in that there were *three* $50,000-a-year scholarships, because we understand that we will not find local mob already enrolled in psychology (as our scholarship currently requires) – we will have to get them into psychology. We also know that we will be addressing people who have families and commitments, so they will have no financial incentive to leave their jobs and study. These scholarships are another first. After Alice is 'covered', we will move on to Cherbourg in Queensland and then Walgett in New South Wales. This is targeting our generationally highest-risk communities – based on the data we have that maps these 'hotspots' of suicides, incarcerations and child removals – so that never again will a child die from a lack of access to services.

Not on my watch.

Never again.

Our focus is now on getting our graduating students back to their communities.

These are runs on the board that are irrefutable and which will change this nation permanently and for the better, with Aboriginal people in the driver's seat, transforming complex human behaviours for the first time.

I see the possibility of a future free of generational child suicides, incarceration and child removals that have become normalised. And, for the first time, I can see that I can do less because our future is becoming assured – my Jilya students are absolutely brilliant, kind and committed. They are everything I hoped for and more. My aim has always been to eventually make myself irrelevant to achieving that great change, and every leader should have that as a goal because leadership is *not* about how much power you can gain for yourself but how much you can gain for others.

11

Explaining the 'Why':
Closing the gap

How can we 'close the gap' when we are not explaining the gap?

We are regularly saturated with headlines of statistics upon statistics telling a seemingly endless trail of horror:

- of Indigenous suicides being double that of non-Aboriginal Australia
- of child suicides being six times that of non-Indigenous children
- of child removals at eleven times the rate
- of incarceration of our youth at twenty-four times the rate, and adults at nineteen times
- of violence against Indigenous women at thirty-five times the rate.[1]

And on it goes. There is no dressing up these statistics.

So, where do we start with all this? How do you get traction on issues so complex that successive governments have failed to 'close the gap'? Frustratingly, the gaps are as evident and unacceptable as they are easily corrected. Too many lives are being lost by this failure while governments continue to throw good money after bad.

The first thing that needs urgent attention is getting the data right. It is a mess across multiple fronts and is the sole cause of the unabated escalation of poor outcomes. The absence of critical data has made it impossible to appraise prevention efforts or to ensure targeted, needs-based funding and accountability of that critical funding. If you capture the right data and analyse existing data in the correct way, it exposes faults in methodology and the unacceptable gaps in our basic knowledge of what is contributing to these statistics.

I've said this *a lot*: 'Statistics tell you something until they don't' – and the statistics we are gathering tell us nothing beyond tracking *what* the problem is. We simply track demographic data and trends only (on child removal numbers, suicide deaths, incarceration numbers), hoping it will provide some magical insight into how to solve these issues. But the simple reality is that we have yet to gather or analyse data in a way that determines unique causal pathways (the 'why' of this over-representation). This would ensure focused, targeted treatments and interventions. We are also not tracking treatment outcomes; we are tracking output (bums on seats and services delivered). And in many instances, we do not have any baseline data against which to determine if critical gaps have actually been closed.

If we address this combination of factors, we will be closer to explaining and then 'closing the gap'. Instead, we wring our hands over the latest headlines and fail to explore how to address any of it. Explaining why Aboriginal people continue to be so over-represented in these statistics has never been a priority and it needs to be. Answer that then treatment and intervention become specific to the actual causes, and this reduction in baseline *causal* factors then becomes our sole focus and outcome metric against which accountability is king.

As someone who is all about prevention, as a psychologist from a remote region, as an Aboriginal person and a taxpayer to boot, it's been extremely frustrating to watch a national 'groundhog day' on repeat every year, particularly when it is about people's lives. I don't expect politicians to be across an issue this complex, but I do expect them to be concerned with applying the best possible science and insisting on transparency from advisers on their allocation of funds and conflicts of interest.

Outcome-based data never lies, but those with opinions about how to 'close the gap' can. During the 2023 Voice referendum we saw too much personal opinion, rather than science and fact, drive conclusions about what are extremely complex issues of human behaviour.

Disagreement can be good. Healthy debate can result in better ideas and outcomes. But if you disagree with science and with evidence, it never leads to better outcomes. And that right there is how Indigenous policy has always been formed. Reactive, personal opinions dominated the Voice referendum, popularised by those who the policy doesn't affect – and the gap widens.

Data can tell you whether a gap has been closed or not, but only if it is the right data. The knock-on effect of gathering the wrong data is that governments don't actually fund prevention. There is not one government-funded program in Indigenous suicide prevention, justice and child protection that has demonstrated it has reduced risk factors. Staggeringly, funding has not been conditional on these programs demonstrating a measurable reduction in risk factors in the communities in which they are delivered. You cannot find any national database on outcomes across any of these critical areas to justify the expenditure.

If governments insisted on that alone, it would have a significant impact. So, why don't they when they are supposed to be all about accountability? The bulk of this critical funding continues to be diverted to reviews upon reviews, roundtables, conferences and resource databases – everything that falls into the category of universal prevention (mental health awareness and promotion), but nothing that meets the classification of selected or targeted prevention.

There is evidence that programs that involve complex interventions reduce risk in our highest-risk offenders, suicidal individuals and families. We have long known that these programs that target established risk factors (rather than general awareness programs) provide our best opportunity of preventing suicides, incarceration and child removals, but we fail to apply this basic scientific standard to our most vulnerable communities.

When we are getting zero traction on suicides, child removals and incarcerations – indeed, they are escalating each year – and yet the same people stay at the helm of these issues, continuing to quarantine all the funding without any questioning of the outcomes, is it any wonder the gap isn't closing?

Instead, we see significant amounts of money for career consultants to rehash literature reviews, develop promotional pamphlets, videos or databases that ultimately recommend the same programs or recommend more reviews that tell us 'what the problem is' or how the problem should be 'reconceptualised' with another 'framework' or infographic. There is clearly comfort in talking to the same people, as well as currency in jostling to be a key adviser. This becomes entrenched when governments don't engage subject-matter experts beyond their selected 'advisers'. So, there are no answers beyond a closed ideology – an echo chamber of the same ideas confined to the same handpicked group.

When I say subject-matter experts, I am talking about those skilled in complex human behavioural change and interventions across multiple Aboriginal communities – the single most unforgiving environment for the average provider. Indeed, there is a puddle of people who meet these criteria in Australia, which speaks to a significant failure in due diligence.

Yet here we are. And here we will remain if we don't completely shift our focus towards the evidence and away from the self-congratulatory opinions of the over-funded few.

As just one example, approximately $7.8 million has been spent on best practice reviews of suicide prevention since 2016.[2] These reviews have failed to find one Indigenous suicide-prevention program in Australia that falls into the category of selected or targeted intervention and demonstrates the required benchmark of risk reduction. Though I produced a peer-reviewed publication on my programs in 2020, I have not been able to deliver them into high-risk communities in over ten years due in no small part to my exclusion from all these best practice reviews. This is politics. It's what happens when the funding mindset is subjective rather than data-determined and objective.

Too many people who sit on advisory committees are disconnected from this reality, with no prerequisite training or track record in working clinically with at-risk Aboriginal clients or delivering outcome-based prevention programs into (usually remote) high-risk Aboriginal communities. There are career advisers with too much power to drive solutions they are not qualified to provide, and there is little questioning of those solutions from a position of objective outcomes. If there was, very little of what is funded would be.

Accountability has never been applied to these decision-makers; instead, it is always unfairly aimed at those at the coalface, those who have little to no influence on desperately needed funds and are blamed for the ongoing 'failures' to 'close the gap'.

That's why bravery to me remains the most important of all the leadership virtues, for it enables all the others. Changing systems that have advantaged those with the most privilege requires bravery.

I wish we had more leaders in this country who were brave.

So where are the gaps?

Despite the horrifying statistics, we have no national data on the prevalence of mental ill-health or suicide behaviours in Australia beyond my PhD research in 2003. This is why the failure to support my WASC-Y/A tools has had a devastating impact on almost all of the 'close the gap' targets. As they are the only clinically and culturally valid tests in the country, they provide the only mechanism of collecting this national data. I have since paid to digitise the tests and, because there are 50,000 practitioners accredited in them, we are now working on memoranda of understanding with organisations to capture data on the nature and prevalence of these critical issues Australia-wide, in real time – and for the *first* time. We have in publication the first-ever data on the mental health and suicide behaviours of 1266 Indigenous youth. We now have the ability to screen an Aboriginal person for risk, just by using a phone. I know this will save many lives.

Because we have never before captured this data, we do not know how much trauma there is in Aboriginal populations, how much depression or suicidal behaviours. Literally, nothing. No organisation government funded in the millions has done this. No university has done this. I have done this by paying for it myself, and Jilya can now ensure that we have our best opportunity for prevention and explaining the gap by capturing the data in real time.

The World Health Organization has long advocated that the best method of reducing the burden of disease is to first – as in, day one on the job – 'define the problem'. If you are not measuring a gap, how can you close a gap? The failure to have any information on the nature, extent and prevalence of mental ill-health and suicidal behaviours has substantial implications, including:

- we have no capacity to measure whether a gap is increasing or decreasing
- we have no ability to argue for a workforce commensurate with need by identifying our most disproportionally impacted communities, which are usually the most remote
- we have no capacity to measure program and treatment outcomes or to develop robust data on what is working
- most critically, we have zero opportunity to be proactive around early intervention and target early signs of distress (for example, trauma or complex attachment in generationally removed families, and depression rather than suicide deaths).

This is our most urgent priority because underlying every major gap target is mental ill-health – child removals, incarcerations and, of course, suicides. Yet millions are funnelled into non-Indigenous organisations to try to validate culturally biased tools, which leads to culturally biased programs. How many children have died as a result? How many have been removed from their families? How many have been put in prison because of trauma reactions?

The problem with assessment tools that have been developed for culturally different populations is what they fail to include in them – and that means they fail to include the different risk variables that lead to Aboriginal people coming into contact with systems, and therefore they fail to incorporate those unique factors in their treatments and intervention. That's why, when it comes to issues this complex, the simple fix is to get assessment right.

All roads lead to assessment

Tragically, these heavily funded organisations churn out reports that mostly completely exclude Aboriginal people from them. Just some unacceptable examples include:

1. the latest clinical norms on attachment classifications in children[3] excluded Aboriginal people from them – this despite Aboriginal people being *eleven* times more likely to be removed from their families and an absence of evidence-based cultural-attachment programs and therapeutic interventions for Aboriginal people.

2. the Australian Bureau of Statistics (ABS) survey[4] on the needs of women experiencing intimate partner violence (IPV) completely excluded Aboriginal women despite them being thirty-five times more likely to be victims of IPV. It is of note that this study concluded that 78 per cent of non-Aboriginal IPV victims stay in these relationships due to financial abuse, whereby control over their income means they do not have the financial means to leave. Given Aboriginal women are consistently at the lowest end of the socio-economic bracket, the cashless welfare card – the government's go-to policy on 'violence prevention' – is likely to put them in even more harmful situations. It is also important to note that there is no data that directly links victim to offender – for example, the ethnicity of

perpetrators is not currently captured. The data does speak to whether IPV victims 'know their perpetrators' – of course, the vast majority (around 90 per cent) say 'yes'.[5] This is then being used to assume that it is Indigenous men who are perpetrating all the IPV.[6] However, in 2011, ABS census data shows that 'mixed couples (opposite-sex couples with one Aboriginal and/or Torres Strait Islander partner and one non-Indigenous partner) made up 74% of all Aboriginal and Torres Strait Islander couples'.[7]

3. a mental-health prevalence study in late 2022 that had *one* Aboriginal person in the focus group and made sweeping generalisations about the prevalence of mental health and suicide behaviours in Aboriginal communities, which I was interviewed about on ABC News.[8]

There is no greater injustice than to feel as if you matter less, as though your pain is invisible. As Aboriginal people, we have an emotional relationship with this data. We would never forget to include Aboriginal people in the necessary evidence base.

The exclusion continues, as my Jilya Institute recently analysed content from all three Australian psychology journals and found that not only did Indigenous-specific content constitute just 1.8 per cent of the 920 published articles since the Australian Psychological Society's 2016 apology to Aboriginal people (ironically, for excluding Aboriginal people from the evidence base), but an alarming 70 per cent of those articles had non-Indigenous psychologists as lead authors.

Capturing this data means that 'calls to action' can now come with clearly defined commitments to outcomes, holding systems accountable for this exclusion. Of note is that only 0.43 per cent of the 920 articles published were from practising Indigenous psychologists. Of those, approximately 70 per cent were my papers. This makes the exclusion of my work from every best practice report, including the Australian Psychological Society guidelines, objectively and scientifically undefendable; but here we are.

Funding continues to be funnelled into big organisations that have no reach into our highest-risk Aboriginal communities. The result is poor data capturing in which only a few communities are sampled and this data is then 'extrapolated' out to define 'all Aboriginal people', when the reality is that there are always going to be some communities with higher prevalence rates than others. The absence of data also fails to answer the 'why' of the over-representation. The methodological inadequacies of the research are so bad as to offend me as a psychologist and from a position of science.

This failure means that the data being captured is inaccurate and so does not set a critical prevention baseline. Instead, the data fits the dominant narrative of blame, and let's not forget that the systems built by non-Indigenous people will always favour non-Indigenous people by affording them better outcomes in those very systems. This means, in essence, that the crime data is not free of racial profiling, racial bias in sentencing and a lack of understanding of the legal process.

Privilege deflates the non-Indigenous crime statistics and inflates the Indigenous statistics. Data should be captured in a way that explains the over-representation and focuses on changing behaviour rather than placing blame.

Suicide prevention gaps

In 2019 we had a heartbreaking spate of suicides across the nation, including the thirteen Aboriginal young people in the Kimberley, where the estimated rate is at seven times that of non-Indigenous Australia.[9] It has been a suicide hotspot for decades. Yet there is nothing that has ever been funded by government that meets the basic definition of suicide prevention – just four successive government inquiries, the most recent of which was the Fogliani inquiry, all while suicides continue to escalate in that region every year. Again, the whole-of-community suicide-intervention programs described in Chapter 8 (which I have not been able to deliver since 2009 due to an absence of funding for their rollout) are still the only programs that have shown risk reduction. Yet, we missed out on funding, again, to upskill three of the highest-risk communities in the country and track suicide risk reduction using my unique tests in 2022 – global-first, significant work. We will now try to find funding for these programs, which I have donated into the Jilya Institute to ensure their rollout.

Despite the national crisis, suicide was not included in the close-the-gap targets until 2020. There remains no coherent strategy for getting us to the 'zero suicide' aspiration. What it says to bereaved Indigenous families is that suicide prevention is not a priority for us as a nation. This is reflected in the lack of public attention on the fact that, in this country, children as young as ten are choosing to die instead of live. Related to this is the lack of any political will to make it a priority.

Our children's lives continue to attract silence from our political leadership.

With incarceration, the gaps get worse

There are days when I hope I am wrong about the gaps in our basic understanding of youth incarceration. In fact, I regularly have days like this.

First, we have no data on *why* Aboriginal kids are in prison. We know what they are being charged with by police, but not what crimes they are being *convicted* of.[10] So, there is a danger in quoting 'youth crime statistics' because they don't show convictions but that police charges 'proceeded'. We do know that around 86 per cent of kids in prison are on remand (not charged with a crime) and most of those kids when they do get in front of a magistrate will not be convicted of a crime.[11]

This is a significant human rights issue that fails to generate public concern because it predominantly affects Aboriginal kids, who are being held on remand for an average of seventy-one days without conviction. Raw local police data is almost impossible to access and we do not break down youth crime data by Indigenous status.[12] Instead, we rely on heavily compromised local police 'data', which seems replete with evidence of racial profiling and other-race effects as factors driving the erroneous charging of Aboriginal and black people generally. Australia incarcerates 'black' people at one of the world's highest rates – five times more than during South African apartheid and 2.5 times the rate of African Americans.[13] With black children it gets even worse, which means that these statistics will worsen for future generations.

Sadly, we do not have the type of research we need on the other-race effect in Australia and must rely on US findings, where they have robust data on the extent to which 'blackness' influences convictions. Innocent black people are seven and a half times more likely to be convicted of murder than innocent white people.[14] Black people who are convicted of murder are also about 80 per cent more likely to be innocent than other convicted murderers. Data also shows that 87 per cent of black death-row exonerees were victims of official misconduct.[15]

Not having this data in Australia means that there remains this view that the system 'has it right' – there is no racism.[16] But what this actually results in is a concretised narrative that Aboriginal people are somehow more predisposed to being criminals than white people. This racist narrative has its roots in eugenics, but it is often dressed up as altruism.

As I've mentioned before, the racial empathy gap means we fail to relate at a human level to the reality that we are putting children in prison. It seems people are all too comfortable locking up ten-year-olds – until it is *their* ten-year-old. Sadly, the majority of the voting public are comfortable in the notion that it never will be their ten-year-old, so why should they do anything about it?

In 2020, I wrote an opinion piece on raising the age of criminal responsibility and ended it with this:

A child at ten:
- loses four baby teeth a year
- knows the complete date
- can name the months of the year in order
- can read and understand a paragraph of complex sentences

- has developed skills in addition and subtraction
- has some skills in multiplying and division

And, in Australia, they can go to prison.[17]

The 'punishment should fit the crime', but what is the crime?

Arguments against raising the age land at this idea that there are so many serious crimes that require children to be locked up. This, despite having little information on what percentage of crimes are at the serious end. Children aged 0–14 represent less than 1 per cent of all homicide perpetrators in the United States, which has by far the highest rates among high-income countries; many of these homicides appear to be preventable, with over 50 per cent being the result of firearm availability.[18]

In Australia, only one child under thirteen has been charged with murder.[19] But if you were to believe some commentators, you would think that this is the standard crime being committed. We do know, for example, that in New South Wales up to 40 per cent of youth charges 'proceeded against by police' are for fare evasion and up to 30 per cent of convictions for Aboriginal people are for 'good order' offences.[20] However, the commentary is all about the so-called criminal rather than the over-policing of Aboriginal people and the harshness of the justice system.

Many of these crimes, if they are not a by-product of poverty, are part of the normal struggles that children have in negotiating peer-group pressure, which are usually trivial and something most of us can relate to.

Show me a person who hasn't done something they regret as a child. At what age do we lose our compassion for children? Well, the government says it is when they turn ten. Yet the irrefutable science tells us that the earlier you incarcerate a child, the greater the likelihood they will have a future of criminality, with 94 per cent of young people going back to prison before they turn eighteen and 45 per cent of adults (and a whopping 70 per cent of Aboriginal adults) returning to prison within two years of release.[21] Given it costs over

$1 million a year to keep a child in prison,[22] if you diverted that to prevention rather than incarceration, you would only need a 6 per cent success rate to justify the expenditure.

We also know that exposure to criminality, while not guaranteeing that future pathway, certainly increases the odds of it, particularly given the virtual absence of early intervention and prevention programs.

But without data, it is difficult to determine trends in youth crime, to develop programs specific to these unique criminogenic needs, to geomap youth crime hotspots and to track local police responses, court outcomes and harshness in sentencing – each of which would be capable of being addressed if there were targets, measurable ones. None of this currently occurs in a way that holds systems accountable for change and improvement. Instead, it is an annual data-reporting exercise used to argue for more policing and harsher responses. Indeed, Australia has the fifth most expensive prisons in the OECD, the seventh-fastest prison-spending growth rate and more police per capita. Corrective services, for example, costs Australia $21 billion, of which $6 billion is spent on prisons with $2.3 billion spent on incarcerating non-violent offenders.[23]

We are left to rely on anecdotal evidence and horror stories, which are too easily dismissed as not being representative of most kids in prison. During my years as a welfare worker, I witnessed daily the realities of children stealing food because they were hungry and being imprisoned for it. This so-called 'criminal activity' was all too often about survival. We then have the reality of the 'other-race effect' and fawn trauma response, in which too many kids were pleading guilty to crimes they had no idea they had committed because 'the copper said I did it, so I must have'.

As a psychologist who has dedicated my life to prevention efforts, the core of my argument is that locking children up is ineffective as a crime prevention measure.[24] So, the 'tough on crime' approach is having the reverse effect. Far from being 'soft on crime' or a 'bleeding heart', I simply ask that the best available evidence direct us when issues this emotional are at play. What is being lost in this debate is that raising the age will force governments to invest in real crime prevention rather than blame-shifting.

Racial bias in assessment

As I've already discussed in relation to the child protection and justice systems, there is significant evidence that mainstream assessment tools inflate risk based on cultural difference, but they continue to be used and result in uniform intervention programs. Flawed assessments lead to flawed treatments, and a failure to develop an evidence-based approach to 'closing the gap'.

In the justice systems of most states, children are not being given basic mental health screening when they enter prison. With an estimated 93 per cent of children in prison having trauma, this is a significant factor in creating an ingrained trauma response.[25] This is particularly so given that kids are being kept in solitary confinement for up to 22 hours each day, with trauma and isolation linked to depression and self-harm.[26]

While there are concerns about kids 'acting out' – such as during the riots at Banksia Hill Detention Centre in May 2023 – there seems to be little concern for those at risk of suicide, depression or self-harm.[27] This assessment data would also ensure that we are treating the kids' trauma, not punishing them for it. My WASC-Y tools are not funded or used for screening in prisons. We are now fixing this by developing memoranda of understanding with justice systems that use the tools. Unfortunately, my home state of Western Australia, which incarcerates Aboriginal people at the highest rate in the country,[28] has demonstrated no interest in this.

In forensic settings, we do not have a culturally and clinically valid test capable of predicting or determining risk for criminality. The WASC-Y/A tools are used in a significant portion of justice settings. Validating them for forensic settings and developing the first large data sets via organisations already accredited in the tools is another focus of Jilya.

In Canada, they have long used Gladue reports for Indigenous offenders and victims. These provide a full picture, explaining the nature, context and seriousness of the crimes, the management of risk to the community and the possibility of rehabilitation. They saw a decrease in their incarceration rate as a result. An equivalent was recommended in the NT royal commission after Don Dale, but it is yet to be implemented.

If we are not developing assessments that tell an entire story – one that Aboriginal people uniquely experience – then we have no possibility of providing specific interventions.

Geomapping those most in need

Based on the statistics, the vast majority of Aboriginal families will – like most Australians – never come into contact with justice and child welfare systems, but this is never depicted in the media.[29] However, for those who do, they carry the greatest burden. This has now become generational.

If you go into any high-risk community, there will be 10–15 families at most that are taking up all the service provision. If you work in the mental health industry for long enough, eventually one of your client's children will become your client. These are generationally incarcerated and generationally removed families, and they exist in every district, in every region. These cohorts make up the bulk of the child protection and crime statistics, and we also know that this is often the trajectory to suicides and mental ill-health. Ensuring access to our highest-risk, most vulnerable communities – such as Alice Springs, Cherbourg, the Kimberley and Walgett – has never been understood, which is why data geomapping is one area that is critical to 'closing the gap'. These communities are so identifiable: the fact that governments have failed to mobilise critical resources into them should be part of our constant accountability narrative.

The way we currently collect data and analyse it ensures it fits a politically convenient view of a problem that is deemed 'unsolvable' and we then get 'othered'. For example, if an Aboriginal person commits an act of violence, it becomes about *all* Aboriginal people being violent. This makes the problem appear bigger and less solvable than it really is.

Geomapping data would involve sharing national information across jurisdictions with data-linking technology. There are certainly good examples of this, with the Australian Institute of Health and Welfare developing a national dataset for child protection data and a NSW study on data linking children across justice, mental health and child protection systems. However, if we did this nationally and across mental health, suicides, crime and child protection systems, based on treatment outcomes that coded families and regions, it would reveal the actual number of affected families, individuals and communities.

When you dig a bit deeper, data from the Northern Territory shows that of the 25,500 notifications of child abuse, 71 per cent involved children already in the system.[30] In looking at child removals in the NT, 92 per cent of kids in care are Indigenous, which gives some much-needed perspective to the claims by Jacinta Nampijinpa Price and Peter Dutton that we need to 'remove more Aboriginal children'. Based on these statistics, we are now officially removing kids at a higher rate than during the Stolen Generations – it's impossible to remove more Aboriginal kids. We continue to deal with the collateral damage of this removal, but some are lauding it as innovative, brave and practical.

In child protection regions, the number of removals is significantly greater in areas with the highest proportion of Aboriginal people per capita. As I first mentioned in Chapter 4, in Western Australia the Kimberley stands out again with 100 per cent of children in out-of-home care identifying as Aboriginal; in the Pilbara it's 96 per cent; the Goldfields, 87 per cent; Mid-West Gascoyne, 86 per cent.[31] However, if we remove these four regions – which are the most remote and the most densely populated Aboriginal areas out of the seventeen child protection districts in the state[32] – Aboriginal child removals fall from 57 per cent to 39 per cent.

When it comes to youth crime, there are approximately 949 kids in prison on any given night across the whole of Australia, with approximately 617 of those being Indigenous. If we geomapped the data, we'd find that those 617 Indigenous kids are the same ones in around 80–90 per cent of cases, and I would hate to think how many would also be in the child protection system.

It seems counterintuitive that when you are in the majority, you are more, not less, oppressed. Similarly, South Africa had apartheid when 80 per cent of South Africans were black. It speaks to individual and group-based oppression when government-enacted legislation enables 'initiatives' like cashless welfare cards and alcohol restrictions that cover whole communities, based on the profiling of a smaller minority.

The NT Intervention engendered learned helplessness in the face of statutory organisations, which have historically wielded considerable power over remote Aboriginal communities. Since its inception, the NT has seen a 160 per cent increase in suicides. If you paternalise people based on their cultural identity, it concretises learned helplessness, which has been consistently shown to be one of the strongest predictors of poor behavioural outcomes and particularly suicides.

If we geomapped data, we could determine the number of people involved across multiple systems and focus our prevention efforts on those most vulnerable in larger communities – those who are over-represented. The Northern Territory, for example, has been calling for needs-based funding for some time.

The other-race effect makes it more likely that an extreme narrative about the broader Aboriginal community is readily believed as factual, despite evidence to the contrary. There are so many distorted and factually incorrect ideas generated about Aboriginal people that are hard to shift. One is that child sexual abuse and child rape are normal and rife in all Aboriginal communities. The extension of that belief is that discussion about solutions also become extreme: for example, if sexual abuse is so 'rife', removal is the only 'safe' conclusion for children. However, we know that 7.3 per cent of abuse in Aboriginal communities is sexual, compared to around 10 per cent for non-Indigenous communities.[33] Yet it becomes easy for the public to demonise whole Aboriginal communities because of the 'othering' that occurs when cases of sexual abuse in an Aboriginal community are reported as normative.[34] Significantly, 79 per cent of notifications of child abuse in Aboriginal populations are based on 'neglect and emotional abuse',[35] warranting an intensive family support response rather than a removal rate eleven times higher.

Research has shown that the racial profiling of Aboriginal families has led to over 60 per cent of notifications ultimately being found to be false.[36] Sexual abuse disclosures in communities have been found to be significantly lower than portrayed in the media, and historically non-Indigenous perpetrators were more likely to be involved.[37] Indeed, the Australian Federal Police has never found a case of an organised paedophile ring orchestrated by Indigenous offenders. We see, for example, significant cases of global paedophile rings that have occurred on the NSW central coast, and yet there was not the widescale, media-generated demonisation of those entire communities, which are predominantly non-Indigenous.

Implicit bias, now measurable, creates differential activity in the amygdala – the region in the brain that deals with perceived threats[38] – in response to black, compared to white, people.[39] These differential patterns in the amygdala are thought to reflect relatively automatic threat responses to black people.

The other-race effect also comes into play in child protection, where the value of Aboriginal staff in the system has never been fully understood. In Western Australia, the last decade has seen a staggering 119 per cent increase in the removal of Aboriginal children, while non-Aboriginal removal rates have had an overall decline of 13.59 per cent.[40]

Importantly, while Aboriginal child removals have blown out, Aboriginal staffing has decreased by almost 50 per cent (from 10.2 per cent to 5.8 per cent). In determining whether these two variables are related, I calculated a correlation coefficient of 0.865. While not causal, it provides some strong initial evidence that the more Aboriginal staff in the system, the lower the Aboriginal child removal rate. Indeed, data from my 2019 state review into cultural competencies of child protection workers demonstrated that Aboriginality strongly predicts cultural competence.

Aboriginal staff have cultural instincts that enable them to understand that Aboriginal parenting and attachment look different. More importantly, the desire and motivation to prevent removals of Aboriginal children speaks to a higher degree of cultural empathy for the impacts of removals on Aboriginal families, given that most Aboriginal people have experienced the impacts of forced removals in their own families.[41]

I was a child protection worker for seven years with a 100 per cent Aboriginal caseload. In that time, *I didn't remove one child.* I also didn't leave a child in an abusive situation. That's because *every* Aboriginal family came to attention *solely* because they were struggling with parenting, trauma, identity or attachment from their own removal from family. So, I proactively did everything in my power to provide the skill and intensive therapy they needed to stay together.

The fact that Aboriginal kids in a horrific 79 per cent of cases are being removed for 'neglect' tells us that removal is entirely preventable from a risk-assessment perspective. Risk has a continuum, from the extreme (remove) to the fixable (neglect); however, we have a system that fails to provide commensurate opportunities for Aboriginal families to heal. This is due to lacking the requirement for staff to be 'culturally competent' and systems that fail to fund anything beyond parenting and attachment-based programs that don't translate culturally. Removal, then, becomes a foregone conclusion once they are flagged by the system.

There is the other reality that, as Aboriginal people who have had removals in their family, we have greater empathy for those at risk – and this makes us, frankly, better at this work. We are more determined to prevent removals because we have seen and experienced the devastation of it. Indeed, numerous inquiries have shown that foster care is no save haven for any child. In fact, Aboriginal children constitute 44 per cent of children abused in care, and there is evidence that Aboriginal children have poorer outcomes than their non-Aboriginal peers when they come into contact with the child protection system.[42] And who is going to care about you when you are sad? Who is going to hug you when you are distressed?

I did a load of parenting and attachment interventions based on my implicit understanding of collective parenting and cultural differences in parenting. I also did a lot of temporary respite for the mums when I could see risk emerging – and this simply meant stress was more evident. Remember, most of these mums did not have parenting models due to removal and often didn't have the associated grandparent support that most Australians rely on.

Obviously implicitly understanding cultural attachment and parenting differences helped significantly, but more importantly I understood how to teach these skills: by modelling appropriate responses and having mum partner up with a parenting mentor. One-on-one with mums was crucial because we understand that it is caregiver responsiveness to children that is still the most predictable pathway to removal. This often means treating depression, identity issues, racial trauma and other kinds of trauma in mums. In one of my cases I got family, extended family and community to praise mum. It sounds odd, but the environment was so negative that mum's self-worth was really low, and this made a significant difference.

As I've said before, change the environment, change the outcome. When community is provided with skills, that community will have them for life.

Solutions: A step-by-step guide

So, to break it down into small chunks, this is how to 'close the gap'. This is our focus at the Jilya Institute.

Step 1: Develop robust causal data to define the problem and identify our highest-risk communities and families. We are doing this at Jilya and will continue for the next three years via some philanthropic research funding.

Step 2: Determine unique causal pathways across two themes:

    i. to inform the development of unique intervention programs and treatments of best practice. At Jilya we plan to do this now that we have digitised the WASC-Y/A, which will enable us to determine what is reducing risk in real time. We will be able to do this for the next three years with the Paul Ramsay Foundation funding.

ii. to determine the causal contribution of cultural competency to outcomes (such as child removals and incarceration rates) in a way that is measurable and improvable over time. For example, do improved cultural competencies statistically reduce child removals? Do improved cultural competencies in the police lead to lower rates of incarceration? Once cultural competency is defined, it then becomes improvable and trackable over time against these outcomes. This is when you are able to 'close the gap' because you have not only explained the gap but set benchmarks that have been shown to cause better outcomes. We are starting this national work at Jilya because we have the only validated tests of cultural competency in the country. It's exciting work.

Step 3: Actually fund prevention.

It's easy to put a child in prison; it's much harder to prevent it. It's easy to remove a child; it's much harder to prevent it. It's easy to track suicide data; it's much harder to figure out how to prevent it.

If I were a politician and I had a pool of, say, $134 million (which is apparently the federal budget for Indigenous mental health), I would put 10 per cent into universal awareness-raising programs (they tend to be cheaper) and allocate 40 per cent for selected intervention programs, which target those exposed to known risk factors, such as suicide, violence and generationally incarcerated families. Finally, I would put the bulk of the allocated funds into targeted interventions focusing on high-risk individuals and families (the long-term incarcerated, perpetrators, suicidal people). This would require that governments identify these programs and, if they do not exist, fund their development and mobilisation into the highest-risk communities. (The IPS programs are the only ones that meet this objective benchmark.)

Step 4: Once identified and/or developed, geomap the data and mobilise these culturally co-designed and clinically validated programs into those communities that make up the bulk of the statistics in 'train the trainer' formats. They are donated because I know that they will be more likely to attract funding.

Step 5: Continue to develop capacity in our highest-risk communities through a model similar to that of my scholarship program.

If we had thirty Indigenous psychologists in Alice Springs, for example, we wouldn't be talking about the 'issues in Alice Springs' for much longer. We know that having culture in common with clients results in significantly better outcomes, so why are governments not taking this permanent skills-development approach with our highest-risk communities? Indeed, one of the biggest urban myths going around is that any psychologist can work in Aboriginal communities without any training to do so. And the fundamental problem is that when Aboriginal people do not share 'power' with those making the decisions, then ensuring culturally informed solutions becomes an impossibility.

We also have the reality that locals never leave. So, why have governments failed to invest in arming a local workforce capable of the type of complex interventions that generational trauma requires?

Step 6: Evaluate the data by tracking treatment outcomes.

We don't need to be rescued

Activism is hard, but black activism is much harder. The sad reality is that we continue to rely on white Australians to amplify black issues and black pain, as white people react more when this happens.

This will always be a difficult reality because if it remains the sole responsibility of the oppressed – those with the least power and privilege – to fix problems created by the oppressor; it places an intolerable burden on those who are already intolerably burdened through grief and policies that removed Aboriginal children from our families, creating a destruction that has never truly been acknowledged or healed. This attachment loss is irrefutably linked to our escalating suicides from intergenerational trauma.

When Australia voted 'no' in the Voice referendum in 2023, it showed us just how fraught this can be. Indeed, my mum, true to her activist roots, was the first to buy her 'yes' shirt, even before any of us really understood what it all meant. As usual, she led the way.

She never once considered Australia would say 'no' – yet all of her non-Indigenous 'friends' told her proudly that they were voting 'no'. When they asked her why she was voting 'yes', she simply said this: 'My entire life as an Aboriginal woman, all I've been told is "no". Just once before I die, I want to hear "yes".'

With well over 80 per cent of remote Aboriginal communities voting 'yes' with my mum,[43] it's hard to reconcile this pain.

Perhaps this is the nexus we needed to see that we cannot rely on government to save us and to stop looking outside our communities for answers. But we lost our belief in what we know works, as governments continue to paternalise us into doubting ourselves. Far too many of us continue to work *within* rather than *outside* of those same systems and being destroyed by them.

Jilya has shown, particularly in light of the Voice referendum, that we have achieved 'yes' many times over through grassroots activism. We are proof that great change can occur when we stop looking outside of our communities to be rescued by the very institutions that created the destruction to begin with.

Change will never occur if we place all our reliance on those impacted the least to tell us how change should look and the pace at which it should occur. We are tired of our communities being stereotyped, demonised and blamed, rather than helped and supported. We are tired of the default response to suicides, abuse and violence being further restrictions on our human rights, rather than funding for the critical prevention programs every Australian has a basic right to. We are tired of governments responding to our pain by inflicting more pain.

To me, Jilya's success, and my own, honours decades of Indigenous leadership showing the value of grassroots activism. This is what Jilya was born from, but too many of those Indigenous leaders' contributions to our country have remained invisible. I acknowledge the strength of their vision and see what has become unburdened because of their individual and collective struggles. It is because of them that we are no longer the 'support act' to the psychologists – we *are* the psychologists.

I hear people constantly scream out: 'We need more Aboriginal health workers!'

I say: 'No, we don't. We need more Aboriginal doctors.'

Or: 'We need more Aboriginal education workers.'

No, we don't. We need more Aboriginal teachers.

If you are sharing space, but not sharing power, it's tokenism.

There are too many systems that like to share space, but not power, with us.

The Jilya dream

With no federal government funding, Jilya is showing what 'yes' looks like. We have achieved 'yes' thousands of times over – as has every Jilya student and decades of black activists who bled for our rights.

To our white allies who choose each day to respect and listen to those of us who understand our communities best, and to the now thousands of Australians who have supported the Jilya dream, I say: 'Yes!'

We are now the 'new Aboriginal'. We are doctors, we are lawyers, we are surgeons. We come from remote communities. We are educated and self-determined. Some of us lead the world in what we do.

The actions we take as leaders should never be about gaining more power for ourselves, but ensuring more power is gained for others. This responsibility for those of us with relative privilege means we need to not only bravely recognise it and defer to others who know more, but also be compelled to act and amplify the pain of others who cannot.

For white allies, this means understanding that being an observer of racism does not make you an equal-status victim of it. White fragility should never trump black pain.

The work I do is an honour and I feel humble when I see the faith that is placed in me every day.

We should all feel like we are falling short and that we have enormous amounts to learn constantly. We should acknowledge when we are failing and be brave enough to get up and fail again.

Because the thing about *hope* is that it has a habit of taking on a life of its own – especially when many more share it with you. Hope is showing us all how a country can come together and be the difference that is so badly needed.

Jilya is the answer.

Jilya is showing what 'yes' looks like.

Acknowledgements

My sincere appreciation firstly to my publisher Aviva Tuffield, who convinced me that I could actually write, and that there was an audience for my words, my work and passions. To the crew at UQP, including Lauren Mitchell for your hard-nosed source editing. Editor Beck Bauert for her input into the early manuscript and being so effortless to work with. The litany of friends and students who indulged me with reading proofs and throwing ideas at them, including Johanna Ramsay, Vanessa Joseph, Robyn Phillips, Associate Professor Lorraine Sheridan. Endorsees Narelda Jacobs, Stan Grant, Troy Cassar-Daley, Lucy Turnbull, Brooke Boney and Julia Baird – I am so grateful for your support.

To my mum, Mavis Westerman, for my education; to my dad, Mick Westerman, for my self-belief; and to my Jilya students for being inspired rather than intimidated by my leadership.

Finally, to the many teachers from Tom Price, who always believed in what I was capable of achieving, well before I knew it. I wish every kid in Australia had the teachers I had.

Notes

Chapter 1: Mum and Dad

1 Bailey, R & Pico, J 2023, *Defense Mechanisms*, StatPearls Publishing, Florida.

2 Paradies, Y 2016, 'Colonisation, racism and Indigenous health', *Journal of Population Research*, vol. 33, no. 1, pp. 83–96.

3 Fani, N, Carter, SE, Harnett, NG, Ressler, KJ & Bradley, B 2021, 'Association of racial discrimination with neural response to threat in Black women in the US exposed to trauma', *JAMA Psychiatry*, vol. 78, no. 9, pp. 1005–12; Paradies, Y, Ben, J, Denson, N, Elias, A, Priest, N, Pieterse, A, Gupta, A, Kelaher, M & Gee, G 2015, 'Racism as a determinant of health: A systematic review and meta-analysis', *PLoS One*, vol. 10, no. 9, e0138511; Paradies, Y, 'Colonisation, racism and Indigenous health'; Priest, NC, Paradies, YC, Gunthorpe, W, Cairney, SJ & Sayers, SM 2011, 'Racism as a determinant of social and emotional wellbeing for Aboriginal Australian youth', *Medical Journal of Australia*, vol. 194, no. 10, pp. 546–50; Priest, N, Paradies, Y, Stewart, P & Luke J 2011, 'Racism and health among urban Aboriginal young people', *BMC Public Health*, vol. 11, article no. 568.

4 Forgiarini, M, Gallucci, M & Maravita, A 2011, 'Racism and the empathy for pain on our skin', *Frontiers in Psychology*, vol. 2, article no. 108.

Chapter 3: Changing Psychology in Australia

1 Gynther B, Charlson F, Obrecht K, Waller M, Santomauro D, Whiteford H & Hunter E 2019, 'The epidemiology of psychosis in Indigenous populations in Cape York and the Torres Strait', *EClinicalMedicine*, vol. 10, pp. 68–77. However, this

study is from Cape York communities in Queensland, which means that the data is extremely limited. Based on my lived experience as a clinician, I believe the true prevalence is likely to be much higher. The following two articles speak to the factors that may increase these rates: Ratana, R, Sharifzadeh, H, Krishnan, J & Pang, S 2019, 'A comprehensive review of computational methods for automatic prediction of schizophrenia with insight into Indigenous populations', *Frontiers in Psychiartry*, vol. 10, article no. 659; Ryder, G 2021, *Why culturally sensitive care for Indigenous populations with schizophrenia matters*, Psych Central, <psychcentral.com/schizophrenia/schizophrenia-indigenous>.

2. My culture-bound syndromes paper was the first to approach this from a perspective of cultural norms manifesting as clinical, diagnostic criteria from the perspective of the DSM guidelines: Westerman, T 2021, 'Culture-bound syndromes in Aboriginal Australian populations', *Clinical Psychologist*, vol. 25, no. 1, pp. 19–35.

3. WA Primary Health Alliance (PHA) 2024, *Kimberley: Needs assessment 2022–2024*, WA PHA, <wapha.org.au/wp-content/uploads/2022/04/Needs-Assessment_Country-WA_Kimberley.pdf>.

4. Daniel, D 2021, 'Universities lose money on psychology degrees as waitlists languish', *The Sydney Morning Herald*, 4 December, <smh.com.au/politics/federal/universities-lose-money-on-psychology-degrees-as-waitlists-languish-20211203-p59ei0.html>; WA PHA, *Kimberley: Needs assessment 2022–2024*.

5. Gøtzsche, PC, Young, AH & Crace, J 2015, 'Does long term use of psychiatric drugs cause more harm than good?', *BMJ*, vol. 350; Kaplan, A 2012, 'On the efficacy of psychiatric drugs', *Psychiatric Times*, 3 April, vol. 29, no. 4, <psychiatrictimes.com/view/efficacy-psychiatric-drugs>.

6. Australian Institute of Health and Welfare (AIHW) 2024, *Mental health-related prescriptions*, AIHW, <aihw.gov.au/mental-health/topic-areas/mental-health-prescriptions>.

7. Garay, J, Williamson, A, Young, C, Nixon, J, Cutmore, M, Sherriff, S, Smith, N, Slater, K & Dickson, M 2023, 'Aboriginal young people's experiences of accessibility in mental health services in two regions of New South Wales, Australia', *International Journal of Environmental Research and Public Health*, 18 January, vol. 20, no. 3, p. 1730.

8. Department of Children, Youth Justice and Multicultural Affairs 2023, *Intensive Family Support: Service model and guidelines*, Queensland Government, <familychildconnect.org.au/ARC/2018/IFS_Service_Model_and_Guidelines.pdf>.

9. Westerman, T, 'Culture-bound syndromes in Aboriginal Australian populations'.

10. I expanded on these four stages in Westerman, T, 'Culture-bound syndromes in Aboriginal Australian populations'.

11. McPhee, R, Carlin, E, Seear, K, Carrington-Jones, P, Sheil, B, Lawrence, D & Dudgeon, P 2022, 'Unacceptably high: An audit of Kimberley self-harm data 2014–2018', *Australasian Psychiatry*, vol. 30, no. 1, pp. 70–3.

12. Australian Bureau of Statistics (ABS) 2019, *Intentional self-harm in Aboriginal and Torres Strait Islander people*, ABS, <abs.gov.au/articles/intentional-self-harm-aboriginal-and-torres-strait-islander-people>.

13 Bertolote JM & Fleischmann A 2002, 'Suicide and psychiatric diagnosis: A worldwide perspective', *World Psychiatry*, vol. 1, no. 3, pp. 181–5.

14 Westerman, T, 'Culture-bound syndromes in Aboriginal Australian populations'.

Chapter 4: Black Identity

1 Reconciliation Australia 2016, *The State of Reconciliation in Australia: Our history, our story, our future*, Reconciliation Australia, Kingston.

2 Conover, C 2023, 'Do Black physicians double the survival odds of Black newborns?', *Forbes*, 10 July, <forbes.com/sites/theapothecary/2023/07/10/do-black-physicians-double-the-survival-odds-of-black-newborns/>.

3 AIHW 2023, *Burden of avoidable deaths among Aboriginal and Torres Strait Islander people 2018*, AIHW, Canberra.

4 Bainbridge, R, McCalman, J, Clifford, A & Tsey, K 2015, *Cultural competency in the delivery of health services for Indigenous people*, issues paper no. 13, Closing the Gap Clearinghouse, AIHW & Australian Institute of Family Studies, <aihw.gov.au/getmedia/4f8276f5-e467-442e-a9ef-80b8c010c690/ctgc-ip13.pdf.aspx?>.

5 Cross, W 1971, 'The Negro-to-Black conversion experience', *Black World*, vol. 20, no. 9, pp. 13–27.

6 Cross, W 1991, *Shades of Black: Diversity in African-American identity*, Temple University Press, Philadelphia.

7 Shutts, K 2015, 'Young children's preferences: Gender, race, and social status', *Child Development Perspectives*, vol. 9, no. 4, pp. 262–6.

8 Dunham, Y, Chen, EE & Banaji, MR 2013, 'Two signatures of implicit intergroup attitudes: Developmental invariance and early enculturation', *Psychological Science*, vol. 24, no. 6, pp. 860–8.

9 Levy, MS 2000, 'A conceptualization of the repetition compulsion', *Psychiatry*, vol. 63, no. 1, pp. 45–53; Westerman, T 2023, 'Psychologist: Colonialism was not all positive for Aboriginal people', *Cosmos*, 27 September, <cosmosmagazine.com/people/society/colonialism-not-positive-for-aboriginal-people/>.

10 Cuéllar, I & Paniagua, F (eds) 2000, *Handbook of Multicultural Mental Health: Assessment and treatment of diverse populations*, Academic Press, San Diego & London.

11 Walker, P 2013, *Complex PTSD: From surviving to thriving: A guide and map for recovering from childhood trauma*, Azure Coyote Publishing, California.

12 Wiener, C & Palmer, T 2021, 'How claims of "consensual rough sex" hide abuse and coercive control from courts', *The Conversation*, 18 December, <theconversation.com/how-claims-of-consensual-rough-sex-hide-abuse-and-coercive-control-from-courts-173683>.

13 Department of Communities 2021, *Child Protection Activity Performance Information 2020–21*, Government of Western Australia, <www.wa.gov.au/system/files/2021-10/child-protection-activity-performance-information-2020-21.pdf>.

14 ABS 2022, *Western Australia: Aboriginal and Torres Strait Islander population summary*, ABS, 1 July, <abs.gov.au/articles/western-australia-aboriginal-and-torres-strait-islander-population-summary>.

15 Department of Communities, *Child Protection Activity Performance Information 2020–21*.

16 Morse, D 2023, 'Alice Springs needs more than band-aid solutions. It needs Indigenous consultation and a new long-term plan, *ABC News*, 4 February, <abc.net.au/news/2023-02-04/alice-springs-needs-more-than-band-aid-solutions/101929654>.

17 Cripps, K 2023, 'These Indigenous women took the risk of calling the police. It didn't save them', *SBS News*, 1 June, <sbs.com.au/news/article/these-indigenous-women-took-the-risk-of-calling-the-police-it-didnt-save-them/tgi2mo39t>; Kerr, A 2020, 'Escaping family violence: How the justice system is failing Aboriginal women', *Precedent (Australian Lawyers Alliance)*, vol. 43, no. 159, pp. 16–21.

18 Westerman, T 2022, 'From love bombing to isolation, the red flags for coercive control can be dangerously difficult to spot before abuse escalates', *ABC News*, 7 August, <abc.net.au/news/2022-08-07/love-bombing-isolation-coercive-control-red-flags-domestic-abuse/101283156>.

19 Walters, A & Longhurst, S 2017, *Over-represented and Overlooked: The crisis of Aboriginal and Torres Strait Islander women's growing over-imprisonment*, Human Rights Law Centre, Melbourne, & Change the Record Coalition, Strawberry Fields, <hrlc.org.au/news/2017/5/10/over-represented-overlooked-report>.

20 Beazley, J 2022, 'Queensland child protection system failing Indigenous domestic violence victims, report finds', *Guardian Australia*, 7 April, <theguardian.com/australia-news/2022/apr/07/queensland-child-protection-system-failing-indigenous-domestic-violence-victims-report-finds>; Jenkins, K 2020, 'Fear of child removal preventing Indigenous women from reporting family violence', *NITV News*, 15 December, <sbs.com.au/nitv/article/fear-of-child-removal-preventing-indigenous-women-from-reporting-family-violence/7uw51v35s>.

21 King, ML 1968, *The Other America*, transcript, Grosse Pointe Historical Society, 14 March, <gphistorical.org/mlk/mlkspeech>.

22 Blay, Z 2015, '4 "reverse racism" myths that need to stop', *HuffPost*, 26 August, <huffpost.com/entry/reverse-racism-isnt-a-thing_n_55d60a91e4b07addcb45da97>.

23 Amnesty International Australia n.d., *Kids in Watchhouses: Exposing the truth*, Amnesty International Australia, <amnesty.org.au/watch-houses/>.

24 Amnesty International Australia 2020, *Indigenous Kids in Prison: Australia's national disgrace*, Amnesty International Australia, <amnesty.org.au/indigenous-kids-in-prison-australias-national-disgrace>.

25 Brennan, D 2023, 'Queensland bail laws driving kids to plead guilty to crimes they didn't commit', *National Indigenous Times*, 28 June, <nit.com.au/28-06-2023/6541/new-bail-laws-driving-kids-to-plead-guilty-to-crimes-they-didnt-commit>.

26 Westerman, T 2021, 'Culture-bound syndromes in Aboriginal Australian populations', *Clinical Psychologist*, vol. 25, no. 1, pp. 19–35.

27 Fryer, B 2020, 'Identity struggles weigh heavily on mental health, experts say', *NITV News*, 3 February, <sbs.com.au/nitv/article/identity-struggles-weigh-heavily-on-mental-health-experts-say/cfbbll0di>.

Chapter 5: Grief and Loss

1 Victor, SE, Schleider, JL, Ammerman, BA, Bradford, DE, Devendorf, AR, Gruber, J, Gunaydin, LA, Hallion, LS, Kaufman, EA, Lewis, SP & Stage,

DL 2022, 'Leveraging the strengths of psychologists with lived experience of psychopathology', *Perspectives on Psychological Science*, vol. 17, no. 6, pp. 1624–32.

2   Christ, GH, Bonanno, G, Malkinson, R & Rubin, S 2003, 'Appendix E: Bereavement experiences after the death of a child', in MJ Field & RE Behrman (eds), *When Children Die: Improving palliative and end-of-life care for children and their families*, National Academies Press, Washington; Fish, WC 1986, 'Differences of grief intensity in bereaved parents', in T Rando (ed), *Parental Loss of a Child*, Research Press Company, Champaign, pp. 415–28; Martison, IM, Davies, B & McClowry, S 1991, 'Parental depression following the death of a child', *Death Studies*, vol. 15, no. 3, pp. 259–67; Rubin, S & Malkinson, R 2001, 'Parental response to child loss across the life cycle: Clinical and research perspectives', in M Stroebe (ed) 2001, *Handbook of Bereavement Research: Consequences, coping, and care*, American Psychological Association Press, Washington, pp. 219–40; Sanders, CM 1980, 'A comparison of adult bereavement in the death of a spouse, child, and parent', *OMEGA Journal of Death and Dying*, vol. 10, no. 4, pp. 303–22; Zisook, S & Lyons, L 1990, 'Bereavement and unresolved grief in psychiatric outpatients', *OMEGA Journal of Death and Dying*, vol. 20, no. 4, pp. 307–22.

3   Queensland Family and Child Commission 2023, *Queensland Child Rights: Report 2023*, The State of Queensland, <qfcc.qld.gov.au/sites/default/files/2023-08/QFCC%20Child%20Rights%20Report%202023%20%281%29.pdf>.

4   Keyes, KM, Pratt, C, Galea, S, McLaughlin, KA, Koenen, KC & Shear, MK 2014, 'The burden of loss: Unexpected death of a loved one and psychiatric disorders across the life course in a national study', *The American Journal of Psychiatry*, vol. 171, no. 8, pp. 864–71.

5   Simon, NM, Shear, KM, Thompson, EH, Zalta, AK, Perlman, C, Reynolds, CF, Frank, E, Melhem NM & Silowash, R 2007, 'The prevalence and correlates of psychiatric comorbidity in individuals with complicated grief', *Comprehensive Psychiatry*, vol. 48, no. 5, pp. 395–9; Shear, KM, Jackson, CT, Essock, SM, Donahue, SA & Felton, CJ 2006, 'Screening for complicated grief among Project Liberty service recipients 18 months after September 11, 2001', *Psychiatric Services*, vol. 57, no. 9, pp. 1291–7; Melhem, NM, Porta, G, Shamseddeen, W, Walker Payne, M, & Brent, DA 2011, 'Grief in children and adolescents bereaved by sudden parental death', *Archives of General Psychiatry*, vol. 68, no. 9, pp. 911–9.

6   Momartin, S, Silove, D, Manicavasagar, V & Steel, Z 2004, 'Complicated grief in Bosnian refugees: Associations with posttraumatic stress disorder and depression', *Comprehensive Psychiatry*, vol. 45, no. 6, pp. 475–82; Neria, Y, Gross, R, Litz, B, Maguen, S, Insel, B, Seirmarco, G, Rosenfeld, H, Suh, EJ, Kishon, R, Cook, J, Marshall, RD 2007, 'Prevalence and psychological correlates of complicated grief among bereaved adults 2.5–3.5 years after September 11th attacks', *Journal of Traumatic Stress*, vol. 20, no. 3, pp. 251–62; Morina, N, Rudari, V, Bleichhardt, G & Prigerson, HG 2010, 'Prolonged grief disorder, depression, and posttraumatic stress disorder among bereaved Kosovar civilian war survivors: A preliminary investigation', *International Journal of Social Psychiatry*, vol. 56, no. 3, pp. 288–97.

7   Cussen, T & Bryant, W 2015, *Research in Practice No. 37: Indigenous and non-Indigenous homicide in Australia*, Australian Institute of Criminology, <aic.gov.au/publications/rip/rip37>.

8   On the media: Buckler, K & Travis, L 2005, 'Assessing the newsworthiness of homicide events: An analysis of coverage in the Houston Chronicle', *Journal of Criminal Justice and Popular Culture*, vol. 12, no. 1, pp. 1–25. On political leadership: Westerman, T 2019, 'Our children's lives deserve more than silence', *NITV*, 6 March, <sbs.com.au/nitv/article/our-childrens-lives-deserve-more-than-silence/nre0lymf2>. On less newsworthiness: Meyers, M 1997, *News Coverage of Violence Against Women: Engendering blame*, SAGE Publications, California, London & New Delhi; Dowler, K, Fleming, T & Muzzatti, SL 2006, 'Constructing crime: Media, crime, and popular culture', *Canadian Journal of Criminology and Criminal Justice*, vol. 48, no. 6, pp. 837–50. On blaming Aboriginal victims: The Quicky 2022, *What Cassius' Family are Pleading with Aussies to Know*, Mamamia Podcasts, <mamamia.com.au/podcasts/the-quicky/cassius-death-racism/>.

9   Cunneen, C 2022, 'The criminal legal system does not deliver justice for First Nations people, says a new book', *The Conversation*, 9 November, <theconversation.com/the-criminal-legal-system-does-not-deliver-justice-for-first-nations-people-says-a-new-book-191005>.

10 For example: Sommers, SR & Ellsworth, PC 2001, 'White juror bias: An investigation of prejudice against Black defendants in the American courtroom', *Psychology, Public Policy, and Law*, vol. 7, no. 1, pp. 201–29.

11 Meyers, M, *News Coverage of Violence Against Women: Engendering blame*.

12 Carmody, J & Barker, J 2022, 'West Australian premier Mark McGowan warns against speculation over death of Cassius Turvey', *ABC News*, 27 October, <abc.net.au/news/2022-10-27/wa-premier-warns-against-speculation-over-cassius-turvey-death/101583520>.

13 Westerman, T 2021, 'Culture-bound syndromes in Aboriginal Australian populations', *Clinical Psychologist*, vol. 25, no. 1, pp. 19–35.

14 Kagi, J 2019, 'WA Parliament turns away from Indigenous youth suicide, despite coroner's urgent plea', *ABC News*, 2 March, <abc.net.au/news/2019-03-02/wa-parliament-turns-away-from-kimberley-youth-suicides/10861250>.

15 Rudin, J 2006, *Aboriginal Peoples and the Criminal Justice System*, Ipperwash Inquiry, <archives.gov.on.ca/en/e_records/ipperwash/policy_part/research/pdf/Rudin.pdf>.

16 Kellermann, NP 2001, 'Transmission of Holocaust trauma – an integrative view', *Psychiatry*, vol. 64, no. 3, pp. 256–67; Kidron, CA, Kotliar, DM & Kirmayer, LJ 2019, 'Transmitted trauma as badge of honor: Phenomenological accounts of Holocaust descendant resilient vulnerability', *Social Science & Medicine*, no. 239, article no. 112524.

17 Wahlquist, C, Evershed, N & Allam, L 2018, 'Half of Indigenous women who died in custody did not receive appropriate medical care', *Guardian Australia*, 10 September, <theguardian.com/australia-news/2018/sep/10/indigenous-women-in-custody-more-likely-than-men-to-have-died-where-policy-not-followed>.

18 Kingston, H 2020, 'How many Indigenous deaths in custody have been recorded?', *Crikey*, 9 June, <crikey.com.au/2020/06/09/how-many-indigenous-deaths-in-police-custody>.

19 Brennan, D 2022, 'Not guilty verdict in police murder case shines light on injustices facing Australia's Indigenous people', *The Diplomat*, 17 March, <thediplomat.com/2022/03/not-guilty-verdict-in-police-murder-case-shines-light-on-injustices-facing-australias-indigenous-people/>.

20 The Herald's View 2020, 'Australia not immune from US-style racial tension', *Sydney Morning Herald*, 2 June, <smh.com.au/politics/federal/australia-not-immune-from-us-style-racial-tension-20200602-p54yru.html>.

21 Guardian Australia 2021, 'Deaths inside: Indigenous Australian deaths in custody 2021', *Guardian Australia*, 5 April, <theguardian.com/australia-news/ng-interactive/2018/aug/28/deaths-inside-indigenous-australian-deaths-in-custody>.

22 NSW Parliament 2014, *The Family Response to the Murders in Bowraville*, Standing Committee on Law and Justice, Sydney, <parliament.nsw.gov.au/lcdocs/inquiries/2131/Bowraville%20-%20Final%20report.pdf>.

23 All in the Mind 2020, *Why We Need More Indigenous Psychologists*, 16 February, <abc.net.au/listen/programs/allinthemind/why-we-need-more-indigenous-psychologists/11954110>.

24 ABS 2023, *Causes of Death, Australia*, ABS, <abs.gov.au/statistics/health/causes-death/causes-death-australia/latest-release>.

25 This is also true of most women, Aboriginal and non-Aboriginal, due to social constructionism in which parents raise girls to be more nurturing of others – for example, looking after baby dolls or learning to cook with their mum.

26 The term was first coined by Aaron T Beck in his 1979 book *Cognitive Therapy of Depression*, Guilford Publications.

27 Hanssens, L 2007, 'The search to identify contagion operating within suicide clusters in Indigenous communities, Northern Territory, Australia', *Aboriginal and Islander Health Worker Journal*, vol. 31, no. 5, pp. 27–33.

28 Mindframe n.d., *Communicating About a Suicide*, <mindframe.org.au/suicide/communicating-about-suicide/mindframe-guidelines/communicating-about-a-suicide>.

Chapter 6: Love, Fear and Attachment

1 All in the Mind 2020, *Why We Need More Indigenous Psychologists*, 16 February, <abc.net.au/listen/programs/allinthemind/why-we-need-more-indigenous-psychologists/11954110>.

2 Bowlby, J 1969, *Attachment and Loss*, Basic Books, New York.

3 Ainsworth, MD 1964, 'Patterns of attachment behavior shown by the infant in interaction with his mother', *Merrill-Palmer Quarterly of Behavior and Development*, vol. 10, no. 1, pp. 51–8.

4 Main, M & Solomon, J 1986, 'Discovery of an insecure-disorganized/disoriented attachment pattern', in TB Brazelton & MW Yogman (eds), *Affective Development in Infancy*, Ablex Publishing, New York City, pp. 95–124; Ainsworth, MDS & Bell, SM 1970, 'Attachment, exploration, and separation: Illustrated by the behavior of one-year-olds in a strange situation', *Child Development*, vol. 41, no. 1, pp. 49–67.

5 Main, M, Hesse, E & Hesse, S 2011, 'Attachment theory and research: Overview with suggested applications to child custody', *Family Court Review*, vol. 49, no. 3, pp. 426–63.

6   George, C, Isaacs, MB & Marvin, RS 2011, 'Incorporating attachment assessment into custody evaluations: The case of a 2-year-old and her parents', *Family Court Review*, vol 49, no. 3, pp. 483–500.

7   Emery, RE, Otto, RK & O'Donohue, WT 2005, 'A critical assessment of child custody evaluations: Limited science and a flawed system', *Psychological Science in the Public Interest*, vol. 6, no. 1, pp. 1–29.

8   Menzies, K 2019, 'Understanding the Australian Aboriginal experience of collective, historical, and intergenerational trauma', *International Social Work*, vol. 62, no. 6, pp. 1522–34; Yehuda, R & Lehrner, A 2018, 'Intergenerational transmission of trauma effects: Putative role of epigenetic mechanisms', *World Psychiatry*, vol. 17, no. 3, pp. 243–57.

9   D'Andrea, W, Pole, N, DePierro, J, Freed, S & Wallace, DB 2013, 'Heterogeneity of defensive responses after exposure to trauma: Blunted autonomic reactivity in response to startling sounds', *International Journal of Psychophysiology*, vol. 90, no. 1, pp. 80–9.

10 Main, M, Hesse, E & Hesse, S 2011, 'Attachment theory and research: Overview with suggested applications to child custody'.

11 Westerman, T 2023, 'As a First Nations psychologist, allow me to unpick Price's claim that there are no lasting negative impacts of British colonisation', *Crikey*, 10 October, <crikey.com.au/2023/10/10/colonialism-no-positive-impact-for-all-aboriginal-people/?su=ZkRFRnI0aHBjV0o4Z2FxalRDcENzZz09>.

12 Haebich, A 2011, 'Forgetting Indigenous histories: Cases from the history of Australia's Stolen Generations', *Journal of Social History*, vol. 44, no. 4, pp. 1033–46.

13 Davies, A 2008, 'Nothing to say sorry for: Howard', *Sydney Morning Herald*, 12 March, <smh.com.au/national/nothing-to-say-sorry-for-howard-20080312-gds4t6.html>.

14 Rose, T & Canales SB 2023, 'Indigenous people "disgusted" by Jacinta Nampijinpa Price's "simply wrong" comments on colonisation, Burney says', *Guardian Australia*, 15 September, <theguardian.com/australia-news/2023/sep/15/jacinta-nampijinpa-price-comments-colonisation-voice-referendum-linda-burney>; Westerman, T, 'As a First Nations psychologist, allow me to unpick Price's claim that there are no lasting negative impacts of British colonisation'.

15 Wheeler, K 2007, 'Psychotherapeutic strategies for healing trauma', *Perspectives in Psychiatric Care*, vol. 43, no. 3, pp. 132–41.

16 Hesse, E & Main, M 1999, 'Second-generation effects of unresolved trauma in nonmaltreating parents: Dissociated, frightened, and threatening parental behavior', *Psychoanalytic Inquiry*, vol. 19, no. 4, pp. 481–540.

17 Hoffman, KT, Marvin, RS, Cooper, G & Powell, B 2006, 'Changing toddlers' and preschoolers' attachment classifications: The circle of security intervention', *Journal of Consulting and Clinical Psychology*, vol. 74, no. 6, pp. 1017–26.

18 Landa, S & Duschinsky, R 2013, 'Crittenden's dynamic-maturational model of attachment and adaptation', *Review of General Psychology*, vol. 17, no. 3, pp. 326–38.

19 AIHW 2022, *Child Protection Australia 2020–21*, AIHW, <aihw.gov.au/reports/child-protection/child-protection-australia-2021-22>; AIHW 2022, *Profile of Indigenous Australians*, AIHW, <aihw.gov.au/reports/australias-health/profile-of-indigenous-australians>.

20 Yoorrook Justice Commission 2023, *Child Protection System Hearing – Government and Departmental Day 8*, <yoorrookjusticecommission.org.au/video/criminal-justice-systems-hearing-government-and-departmental-day-8/>.

21 McKenna, K 2020, '"Racially biased" screening tool used in the child protection system places more Indigenous children in custody, critics say', *ABC News*, 10 July, <abc.net.au/news/2020-07-10/queensland-discriminatory-tool-indigenous-child-protection/12434784>.

22 Indigenous Psychology Service 2019, *Cultural Competency Audit of Child Protection Staff and Foster Care and Adoption Manual*, Department of Communities, Government of Western Australia, Perth, <wa.gov.au/system/files/2022-02/Cultural-Competency-Audit.pdf>; Westerman, T 2020, *Statement of Dr Tracy Westerman*, Royal Commission into violence, abuse, neglect, and exploitation of people with disability, <indigenouspsychservices.com.au/wp-content/uploads/2021/05/DRC-OSA-Final-witness-statement-20201124-Dr-Tracy-WESTERMAN_.pdf>; Westerman, T 2022, 'Opinion: Fixing the broken system of Indigenous child removal', *NITV*, 22 March, <sbs.com.au/nitv/article/opinion-fixing-the-broken-system-of-indigenous-child-removal/im1h0cyi9>.

23 Westerman, T 2022, 'From love bombing to isolation, the red flags for coercive control can be dangerously difficult to spot before abuse escalates', *ABC News*, 7 August, <abc.net.au/news/2022-08-07/love-bombing-isolation-coercive-control-red-flags-domestic-abuse/101283156>.

24 Alhalal EA, Ford-Gilboe, M, Kerr, M & Davies, L 2012, 'Identifying factors that predict women's inability to maintain separation from an abusive partner', *Issues in Mental Health Nursing*, vol. 33, no. 12, pp. 838–50, <pubmed.ncbi.nlm.nih.gov/23215985/>.

25 McGrath, V 2019, *Narcissist mirroring: How narcissist manipulates you into loving them*, The Minds Journal, <themindsjournal.com/narcissist-mirroring/>.

26 Connell, C 2022, 'NSW government releases draft coercive control bill, proposes seven-year jail term', *ABC News*, 20 July, <abc.net.au/news/2022-07-20/cocercive-control-laws-nsw-draft-bill/101253266>.

27 Gleeson, H 2022, 'Police are still misjudging domestic violence and victims are suffering the consequences', *ABC News*, 31 March, <abc.net.au/news/2022-03-31/police-misidentifying-domestic-violence-victims-perpetrators/100913268>.

28 Buschman, H 2019, *Large study reveals PTSD has strong genetic component like other psychiatric disorders*, UC San Diego Health, <health.ucsd.edu/news/press-releases/2019-10-08-study-reveals-ptsd-has-strong-genetic-component>.

29 Westerman, T, 'Opinion: Fixing the broken system of Indigenous child removal'.

30 Yoorrook Justice Commission, *Child Protection System Hearing – Government and Departmental Day 8*; Westerman, T, *Statement of Dr Tracy Westerman*; Westerman, T, 'Opinion: Fixing the broken system of Indigenous child removal'; Atkinson, J 2002, *Trauma Trails, Recreating Song Lines: The transgenerational effects of trauma in Indigenous Australia*, Spinifex Press, North Melbourne.

31 Westerman, T, 'Opinion: Fixing the broken system of Indigenous child removal'.

32 Department of Children, Youth Justice and Multicultural Affairs 2023, *Intensive Family Support: Service model and guidelines*, Queensland Government, <familychildconnect.org.au/ARC/2018/IFS_Service_Model_and_Guidelines.pdf>.

33 Grossmann, KE, Grossmann, K & Waters, E (eds) 2005, *Attachment from Infancy to Adulthood: The major longitudinal studies*, Guilford Press, New York.

34 Shmerling, E, Creati, M, Belfrage, M & Hedges, S 2020, 'The health needs of Aboriginal and Torres Strait Islander children in out-of-home care', *Journal of Paediatrics and Child Health*, vol. 56, no. 3, pp. 384–8.

35 Westerman, T 2003, 'The development of an inventory to assess the moderating effects of cultural resilience with Aboriginal youth at risk of depression, anxiety and suicidal behaviours', PhD thesis, Curtin University, Western Australia, <indigenouspsychservices.com.au/wp-content/uploads/2020/05/ABSTRACT.pdf>; Westerman, T, 'Opinion: Fixing the broken system of Indigenous child removal'; Westerman, T, *Statement of Dr Tracy Westerman*; Ridani, R, Shand, FL, Christensen, H, McKay, K, Tighe, J, Burns, J & Hunter, E 2015, 'Suicide prevention in Australian Aboriginal communities: A review of past and present programs', *Suicide and Life-Threatening Behavior*, vol. 45, no. 1, pp. 111–40.

36 Funston, L. & Herring, S 2016, 'When will the Stolen Generations end? A qualitative critical exploration of contemporary "child protection" practices in Aboriginal and Torres Strait Islander communities', *Sexual Abuse in Australia and New Zealand*, vol. 7, no. 1, pp. 51–58.

37 Maclean, MJ, Taylor, CL & O'Donnell, M 2017, 'Relationship between out-of-home care placement history characteristics and educational achievement: A population level linked data study', *Child Abuse & Neglect*, vol. 70, pp. 146–59.

38 Funston, L & Herring, S, 'When will the Stolen Generations end?'.

39 Territory Families, Housing and Communities 2020, *Territory Families Annual Report, 2019–2020*, Northern Territory Government, <tfhc.nt.gov.au/__data/assets/pdf_file/0003/943923/territory-families-annual-report2019-20.pdf>.

40 Department of Children, Youth Justice and Multicultural Affairs, *Intensive Family Support: Service model and guidelines*.

Chapter 7: Trauma, Racism and Violence

1 MedlinePlus 2022, *Is temperament determined by genetics?*, National Library of Medicine, National Institutes of Health, U.S. Department of Health and Human Services, <medlineplus.gov/genetics/understanding/traits/temperament/>.

2 Garcia-Arocena, D 2015, *The genetics of violent behavior*, The Jackson Laboratory, <jax.org/news-and-insights/jax-blog/2015/December/the-genetics-of-violent-behavior>.

3 Bowlby, J 1969, *Attachment and Loss*, Basic Books, New York.

4 Innocence Staff 2020, 'How eyewitness misidentification can send innocent people to prison', *The Innocence Project*, 15 April, <innocenceproject.org/how-eyewitness-misidentification-can-send-innocent-people-to-prison/>; Yaros, J 2020, *The other race effect and face perception*, Yassa Lab, UCI Translational Neuroscience Laboratory, <faculty.sites.uci.edu/myassa/research/the-other-race-effect-and-face-perception>.

5 Heffernan, E, Andersen, K, Davidson, F & Kinner, SA 2015, 'PTSD among Aboriginal and Torres Strait Islander people in custody in Australia: Prevalence and correlates', *Journal of Traumatic Stress*, vol. 28, no. 6, pp. 523–30; Cénat, JM,

2023, 'Complex racial trauma: Evidence, theory, assessment, and treatment', *Perspectives on Psychological Sciences*, vol. 18, no. 3, pp. 675–87.

6 Levi, O 2019, 'The role of hope in psychodynamic therapy (PDT) for complex PTSD (C-PTSD)', *Journal of Social Work Practice*, vol. 34, no. 3, pp. 237–48.

7 Center for Substance Abuse Treatment 2014, 'Understanding the impact of trauma', in *Trauma-Informed Care in Behavioral Health Services*, Substance Abuse and Mental Health Services Administration, Rockville, pp. 59–89, <ncbi.nlm.nih.gov/books/NBK207191/>.

8 Center for Substance Abuse Treatment, 'Understanding the impact of trauma'.

9 Davis, S 2022, *Rejection trauma and the freeze/fawn response*, The Foundation for Post-Traumatic Healing and Complex Trauma Research, 21 February, <cptsdfoundation.org/2022/02/21/rejection-trauma-and-the-freeze-fawn-response>.

10 Paradies, Y 2016, 'Colonisation, racism and Indigenous health', *Journal of Population Research*, vol. 33, no. 1, pp. 83–96; Smallwood, R, Woods, C, Power, T & Usher, K 2021, 'Understanding the impact of historical trauma due to colonization on the health and well-being of Indigenous young peoples: A systematic scoping review', *Journal of Transcultural Nursing*, vol. 32, no. 1, pp. 59–68; Westerman, T 2003, 'The development of an inventory to assess the moderating effects of cultural resilience with Aboriginal youth at risk of depression, anxiety and suicidal behaviours', PhD thesis, Curtin University, Western Australia, <indigenouspsychservices.com.au/wp-content/uploads/2020/05/ABSTRACT.pdf>.

11 On the long-term impacts: Nasir, BF, Black, E, Toombs, M, Kisely, S, Gill, N, Beccaria, G, Kondalsamy-Chennakesavan, S & Nicholson, G 2021, 'Traumatic life events and risk of post-traumatic stress disorder among the Indigenous population of regional, remote and metropolitan Central-Eastern Australia: A cross-sectional study', *BMJ Open*, vol. 11, no. 4, e040875; Carter, RT 2007, 'Racism and psychological and emotional injury: Recognizing and assessing race-based traumatic stress', *The Counseling Psychologist*, vol. 35, no. 1, pp. 13-105; Carter, RT & Forsyth, JM 2009, 'A guide to the forensic assessment of race-based traumatic stress reactions', *The Journal of the American Academy of Psychiatry and the Law*, vol. 37, no. 1, pp. 28–40. See also: Blum, RW, Harmon, B, Harris, L, Bergeisen, L & Resnick, MD 1992, 'American Indian-Alaska native youth health', *JAMA Psychiatry*, vol. 267, no. 12, pp. 1637–44; Radford, AJ, Harris, RD, Brice, GA, Vann der Byl, M, Monten, H, Matters, D, Neeson, M, Bryan, L & Hassan, R 1991, 'Social health among urban Aboriginal heads of households in Adelaide, with particular reference to suicide attempts', *Aboriginal Health Information Bulletin*, no. 15, pp. 20–25.

12 Cénat, JM, 'Complex racial trauma: Evidence, theory, assessment, and treatment'.

13 Perry, B 2013, 'Complex traumas in children: Assessment and treatment', *3rd Annual Child's Eye View Conference 2013*, 3 June, Kilden.

14 Heffernan, R, Ward, T, Vandevelde, S & Van Damme, L 2019, 'Dynamic risk factors and constructing explanations of offending: The risk-causality method', *Aggression and Violent Behavior*, vol. 44, pp. 47–56.

15 Senate Select Committee on Regional and Remote Indigenous Communities 2010, *Indigenous Australians, Incarceration and the Criminal Justice System*, Discussion paper prepared by the committee secretariat, <aph.gov.au/~/media/wopapub/senate/committee/indig_ctte/Final_RRIC_pdf.ashx>.

16 Commonwealth of Australia 2017, *Report of the Royal Commission and Board of Inquiry into the Protection and Detention of Children in the Northern Territory: Findings and Recommendations*, Commonwealth of Australia, <royalcommission.gov.au/system/files/2020-09/findings-and-recommendations.pdf>.

17 ABS 2023, *Prisoners in Australia*, ABS, <abs.gov.au/statistics/people/crime-and-justice/prisoners-australia/latest-release>.

18 Perry, BD & Szalavitz M 2017, *The Boy Who Was Raised As a Dog*, 3rd edn, Basic Books, New York.

19 Perry, BD & Szalavitz, M, *The Boy Who Was Raised As a Dog*.

Chapter 8: The Communities and Suicide Prevention

1 Darvishi, N, Farhadi, M, Azmi-Naei, B & Poorolajal, J 2023, 'The role of problem-solving skills in the prevention of suicidal behaviors: A systematic review and meta-analysis', *PLoS One*, vol. 18, no. 10.

2 AIHW 2020, *Mental Health Workforce*, AIHW, <aihw.gov.au/getmedia/336a8730-fe0d-484b-8812-4cad6d3e893f/mental-health-workforce-section.pdf.aspx>.

3 Eades, D 1992, *Aboriginal English and the Law*, Queensland Law Society, quoted in J Hunyor, 2007, 'Commission submission: On common difficulties facing Aboriginal witnesses', Australian Human Rights Commission, <humanrights.gov.au/our-work/legal/commission-submission-common-difficulties-facing-aboriginal-witnesses>.

4 Brüdern, J, Stähli, A, Gysin-Maillart, A, Michel, K, Reisch, T, Jobes DA & Brodbeck J 2018, 'Reasons for living and dying in suicide attempters: A two-year prospective study', *BMC Psychiatry*, vol. 18, no. 1, p. 234.

5 ABS 2019, *Intentional self-harm in Aboriginal and Torres Strait Islander people*, ABS, <abs.gov.au/ausstats/abs@.nsf/Lookup/by%20Subject/3303.0%7E2017%7EMain%20Features%7EIntentional%20self-harm%20in%20Aboriginal%20and%20Torres%20Strait%20Islander%20people%7E10>

6 Westerman, T 2020, 'Opinion: "Funding football programs is not suicide prevention"', *National Indigenous Times*, 2 April, <nit.com.au/02-04-2020/488/opinion-funding-football-programs-is-not-suicide-prevention>.

7 Reid, J & Trompf, P (eds.) 1991, *The Health of Aboriginal Australia*, Harcourt Brace Jovanovich, Sydney.

8 Sheldon, M 2001, 'Psychiatric assessment in remote Aboriginal communities', *Australian & New Zealand Journal of Psychiatry*, vol. 35, no. 4, pp. 435–42; Vicary, D & Andrews, H 2001, 'A model of therapeutic intervention with Indigenous Australians', *Australian & New Zealand Journal of Public Health*, vol. 25, no. 4, pp. 349–51; Westerman, T 2003, 'The development of an inventory to assess the moderating effects of cultural resilience with Aboriginal youth at risk of depression, anxiety and suicidal behaviours', PhD thesis, Curtin University, Western Australia, <indigenouspsychservices.com.au/wp-content/uploads/2020/05/ABSTRACT.pdf>.

9 Slattery, G 1994, 'Transcultural therapy with Aboriginal families: Working with the belief system', *Australian & New Zealand Journal of Therapy*, vol. 8, no. 2, pp. 61–70.

10 Evans, WP, Marsh, SC & Owens, P 2005, 'Environmental factors, locus of control, and adolescent suicide risk', *Child and Adolescent Social Work Journal*, vol.

22, nos. 3–4, pp. 301–19. See also: Sheldon, M, 'Psychiatric assessment in remote Aboriginal communities'; Vicary, D & Andrews, H, 'A model of therapeutic intervention with Indigenous Australians'; Westerman, T, 'The development of an inventory to assess the moderating effects of cultural resilience with Aboriginal youth at risk of depression, anxiety and suicidal behaviours'.

11 Kearins, JM 1981, 'Visual spacial memory in Australian Aboriginal children of desert regions', *Cognitive Psychology*, vol. 13, no. 3, pp. 434–60.

12 Mpinga, K, Rukundo, T, Mwale, O, Kamwiyo, M, Thengo, L, Ruderman, T, Matanje, B, Munyaneza, F, Connolly, E, Kulisewa, K, Udedi, M, Kachimanga, C, Dullie, L & McBain, R 2023, 'Depressive disorder at the household level: Prevalence and correlates of depressive symptoms among household members', *Global Health Action*, vol. 16, no. 1, 2241808.

13 Institute of Health Metrics and Evaluation 2019, *Global Burden of Disease Results*, Global Health Data Exchange, <vizhub.healthdata.org/gbd-results>.

14 American Psychiatric Association 2003, *Practice Guideline for the Assessment and Treatment of Patients with Suicidal Behaviors*, American Psychiatric Association Publishing, Arlington.

15 Westerman, T & Sheridan, L 2020, 'Whole of community suicide prevention forums for Aboriginal Australians', *Australian Psychologist*, vol. 55, no. 4, pp. 363–74.

16 Westerman, T 2019, 'Aboriginal suicide prevention. Where is the funding going?', *IndigenousX*, 18 January, <indigenousx.com.au/aboriginal-suicide-prevention-where-is-the-funding-going>.

17 Chandler, J 2021, *High risk household items that can be used to get high*, Muse Treatment, 2 April, <musetreatment.com/blog/household-items-used-to-get-high/>.

18 Department of Justice 1996, *Mental Health Act 1996*, Government of Western Australia, <legislation.wa.gov.au/legislation/statutes.nsf/RedirectURL?OpenAgent&query=mrcmp_20621.pdf>.

Chapter 9: Indigenous Psychological Services

1 Westerman, TG & Dear, GE 2023, 'The need for culturally valid psychological assessment tools in Indigenous mental health', *Clinical Psychologist*, vol. 27, no. 3, pp. 284–9.

Chapter 10: The Future

1 Conover, C 2023, 'Do Black physicians double the survival odds of Black newborns?', *Forbes*, 10 Jul, <forbes.com/sites/theapothecary/2023/07/10/do-black-physicians-double-the-survival-odds-of-black-newborns/>.'

2 Macklin, J 2018, 'How we said sorry: Reflecting on the apology, a decade on', *Meanjin*, 7 February, <meanjin.com.au/essays/how-we-said-sorry-reflecting-on-the-apology-a-decade-on>.

Chapter 11: Explaining the 'Why'

1 Al-Yaman, F, Van Doeland, M & Wallis, M 2006, *Family Violence Among Aboriginal and Torres Strait Islander Peoples*, Australian Institute of Health

and Welfare, Canberra, <aihw.gov.au/reports/indigenous-australians/family-violence-indigenous-peoples/summary>.

2 Dudgeon, P, Milroy, J, Calma, T, Luxford, Y, Ring, I, Walker, R, Cox, A, Georgatos, G & Holland, C 2016, *Solutions That Work: What the evidence and our people tell us*, Aboriginal and Torres Strait Islander Suicide Prevention Evaluation Project (ATSISPEP), <atsispep.sis.uwa.edu.au/__data/assets/pdf_file/0006/2947299/ATSISPEP-Report-Final-Web.pdf>.

3 McIntosh, JE, Opie, J, Greenwood, CJ, Booth , A, Tan, E, Painter, F, Messer, M, Macdonald, JA, Letcher, P, Olsson, CA 2023, 'Infant and preschool attachment, continuity, and relationship to caregiving sensitivity: Findings from a new population-based Australian cohort', *The Journal of Child Psychology and Psychiatry*, vol. 65, no. 1, pp. 64–76.

4 ABS 2023, *1 in 5 Australians have experienced partner violence or abuse*, ABS, <abs.gov.au/media-centre/media-releases/1-5-australians-have-experienced-partner-violence-or-abuse>.

5 AIHW 2023, *Family, domestic and sexual violence: Aboriginal and Torres Strait Islander people*, AIHW, 24 November, <aihw.gov.au/family-domestic-and-sexual-violence/population-groups/aboriginal-and-torres-strait-islander-people>.

6 AIHW, *Family, domestic and sexual violence: Aboriginal and Torres Strait Islander people'*.

7 ABS 2013, 'Changes in family dynamics', *Census of Population and Housing: Understanding the increase in Aboriginal and Torres Strait Islander Counts, 2006–2011*, ABS, <abs.gov.au/ausstats/abs@.nsf/Lookup/2077.0main+features72006-2011>.

8 *ABC News* 2022, Australian Broadcasting Corporation, 24 November, <indigenouspsychservices.com.au/wp-content/uploads/2022/12/1.mp4>.

9 AIHW, *Suicide&self-harmmonitoring:DeathsbysuicideamongFirstNationspeople*, AIHW, <aihw.gov.au/suicide-self-harm-monitoring/data/populations-age-groups/suicide-indigenous-australians>.

10 Westerman, T 2021, 'We must raise the age of criminal responsibility, here is why', *IndigenousX*, 11 May, <indigenousx.com.au/we-must-raise-the-age-of-criminal-responsibility-here-is-why>.

11 Amnesty International Australia, *Human rights abuses against kids in the Brisbane city police watch house*; Amnesty International Australia, *Indigenous kids in prison*.

12 ABS 2023, *Recorded crime – offenders*, ABS, 9 February, <abs.gov.au/statistics/people/crime-and-justice/recorded-crime-offenders/latest-release>.

13 Graham, C 2009, 'We jail black men five times more than apartheid South Africa', *Crikey*, 2 July, <crikey.com.au/2009/07/02/we-jail-black-men-five-times-more-than-apartheid-south-africa>; Jericho, G 2020, 'No, Australia is not the US. Our shocking racial injustice is all our own', *Guardian Australia*, 7 June, <theguardian.com/business/grogonomics/2020/jun/07/no-australia-is-not-the-us-our-shocking-racial-injustice-is-all-our-own>; Shields, T 2023, 'The Voice offers new way forward to end Australia's appallingly high incarceration rates', *The Australia Institute*, 20 September, <australiainstitute.org.au/post/the-voice-offers-new-way-forward-to-end-australias-appallingly-high-incarceration-rates>.

14 Gross, SR, Possley, M, Otterbourg, K, Stephens, K, Weinstock Paredes, J & O'Brien, B 2022, *Race and Wrongful Convictions in the United States 2022*,

National Registry of Exonerations, <law.umich.edu/special/exoneration/ Documents/Race%20Report%20Preview.pdf>. (This research also found that official misconduct, false accusations or perjury were more likely to occur if the defendant was black.)

15 Dunham, R 2017, *The most common causes of wrongful death penalty convictions: Official misconduct and perjury or false accusation*, Death Penalty Information Center, 31 May, <deathpenaltyinfo.org/stories/dpic-analysis-causes-of-wrongful-convictions>.

16 Collard, S 2023, 'NSW police reject suggestion "racism is rife" in force and say "lessons learned" after Bowraville murders', *Guardian Australia*, 28 July, <theguardian.com/australia-news/2023/jul/28/nsw-police-reject-suggestion-racism-is-rife-in-force-and-say-lessons-learned-after-bowraville-murders>.

17 Westerman, T, 'We must raise the age of criminal responsibility, here is why'.

18 Hemenway, D & Solnick, SJ 2017, 'The epidemiology of homicide perpetration by children', *Injury Epidemiology*, vol. 4, no. 1, p. 5.

19 Molloy, S 2023, 'A 12-year-old girl charged with murder was "prostituted out" for as long as a year but police ignored multiple pleas for help', *news.com.au*, 21 November, <news.com.au/national/victoria/crime/a-12yearold-girl-charged-with-murder-was-prostituted-out-for-as-long-as-a-year-but-police-ignored-multiple-pleas-for-help/news-story/2efb8ef4df76a4db269fc9a37d437696>.

20 ABS 2024, *Recorded crime – Offenders: 2022–23*, ABS, <abs.gov.au/statistics/people/crime-and-justice/recorded-crime-offenders/latest-release>; Aboriginal and Torres Strait Islander Social Justice Commissioner, Human Rights and Equal Opportunity Commission 2003, *Issue 3: Law and public order, including juvenile justice – Submission to the United Nations Committee on the Rights of the Child for their Day of General Discussion on the Rights of Indigenous Children*, Australian Human Rights Commission, <humanrights.gov.au/our-work/aboriginal-and-torres-strait-islander-social-justice/issue-3-law-and-public-order>; Fernandes, A 2021, 'Aboriginal people keep dying in police custody. More than half are accused of a minor crime', *SBS News*, 15 April, <sbs.com.au/news/article/aboriginal-people-keep-dying-in-police-custody-more-than-half-are-accused-of-a-minor-crime/6m2krb5vx>.

21 Western Australian Association for Mental Health, Western Australian Council of Social Service & Western Australian Network of Alcohol and other Drug Agencies 2013, *Submission to the Senate Legal & Constitutional Affairs Committee Inquiry: Value of a justice reinvestment approach to criminal justice in Australia*, <aph.gov.au/DocumentStore.ashx?id=3d698e1e-9d5a-4164-8c5a-93260b4afaee&usg=AOvVaw2DMz-BHf4pSUcJTepqCcRH>.

22 Brennan, D 2024, 'New data shows youth incarceration costing public over $1 million per child, experts urge "Raise the Age"', *National Indigenous Times*, 25 January, <nit.com.au/25-01-2024/9449/new-data-shows-youth-incarceration-costing-public-over-1-million-per-child>.

23 Schlicht, M 2023, *The Cost of Prisons in Australia: 2023*, Institute of Public Affairs, <ipa.org.au/wp-content/uploads/2023/07/IPA-Cost-of-Prisons-Report.pdf>.

24 Aizer, A & Doyle, JJ 2015, 'Juvenile incarceration, human capital, and future crime: Evidence from randomly assigned judges', *The Quarterly Journal of Economics*, vol. 130, no. 2, pp. 759–803>.

25 Honorato, B, Caltabiano, N & Clough, AR 2016, 'From trauma to incarceration: exploring the trajectory in a qualitative study in male prison inmates from north Queensland, Australia', *Health & Justice*, vol. 4, no. 3.

26 Collard, S 2023, 'Children self-harming to escape prolonged confinement in cells, South Australian watchdog says', *Guardian Australia*, 30 June, <theguardian.com/society/2023/jun/29/children-locked-in-cells-for-up-to-23-hours-at-south-australias-youth-detention-centre>; Juvenile Law Center n.d., *Solitary confinement and harsh conditions*, Juvenile Law Center, Philadelphia, <jlc.org/issues/solitary-confinement-other-conditions>.

27 Burmas, G, Carmody, J, Weber, D & Bazeer, Z 2023, 'Banksia Hill Detention Centre riot over as armed officers move in to arrest teenagers on roof', *ABC News*, 10 May, <https://abc.net.au/news/2023-05-10/fires-lit-at-banksia-hill-detention-centre-in-major-disturbance/102325284>.

28 ABS 2024, *Corrective services, Australia*, ABS, <abs.gov.au/statistics/people/crime-and-justice/corrective-services-australia/latest-release>.

29 Amnesty International Australia 2022, *The Overrepresentation Problem: First Nations kids are 26 times more likely to be incarcerated than their classmates*, Amnesty International Australia, <amnesty.org.au/overrepresentation-explainer-first-nations-kids-are-26-times-more-likely-to-be-incarcerated>.

30 Territory Families, Housing and Communities 2020, *Territory Families Annual Report, 2019–2020*, Northern Territory Government, <tfhc.nt.gov.au/__data/assets/pdf_file/0003/943923/territory-families-annual-report2019-20.pdf>; Territory Families, Housing and Communities 2023, *Territory Families Annual Report, 2022–2023*, Northern Territory Government, <tfhc.nt.gov.au/__data/assets/pdf_file/0011/1291088/territory-families-housing-and-communities-annual-report-2022-23.pdf>.

31 Department of Communities 2021, *Child Protection Activity Performance Information 2020–21*, Government of Western Australia, <www.wa.gov.au/system/files/2021-10/child-protection-activity-performance-information-2020-21.pdf>.

32 ABS 2022, *Western Australia: Aboriginal and Torres Strait Islander population summary*, ABS, <abs.gov.au/articles/western-australia-aboriginal-and-torres-strait-islander-population-summary>.

33 AIHW 2022, *Child protection Australia 2020–21*, AIHW, <aihw.gov.au/reports/child-protection/child-protection-australia-2020-21/contents/summary>.

34 O'Callaghan, K 2015, 'Reality of Aboriginal child abuse far worse', *The West Australian*, 30 March, <thewest.com.au/news/reality-of-aboriginal-child-abuse-far-worse-ng-ya-103684>.

35 AIHW, *Child protection Australia 2020–21*.

36 Yoorrook Justice Commission 2023, *Child Protection System Hearing – Government and Departmental Day 8*, <yoorrookjusticecommission.org.au/video/criminal-justice-systems-hearing-government-and-departmental-day-8/>.

37 Salter, M, Woodlock, D, Whitten, T, Tyler, M, Naldrett, G, Breckenridge, J, Nolan, J & Peleg, N 2023, *Identifying and Understanding Child Sexual Offending Behaviours and Attitudes Among Australian Men*, Australian Human Rights Institute,

<humanrights.unsw.edu.au/sites/default/files/documents/Identifying%20 and%20understanding%20child%20sexual%20offending%20behaviour%20 and%20attitudes%20among%20Australian%20men.pdf>.

38 Davis, M 1992, 'The role of the amygdala in fear and anxiety', *Annual Review of Neuroscience*, vol. 15, pp. 353–75; Whalen, PJ 1998, 'Fear, vigilance, and ambiguity: Initial neuroimaging studies of the human amygdala', *Current Directions in Psychological Science*, vol. 7, no. 6, pp. 177–88.

39 Hart, AJ, Whalen, PJ, Shin, LM, McInerney, SC, Fischer, H & Rauch, SL 2000, 'Differential response in the human amygdala to racial outgroup vs ingroup face stimuli', *Neuroreport*, vol. 11, no. 11, pp. 2351–5; Wheeler, ME & Fiske, ST 2005, 'Controlling racial prejudice: Social-cognitive goals affect amygdala and stereotype activation', *Psychological Science*, vol. 16, no. 1, pp. 56–63.

40 Westerman, T 2022, 'Opinion: Fixing the broken system of Indigenous child removal,' *NITV*, 22 March, <sbs.com.au/nitv/article/ opinion-fixing-the-broken-system-of-indigenous-child-removal/im1h0cyi9>.

41 Indigenous Psychology Service 2019, *Cultural Competency Audit of Child Protection Staff and Foster Care and Adoption Manual*, Department of Communities, Government of Western Australia, Perth, <wa.gov.au/system/files/2022-02/ Cultural-Competency-Audit.pdf>.

42 AIHW 2021, *Safety of children in care 2020–21*, AIHW, <aihw.gov.au/reports/ child-protection/safety-of-children-in-care-2020-21/contents/how-many- children-are-abused-in-care>; Department of Communities and Justice, *Comparing Outcomes for Maltreated Children: Out-of-home care versus remaining at home – a literature summary*, NSW Government, <facs.nsw.gov.au/__data/ assets/pdf_file/0003/832566/Comparing-Outcomes-for-Maltreated-Children- Brief.pdf>.

43 Charles, B & Knowles, R 2023, 'The referendum failed. But data shows the majority of Indigenous communities voted yes', *NITV*, 16 October, <sbs. com.au/nitv/article/the-referendum-for-a-voice-to-parliament-failed- but-what-outcome-did-most-indigenous-voters-support/i2reavyqn>.